The Roman Alexander

This book seizes on one of the eternal objects of widespread attention in ancient history and turns the tables on the scholarship that has shaped and dominated the field.

Instead of scrutinizing the documents in order to reconstruct the biography and assess the historical significance, Diana Spencer traces the deployment and development of the mythical figure of Alexander. She explores and synthesizes a selection of Latin texts, from the Late Republic to Hadrian, to form a series of themed discussions which investigate the cultural significance of Alexander for Rome.

The selected texts—drawn from verse and prose, history, epic and oratory—are presented alongside their English translation, and provide an insight into a world where to think about Alexander was to engage with the burning ideological issues of Rome during a period of intense and often violent political and cultural change. The book makes clear how particular texts and issues may be readily accessed, providing a valuable resource for teachers and their students, whilst also offering a new approach to cultural histories of Rome and Alexander.

Diana Spencer is Lecturer in Classics at the University of Birmingham.

Frontispiece: *The Alexander Mosaic* from the House of the Faun of Pompeii. As in Le Brun's *The Battle of Arbela* (Fig. 5), we find Alexander and Darius divorced from the turmoil through the semiotics of their depiction; Alexander both is, and is not, embroiled in battle, Darius is eternally poised for flight. Both are on the cusp of dramatic changes in fortune.

The Roman Alexander

Reading a Cultural Myth

Diana Spencer

UNIVERSITY
of
EXETER
PRESS

First published in 2002 by
University of Exeter Press
Reed Hall, Streatham Drive
Exeter EX4 4QR
UK

www.exeterpress.co.uk

Reprinted 2003, 2008

British Library Cataloguing in Publication Data
A catalogue record of this book is available
from the British Library.

Hardback ISBN 978 0 85989 677 1
Paperback ISBN 978 0 85989 678 8

Typeset in 10.5 on 12.5 pt Sabon by Exe Valley Dataset Ltd, Exeter

Printed and bound in Great Britain by
CPI Antony Rowe, Chippenham, Wiltshire

Libellum auctori meo dono

Kevin Spencer

1933–1997

CONTENTS

READINGS

ILLUSTRATIONS

Cover: Andy Warhol, *Alexander the Great* (1982): synthetic polymer paint and silkscreen ink on canvas 40×40 inches (© The Andy Warhol Foundation for the Visual Arts, Inc./ARS, NY and DACS, London 2002).

Frontispiece: 'The Alexander Mosaic' *La Battaglia d'Isso* (photograph used with the permission of the Soprintendenza Archeologica della Provincia di Napoli e Caserta) from the House of the Faun at Pompeii.

MAPS

Acknowledgements

Without the assistance of a vast number of people, this book would never have undergone the immense transformation that developed it from a chapter of my PhD thesis into something entirely different. My main debt, as so often, is to John Henderson: his unfailing ability to encourage my flagging efforts, and to reignite my enthusiasm for Roman Alexanders is to a large extent responsible for everything that sparkles in this book. But numerous others have offered help along the way. Closest to home, I have been lucky enough to have a wonderfully supportive group of colleagues at the University of Birmingham (in particular, Matthew Fox, Niall Livingstone and Elena Theodorakopoulos), who have provided an invaluable safety net at moments of crisis. I also owe a particular debt to a succession of undergraduate students at Cambridge and Birmingham, whose interest in my classes on the reception of Alexander, and whose responses to my investigations, have helped to shape many of the concerns of this book.

Christina Kraus has not only helped to tease out some of my ideas on various occasions: she has also read various drafts of the book-in-progress, offering intellectual support and good humour far beyond anything I might have expected. A chance meeting triggered an ongoing series of exchanges on Statius with Carole Newlands, whose interest and sharing of readings has produced a much more detailed (and far more stimulating) engagement with the *Siluae* than I had originally foreseen. Finally, some years of moral (and intellectual) support from Alison Sharrock have reminded me that the struggle of being a classicist can also be fun.

Two other readers have offered welcome advice and encouragement. From a classicist's perspective, Gideon Nisbet, who often asked the questions I hadn't thought of answering and whose perseverence and toil helped bring the index to life. From the perspective of a non-classicist (who probably received a larger bundle of pages than he had expected), Alistair Newall. Thank you both.

University of Exeter Press has been consistently efficient and patient, and Peter Wiseman has offered acute and careful criticism, the results of which I hope I have been able to incorporate into the finished work. I am particularly grateful to the Press for its help in obtaining permission to use the cover image, and to the Department of Classics at Birmingham for its subsidy towards the costs of using this technicolour Alexander, which sums up so many of his contradictions and fascinations.

On a more personal level, I would like to thank Daniel Lea, who has seen this book through from its beginnings ten years ago, has read more versions of it than I can bear to count, and who has suffered with me through its frequently painful birth pangs. Without Daniel, it would never have been started.

Introduction

The Empty Bottle

Just by writing and reading the name 'Alexander the Great' we are invoking a weighty burden of cultural baggage, ranging from imperialist dreams of world dominion and military glory to visions of a mystical quest, pushing back the boundaries of everyday, experiential reality. This is a book about the ways in which Alexander came to be an important figure in the Roman world, but in a broader sense it will also engage with our own twenty-first century relationship with Alexander, Rome and the changing discipline of Classics.

Alexander is a figure who continues to fascinate and enchant, but as the coming chapters discuss, the allure that surrounds him was beginning to be constructed even during his own lifetime, and under his own auspices. Thus, in Alexander, we find an appropriate model for the increasing importance of celebrity and media manipulation in public life. The publication of this book illustrates a continuing cultural preoccupation with the model of Alexander as both classical and contemporary icon. We, as readers and writers, are all complicit in the creation of Alexander, and becoming involved in this discourse means becoming involved in the perpetual cycle of recreating Alexander.

The German historian Ulrich Wilcken's perceptive characterization of Alexander as symbolizing all things to all men exemplifies the flexibility of the Alexander myth as a significatory paradigm. Developments of this idea have led to Alexander being described metaphorically as a bottle that can be filled with any 'wine'.[1]

Given the alcoholic excesses that play a major part in almost all stories of Alexander's life, this metaphor has an (apparently) unintentional, yet biting, irony, but within the metaphor there also lurks a significant point about the way in which the greater story of Alexander has come into being. During the past century, interest in theories of historiography and historical method has increased rapidly, and to extend the metaphor further, if Alexander is a bottle that can be filled with any wine, then the historian becomes the 'winemaker', blending literary skills and source study into a final bottled product. It is to this vision of historiography as a creative process that the title of this chapter refers, the process by which Alexander's story has developed and continues to hold relevance.[2]

We all bring our own assumptions to bear on our interests and this book is closely concerned with the way in which such individual approaches have shaped the history of Alexander the Great. The kinds of discourse encompassed include the rhetorical, biographical and historiographical material that was already saturating ancient consciousness and continues to permeate scholarly research and the popular media today. Through a discussion of a selection of texts we can examine the proliferation of versions of Alexander in the Roman world, and establish why preference is given to particular accounts. In this way we can approach sources with an awareness of what they may want (and not want) to tell us. Ultimately, we will be able to read a story of the development of a textualized Alexander and his impact on Roman political evolution, whilst also gaining a sense of the semiotics of Alexander in the modern world. By engaging with the issues of historical and biographical truth raised when an author writes and a reader consumes a text, this study traces the Roman story of Alexander and its continuing impact on the twentieth and twenty-first centuries. It demonstrates that even if the construction of a defining, consistent history of Alexander recedes as a goal, we will still retain an understanding of the degree of parallelism between ancient and modern mythmaking. This parallelism has led not only to the enduring fascination of the figure of Alexander, but also forms part of a perennial reading of Rome and Alexander as models of power and conquest in state and individual.

The rationale for a study of Roman engagement with Alexander is twofold: in the first place, the early story of Alexander as we receive it today is essentially a Roman story, constructed and developed during the period of Roman domination of the Mediterranean world. Secondly, Rome and the Roman Empire in differing modes and guises continue to grip the modern imagination. Given Alexander's intimate and persistent connexion with power and empire at Rome, and contemporary fascination with Rome as the quintessential imperializing western state, there is an immediate and clear relevance for a study of Roman engagement with Alexander. The vital connecting factor for interest then and now is the pervasive and continuing interplay between ancient and modern mythologizing. Our primary literary sources for Alexander, although composed in both Greek and Latin, are all inextricably texts of and about the Roman world that produced them, and therefore texts engaged with a man and a myth that were historical even in their own eras. More importantly, these texts were even then concerned with the story of a past before Roman domination of the Mediterranean, before the *imperium sine fine* (unlimited power) of the Augustan worldview, and before the revival of Hellenism in the late first and early second centuries CE. The Alexander that we know and reinterpret is himself a 'Roman' construct, a product of Roman sensibilities and worldview; it was the Romans who made him 'the Great'. At the same time, our interest in Roman negotiations of power, politics and imperialism is intrinsically related back to Alexander as an archetype for power and imperialism in the Roman world.[3]

Over the course of Chapters 2 to 4, this study presents a selection of texts, commencing in the first century BCE, and drawing on material up to the reign of the Emperor Trajan in the second century CE. These chapters provide themed discussions, exploring the literary and cultural contexts of the authors discussed, and examining the different ways in which Alexander persists as a popular icon. Based on the readings of these chapters, Chapter 5 develops their literary analysis into a discussion of a broad spectrum of engagement with Alexander on the part of Roman politicians, generals and emperors, focusing on Scipio, Pompey, Caesar, Augustus, Germanicus and Nero. By the conclusion of this study, we will have considered a selection of key texts on Alexander, texts which provide a comparative framework for a wider understanding of developing Roman concerns and for the interrogation of a discourse of government and power in which Alexander was a recurring protagonist. This study requires of its readers an intellectual shift, from the process of accessing ancient material on Alexander as historical sources to be mined for cross-referential, objective, scholarly accounts of Alexander's life, to an appreciation of their place as cultural texts in their own right, available for literary and contextual study as part of the greater (and ever-developing) story of 'Alexander'. This study is not about the recovery of History, rather, it is concerned with discussing the responses, ideas and intellectual requirements that led authors into ideological bias when collating and editing their collections of fact, hearsay, myth, prejudice and literary artifice into textual form. Not all of the texts examined in this study are wholly concerned with Alexander, and most make no claims to represent the minutiae of his whole life-story; rather, they attempt to create an impression of what 'Alexander' can mean by reworking and reusing motifs from the stock of available stories. This process of 'cultural mythmaking' forms the basis for the following chapters.[4]

Chapter 1 provides a background discussion to the texts discussed in Chapters 2 to 4, suggesting some of the ways in which Alexander's story, bursting with reinterpretations of kingship, was focal in the changing pattern of Roman politics. Roman expansion east in the first century BCE brought Roman generals into contact with the Hellenistic kingdoms of the Successors of Alexander. Alexander's generals had founded these states after his death, men who could use their close association with him as a justification for seizing power, generals who carved out individual territories from the territory he had conquered. The political development of these states offered a stark contrast to the abhorrence of monarchical government that epitomized Roman republican ideology. Association with Alexander during his lifetime had offered his generals a route to supreme power, and a validation for retention of that power by their heirs in the wake of his deification. For Rome, these kingdoms demonstrated how a country founded in battle and based on conquest could offer a rapid route to power for a charismatic military leader. As any map of the Mediterranean will make tellingly clear, Alexander and Rome—via the kingdoms of the Successors—were on a geographical and cultural collision course (see Maps 1 and 2). Geographically, Roman expansion east, first into Greece and Macedon, later into Parthia, meant that the two empires had the potential to be co-terminous. Aside from the military and political synchronization as empire-builders, Rome and Alexander had another point in common, both had significant representation as *cultural* imperialists, spreading western culture in the decadent and barbarous East. Worryingly, however, both also suffered from the two-way nature of the cultural interchange set in motion. Roman national self-definition as a state that had expelled kings, that glorified victory and required military service, meant that Alexander's imagery as the ultimate western conqueror of the East was bound to surface.

One of the reasons why Alexander has retained such an enduring popularity is that like the semi-divine heroes of myth and epic, he emerges as an exciting, dangerous figure. But unlike the heroes of myth, we believe that we can locate him in a 'real', historical past. An inescapable fascination with Alexander the man has led to a preponderance of studies that attempt to peel back layers of historical material, mining source texts with the tacit assumption that there was some real, quantifiable and ultimately available 'Alexander' awaiting discovery beneath the narratives and legends. Over the course of this study I will be suggesting ways in which we can side-step the endless stream of *Quellenforschung* that makes up such a large portion of the Alexander industry, and return to the narratives presented by literary and cultural texts that have created the iconic Alexander who still exists today. We may want to know more about Alexander, but we have to accept that his may not be the only story that our sources are necessarily trying to tell. Instead of trying to force the 'real' Alexander to step forward, this study suggests critical strategies for reading the stories that our texts do offer. These strategies are based in contextualization—both for composition and for the textual Alexander—and on an investigation of the implicit or explicit commentary offered by the author/narrator. Awareness of a dichotomy between the roles of author and narrator is a prerequisite for this study, and the reader must beware (and be aware) of such a distinction when reading the texts on offer.

A vast bibliography on Alexander the Great already exists, and this book is not about adding to the sum of knowledge about the historical Alexander. Nor, despite the historical introduction that dominates Chapter 1, is it a book that tries to narrate a linear, chronological history of Rome. Indeed, many readers may find that they already know a story of late republican and early Roman imperial history so well that a large chunk of Chapter 1 seems superfluous. For some readers, this may in fact be the case, but having decided to write a version of Roman history that complemented the changing tradition of Alexander, I discovered that many of the 'facts' that I had previously taken for granted were up for intellectual grabs in a way that I had never contemplated. And as certainties dissolve and patterns of historical narrative undergo a process of realignment, new stories emerge. This book highlights a process of appropriation of Alexander whereby he becomes a key figure in the enormous political and cultural changes taking place in Rome towards the end of the Republic and in the early imperial period. Reading any history of Rome opens up a wide vista of potentially available stories to tell, and the version of Rome that develops in Chapter 1 is designed to offer a clear backdrop for thinking about the texts and personalities of Chapters 2 to 5, suggesting ways in which historical information can be realigned and reinterpreted on the most basic level, and foregrounding the role of the author *qua* inventor in preparation for the main body of this book. If Chapter 1 juggles with facts and their interpretation in order to suggest ways of reading history more actively, then the next three chapters suggest how the texts upon which historical narratives are based are themselves equally open-ended. Although not encyclopaedic, the texts that I have selected provide a series of semi-transparent windows through which a gradually developing story of Roman interest in Alexander can be perceived.[5] But to speak in linear, developmental terms sends out the wrong interpretative signals. The impression is frequently of *mise en abîme* rather than progression, and despite the artificiality of imposing a linear framework on such an inherently unruly and tangled web of interconnecting stories and impressions, this book suggests that it is possible, and can even perhaps be elegant, to use an engaged and self-reflexive textual format to interrogate the narrative and textual layers that make up our historical and cultural consciousness. With Walter Blackett, one of the characters in J.G. Farrell's *The Singapore Grip*—set at the moment of collapse of British power in Singapore—we might begin this exploration with a consideration of:

> . . . what makes up a moment of history; if you took a knife and chopped cleanly through a moment of history what would it look like in cross-section? Would it be like chopping through a leg of lamb where you see the end of the muscles, nerves, sinews and bone of one piece matching a similar arrangement in the other? Walter thought that it would, on the whole. A moment of history would be composed of countless millions of events of varying degrees of importance, some of them independent, others associated with each other. And since all these events would have both causes and consequences they would certainly match each other where they were divided, just like the leg of lamb. But did all these events collectively have a meaning?
> Most people, Walter believed, would have said 'No, they are merely random.' Perhaps sometimes, in retrospect, we may stick a label on a whole stretch of events and call it, say, 'The Age of Enlightenment' the way we might call a long hank of muscle a fillet steak, but we are simply imposing a meaning on what was, unlike the fillet steak whose cells are organised to some purpose, essentially random. Well, if that was what most people thought, Walter did not agree with them.
> Farrell 1978, 423–24

The conceit is striking in its invocation of a gristly and organic historiographical process, one in which order and iconography can be simultaneously inexplicable, random, and susceptible to a grand perspective. In this analogy we find a historical model that can encompass history as minutiae, apparently haphazard combinations of sinew and capillary which are still susceptible to reinterpretation on both molecular and macrocosmic levels. It is to this model, with its tension between 'natural' and structured conceptual history, that I suggest we turn when thinking about the tradition of Alexander, a tradition which demands that we engage with an ongoing process of reception and revitalization, a history written on the body, with a politicization of appearance and identity that can shift from personal to public and national significance with the polyvalence of Alexander himself.

Reading Alexander

An understanding of context and historical background is vital if we are to engage with texts in a manner approaching the complexity of nuance and evocation within which they have been successively read. The main texts that form the basis for our understanding of the different meanings of 'Alexander the Great' are texts of the Roman world, and are therefore also texts that inform us not just on Alexander, but also on the agendas and interests of a world in which Alexander remained a vital and significant figure. With an appreciation of their compositional context in place, we can get down to *how* we focus on Alexander. The extant textualized story of Alexander begins, for us, in the narratives and concerns of Roman authors. This should warn us that even if we want to establish a linear and sequential set of headings for considering reception, we will immediately be faced with a problem. For these authors, the construction of a linear and externally consistent narrative was not, in many cases, a priority. Instead, what drove many authors to write about Alexander was the susceptibility of his life to periodization, to episodicization, and most of all, to a treatment as a rich source of excerpts and exempla, waiting to be plundered for use in specific discursive contexts. The vitality of 'Alexander' as a signifier was a function of his cultural polyvalence, demanding that each narrator exercise a series of choices: to whom and in what successive contexts was Alexander most important? This in turn excludes a wide variety of references, texts and contexts, just as it valorizes those elected. This dilemma, if allowed to become too onerous, could preclude any attempt to undertake this project, and indeed almost every culturally and contextually constructed recuperative project is similarly constrained. My approach has been to focus on a themed selection of texts, but having decided upon a thematic framework, the first task is to choose appropriate themes. The themes that drive Chapters 2 to 4 are arranged in order to return us to the basic question that underlies this book—why be interested in Alexander? The answers that recur are that he provides an archetype for monarchy and charismatic autocracy that continues to have implications even for present-day leaders, that his brand of media-wise power prefigures all subsequent political propaganda, and that the mythic status of his doomed eastward campaign, his gilded youth, excess and early death persists in the mythography of celebrities who die young. These unfinished lives remove them from the natural cycle of death, decay and disintegration. The final chapter picks up these themes and refocuses them on the Roman Alexanders who have formed a backdrop to the textual and historical explorations of the rest of the book.

Map 1

The Roman World: From Republic to Empire

Rome's control over the Mediterranean world and near east ebbed and flowed during the time-span covered by this book (100 BCE to 117 CE). This map locates the key scenes for authors, texts, and the playing out of the Roman imperial adventure, illustrating how Alexander's world collided with and merged into the Roman experience.

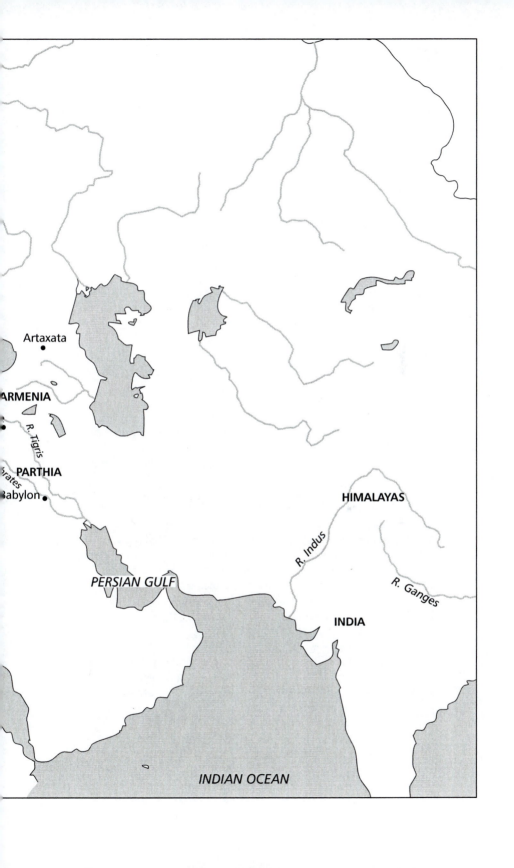

Artaxata

ARMENIA

R. Tigris

PARTHIA

Babylon

HIMALAYAS

R. Indus

PERSIAN GULF

R. Ganges

INDIA

INDIAN OCEAN

Chronology of Alexander

356   July: birth; parents Philip II and Olympias.

340/39 Appointed Regent by Philip whilst Philip besieges Byzantium; founds Alexandropolis in Thrace.

338   August: commands the right wing at Chaeronea.

336   Succeeds to throne after Philip assassinated; marches south against Greek states; confirmed as leader of League of Corinth.

335   Spring: campaign in Thrace.
June: marches to Illyria.
August/September: revolt of Thebes.
October: capture and destruction of Thebes.

334   Spring: crossing into Asia.
May: battle of Granicus. On through Sardis, Priene, Ephesus . . . lays siege to Miletus, Halicarnassus.
Autumn: marches into Caria, then Lycia, Pamphylia; Parmenion sent to Phrygia via Sardis.

334/3 Winter: moves to Milyas, then Phaselis, Side, Celaenae.

333   Spring: marches north to Gordium. Then marches east to Ancyra, then south to Cilician Gates, Tarsus. Taken ill with fever at Tarsus; action at Soli; news of capture of Halicarnassus.
November: battle of Issus. Parmenion captures Damascus; on to Phoenicia—Marathus, Byblus, Sidon.

332   January: siege of Tyre.
July/August: capture of Tyre.
September: siege of Gaza.
November: capture of Gaza. Marches on Egypt—Pelusium, Memphis; coronation as Pharoah. Foundation of Alexandria.

332/1 Winter: visit to Siwah (oracle of Ammon); return to Memphis; organization of Egypt.

331   Spring: marches north from Memphis to Tyre.
May: news of 'revolt' of Agis of Sparta.
July/August: marches east to Thapsacus on Euphrates.

20 September: eclipse of moon, two days after crossing of Tigris.

1 October: battle of Gaugamela.

Late autumn: Agis defeated by Antipater at Megalopolis.

October/November: moves south to Babylon, where Alexander waits.

December: arrival at Susa.

End December: move east through land of Uxii and Persian Gates to Persepolis.

330   January/April: stay in Persepolis.

April: campaign in interior of Persia.

May: return to Persepolis; burning of palace and departure for Ecbatana. At Ecbatana: Greek allies dismissed; marches north-east to Caspian Gates.

July: death of Darius; capture of body.

Late summer: advances to border of Hyrcania; reception of Persian nobles. Alexander acts as Great King and adopts Persian/Median dress. To Zadracarta, towards Bactria, but diversion to Artacana (revolt of Satibarzanes).

Autumn: trial and death of Philotas; murder of Parmenion. Trial of Amyntas and his brothers. Marches through land of Ariaspes. Arrest of Demetrius the bodyguard; move to Arachosia.

November: through Paropamisadae.

330/29 Winter: foundation of Alexandria (Kandahar?).

329   Early spring crossing of Hindu Kush. Move to Drapsaca and Bactria; older men and Thessalian volunteers sent home. Crossing of Oxus; capture and execution of Bessus. To Maracanda (Samarcand).

Summer: moves to river Jaxartes; foundation of Alexandria Eschate. Mid-summer: revolt of local tribes and Sogdiana; campaigns v. Spitamenes.

329/8 Winter: at Zariaspa; embassies from Scythians and Chorasmians.

328   Summer: trouble in Sogdiana with Massagetai and Spitamenes.

Autumn: detachment left with Coenus in Sogdiana for winter. Spitamenes killed by Massagetai. Returns to Maracanda; murder of Clitus the Black.

328/7 Winter: winter quarters at Nautaca.

327   Early spring: capture of rock of Sogdiana.

Spring: capture of rock of Choriene. To Bactria; defeat of Catanes and Austanes, last opposition in Paraitacene. Pages' Conspiracy; arrest of Callisthenes the historian.

Late spring: departure from Bactria. Capture of Massaga, and then of rock of Aornus.

Autumn: departure for India. Late in year death of Callisthenes.

327/6 Winter: quarters in Assacene.

326   Early spring crossing of Indus; to Taxila. River Hydaspes reached.

May: battle of river Hydaspes; death of Bucephalus.

May/June: halt in kingdom of Porus.

Late June: advances to river Acesines, then Hyphasis; revolt of army. Returns to Hydaspes; death of Coenus; construction of fleet.

November: journey downstream begins. Subjugation of Malli tribe; Alexander wounded in lung.

325   Mid-July: arrival at Patala.

August: moves downstream from Patala; Nearchus delayed by winds.

September: Alexander reaches the Oritae.

September/October: Nearchus leaves on voyage. Alexander marches through Gedrosia and reaches Pura.

December: Nearchus reaches Hormuz and rejoins Alexander.

324   January–March: Nearchus leaves Hormuz, to rejoin Alexander at Susa.

April?: mass marriages at Susa; repayment of soldiers' debts; voyage up Tigris to Opis.

June?: mutiny at Opis; banquet of reconciliation.

August/September: Exiles' Decree published by Nicanor at Olympic Games.

October: to Ecbatana; death of Hephaestion.

324/3   Winter: expedition against Cossians. To Babylon; preparations for Arabian expedition.

323   c.1 June: Alexander taken ill.

10 June, Babylon: death of Alexander.

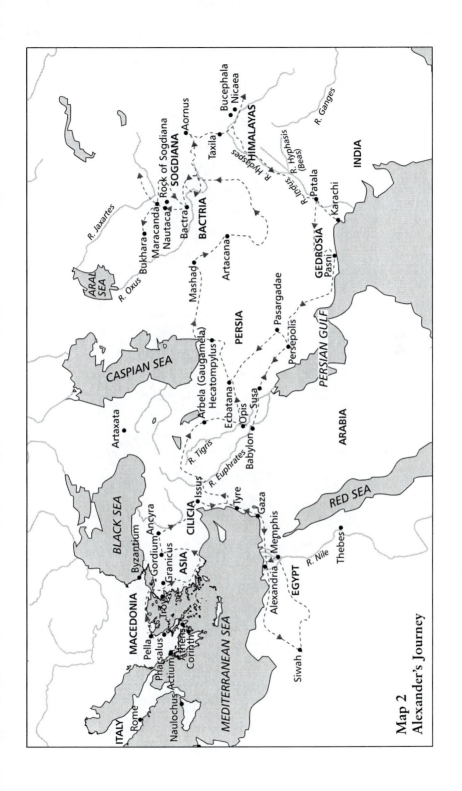

Map 2
Alexander's Journey

1. The Master of the Griselda Legend, *Alexander the Great* The languid downward gaze and flowing locks of this Alexander (probably dating from the early sixteenth century) add to the unusual tranquillity of this portrait. Here, Alexander is every inch the Renaissance Prince. The Latin caption reads: 'I, Alexander, who conquered the whole world with my own strength, shook off the flames of desire from my heart. It is of no avail to rejoice in the outward triumphs of war if the mind lies sick, and rages within.'

1

History into Story

Starting at the beginning: what's in a name? What is it that initially grabs our attention about this particular 'Alexander', what makes him stand out from any other previous or subsequent Alexanders? The answer, on the level of primary reflex, is in the sobriquet. Our Alexander is 'Alexander the Great', but his by-line—'the Great'—was a relatively late arrival on the Roman scene.[1]

In this chapter I will be teasing out some of the implications of this magnification of Alexander for Rome and Greece alike, and examining the way in which even the most basic act of transliterating 'Alexander' from Greek into Latin characters could make a difference to the semiotics of a Latin text. This change in language, and the complexity of associations that particular linguistic modes of expression evoke, is vitally important to our understanding of the ways in which 'Alexander' persists as a name to conjure with. This chapter considers the centrality of this potential for slippage at the heart of Alexander-mythology. The second part of this chapter will consider the ways in which the Hellenistic kingdoms of the Successors developed a public and political role for history in the creation of monarchical and national identity, leading ultimately to the ways in which 'making' history came to be a primary function of the Roman senatorial elite from the first century BCE onwards. By exploring the development of Roman configurations of what it meant to be a historical people we can investigate whether Roman identity as a people and the political reality of the state were always at stake, whenever Alexander was brought into play. In the wake of late republican Alexanders such as Pompey and Caesar, Roman emperors were required to make a choice, sometimes explicitly, about the kind of Alexander they would accept or have thrust upon them as a model. This takes us back to the starting premise of Alexander's title. We think of him generally as 'the

Great', and sometimes as Alexander (III) of Macedon, but in his iconic career in the Roman world his regular slippage from king, commander and statesman to degenerate, murderous tyrant, was a key element in his enduring relevance as a prototype for Roman experience.[2]

What's in a Name?

In order to explore nomenclature a little further, we can test out what happens if we rename our Alexander the Great. If we call him 'Alexander of Macedon', we immediately connect with a geographical and ethnographic debate that has continued to surround 'Macedonia' to the present day.[3] This name change ties Alexander to a small and previously obscure state in Mediterranean terms, a state which only emerged as a leader of Greece under his father Philip.[4] Until then, we could argue, Hellenic (and particularly Athenian) perceptions of Macedon dismissed it as a cultural wasteland, ruled over by kings and distinguished more for small-scale raids on neighbouring states than for any intellectual or ideological advances.[5] From a 'Greek' perspective, Macedon functioned as a barbarous land to the north, which fulfilled barbarian reputation by sweeping down on the obdurate nations that refused to fall in with its hegemony, a country where heavy drinking was endemic, polygamy was tolerated, and the arts disdained. Nevertheless, not all potential Greek interpretations of Alexander 'of Macedon' need be negative, and Alexander himself was to invoke some of these more positive associations when mustering support for his Persian expedition from amongst the Greek states. Alexander of Macedon leading a Greek army could be represented as leading a unified, Hellenized West, in a cultural clash with the East. Macedonian military aggrandizement could be reconfigured as a civilizing mission to spread Greek culture to the Persian Empire as payback for Persian aggression. This means that *this* Alexander can represent both barely civilized barbarian *and* Greek saviour. That Persia had on occasion joined forces with Sparta, Athens' main rival before Philip of Macedon changed the balance of power, would add spice to the inter-Greek rivalries involved.[6]

For a Roman in the first century BCE, the combination of Alexander's Greek identity with Rome's victory over the Greek world, makes Alexander a proto-Aeneas figure; Trojan Aeneas and 'Macedonian' Alexander both, in their different ways, prefigure Roman expansion into the Mediterranean and Asia. For Rome,

Alexander had *always* been there first. Evoking Alexander's intimate connexion with such a lowly state is part of a discourse of diminution of his achievements that we find in authors such as Lucan and Juvenal,[7] and it is a discourse that carries a double-edged meaning. Macedon was a small state that came to dominate the Greek world, and as Livy's use of Pyrrhus as a quasi-Alexander suggests, Macedon could still signify 'Greece', or even Alexander's 'East' in a Roman worldview. For Rome, the ascendant Mediterranean power, the glories of Alexander's conquests and Macedonian supremacy were short-lived, and so by conjuring with Alexander 'of Macedon', Romans were also, paradoxically, evoking an inbuilt discourse of the transitory nature of imperial greatness. This complexity of meanings surrounding Alexander's description meant that the conquest of Alexander's birthplace could diminish his glory in the light of Roman triumphs (the conqueror conquered), whilst also aggrandizing Roman achievement. The dialogue between both interpretations makes available a sense of the impermanence of empire and divine favour. In this discourse, as we shall see when looking at Livy, the role of Alexander's conquests is to be simultaneously impressive and puny in comparison with the might of the Roman war-machine. An alternative model that is also implicit in comparisons between Rome and Alexander suggests that if the empire conquered by Alexander stands as an interpretative model for Roman imperialism, it can offer a paradigm for the victory of a young, warlike nation over the decadence of an ageing civilization. In this cyclical scenario, the fall of the ageing, decadent, Hellenized East offers a warning against the dangers of over-expansion—Alexander's empire (like all empires?) became what it had conquered. This flexibility—an important feature for the development and enduring popularity of Alexander—meant that 'Alexander' was at once available to those who wished to provide a critique of imperial policy or behaviour (e.g. the younger Seneca) and to those favourable to Roman achievements (e.g. Livy).

A second result of the removal of Alexander's 'Great' is a playing down of the personality cult that surrounded Alexander—probably with his encouragement, if he was as canny a ruler as we are led to believe. Instead of standing alone as 'Alexander the Great', he becomes a Macedonian ruler, reconfigured as a leader of his countrymen rather than a spectacular individualist. Such an interpretation also tones down Alexander's role as political maverick and reformer, a man who turned a traditional Macedonian monarchy into a charismatic autocracy, with a divine leader at its head. The end result of this shift suggests that we might re-view his life as an attempt to build a Greater

Macedonian Empire, rather than as the one-way trip of a doomed young hero, who conquered the gorgeous East only to be ensnared by its perilous luxury and decadence. If we consider this shift in Roman political terms, the implications for late republican and imperial politics become even more crucial. Alexander begins to shed his role as a unique figure, and is transformed into one in a line of rulers, similar to the list of Roman super-Alexanders that Livy proposes in his history of Rome (Readings 2.1 and 2.2). By (linguistically) limiting his empire to 'Macedon', we remind ourselves of his lack of lasting military success: he may have conquered Persia, but he never consolidated his possessions, and—perhaps ironically—can still be defined by his country of birth rather than by his imperial domain.

Names matter. Leading a 'Greek' army and championing a 'Greek' cause, Macedon could stand for Rome's Greece *and* Rome's gateway to Alexander's empire. Alexander was the ultimate western conqueror in the East; Rome's eastern aspirations would always demand evaluation on his terms. The seeds of the rapid political change undergone in Rome in the first century BCE are evident in Rome's growing domination of the Mediterranean, and particularly the conquest of Greece in the second century BCE.[8] As more and more of the Mediterranean world changed from a collection of independent kingdoms and states into client kingdoms, and ultimately provinces of the Roman Empire, the fluidity of national identity became an increasingly important political issue. For Rome, it was necessary that these states have a fluid identity that could be merged successfully with Roman government and political organisation; but once this potential for transience and impermanence had been established, how could Roman imperium be regarded as any more secure than previous settlements, or indeed, Alexander's? If Alexander is 'the Great', how can it have happened that his personal legacy became so ambiguous, and that his empire disintegrated so quickly after his death, and what does this say about all 'Greatness'? In order to consider use of Alexander as a Roman cultural icon, we first need to think broadly about what sort of milieu for appropriation of Alexander existed in Rome, and what expectations a Roman audience might have had from stories of Alexander. The ultimate joke in all this must be that the 'original' Alexander is not Alexander the Great, but *Paris of Troy*, wife-stealer and anti-hero *par excellence*. So the first 'Alexander' who *did* accomplish a westward smash-and-grab raid, lurks, ever-contemporary, behind all successive models. A succession of potential Roman Alexanders saturated Rome during the first century BCE, but in order to gain some understanding of how these characters were able to tap into a cultural awareness of what Alexander could mean, we need to look a little further back. We must consider the years after Alexander's death and the establishment of personal kingdoms by his generals, the Successors.

First, this involves an investigation of how and why the kinds of political settlement achieved by the Successors might have had particular significance for the expanding Roman Empire.[9] Second, the use of 'Alexander' as narrative shorthand for a bundle of political and cultural associations can also suggest ways in which Rome could have become intimately involved in an ongoing discourse concerning political stability and cultural superiority. Effectively, we need to engage with the different ways in which 'succession' becomes integral to political developments at Rome. Initially, Rome as a collective becomes 'successor' to Alexander via conquest of the Hellenistic kingdoms in the East. Eventually, the Roman state becomes positioned not just as heir to their (and his) empire-building ambitions, but also has to come to terms with a system based around direct transference of power from one generation of a family to the next. In this way, we can see that geographical and political empire are not the only reasons why 'succession' becomes a live issue at Rome; Rome is also involved in a complex transition from oligarchy to autocracy in a manner that echoes the literary narratives of Alexander's political career. Rome itself, therefore, becomes a Successor kingdom of sorts. In the next section I suggest how this greater pan-Mediterranean political and historical context for Roman appropriation of Alexander can allow us to gain an awareness of some of the possible reasons for the inescapable potency of Alexander as a political and cultural construct. With this background in mind, we can then trace the ways in which the developing Roman appropriation of Alexander gradually shifted emphasis from state (Macedon) to would-be dynast ('the Great') as the Republic crumbled and the Principate became more firmly established.

Alexander and the Successors: Making History

With Alexander (and to a lesser extent, his father Philip), official control of information and media develops into an important function of autocracy. This means that the way in which historians recorded their actions became an integral function of their reigns. The high level of control over his own image that Alexander appears to have achieved became formalized in the Hellenistic kingdoms, developing into a significant element in the burgeoning propaganda machines of these emerging states. When Alexander succeeded his father Philip, Macedon was just beginning to have a major impact on the Greek world. Philip had unified his country and pushed south, drawing the Greek states into a Macedonian hegemony. In so doing, he had engineered Macedonian domination of a world that portrayed his people as uncivilized, and his country as a place of warring families and primitive, monarchical government. Even in the face of Macedonian military supremacy, the Greek world was reluctant to accept this obscure northern land as the head of a Hellenic coalition. It was in the wake of this reluctance that either Philip himself, or Alexander, established the grand scheme of a war against Persia. This war could be marketed as a means of retaliation for Persian invasion of Greece. By constructing a propagandist campaign against Persia in terms of Greek revenge against the eastern invader, it became possible to use it as a rallying cry for Greek unity behind a common cause. Macedon and its ruler could be repositioned from non-Greek ('barbarian') to 'Greek' figurehead, or even pin-up. Perhaps surprisingly, in the light of the significance of this pan-Hellenic propaganda, we lack contemporary sources for Alexander's eastern campaign. I say surprisingly, because one of the key features of the imagery that has come down to us about Alexander is his media awareness. Alexander was accompanied on campaign by the historian Callisthenes, Aristotle's nephew, who seems to have been expected to put together an on-the-spot record of the progress of the adventure.

This careful consideration for how the Persian campaign would be perceived, both at the time and posthumously, taken alongside Alexander's control of how he was represented visually, suggests that he was highly conscious of the ways in which image-making needed to be centrally controlled.[10] His admiration for Homer, and particularly the Homeric Achilles, stemmed in part from his belief that he was descended from Achilles, but also seems to have been tied up in a recognition that without someone to record heroic exploits effectively, their value for posterity would be minuscule.[11] Thus, fairly or not, we have a sense of Alexander as someone who was highly concerned with his reputation, both during his lifetime and posthumously, and who was also aware of the kinds of behaviour necessary to ensure its enhancement. This is likely to have been a knowing awareness, meaning that before we dismiss some episodes in the story of Alexander as demonstrating his divine monomania, his abandonment of 'Greek' customs for the trappings of eastern monarchy, his delusory belief in his soldiers' willingness to follow him whatever the human cost, we should also take another side of these vignettes into account. It is these images of excessive behaviour, of marvellous good looks and bravery, of drunken debauchery and magnificent military feats, combined with a crusade into the unknown, that have kept Alexander 'great'. So before we wonder at the inability of such a media-conscious monarch to manage his reputation more successfully, we should remember that having such a vibrant and cross-cultural reputation for anything, at this temporal remove, is a marvellous feat in itself. Moreover, as we can now take into consideration, Alexander was not the only figure on the expedition with an eye to history.

The source most commonly cited for Alexander is Arrian, and although his reputation as the only 'good' source for Alexander has diminished in recent years,[12] his is still the account most often turned to for information about Alexander's campaigns. Arrian provides us with an immediate gateway to those other campaign historians whose accounts provided some of the basis for the narratives of later writers, and these primary historical accounts were written by a group of men who were to become politically significant after Alexander's death. In his Preface, Arrian highlights his dependence on Ptolemy, and claims that he considers him to be the most trustworthy source for Alexander because Ptolemy was not just one of Alexander's generals and an important figure in the Macedonian hierarchy, he was also one of the men who carved out a kingdom for himself in the aftermath of Alexander's death at Babylon in 323 BCE. Arrian, writing in the second century CE, believed (or claimed to believe) that because Ptolemy became a king, his narrative was intrinsically the most credible, because for a king to lie would be particularly shameful. To us, this may seem naïve and even bizarre, but it raises important questions regarding the ways in which Alexander's 'greatness' was modulated and translated in the Hellenistic period, and how the political and cultural changes that took place in the territory conquered by Alexander were to have a direct impact on the development of Alexander-imagery in the Roman world. Furthermore, it suggests that ancient concepts of 'truth' and 'fiction', and how these concepts related to the production of history, were strikingly different to modern criteria for the evaluation of historical material and texts. These changes, and the relationship between Alexander's campaigns, his generals and the Hellenistic kingdoms, were to have a fundamental effect on the public and official role of history and its textualization in a way that would alter the development of political history at Rome.

Before we can consider what kinds of agenda may have informed the posthumous histories and accounts, we first need to think about the ways in which Alexander's campaigns may have been being recorded as they happened, in 'real-time'. We may want to assume that the narratives written by Alexander's generals were compiled in some form during the campaign, but information concerning their compositional history is lost to us.[13] The obvious place to start looking is with the historian Callisthenes, who was brought on the expedition by Alexander as an 'official' historian for the project. He wrote up ongoing accounts of the campaign in some form, but was executed by Alexander on a charge of treason, unconnected, as far as we know, to what he wrote. This history must have remained incomplete, although probably still available in some form to other authors. Alongside Callisthenes' 'official' history, it is thought that some form of campaign log or daybook was also kept. This is usually referred to as the *Ephemerides*, but there is no consensus as to whether this was kept up from the start of the expedition, or commenced at a later point. Nor do we know exactly how it was written, whether some one person was responsible for putting together material on a daily, weekly or monthly basis, or even what form the narrative may have taken. Nevertheless, it seems that there was some kind of record of the campaign available to Hellenistic authors, and the *Ephemerides* may have formed part of it.[14] Also available may have been individual generals' personal records, focusing on their achievements or their relationship with Alexander. For the Hellenistic court historians, any such sources of information must have been highly significant: these narratives were written in the first instance for a group of men, or their descendants, who had used their role in Alexander's conquests as arguments for the legitimacy of their own right to rule. But the kind of representation of Alexander that might emerge from these histories could not be straightforward. On the face of it, men who were basing their right to monarchical power on their connexion with Alexander might want to improve his posthumous standing in order that their own reputations would gain some reflected glory, but the situation was more complicated that that. In the first place, prior association with Alexander and some level of general acceptance as one of his key generals was vitally important in order to gain support, to motivate and command troops, and to justify some right of succession. This focalization of the memory of Alexander is particularly evident in Ptolemy's speedy hijacking of Alexander's corpse, removing it for burial in Alexandria. Alexandria was Alexander's first self-reflexively named civic foundation, but also Ptolemy's new HQ, and in maintaining this link Ptolemy made a significant claim to an 'imperial' destiny. Ptolemy's possession of the corpse of the divine Alexander, and his focusing of Alexander's cult on Alexandria, emphasized the deceased Alexander's presence at Ptolemy's side.

Once these newly forged kingdoms had survived the first turbulent years after Alexander's death, needs began to change. The ruling family required the focus of power and popular adoration to shift from the 'mythical' founder (Alexander) to themselves, and this brought about a shift in the way in which Alexander was used. His conquistadorial role decreased in importance and he gained in divine authority, gradually being subsumed into the role of divine AdC for the first generation. For successive generations he came to function as a model ruler who was divinely ordained to monarchy. In other words, the focus for these Successor kingdoms shifted from proving the right of the first king to rule, to establishing a dynastic monarchy in which each successive ruler needed to be tied back to familial authority and inheritance rather than to direct association with Alexander.[15] It was this need to articulate a rationale for power that made the creation of textualized history of such paramount importance as a propaganda tool for dynasticism. When a dynastic ideology was being developed, all historians working on the story of Alexander needed to take into account the changing needs of their patrons, and these patrons required their own roles as victorious generals and leaders to be emphasized, perhaps causing Alexander's role to undergo a comparative diminution. In this way, the story of Alexander's adventures in the East underwent a subtle shift. Hero-focused stories were no longer required; instead what established rulers needed was evidence that the campaign's successes were direct results of their participation in Alexander's expedition. Furthermore, the fame and glory attached to Alexander's name (glory that had helped them to power in the first place) needed to be subordinated to their own victorious roles in the empire Alexander had carved out.

Rome and the 'East': Cultural Context

What kinds of intellectual preconception are revealed by our engagement with the East? For the Greek states, the East could be a land of wonder, wealth, and magic, and also a land of barbarians, of other peoples who spoke non-Greek languages, who were ruled over by kings, and whose culture could be antithetically opposed to that of the Hellenic world. This opposition is enacted on a grand scale in the story of Alexander, who drew together the warring Greek states under his leadership with the promise that this coalition would present a united front against the Persian enemy and avenge the Persian invasions of Greece. In Alexander we find a figure who could, temporarily at least, unite the Greek world under one banner, but in doing so he committed 'Greece' to a monarchy; monarchy was always susceptible to accusations of despotism, of orientalism and excess. Conceptualizations of the geographical east in terms of a mythical 'East', a land of mystery and marvel, of Dionysus, of Amazon warriors, of fabulous wealth and decadence, coexisted with a sense of the East as actively opposed to the cultural assumptions of Athens and the ideals of democratic government. This tension between East and West was left unresolved at Alexander's death, only to re-emerge in Rome. It developed through the European tradition, gaining force when the Far East began to be opened up to the European West in the seventeenth and eighteenth centuries.[16]

For Rome, a deep undercurrent of ambivalence complicated the relationship between East and West. On one level, the Greek states held the status of cultural shrine, but they still occupied an ambivalent geographical 'East' in relation to Italy. This was further problematized by the way in which reception of Alexander tended to associate him with divine monarchy and assimilation of eastern customs, whilst simultaneously making him the archetypal Greek hero and disseminator of Greek culture. One way in which we can approach the ambivalent Roman relationship with these ideas is through the Trojan foundation myths embedded in Virgil's *Aeneid*. In the *Aeneid*, Virgil confronts a legend buried in Roman self-consciousness, a legend of a mythical connexion between early Rome and Greece, binding Greeks and Romans together through literary continuity and the development of a Roman foundation myth that made the first Romans the direct heirs of the fallen Troy. From the increasingly Rome-dominated Mediterranean of the third century BCE, this myth demanded that Greeks should ally themselves with a growing power that celebrated its foundation by refugees from their one-time eastern enemies, the Trojans. The newly constructed eastern enemy, taking the place of Troy or even Persia in the discourse of a clash between East and West, was the Phoenician-founded Carthaginian Empire. In this way Carthage was inexorably forced into a nexus of ancient, mythological, cultural and literary myths that would demand an eastern enemy not just for the Achaeans, for the Greek states, or for Alexander, but also for Rome.

In the 260s BCE, Rome was desperately trying to secure Sicilian support against Carthage, and specifically, the support of the Sicilian Greek community.[17] The construction of a mutual 'Greek' heritage based upon common participation in the Trojan cycle fostered an inter-relatedness between the two peoples that could exclude the Carthaginians. This exclusion forced Carthage into the position of othered enemy, laying the foundations for a Roman distrust of north Africa that would culminate in the demonization of Ptolemaic (and therefore Alexandrian) Egypt during the civil war between Antony and Octavian. To untangle this network of literary, political and cultural associations, the figure of Alexander is vitally important. In Alexander we find a bridging link, a figure who by convention was allied with the Greek states, who idolized Achilles, who travelled everywhere with his Homer, and who set the Greek 'West' against the Carthaginian mother city of Tyre. Alexander could represent the great rewards that could attend international co-operation, but attached to him also could be the frisson of danger, the threat of degeneracy into the mores and luxury of a great defeated enemy. Where Alexander went east, and never returned, Aeneas, the Trojan hero, could come west and become Roman, could defeat the 'joint' Greek and Roman enemy, and could found Rome, a city and power that would outstrip Alexander's Egyptian city. Each literary adaptation of the Trojan myth of origins had to bear the weight of previous treatments, and increasingly, in the first century BCE, had also to be alive to the political significance that was building up around the story of Aeneas.

The Legacy of the Punic Wars

The Trojan legend first came to literary prominence at Rome in the third century BCE, when Naevian and Ennian treatments of this story were put to contemporary use as a parallel and aetiology for Rome's fate as an enemy (and conqueror) of Carthage. But by the late first century BCE a whole new set of accretions had built up. Caesar had resurrected his family's claims to descent from Venus, and in his construction of a temple to Venus Genetrix close to the Forum Romanum, he had made a monumental public statement to the citizen body about the continuing political vitality of the Trojan foundation legend. Octavian had also defeated Antony (whom we might read as an Aeneas *and* Alexander gone to the bad) and Cleopatra, reinforcing his adoptive father's steadfastness of character in leaving her for the greater good of Rome. Antony, incapable of disentangling himself from Cleopatra, could therefore be portrayed as never having been a true and *pius* Roman at all. Most importantly, from a battle against external eastern enemies, Rome had turned upon itself in a series of

bitter and costly civil wars. This shattered the illusion of the permanently 'other' foreign enemy, and forced the propagandist contortions
that sought to prove that war against Antony was war against
Cleopatra, while the Romans who fought on her side were characterized as bewitched, un-Roman, or mercenary turncoats. These factors
inexorably bound Greece, Rome and Alexander together, and are also
the prerequisites for any investigation of Alexander's significance to
Rome.

As Rome became an imperial nation, opportunities for making
money, through trade, through slavery and through the taxation
levied on the wealthy provinces of the east, made a dramatic impact
on society. No longer could Romans claim (if, indeed this was ever
more than a seductive culture-myth of nostalgia) to be an agricul-
turally based nation of hard-living, hard-hitting citizen farmers. The
monetary wealth that was pouring into Rome brought with it a new
cultural diversity for those who now had the money and the leisure to
afford it. At first through soldiers, then administrators and merchants,
the artistic and cultural delights of the inviting new imperial landscape came back to Rome. Eventually, through the educated house
slaves who began to take over the training of young Romans, to
attend on their masters as secretaries, to act as hairdressers, pet
philosophers and stewards, and finally, as the new provinces were
pacified, through travel, Rome changed. Roman victory in the first
Punic War (241 BCE) stands as a decisive moment in the development
of Roman imperial consciousness, and the first Roman epics date to
this period. Naevius (*c*.270–201 BCE), who fought in the first Punic
War, wrote an epic poem (*Punica*) about the conflict. This poem seems
to have been both the first major Latin epic poem *by a Roman*, and
also the first great national epic for Rome.[18]

Victory in the first Punic War provided an impetus for Roman
expansion in the Mediterranean. Victory over the powerful and wealthy
Carthaginian Empire seems to have given Rome a sense of what was
attainable, and Roman domination over the Mediterranean was to be
ensured with the second Punic defeat (201 BCE). Naevius took as his
starting point the mythological origins of Rome in Troy, and brought
his story to a climax with the first defeat of Carthage. This suggests
that Roman epic had its genesis in a literary form closely concerned
with the city itself, and its power and place in the world. This Naevian
epic also demonstrates another concern that was to continue to be
central to later Roman epics: an interest in origins and the linear progression of history. Naevius' epic is extant only in fragmentary form,
but he seems to have dealt at some length with Aeneas and the

construction of a Trojan aetiology for the wars. The vital importance of these wars in a growing sense of Roman self-awareness and self-definition as a powerful nation state makes such an aetiological interest on his part highly attractive to us, but not enough has survived of Naevius' treatment of the Trojan material to make any definite judgements. The significance of Naevius for our analysis of Roman engagement with Alexander and the East is that he connected Roman myths of a Trojan foundation into the contemporary military and political scene, fusing this with a myth of Roman opposition to a great 'other' and magnificent enemy.

The indemnities demanded and received by Rome in the aftermath of the first Punic War were humiliating and crippling to Carthage. Retaliatory Carthaginian expansion into Spain by Hamilcar, who founded New Carthage and captured the Roman allied city of Saguntum, provided a suitable story to explain Rome's eagerness for a second Punic War (218–201 BCE). A second poet to deal with the Trojan myth in connexion with the Punic Wars was Ennius (239–169 BCE), an Italian who served in the Roman army in this second phase of the conflict. Now, battle was carried into Italy, and Hannibal, the Carthaginian general who rampaged through the Italian countryside, is a significant model in the developing pattern of Roman engagement with Alexander. Hannibal's quasi-mythical crossing of the Alps stands alongside stories of Alexander's endurance of frozen marches at his troops' side, whilst his youth, speed of action, and particularly his army's crushing defeat of Rome at the battle of Cannae, did more than just make him an obvious bogeyman for Rome. They also opened him up to potentially Alexandrian comparisons. Despite these possibilities, Hannibal did not become a westward-ranging Alexander figure at Rome during this period. The probable reason that a comparison between the two remained implicit rather than explicit was the military success of P. Cornelius Scipio (Scipio Africanus), a future patron of Ennius, under whose command Rome eventually defeated Carthage at the battle of Zama (202 BCE).

The second Punic War was a conflict dominated—at least in retrospect—by personalities: Hannibal and Scipio, both of whom feature in the continuing stories of Alexander that I discuss in the following chapters. For over fifteen years Hannibal and his army terrorized the Italian land that had only become Roman territory in the years after the first Punic War, but it was on African soil that the contest between Rome and Carthage would finally be decided. The aftermath of this conflict can be seen in the first Macedonian War, triggered by an agreement forged between Hannibal and Philip V of

Macedon in 215 BCE, which dragged Alexander's homeland directly into the struggle. The damage caused to Roman power and military confidence by the massive defeat suffered at Cannae was only beginning to be reversed when a Roman took centre stage in a war previously dominated by the force of Hannibal's personal exploits as leader. The rise of Scipio marks a clear turning point from a propagandist point of view. P. Cornelius Scipio had first come to public notice when in 210 BCE as proconsul, his first public office, he captured New Carthage in Spain. By taking this strategically resonant city and holding the port of Saguntum, Scipio opened up the possibility of a naval expedition against Carthage itself. After gaining the consulship for 205 BCE he was granted the province of Sicily, and the means to take the war to Africa. His African plans had met with opposition at Rome, but after the decisive victory won at Zama, peace was agreed in the following year. Scipio's victory was highly significant politically and culturally in addition to its important military implications. This war had left Rome seriously depleted, but it had also, despite the focus on personalities, strengthened the institution of the Senate and formalized its hierarchical recruitment. Scipio did not use his military authority to place himself outside the traditional republican governmental structures, but as we shall see (Chapter 5) his popular success and his courting of popular esteem foreshadow the rise of the generals and leaders of the first century BCE.

Ennius' poem on this war (the *Annales*) exists only in fragmentary form (about six hundred lines, probably less than 5 per cent of the full text). As with Naevius' poem, the Trojan cycle played a major part in Ennius' narrative. The epic probably commenced with a Trojan foundation myth, leading into the Romulus legend, then moving on to the regal period, the foundation of the Republic, the Gallic invasions (early fourth century BCE), and the Samnite Wars and war against Pyrrhus of Epirus (early third century BCE).[19] One of the most notable features of Ennius' poem is the dream sequence with which it seems to have begun, in which Homer encounters Ennius and tells him that his soul has been reborn in the Roman poet. This poem suggests a sense of heightened focus on the position of Rome (and Roman authors) in the cosmic scheme of things, demonstrating the historical continuum whereby especially talented or heroic souls transmigrate from one generation to the next.[20] A cyclical process of rebirth will necessarily line up potential Alexanders, ultimately forcing a confrontation with the notion that reborn Roman Alexanders—even Hannibals—will always be waiting in the wings.

The second century BCE saw the continuing shift of power to Rome, as the republic gradually became a territorial Empire spanning the 'barbarous' peoples of the West and the old Hellenistic kingdoms of the east. Greece and the former Carthaginian territories were finally annexed in 146 BCE, Greece after a series of wars with Macedon, and a Greek uprising, Carthage after a final Roman victory in a third Punic War. During this period the Roman provinces of Asia (133–126 BCE), and Transalpine Gaul (121 BCE) were formed, whilst from Africa another rampaging anti-Roman brought personal conflict back to the fore: Jugurtha. Jugurtha was defeated in 105 BCE, and the two men finally responsible were Marius and Sulla.

Rome in the First Century BCE

During periods of political flux, interpreting and formulating governmental structure take on vital importance. The Trojan foundation myth was already of great significance for the Punic conflict, but where it had acted as a national foundation myth in the third century, by the first century BCE it was being put to use by individuals and families in order to legitimize their right to power within the Republic. For politicians whose power was primarily non-traditional (i.e. with a strongly populist or military basis), the justification of origins was crucial. From our perspective, the first century BCE was dominated by a series of increasingly powerful and power-hungry dynasts. These men, and this era, have become for us a series of mythological landmarks that narrates a period of political and cultural revolution at Rome, but this particular 'heroic' narrative is itself a retrospective product of post-Julius Caesar narratology. The rise of these men and the new focus on the individual as historical agent are intimately connected to the cultural changes sparked by exposure to new countries, by increasing wealth, and by the growing interest in Hellenistic art, philosophy and literature. These changes had important political consequences. By the end of the second century, personal political ambitions were increasingly coming to be focused outside the traditional framework of the Senate and *comitia*. The length and scope of the Punic Wars were also making it increasingly difficult to reconcile the reality of Roman imperial success with a wholly citizen militia.

The story of Marius, a *nouus homo* ('new man') who was elected consul for 107 BCE in the teeth of traditionalist senatorial opposition, marks the real beginning of our supercharged vision of the new era of great loners. Our story recounts how Marius seized the opportunity to make sweeping and anti-traditionalist military reforms, lowering the wealth qualification and allowing the *proletarii* to serve, thereby jump-starting a direct bond between a powerless underclass and military high-command. Military service would be voluntary, but soldiers would be paid, entitled to a share of the spoils at the end of a campaign, and would receive a land grant on discharge. This marked a clear break with the previous notion of a wealthy citizen militia: now a new military class would automatically owe primary allegiance to their commander, the man who gained and distributed their booty, donated gifts if celebrating a triumph, and fought for their plots of land on discharge. What had been the army of the Republic became the army of Marius, of Sulla, of Pompey, and ultimately of Caesar, but the basis for their extraordinary authority is complex. Marius, with Alexander's legendarily close relationship with his troops in the background, is the primary model for this development, but a key factor that connects all these men is the length of time that they had in control of armies in the field. Without this, political domination would have been impossible to sustain, yet paradoxically, we also see a repeated pattern of commanders being drawn back to Rome, and losing control.

In the wake of his military success against Jugurtha in Africa, and against German tribes in Gaul, Marius was re-elected as consul in 105 BCE, and he was re-elected again each year until 100 BCE. His seven consulships and their consequent heightening of the cult of personality and personal prowess above communal, civic glory, highlighted a political fact that was already becoming clear: the state 'needed' these men (or at least manipulation of public opinion had made them seem indispensable). Yet increasingly, they were outgrowing the traditional political structures that they had been elected to conserve. Moreover, these multiple consulships allowed Marius to build up a vast network of personal *auctoritas*; but despite these developments, the story of Marius becomes one of defeat snatched from the jaws of victory. Returning to the issue of historical perspective, this makes sense. All leaders in any first century BCE narrative are inevitably reconfiguring the past in preparation for the greater adventure of Julius Caesar that is still to come. This makes Marius' apparent vacillation, and inability to consolidate political power, an ideal prequel for Caesar's ability to combine politics with military success.[21]

The man who 'succeeded' Marius, Sulla, was from a very different background: an aristocrat from an old and patrician family. His image was of the cultivated diplomat and military tactician.[22] In 88 BCE Marius became involved in a dispute with Sulla over the command of an expedition against Mithridates VI Eupator of Pontus. The Senate had entrusted Sulla with command, but Marius, though old (72) and ill, was the experienced general and the 'popular' choice. The ensuing bloody and long-drawn civil struggle marks a further watershed in our historical narrative. Sulla's march on the city of Rome and its eventual capture were a major blow to republican tradition. A consul under arms was forbidden to enter the city, and this was the first time that a Roman general had entered Rome in command of an army. Marius died at the beginning of his seventh consulship in 86 BCE.

Even at this early stage, a recurring pattern begins to emerge, whereby conquest in the 'East' provides a platform for personal power at Rome. This pattern first became evident in Scipio's African adventures, then Marius achieved immense prestige and successive consulships based on his success against Jugurtha. On Sulla's victorious return to Italy from the east there was bitter fighting until in late 82 BCE Sulla took Rome. In the aftermath of Sulla's proscriptions, from 82–79 BCE, he held the office of dictator. This marks a sharp developmental contrast with Marius' multiple consulships. In Marius' case, annual re-election was still necessary, but for Sulla, no time limit was placed on his powers; his past actions were legalized, and he was given powers of execution, and the right to distribute public land and found colonies. Sulla did in fact 'restore' many so-called traditional powers to the Senate, strengthening its authority and curtailing the tribunes' rights, but he also doubled the numbers of senators, and packed the ranks with his partisans. After a magnificent Triumph in 81 BCE, Sulla surrounded himself with a train of twenty-four lictors (doubling the number who attended upon consuls), and Sullan propaganda presented him as Sulla *Felix*: beloved of the gods and a special protégé of Venus.[23] With hindsight, we can see Caesar's emphasis on Venus as the ancestor of the Julian family following in the wake of this earlier Sullan appropriation, but Sulla's use of Venus is the first recorded direct propagandist use of a deity to serve the personal ambition of an *imperator*. Furthermore, Sulla's relationship with his notional fellow-senators (purge, then champion) is highly reminiscent of Philip's (and then Alexander's) treatment of the Greek States: first conquer and subdue your rivals, then reposition yourself as their messiah. Sulla retired in either 80 or 79 BCE, suffering from ill health, and he died in 78 BCE.

As becomes clear, the power figures that dominated Rome in the first century did not exist in isolation, and each was closely involved with his older contemporaries. Pompey was born *c*.105 BCE, into an influential equestrian family from Picenum. He had the foresight to

side with Sulla when he landed at Brundisium in 83 BCE, and after
success in fighting against the Marian veterans he was acclaimed
Magnus by his troops. This, together with Pompey's supposed cultivation of an Alexandrian appearance, emphasizes the developing association between 'Alexander' and potential Roman greatness. He was
already a sufficiently significant figure in the Roman consciousness for
his appropriation by Pompey to be useful, and the main associations
must also still have been positive. A second associative level is invoked
by the story that Pompey's *'magnus'* (The Great) was awarded to him
'spontaneously' by his soldiers. This idea of the general as 'one of the
men', a commander who had the complete and utter loyalty of his
troops and who shared their dangers and triumphs, tied him directly
to images of Alexander the Great as an all-conquering general and
ruler. These two areas of comparison are completed by the tradition
that Pompey deliberately cultivated an Alexander-style image, longish
curling hair, and an upward tilt to the head, in his portraiture. In this
development of attributes of Alexander we can see how Alexander as
ultimate eastern conqueror, favoured by the gods, is coming to form
an important model for Roman power-seekers.[24] It is not until the end
of Caesar's life and the propaganda battle between Antony and
Octavian that we find the negative comparisons with Alexander being
brought into play, for example: drunkenness, tyrannous monarchy,
obsession with personal glory, and aspirations to divinity.

Pompey put himself forward for the consulship in 79 BCE, aligning
himself with the *nobiles* against Sulla, who by this stage was struggling to legitimize his own shaky history, and was trapped in an ultra-
traditionalist role. This left the way clear for Pompey, the new
'Alexander'. Rather than settling down to a political career at Rome,
Pompey embarked upon a succession of military engagements, notably
defeating Sertorius' rebel army in Spain, and with the assistance of M.
Licinius Crassus, Spartacus' slave revolt in Italy. Pompey and Crassus
then forced the Senate to accept their joint candidacy for the consulship of 70 BCE. The Senate's agreement marks another significant
moment in the continuing erosion of republican institutions, and the
two consuls went on to repeal much of Sulla's legislation. There were
growing problems in the east during these years: pirates threatening
shipping in the Aegean, Thracian incursions in Macedonia, and fresh
aggression from Mithridates and his son-in-law Tigranes of Armenia.
Pompey had himself granted exceptional powers by the *lex Gabinia*
of 67 BCE, with the backing of the young senator Gaius Julius Caesar,[25]
and this allowed him three years' supreme command over all seas and
coastal areas. This was the first such overarching power to be granted

to an *imperator*, essentially placing Italy and Rome under his sole
authority. Having subjugated the pirates in one campaign in 67 BCE,
he then proceeded to deal with Mithridates, armed with the *lex
Manilia* which confirmed his *imperium* with unlimited duration, gave
him full command of the war and the power to conclude alliances and
treaties. At this point, Cicero had delivered his speech *De imperio Cn.
Pompei*, eulogizing the qualities and 'fortune' of Pompey, and presenting him in Sullan guise as a favourite of the gods and protected by
Venus Victrix. By now, Pompey was not *just 'magnus'*, he had *maius
imperium*.

Pompey returned to Rome in 61 BCE having conquered Mithridates,
Syria and Jerusalem, reorganized the provinces, and built up a net-
work of client states between Roman territory and the Parthian
Empire. Pompey returned, in other words, from a tour of duty as a
Roman Alexander, fighting his way into the territory that was still
physically and intellectually dominated by Alexander's campaigns.
But he seems to have stopped short of overt royal aspirations, making
an effort instead to work within the traditional framework of power.
During his eastern absence, Caesar had been busy building up his own
power base, and rather than opposing Caesar directly, Pompey dismissed his army and celebrated a stupendously lavish triumph in
September 61 BCE. He also commenced a building programme on the
Campus Martius. This included a temple to Venus Victrix, attached to
the first permanent stone theatre in Rome. There was also a garden
surrounded by a colonnade and ornamented with fifteen colossal
statues: fourteen for the nations Pompey had defeated, and one of
Pompey himself, depicted nude in the heroic Greek manner and
holding in his hand a globe as symbol of his position as *kosmokrator*,
or master of the world. The temple itself acted almost as an annex to
Pompey's theatre, yet again forcing home an association between
Venus and an aspirant Roman Alexander. Conquest is sexy, and the
gods love extravagant conquerors. We could see in this, coupled with
Cicero's speech, an early foreshadowing of the growing importance of
monumental and written propaganda, but what it also demonstrates
is a growing awareness of the visual signs of 'Alexander' that were
coming to populate the public spaces of civic Rome.

In 60 BCE Pompey, Caesar and Crassus formed an unofficial coalition, now termed the 'First Triumvirate'. This was to last until 54 BCE.
While Pompey had been in the East, Rome had again suffered from
factionalist violence; Caesar and Crassus had been engaged in personal
conflict for power, and the partisans of the *populares* and *optimates*
had been causing general civil disturbance. Although Caesar was from

a patrician family, he took the side of the *populares*, and he had also manoeuvred himself into the key priesthood of the *pontifex maximus*, providing additional public and civic backing for his cause. Crassus' role in all this tends to be presented as that of the financial backer, who finally—and fatally—bungles things when he attempts to shift from finance and politics to war. The three co-operated on legislation, and backed each other for the consulship (Caesar *cos.* 59 BCE, Pompey and Crassus in 55 BCE). The situation at Rome heated up even further in 54/53 BCE with street fighting and electoral disruption, and the Senate responded by appointing Pompey, now reconfigured as the senatorial candidate, as sole consul for 52 BCE, with proconsular *imperium*.

In the wake of Pompey's initiatives in the states immediately separating Rome from Parthia, Crassus' expedition against the Parthian Empire is particularly significant. Given Pompey's eastern glory, and Caesar's conquest of the West, it might appear that the whole world was under their control, but with hindsight, Crassus' defeat becomes a dominating theme for the rest of the century. Why did he go? Perhaps he wanted a share in the military *kudos*, or perhaps the lack of clear rationale is part of a greater story of the 'inevitability' of Roman aggression in the East. Whatever his motivation he left Rome for the East before the end of his consular year in 55 BCE. He had some early success in Mesopotamia in 54 BCE, and in the following year he marched against the Parthian forces in the desert to the east of the river Euphrates. The two armies met near Carrhae, and the Romans were overwhelmed. Crassus was forced to come to terms with the Parthians, but he rode into a trap and was killed. Of the soldiers who made it through, many were forced to settle as prisoners in Parthia. The legionary standards were lost to the enemy. Crassus stands as the first significant unsuccessful Roman Alexander. Apart from the immediate political consequences, his failure, the humiliation of captured Romans living as Parthians, and the loss of the legionary standards by a Roman expeditionary force continued to haunt Roman policy in the East long after Horace had compared the Parthian PoWs to Romans captured during the first Punic War.[26] Suddenly, to go east was not to encounter an exciting new world, open to conquest by superior western force; instead, the 'East' was a place where Romans might be at a disadvantage, intellectually and even psychologically. The landscape itself might be their enemy, and disgrace rather than triumph might await. This shift becomes evident in the lack of senatorial enthusiasm for Caesar's Parthian plans, and is further demonstrated in the aftermath of Antony's losses. The death

of Crassus, the annihilation of his army and the Parthians' capture of
the legionary standards marked an end to the 'triumvirate', but a final
split between Pompey and Caesar did not occur until 50 BCE. In
January 49 BCE Caesar, returning from Gaul with his legions, illegally
crossed the Rubicon and marched on Rome. Civil war broke out
again. Caesar took control of Rome and the consulship of 48 BCE.
Pompey went on a recruitment drive in Asia, but was eventually
defeated in Greece at Pharsalus in 48 BCE, and fled to Egypt, where he
was assassinated.

A revealing episode in the development of Caesar's Julian
propaganda can be seen in the funeral eulogy he delivered for his Aunt
Julia in 69 BCE, as Suetonius records:

> 'On her mother's side, my aunt Julia's family was
> descended from kings, and on her father's, her ties were
> with the immortal gods. Indeed the Marcius Rex family
> come from Ancus Marcius, which was her mother's name;
> the Julii are descended from Venus, of which family ours is
> a branch. Thus in us is combined the sacred character of
> kings, who are the masters of men, and the sanctity of the
> gods, to whom even kings must submit.'

'Amitae meae Iuliae maternum genus ab regibus ortum, paternum cum
diis inmortalibus coniunctum est. Nam ab Anco Marcio sunt Marcii
Reges, quo nomine fuit mater; a Venere Iulii, cuius gentis familia est
nostra. Est ergo in genere et sanctitas regum, qui plurimum inter homines
pollent, et caerimonia deorum, quorum ipsi in potestate sunt reges.'

SUETONIUS,* *Iulius Caesar* 6.2

We cannot know to what extent Caesar's success was carefully
planned, and to what extent he was a clever and inspired opportunist,
but until 49 BCE his main aim seems to have been to avoid a hasty
return to civil wars. After securing Rome, he did not make Pompey's
mistake: rushing headlong towards the now dangerous East. Instead
he remained to consolidate his own power base, promising financial
donatives and distributing grain, whilst also granting citizenship to all
free men in Cisalpine Gaul, gaining a vast new clientele and new
legionary recruits at a stroke. After his defeat of Pompey, Caesar
turned Egypt into a Roman protectorate, sealing a key Alexandrian
locus into the Roman world, and he created a new province of Africa
Nova (Numidia). In 47 BCE Caesar made himself Dictator for a year,
and in August and September 46 BCE, the year of his third consulship,
he celebrated triumphs over Gaul, Egypt, Pontus and Africa. He cele-

brated a fifth triumph in October 45 BCE after his victory at Munda, and also took the consulship for that year, whilst he 'mopped up' the remnants of civil war across the *imperium*.

The physical transformation of Rome that Pompey had made such a key feature of his cult of personality continued under Caesar. This was evident not only through his construction of monuments dedicated to his victories, but more pervasively, through the heightened personal *auctoritas* that his increasing powers allowed him to command. In 46 BCE he had been granted the Dictatorship for ten years, and in February 44 BCE, during his fifth consulship, this ten years was extended to life. Perhaps unsurprisingly, the accounts of physical and propagandist changes that we so frequently see ascribed to Caesar during this period date almost entirely to the late first century BCE and after, with Suetonius, Dio and Appian the key sources. From their accounts (combined with some 'eye-witness' testimony from Cicero), we get a striking picture. He had adopted a purple toga and wore a laurel wreath, and his effigy was placed on coinage, sometimes with a golden wreath. This assimilation of a 'crown' into Caesar's imagery, with its monarchical and eastern symbolism, in conjunction with the transgressive portrayal of a *living* citizen rather than a god on coinage, focuses attention firmly on an increasing trend towards Alexander-style divine monarchy. Furthermore, the oath of loyalty was sworn on his name (previously sworn only on Jupiter's name), and his statue was placed on the Capitol beside the seven kings of Rome. He also received the title *parens patriae*. In all but name and diadem, he was king.[27] If these echoes of Alexander are not striking enough, two further, specific (though posthumous) comparisons emerge. According to Suetonius (*Iulius* 7.1) Caesar had compared himself to a statue of Alexander at Gades in Spain in 69 BCE, and Nicolaus of Damascus likened Caesar's conquests to Alexander's in that both men pushed their conquests as far as the Ocean.[28] In conjunction with a strong emphasis on Caesar's popularity with his troops and his reputation for swift attack and fighting his own battles, we can see potential similarities with Alexander becoming more inevitable. And with Alexander-style military success comes the possibility of Alexander-style aspirations to divinity.

In the wake of increasingly autocratic moves on Caesar's part, from about 45 BCE onwards, opposition had been growing. For a coalition of opposition factions, Caesar's plans for a war against Parthia provided a convenient *ne plus ultra* against which discontent with his autocracy could be modelled. In this resistance to Caesar's desire to conquer Parthia we can see echoes of some of the problematic issues raised by Alexander's eastern campaign: issues of the stability of national identity, and the way in which personal characteristics could deliquesce in the face of the luxury of the East. Increasingly, aspirations to eastern conquest and Alexander-style success were perceived to be dangerous rather than glorious for Roman leaders, marking a shift from the still positive overtones invoked by Pompey. On 14 February 44 BCE, at the time of the *senatus consultum* granting him lifelong Dictatorship, Caesar received the senators in front of his Temple of Venus Genetrix. He was poised on a gold seat, at the foot of a statue of himself. The significance of the visual rhetoric of this scene is striking. From Pompey's post-Sullan role as favoured by Venus, we have a ruler who claims direct descent from Venus, and locates this 'familial' relationship within a reconfigured public space in which the Julian family rather than the Roman people is prioritized. On the 15th, and this was during the Lupercalia Festival, the famous scene on the Rostra occurred where he was offered a diadem by Antony, and refused, but this attempt at spin came too late. The corrupting 'East' had sealed the fate of another Alexander. On the Ides of the following month, March, at a meeting of the Senate held at Pompey's theatre, he was assassinated.

The thirteen years between Caesar's assassination and Octavian's triumph over Antony at Actium were a period of civil and political bloodshed, and rapidly hardening positions. Although Antony initially seized the initiative by making Caesar's will public and organizing rousing funeral ceremonies for the Dictator, the young Octavian, born in 63 BCE, and Caesar's great nephew and posthumously adopted son, quickly set himself up in the role of Caesar's successor. Again we see in this idea of Octavian as Caesar's successor a warping of the traditional features of Roman governance. The essentially aristocratic senatorial system had worked against sudden shifts in power towards any *noui homines*, so that power and influence at Rome had a strong familial basis. Octavian's distortion of this pattern allowed him to base his claim to the loyalty, popularity and *auctoritas* of Caesar on a right of succession and inheritance, and there was nothing new about adoption as a device for strengthening and securing a family. This adoption, however, crucially exposed the artifice of the strategic mechanics of adoption when it played a key role in the reality of a 'First Family' at Rome. How would Rome deal with the adopted son of a god? Octavian's foundation of a temple to Caesar in the heart of the Republican forum hammers out the centrality of this paradox and the startling new dimension that Caesar's deification added to the volatile political situation.

Cicero and the Senate sided with Octavian, and defeated Antony, who abandoned Rome. Octavian, appointed propraetor, took advantage of a power vacuum caused by the death of the two consuls, and marched on Rome, seizing the Treasury. He then had himself elected consul, and came to terms with Antony. In 43 BCE they formed a 'Second' Triumvirate, along with M. Aemilius Lepidus. The *lex Titia* formally acknowledged their five-year triple magistracy, and provided for its renewal in 37 BCE. Proscriptions on a grand scale (once again) followed this apparent settlement. The Triumvirs held the West, whilst the East was in the hands of the assassins of Caesar, led by Brutus and Cassius. While Brutus and Cassius controlled the East, its wealth and resources were closed to the Triumvirs and Rome. With victory at Philippi in 42 BCE the stakes were immediately raised.

The Roman world was again divided: again, Antony's partiality for eastern conquest seems to be in evidence in a split that gave Octavian the West, gave Gaul and the East to Antony, leaving Lepidus only with Africa. In the face of Parthian incursions into Syria and Asia Minor, Antony took over Caesar's Parthian plans, and went east to raise funds and troops. It was during this period that Antony became involved with Cleopatra, whilst canvassing for support and money for his Parthian war. Initially, Antony was successful against the Parthians, and drove them back across the Euphrates, but when he launched a full-scale assault in 36 BCE he met with disaster, and although he did capture Armenia two years later, Crassus' defeat at Carrhae remained unavenged. After Armenia, Antony returned to Alexandria where he (scandalously) celebrated a triumph—a Roman triumph could only have positive meaning when enacted within the cultural and religious topography of the city itself, and this is bound to have been milked for its propagandist value by Octavian. Not only had Antony allotted Rome's eastern provinces to his children with Cleopatra (*Alexander* Helios and Cleopatra Selene), and proclaimed her son Caesarion as Caesar's legitimate heir, he had also committed the unthinkable. By celebrating a triumph outside Rome itself, Antony was effectively divorcing the victory from the physical city and its collective citizen body, and de-centring its position as imperial capital. Such an apparent abandonment, coupled with Octavian's 'disclosure' of Antony's will, stating that he wished to be buried in Alexandria, puts a final, detrimental gloss of Alexander on Antony's public image.

This would certainly be the spin we would expect to find Octavian placing on Antony's activities, and this reading is reinforced by post-Actian rhetoric of an 'orientalized' Antony, corrupted by Cleopatra. This also marks the first explicitly negative association of Alexander-type qualities with a Roman leader, although events in 45 and 44 BCE under Caesar had paved the way for such a cultural shift. Suddenly, rather than focusing on the positive, expansive and empire-building elements of Alexander-imagery, we are effectively being presented with a turning point. The 'new' Rome, as reconstructed by writers of the Augustan era, was beginning to focus on how these autocrats were conducting themselves at Rome, and how they were relating themselves to the *mos maiorum*. The Triumvirate finally disintegrated in January 32 BCE, and Octavian's control of Rome was complete when the consuls, partisans of Antony, fled to Ephesus with 300 senators.

In July 32 BCE a senatorial decree declared war on Cleopatra, and stripped Antony of all powers, whilst Octavian was elected consul for 31 BCE. Significantly, war was declared on Cleopatra rather than on Antony: Romans could not be asked explicitly to engage in civil war. On the other hand, Octavian was outrageously permitted to require the swearing of an oath of loyalty to him *personally*, in Italy and the western provinces, giving him complete command of the war. Both sides engaged in an intensive propaganda campaign, with Octavian accusing Antony of being enslaved by a foreign and degenerate woman, being a drunkard and a lecher, wanting to shift the capital from Rome to Alexandria and to put Rome into Cleopatra's power: all tapping into different elements of Alexander's mythology. Antony no doubt accused Octavian of effeminacy, impiety, treachery, self-interest and poor leadership and military qualities, but since the victory was Octavian's, little negative propaganda about him survives. Even the gods with whom they associated themselves took on increasing importance: Antony's 'choice' of Hercules and Dionysus laid him open to propagandist implication in the most negative characteristics and eastern associations of their divinity, and he was also linked, through this association, with Alexander, another devotee. Octavian, aligned with Apollo and Jupiter, seems to have assigned to himself the place of rational, Roman and considered action. So alongside the terrestrial contest, a parallel divine battle was also taking place.

The two sides met at the sea battle of Actium in September 31 BCE, below a promontory dominated by a temple to Apollo. Part of Antony's forces retreated following the withdrawal of the Egyptian fleet, and the abandoned land and sea forces surrendered. Antony and Cleopatra remained at Alexandria until Octavian's march on Egypt in 30 BCE. The victors' story then presents a plot that has all the hallmarks of romantic fiction: Cleopatra tried to negotiate a settlement, but Octavian played for time, and Antony, believing himself betrayed and Cleopatra dead, committed suicide. Once Octavian had gained control of the treasury, Cleopatra followed Antony's example. The subsequent mythologization of Antony and Cleopatra emphasizes the fictive, mythic quality that this story has taken on. When Suetonius tells us of Octavian's determination to visit the tomb of Alexander the Great whilst in Alexandria, he is not just demonstrating the way in which Alexander still provided an image of enduring fascination (*Augustus* 18). He is providing an example of the centrality of an opposition between 'Alexander' and the Emperor to Roman imperial discourse. Without Alexander-Antony, a narrative of 'Augustus' falls flat. Egypt was then reduced to an imperial 'province' and senators were prohibited from going there without authorization. This tacitly acknowledged its financial significance *and* its importance as a potential pilgrimage destination for any future Roman Alexanders.

In 42 BCE the *lex Rufrena* had organized Caesar's cult throughout Italy, and the kind of sanctification of power that Caesar had approached was fully developed by Augustus who collected up all the major priesthoods, finally succeeding to the life-appointment of *pontifex maximus* in 12 BCE. In the aftermath of the victory at Philippi, couched in terms of avenging Caesar's murder, he vowed a temple to Mars Ultor (finally dedicated in 2 BCE), and following his defeat of Sextus Pompey in 36 BCE he vowed a temple to Apollo, his 'protector', on the Palatine. This temple, completed in 28 BCE, would indissolubly link personal, public, cultural and religious power when it was built, because it was linked with Octavian's own house on the Palatine, and also contained a magnificent library.

After the fall of Alexandria, most of the eastern kingdoms quickly fell into line behind Octavian, and he arrived back in Rome in summer 29 BCE, consul for the fifth time, to a city that had already inserted his name into the chants sung by the ancient Salian priesthood, had ratified all his actions, and granted him so-called tribunician power for life. A concrete expression of Octavian's deployment of symbolic rhetoric is the closure, in January, of the doors of the Temple of Janus in the Forum. In August of 29 BCE Octavian celebrated a triple triumph over Illyria, Actium and Egypt, and dedicated a temple to *Diuus Iulius* in the Roman Forum. This further signifies the radical changes being implemented by Octavian to the fabric of Roman political life, and highlights how far the community had already shifted from the *mos maiorum* in its willingness to accept a son's deification of his father. State cult had no analogy for deification since Romulus, yet Caesar's temple was located at the heart of the republican Forum. The Forum was further changed by the opening later that month of a new Curia, in which stood a statue of Victory and an altar, to remind the assembled senators of Actium. Immediately in the wake of Actium, Octavian erected two trophies, one in the Temple of Apollo overlooking Actium, the other on the site of his camp, and raised to Mars, Neptune and Apollo. These trophies attested the wider religious and physical significance of the victory, and highlighted Octavian's success as having been achieved under the auspices of all three gods. Also, facing Actium a city called Nikopolis was founded (echoing similar foundations by Alexander), and a great shrine to Apollo was dedicated, intended to serve as the focal site for Actian games (first celebrated in 28 BCE). Coins carrying the image of Victory bearing trophies were minted. Echoes of the huge popular import of Actium can be seen in the works of Horace, Propertius and Virgil, with *Aeneid* 8.680–81 offering a good example.

This emphasises the role of Victory, and specifically a victory directly related to and dependent upon the Olympian gods, as an integral and basic feature of Octavianic ideology. By focusing on the defence of Hellenism (initially) and ultimately Roman values in the face of Eastern and Egyptian barbarism, and drawing a parallel between the battles of Salamis and Actium, Octavian cleverly opened up the possibility of reconciling the Greek East and the Roman West under his authority. Further to this we may note that Virgil has Aeneas hold his Trojan games on the shores of Actium. As was the case with Caesar, Octavian engaged in a major building and public works programme, completing many of the projects left undone at Caesar's death (e.g. the Curia Julia, and the stone theatre that would become the Theatre of Marcellus), and engaging in widespread restoration of old temples and buildings, and the construction of new buildings. He also, in the early stages, gave support to public works by other citizens, such as Rome's first stone amphitheatre, and Agrippa's aqueducts. In this way we can see how gradually, through the first century BCE, the safety and well being of *imperatores* was becoming closely identified with the security and continuing greatness of Rome, on divine and human levels. If the gods smiled so favourably on these men, maybe it *was* acceptable to allow them extraordinary honours and authority. Rather than conceptualizing this as an inevitable state of decline, Rome was ready for a new ideology that would foreground a cyclical rather than a linear conception of history: the city was being reborn through a great purge, rather than edging into terminal decay. The problem with this was that in the early phase of his Principate at least, History needed to stop with Augustus, signalling the historical inevitability of his authority for a potentially unconvinced audience. This tension becomes more evident towards the end of the century as succession and dynasticism gain prominence, and the early emphasis on continuity through change took on a new significance.

Despite Antony's death, Octavian's military victories were no guarantee of political success. The Senate had preserved much of its prestige, even if its actual power was diminished, and the influential senatorial families could still mobilize stiff opposition if it seemed that their guardianship of the traditions and ethos of the Republic was going to be denied. Moreover, the title and regalia of monarchy were still highly charged with negative symbolism in the wake of Caesar's assassination, making any assertion of autocracy problematic. Finally, even allowing for his successful propaganda, there was still scope for the assertion that, unlike Caesar, the proven military genius, Octavian was trading mostly on his name and heritage, without any serious and impressive personal military charisma behind his rhetoric. Octavian's may have been the name and fame to conjure with, but looking over the major successes of the 30s BCE—Mylae and Naulochus (36 BCE), the Illyrian War (35–34 BCE), and of course most significantly, Actium itself (31 BCE)—and despite subsequent propaganda, Agrippa was the commanding military force.[29] Octavian's ruthlessness as a civil war faction leader, combined with the relative obscurity of his family, the Octavii, could well have provided further stumbling blocks. All of these factors combine to make Octavian's position still uncertain after Actium, and it can have been by no means clear what political settlement would ultimately result from his civil war victory. This was reinforced in 28 BCE when M. Licinius Crassus, grandson of the Triumvir, asked to celebrate a triumph and be awarded the *spolia opima* for having slain an enemy general in battle. Livy refers to this incident indirectly, linking Octavian to the *spolia opima* by involving him in a debate about whether one had to be a consul in command of an army to win them.[30] This might suggest that although Octavian's conquest of Egypt was accepted, there may still have been undercurrents of resistance to his assumption of military autocracy. It may even have been the case that this apparently arcane debate over the rights to the *spolia opima* was tapping into a tacit and potentially subversive rhetoric centred on Octavian's assumption of the credit (and triumphs) for conquests carried out in his name.[31] As long as Octavian had the support of the army, he was relatively secure, but this meant that he needed to retain a unified military command in his own hands, rather than allowing provincial governors to gain their own armies. This in itself was a revolutionary moment in terms of Roman tradition, and if he appeared to be too much the monarch, then he might provoke resistance anyway.

The Augustan Principate stands as a winning fiction based on the balancing act that was necessary to sustain it; it had no written constitution or basis, other than the laws promoted by Augustus (and inscribed in the *Res Gestae*). In 27 BCE in the wake of the magnificent choreography of his post-Actium triumphs, the public works and land settlements, the Senate 'offered' Octavian the title Augustus, which he accepted. He had suddenly renounced all his powers, and the protests and disturbances this set in motion brought the Senate to offer him proconsular imperium. A golden shield was set up in the Senate proclaiming his virtues, valour, clemency, justice and piety. His door was decorated with laurel and oak symbolizing his saving of Roman citizens, and the month Sextilis was renamed for him. Octavian the Triumvir became Augustus the Princeps (first citizen), a republican term of respect for outstanding citizens. He remodelled the Senate in 18 BCE, cutting its numbers to 600, and through the Julian laws he attempted to encourage marriage, make adultery a public offence and promote the bearing of legitimate children (*c.*18 BCE). In 17 BCE, the Saecular games were staged, officially marking the dawn of a new era of peace, for which Horace wrote an official hymn, the *Carmen Saeculare*.

This brief story of the significant moments in Roman history leading up to the foundation of the Principate offers an interpretation of the background to the texts that will be discussed in Chapters 2 to 4. It is not comprehensive, and many of the texts will post-date the events I have been discussing. Nevertheless, this historical panorama fulfils an important function: it demonstrates a pattern that developed at Rome in the last centuries of the Republic, a pattern that would ultimately lead to the individual power of the emperor, while at the same time making his role highly problematic. Romans were slow to come to terms with even the trappings of monarchy, and the descriptor 'king' (*rex*) remained taboo; yet bound up in the Roman sense of self as a warrior people, destined to wage war successfully and to take on the role of a vigorous, moral and essentially simplicity-loving nation, was the quest for personal power and glory that would inevitably bring successive Roman power figures into association with Alexander. With this came the trope of the great king brought low by the degenerative effects of success.

Augustus and the Succession

A rhetoric of boundless empire characterizes Augustan literature, and early in the *Res Gestae Diui Augusti* (*Deeds of the Divine Augustus,*

3) we find an emphatic statement of Augustus' self-presentation as world-saviour. But the emphasis of Augustus' self-construction as *imperator* is closely focused on representing the inevitability of his victories and military triumphs, rather than concentrating on the highly charged and meteoric career-path allotted to Caesar. His catalogues of successes (4, 25–33) suggest a careful and concerted integration of personal and familial achievement whereby 'sons' (Gaius and Lucius 14, Marcellus 21, Tiberius 27) are interwoven in a narrative of the inevitability of an ongoing, posthumous role for Augustus, through the persons of his successors. Augustus the world-conqueror becomes Augustus the founding father. In this scheme, Augustus' overarching success is to have perpetuated himself through a complex programme of dynasticism and 'family values' which allows his success to be represented as greater than that possible to achieve in any one lifetime. These ideas become particularly relevant for the discussion of succession in Chapter 5 (pp. 175–8), and will recur throughout Chapters 2 to 4, but for the purposes of this introduction, an overview of what happened next sets the scene for some of the post-Augustan Alexanders.

Inevitably, the death of Augustus marked a new phase in Roman politics. Despite Augustus' self-modelling as Caesar's heir, the transmission of power to Tiberius was the first direct instance of a dynastic appropriation of supreme power since early Roman monarchical history. Autocracy tends to suggest a move towards a standardization that leads to an apparent closing down of opportunities for a discourse of opposition, but as Tacitus' 'normative' history of the aftermath of Augustus suggests, oppositional rhetoric can also take on authoritative status. The exceptional honours granted to Augustus' grandsons Gaius and Lucius Caesar made the eventual succession of Tiberius particularly problematic.[32] Tiberius really did have an impressive military reputation of leadership in the field, and Horace *Odes* 4.4 and 4.14 demonstrate an attempt to integrate the Claudian heritage of Drusus and Tiberius into Augustan mythology, but as Tiberius' self-enforced exile on Rhodes suggests, Horace was fooling nobody as regards Augustus' priorities. Augustus consistently preferred his nephew, and then his grandsons, to Livia's son Tiberius. Tiberius' second triumph (Pannonia and Dalmatia, CE 12), after his adoption by Augustus, probably marked an official acceptance of his position and enforced his military credentials, but his enforced adoption of the sons of Drusus and Agrippa (Germanicus and Agrippa Postumus) suggests that there may well have been a sense that Tiberius was only a stopgap. Tacitus' emphasis on the hopes and expectations roused by Germanicus suggest at the very least that a senatorial version would attempt to downplay direct and automatic succession in favour of the selection of an exceptional and deserving heir. This underlines how Germanicus rather than Tiberius could become Tacitus' 'perfect' candidate for power. Like Tiberius, he could be represented as having personal military success, but unlike Tiberius he was uncontaminated, retrospectively, by actual imperial power. Furthermore, like Alexander, his youthful death provides an appropriately elegiac note with which to commence a narrative of imperial decline.[33]

History and Identity

A key question in the development of a national historiographical voice is: 'Who are we?' Many of the texts examined in this book are not histories, but in their reference to Alexander they draw upon and partake of both history and cultural myth. From Alexander's popularity in first century BCE Roman narratives, we can deduce that a ready-primed audience for his inclusion existed. This interest seems to have been part of a wider interest in the consumption of textualized history drawn from a growing need to define the nature of Rome's historical progression. The production of history was not the only area of cultural expansion in the final two centuries BCE. Roman culture as a whole underwent an extraordinarily rapid development; this was founded on the essentially competitive nature of the Roman ruling elite (the major recipients, arbiters and producers of culture), and catalysed by Roman expansion into Greece. The resultant broadening of cultural horizons coincided with a vast influx of wealth and an increase in potential areas for competition and rivalry. Not only did this affect intellectual patronage and development, it also caused a massive shift in the political dynamic, offering a far wider stage for political ambition and the resources to back a succession of increasingly polarized struggles for overall power. As we have already seen, a secondary area where Rome's dominance of the Mediterranean was eventually solidified, with significant literary implications, was in the wars against Carthage. The Punic Wars of the third century BCE play a key role in the development of a Roman epic consciousness, but are also cited as having a wholly negative moral effect on the Roman people. We might argue that where conquered Greece was absorbed into and played a key part in kick-starting Roman cultural change, Carthage was made emblematic of the kind of degenerative ethical results of becoming *the* major imperial power in the Mediterranean world. In this way, the developing conflation of Trojan,

Homeric origins with fated antagonism between Rome and Carthage, commences an epic justification for a Roman imperial destiny as leader of Greek and Roman peoples in a joint exercise.

This means that what we find in Rome is a situation where the expanding state and the potential dynasts were rapidly seeking some new means of self-definition, whether in Roman or Hellenistic terms. For national and personal imperial power, the creation of an over-arching sense of historical destiny was a key factor—an expanding empire needs an ideology on a grand scale. As heralded by Livy, the Roman discourse of power (vested in an autocrat) is inextricably entwined with a traditional Roman hostility to monarchy.[34] Despite this, Livy's monumental history was composed in the aftermath of Octavian's victory and the relative stabilization of Roman politics achieved by the Principate.[35]

There has been much debate on levels of literacy in antiquity,[36] but there is a real possibility that although textualized history may primarily have been aimed at political and social elite groups, a more popular audience, accessing history through readings and perform-ance, would have been an important secondary concern. Alexander's meteoric career may have changed the nature of textualized history by decreasing the level of participation in government available to his subjects—when so much emphasis is placed upon an unelected ruler, the stature of the citizens/subjects is necessarily diminished. Histori-ography concentrated on affairs of state, on politics, battles and power figures. In a democracy, the People were necessarily key players in national decision-making and strategy, yet even in 'democratic' history, individual leaders such as Pericles still stand out precisely because they are presented as remarkable individuals. When a solitary ruler such as Alexander (or the Successors) has sole responsibility and apparently divinely sanctioned authority, it may have seemed that mass popular participation in history (where textualized history functions as a moral primer for the political citizen) was being eroded. If written history was aimed primarily at the elite of the Hellenistic world, and therefore concentrated on elite concerns, this may have been mirrored in a growing emphasis on the role of Τύχη (Fortune) in Hellenistic histories: the ruler's fortune and relationship with the divine came to be of paramount importance in the immediate wake of Alexander's construction of a vocabulary of divine monarchy.[37] During the Hellenistic period, 'official' court historians became increasingly important, and it is in this context that we can interpret a developing official role for history. In the Hellenistic kingdoms of the Successors, Alexander's ideology of divine monarchy underwent a change whereby, gradually, the dynasties established by Alexander's generals shed their primary justification as heirs of Alexander, and took over his direct line to the gods. This allowed them to absorb 'public' civic history into their own imagery and justification for power. Nevertheless, their right to power could still be bolstered through association with Alexander and his successful conquests. These Successors created a world where divine legitimization coupled with military prowess determined monarchical government and the identity of the king. Praise of these rulers could symbiotically become praise of the state they embodied.[38]

Between the Hellenistic world and Roman Greece stands Polybius, mediating the new power for the old, and prefiguring some of the cultural ambiguities of second century CE Greek authors. Polybius (1.1.2) suggests that his work will teach men to accept the vicissitudes of fortune by demonstrating the reversals suffered by others.[39] Interpreting Rome for Greece, and writing as a 'client' of Scipio, Polybius seems to imply that Greek participation in at least a rhetoric of power is still possible. By learning to deal with Rome in Greek terms Polybius is in effect defining each nation for the other, and offering a cultural template for the Greek world in the hope that this translation can aid mutual co-operation. But Scipio's looming presence should never be far from our 'reading' of Polybius' scheme; his version of Greek expectations and areas of interest in Rome illuminates Greek concerns as much as Roman reality. Like an ancient Baedeker, Polybius' *History* will focus on the concerns of the Hellenistic 'explorer' in a new and fast-changing Roman Mediterranean world, yet the situation is complicated by Roman appropriation of Greek culture as well as territory. When Scipio forces Rome to acknowledge his individual importance he is not just breaking with Roman tradition, he is stepping across cultural boundaries that separate Rome from the East. When the Greek literary heritage is taken over, how are Greek versions of Roman power and identity to be interpreted? Particularly when we remember that this era saw increasing Roman demand for narratives of *Roman* national identity. We might consider that in his *History*, Polybius pre-packages Rome the new ruler, complete with ready-made interpretative 'biography'. Thus in Polybius we may be seeing the beginning of the story that would later have Livy characterize Rome itself as a super-Alexander.

The Hellenistic world largely accepted charismatic kingship—rulers *need* subjects and courtiers, and the mutual dependence seems to have offset the decreasing opportunities for organized participation in political affairs for citizens, but since Greek and Roman affairs were increasingly becoming entwined, we should now be asking: what was happening in Rome? Increasingly, power was concentrated in the hands of individuals, who through popular politics and military success—and on the back of Roman imperial expansion—were destabilizing the republican system of government. For a first century BCE Roman, Alexander's country was part of the newly conquered 'near' East, and a Roman province, but also symbolic of western victories in the Persian East. Constructing the East as a place of decay and decadence, of splendour and seduction, was already an established trope, so Alexander could fulfil both expectations of Roman victories *and* fears of political instability. Roman defeat of his successors could still have great national resonance. Would Rome, this potential new Macedon, march on to victory in the Parthian East? For late republican generals, Alexander's military glory was paramount in his use as a positive comparison, but for Julius Caesar and *his* successors, the required imagery became more confused. Military glory began to lose its importance and style and representation of government became vital. Constantly, we find examples of attempts to refine the nature of *Romanitas*, to work with the new power figures and to accommodate the changing situation. Augustus could offer peace, in conjunction with the promise of a semblance (or actuality) of a restored Republic; some might have accepted the 'reality' of this governmental formula, others would have thought it a reasonable, and probably the only effective, solution.[40]

As demonstrated by Crassus' Parthian debacle, fears surrounding Caesar's plans to campaign in Parthia, and Antony's disastrous Parthian losses, going east in the late first century BCE was gaining significant negative overtones, and these are clearly reflected in a parallel negative tradition using Alexander as an *exemplum*, warning of the dangers of over-identification. This is made explicit in Cicero's comments to Crassus' son Publius (*Brutus*; 46 BCE), where Alexander and Cyrus are the complicated models for Crassus Junior's ambition. Perhaps tactically, Cicero chooses not to make clear whether their inspirational roles are wholly negative.[41] For a Roman, going east was gradually losing its conquistadorial gloss, and gaining a discrete set of dubious if not outright negative associations. The republican system had allowed an acceptable power-struggle and outlet for ambition to a limited portion of society (senators, and equestrians in pursuit of senatorial standing), with the annual magistracy of the consulship the ultimate goal. Not everyone could win, but the aspirational structure suggested that for the upper levels of society, power was not unattainable. Traditionally senatorial families could compete for power in the knowledge that the consulship carried real authority, even if circumscribed by its annual nature. The early years of the Principate amounted to a curtailment of political aspirations among the former ruling class, cutting off legitimate political aspirations and affecting any subsequent potential for personal identification with images of Alexander. Under a supreme ruler, models of 'greatness' had to be reconfigured to focus on *his* state and civic symbolism, and that of the imperial house. The *auctoritas* of the *princeps* was not confined within specific limits, and once it had been allowed, no amplification or further discretionary powers were needed. Ironically, once the principle of autocracy was in place, aiming for imperial greatness opened up a whole new realm of competition.[42]

Narrative history developed relatively late in Rome, and the early Roman historians produced versions of the past that tended to focus on achievements of cities and rulers. They represented Rome, the new Mediterranean power, for Romans and new subjects alike.[43] The annalistic tradition, commencing in the late second century BCE, offered chronological accounts of Rome from the origins of the city to the present (although there was some disagreement concerning the nature of the earliest origins).[44] In comparison with earlier works, these were vast productions, and while we do not know for certain what prompted this new direction in history-writing, we could hazard a guess. Rome's new dominance came to demand an explanation, a justification, in a development comparable to that traceable in the kingdoms of the Successors. In collision with the highly developed identities of the Greek states, Rome as a nation *needed* a history.

Two figures that played an important role in the development of a historical consciousness at Rome were Diodorus Siculus and Dionysius of Halicarnassus. Like Polybius, both wrote in Greek, and again both are providing narratives of Roman history from a foreign perspective. Diodorus' universal history presents itself as a complete account of world history from mythological times to the 'present' (60 BCE), but in effect, what he gives us is a bifocal narrative, in which 'Greek' history gives way to 'Roman' history with the first Punic War. Diodorus' *Library* was probably completed in about 30 BCE, making it a significant text for the polyphonous 'Histories' of the Augustan period. The narrative attempts to create a sense of parallelism between Greek and Roman historical imaginations through its annalistic synchronization of the two chronological systems, but Diodorus' interest in the Hellenistic, Successor Kingdoms, is particularly relevant here. It suggests that his interpretation of more recent Roman history would have modelled the late republican political changes onto a scheme that promoted the benefits of benevolent autocracy. The final books, which contained his account of the most 'recent' past, are fragmentary, but his concern with the relationship between the individual and the state, and the role of the individual in society, suggest that he was in tune with the kinds of anxiety that were plaguing late republican Rome. Dionysius, the second of these historians, published his *Roman Antiquities* about twenty-two years after his arrival in Rome, shortly after the battle of Actium, and dealt with Rome from its legendary origins until the first Punic War. For Diodorus, Roman history is a function of Roman expansion; for Dionysius, Rome's Trojan foundation revises the historical process, reinterpreting Rome as a function of 'Greek' expansion. By rewriting Rome as a Greek city-state, Dionysius presents us with the tempting promise of cultural and intellectual coherence if only, as Romans, we accept that we are Greeks. That this was a troublesome and lively theme in the aftermath of Actium is further enforced by Virgil's struggles to explain the role of Troy and the transformation undergone by Aeneas and his people that changed them from Trojan (and hated by Juno) to Romans, destined to rule the entire world. So right at the start of the 'Augustan' era we have the publication of Diodorus' Greco-Roman historical coalition, Livy writing the first pentad of his *History of Rome*, and Dionysius' arrival and commencement of a new historical project.

In the years around Actium, there was a boom in annalistic history. In the context of Cicero's claim for the universal appeal of history (*de Fin.* 5.52), we are confronted by a world in which there is a wide potential audience, hungry for appeals to and explanations of the past; parallels with the fourth century Hellenistic experience are clear.[45] Powerful men become the focal points for late republican historiography and suddenly both past and more recent power-figures, Roman and foreign, take centre stage in a newly developing historical matrix. The way in which this shift took place, focusing audiences on a growing indivisibility of leader and state, with a sense of merging between the interests of the two, or conversely, demanding that the audience recognize and negotiate the ways in which the two are at odds, was never before available in literary form to the massed ranks of the consuls. This refocusing of historical needs from the interests of the state onto those of the powerful individual who stood for the state, has its roots in the way in which Romans negotiated their bond with the state via their ancestors and family. We have already looked at Suetonius' account of Caesar's speech at his aunt's funeral, and the importance of this funeral and his self-

positioning at it, and it was on these occasions that Roman relationship with the past, familial and civic, was constantly renegotiated.

Formal legitimate political participation may have been endan-
gered, but for a powerful few, popular politics and military prowess
combined to offer unprecedented opportunities for personal aggrandizement. Both the elite and the lower orders were eventually to be
effectively disenfranchized from their traditional roles. Appian could
still speak of history as useful (*BC* 1.24; *Syr.* 207) but in general by
the second and third centuries CE, histories are saturated with a need
to come to terms with freedom and autocracy, the existence of one
demanding an understanding of its opposite. From Trajan onwards
and in the second century CE we find a renewed interest in Alexander,
as acceptance of one-man rule demanded a renegotiation of understanding of freedom and tyranny, and among Greek authors, we find
Alexander revived as the embodiment of glorious, untarnished Greek
heroism.[46]

For a Greek living under the rule of Rome, Alexander could represent a great Greek saviour, a disseminator of culture to the barbarians
(overtly, the Persians, but also tying in notions of Greek cultural
supremacy over Rome). He could stand for the cultural supremacy of
Greece, and Greek military prowess, and his fame could demonstrate
the lasting greatness of a Greek over Rome. This becomes particularly
important after the Julio-Claudians and in the second century CE,
when philhellenism regained respectability. It may seem obvious that
'Roman Greeks' of this period might want to rewrite past and present,
each in terms of the other, and fuse present Roman power with
Hellenistic origins, but why should Hellenism have gained respectability? The Emperor Nero's admiration for Greek culture may have been
one trigger, but other factors are also involved.

The Greek world was recovering from the turmoil of Roman
expansive imperialism and civil war, and a trend in confident Hellenic
self-definition seems to have paralleled renewed Roman interest. After
the troublesome dynasticism of the Julio-Claudians, it was clear that
the army and military success were key elements in the attainment and
consolidation of power. This had also, of course, been the case for
Octavian, but he had sought to muddy the issue with his talk of
'restored' republic and his refusal to spell out an ideology for the
transference of power. Instead he had sought to imply that the Senate
still held the ultimate veto. By the end of the first century CE, the role
of the Senate was manifestly subordinate to the power of the army,
and we find a situation developing reminiscent of that in the
Hellenistic kingdoms after Alexander. Links with republicanism were

becoming more attenuated, and Greek culture, with its developed
vocabulary and rhetorics of monarchical power, was gaining relevance. The texts discussed in the following chapters suggest how the
kinds of literary reinvention of Alexander that were taking centre
stage during the last century of the Roman Republic, might have
offered a basis for Roman appreciation of these developments. Moreover, the movement loosely termed the Second Sophistic is prefigured
in Rome by the elder Seneca, whose *Suasoriae* offer a window onto a
world where Greek rhetors and Greek dialogic forms are an everyday
part of Roman life.[47] The Greek orator Dio Cocceianus (Chrysostom—
Golden Mouth) flourished in Rome under Nerva and Trajan (he had
previously suffered banishment by Domitian for conspiracy). Dio
epitomizes the fusion of Greek cultural revival and Roman political
ideology and vocabulary that characterizes this period, and in his
orations on kingship, addressed to Trajan, we find a Greek counterpart
for Pliny's *Panegyric* to the same emperor. In a world of Greek chic,
Arrian's choice of Alexander as a subject for full-length treatment is
unsurprising.[48] That Arrian also wrote a work (no longer extant) on
the world in the wake of Alexander's death suggests that this fall-out
was itself of interest in the changing ideology of Roman Empire.

Readings—Alexander *Rex*

It should come as no surprise that when we think about contexts for Alexander, administration and bureaucracy do not feature prominently in the narrative tradition. The business of consolidating and *governing* an empire falls to the post-conquest phase. We might argue that the whole point about being Alexander is this constant closural problem. Alexander's early death at Babylon in 323 BCE sets up a narrative dynamic which demands explicit authorial engagement with what *might* have happened next.

The open-endedness generated by this lack of a post-conquest phase makes Alexander a particularly problematic and at the same time extremely attractive model for Romans thinking about paradigms of power. He becomes endlessly available as a model for speculation as to how successfully a supreme commander can hold on to empire, whether new military targets and exploratory quests will constantly be required in order to justify his rule, and how political settlement can be negotiated when and if he 'settles down' to govern.[1] In Alexander we have a figure whose role as king is restricted to what might be defined in narrative terms as its introductory, military phase. By dying young, he ensured that the image of the eternally youthful leader persists, but thinking about Alexander *Rex* involves more than glamour and charisma. It is far more complicated than that. Whether or not our sources present Alexander as a 'good' king depends upon complex constructions of the Macedonian monarchy as in some way 'democratic', and of his power as dependent upon his exploits, his fame and his ability to retain a bond of apparent intimacy with his soldier-citizens. And this brings us to another significant element in any reading of Alexander the king: once he crosses into Asia, leaving a sullenly unified Greece in the hands of his regent, Antipater, his citizen body is entirely made up of his army, itself an amalgam of Macedonian, Greek and, increasingly, Asian troops.

2. Pietro della Vecchia, *Timoclea Brought Before Alexander* (*c.* 1640) Scenes of Alexander with women tend to be focused on supplication rather than sex, although the erotic subtext of this scene is barely concealed. Timoclea demands justice from Alexander after her rape during the Battle of Thebes, yet her sensual distress and dramatic position, coupled with our glimpses of her flesh and Alexander's *déshabille*, make this picture an eloquent witness to the powerful symbiosis between sex and violence.

For Romans in the first century BCE, recasting the dynamic Alexander—a successful one-way *triumphator* in the east—as a Roman general who makes the return trip, contaminates him with the ensuing horror of civil war and bloodshed. Negotiating whether and why the development of personality cults, autocracy and extra-republican powers has to be a corollary of the increasingly imperialistic and expansive nature of the Roman state becomes a question of vital political and cultural importance. It is during this period that we start to see Romans questioning and exploring the nature of their political framework, and investigating what differentiates their system from those of the states with which they are increasingly coming into contact and conflict. King Alexander, the subject of this chapter, is a topos that encompasses all of the fundamental elements of his Roman appropriation: absolute monarch, military genius, uncontrollable madman and conquistador *par excellence*. The texts discussed in this chapter focus on the points of intersection between these different versions of Alexander, and how they feed into an ongoing negotiation of how to hold power at Rome. Alexander's leadership skills and ability to govern his people function as vital elements in his Roman imagery, and prime questions to ask of the first of these texts are how and why the leadership model constructed around Alexander was to have such continuing potency for Roman politics.

Alexander v. Rome? What if . . .

This group of texts spans the late Republican period, taking us up to the mid first century CE, highlighting the modulations taking place in a pattern of ongoing reinvention of Alexander as a model for the interrogation of power and authority at Rome.

Alexander plays a significant role in Livy's investigation of what it means to hold power in Rome, albeit potentially neutralized by a 'safe' early republican context. Livy's comments on the nature of Alexander's power implicate him in a tangled nexus of Roman concerns about how military and political supremacy in the Mediterranean have been achieved, and the presence of Alexander in such a discourse poses some awkward questions. If Alexander's conquests were inextricably linked to his increasing loss of Greek (or Macedonian) self, then how can anyone guarantee that a similar fate will not overtake everyone who assumes his role? Similarly, if the eastern peoples (and particularly the Persian king, Darius) whose

mores and customs gained such a stranglehold over him were themselves in some way 'inferior', then the potential glory attendant upon
eastern conquests becomes directly implicated in a set of complicated
issues of ethnicity and national identity.

READING 2.1
LIVY,
From the
Founding
of the City
9.18.1–7

(1) I am speaking about Alexander at a time when he was
not yet overwhelmed by the tide of favourable events,
because there was no-one who was more incapable of
dealing with prosperity of this kind.

(2) If he is judged according to the nature of the new
fortune and new character which he assumed, so to
speak, as a victor,

(3) then he would have come to Italy more in the manner
of Darius than of Alexander, and would have brought
with him an army that had forgotten Macedonia and
that was already falling into Persian ways.

(4) It is unpleasant, in the case of so great a king, to have
to recount his arrogant alteration of his clothing and his
desire that those fawning upon him should prostrate
themselves on the ground, which even had they been
vanquished must have been humiliating for the
Macedonians, and how much more so given that they
were victors; it is distasteful to recount the repugnant
punishments he inflicted, and the murder of his friends
at the banqueting table and the vanity of his fabrication
of his parentage.

(5) What would have happened if his love of wine had
become greater as time went on? What if his savage
anger had blazed more brightly as he grew older? And I
am only recounting facts about which there is no dispute
amongst authors. Are we to regard none of these things
as a drawback to his excellence as a commander?

(6) Was there really a danger, as the most frivolous amongst
the Greeks, those who promote the Parthians in the face
of everything that Roman glory entails, rehash at every
opportunity, that the Roman people would not have
been able to resist the majesty of Alexander's name?
Despite the fact that I don't think he was even known to
them by repute, would not one out of all the Roman
leaders have given voice to his true feelings against him,

(7) even though men dared to speak out freely against him in Athens, in a city shattered by Macedonian arms (and with the smoking ruins of nearby Thebes a visible warning) as the records of their speeches make clear?

(1) Et loquimur de Alexandro nondum merso secundis rebus, quarum nemo intolerantior fuit. (2) Qui si ex habitu nouae fortunae nouique, ut ita dicam, ingenii, quod sibi uictor induerat, spectetur, (3) Dareo magis similis quam Alexandro in Italiam uenisset et exercitum Macedoniae oblitum degenerantemque iam in Persarum mores adduxisset. (4) Referre in tanto rege piget superbam mutationem uestis et desideratas humi iacentium adulationes, etiam uictis Macedonibus graues, nedum uictoribus, et foeda supplicia et inter uinum et epulas caedes amicorum et uanitatem ementiendae stirpis. (5) Quid, si uini amor in dies fieret acrior? Quid, si trux ac praeferuida ira?—nec quicquam dubium inter scriptores refero—nullane haec damna imperatoriis uirtutibus ducimus? (6) Id uero periculum erat, quod leuissimi ex Graecis qui Parthorum quoque contra nomen Romanum gloriae fauent dictitare solent, ne maiestatem nominis Alexandri, quem ne fama quidem illis notum arbitror fuisse, sustinere non potuerit populus Romanus; (7) et aduersus quem Athenis, in ciuitate fracta Macedonum armis, cernente tum maxime prope fumantes Thebarum ruinas, contionari libere ausi sunt homines, id quod ex monumentis orationum patet, aduersus eum nemo ex tot proceribus Romanis uocem liberam missurus fuerit.

In this amazing and utterly unexpected passage, Livy sets up an imaginary contest between Alexander and Rome, a conceit that recalls the set-piece topos of the rhetorical exercise as reflected in the Elder Seneca's *suasoriae*. Here, the emphasis is complicated by the 'real' historical context within which the parameters for this potential conflict are configured. For a start, the textual locus of this intersection between the history of Rome and the imaginary history of Alexander (although we might want to consider applying the term 'imaginary' to both sets of historical narrative, even if in slightly different ways) is highly significant. Livy sets this digression on Alexander after Alexander's death, thereby interpolating the imaginary meeting between the two forces at a point when Alexander might have been expected to attempt to extend his empire in a westward direction. This nod towards a 'reality effect', a sense that Livy is narrating for his readers what might legitimately have been an expected outcome to Alexander's abortive return from the East, is made all the more gratingly 'real' by its inclusion in a history of Rome that commences with the foundations of the city, indeed, with the pre-history of the space that would eventually be Rome. An impossible future for

Alexander intersects with Livy's refoundation of the Roman state, but like Alexander's abortive plans for a westward campaign, the future of the Republic might also be construed as having come to an end stop. Livy's musings on Alexander in Book 9 fall in the midst of his narration of the Samnite Wars (and the settlement of Latium) which were to result in Roman domination of the Italian peninsula by the early third century BCE.[2] In this way, Livy presents for his audience a meditation on how power corrupts, in a manner that simultaneously foreshadows the ongoing development of Roman history and his own historical narrative whilst also dislocating the reader from the apparent linearity of the historical progression. Alexander is absorbed into a developing story of a Roman past whilst remaining a figure of (disturbing) ongoing vitality in an Augustan 'present'.

If Alexander offers a useful model for the construction of a point of intersection between contemporary and historical Romes, Livy's configuration of this significatory role makes some important, if implicit, demands upon his audience. To begin with, Alexander's meteoric rise and dramatic downfall offer a not particularly subtle warning of what *can* happen when power is entrusted to one man. Livy's league of Roman super-heroes allows for this, and repudiates its relevance for Rome by suggesting that the degeneration suffered by Alexander was a function of his autocratic position. Yet Livy was composing his history at a time when Rome was also under the control of one man, but when Roman commentators seem to have believed that the preconditions for this departure from republican tradition were a result of growing foreign infiltration rather than vice versa. In this way, Livy's model apparently equates a pre-conquest King Alexander with the safely republican values that preceded the political disturbances of the first century BCE. This kind of bifocalism, whereby Alexander *before* Persia can be allowed to function as a potential parallel for a (long defunct) Rome, governed according to solidly republican principles, presents us with a paradox. How can any state retain its sense of identity and traditions of freedom in the face of an inevitable decline and corruption once the concentration of powers in one man reaches a certain critical mass? The final comments of passage 2.1 offer one way in which Livy is suggesting that excessive power can be countered—through a determination to exercise freedom of speech, and to ensure that subversive and anti-establishment critiques are written down in some form. In this way, Alexander the degenerate and excessive monarch becomes an important trigger for an implicit, but still programmatic statement of Livy's historical agenda. The speeches of Athenian opponents of Alexander were recorded, and in this way a tradition of resistance to Alexander has remained intact (9.18.7); it is in their continuing vitality that Livy vests their importance. Similarly, in Livy's reification of the historical process, refusal to admit to fear of Alexander is implicitly defined as a refusal to be silenced.[3] Livy uses this story of Athenian resistance to Alexander in order to construct the act of textualization of oppositional rhetoric as a form of resistance in itself, and one that has the potential to outlast the oppressor whose power triggered their composition. The enormity of Alexander is matched, here, by the bravery of those who defied him, but the one cannot completely exist independently of the other. Alexander the Great only figures in Livy's version of Rome because of the magnitude of his greatness and the parallel depths of degeneracy into which he was portrayed as having fallen.

Livy, writing at the very beginning of the Augustan Principate, provides us with a sense of the immense political complexity that all Romans had to learn to negotiate in the wake of Octavian's triumph at Actium. Perhaps as a consequence, Livy's version of how and why Alexander's 'degeneracy' is relevant to Rome is connotative rather than explicit, but it is astonishing that his sole piece of explicit dialectic makes the Alexander 'issue' *the* problematic of Roman history.[4]

READING 2.2
LIVY,
From the
Founding of
the City
9.18.8–19

(8) As imposing as his magnificence may seem to us, it is still the magnificence of one solitary man, the end result of a little over ten years' good fortune.

(9) Those who go into raptures on the basis that although the Roman people have never lost a war, they have still suffered many defeats in battle whereas fortune never abandoned Alexander in a fight, fail to realize that they are comparing the achievements of one young man with the feats of a people already in its fourth century of warfare.

(10) Should we be surprised, then, if when counted up, the generations on one side outnumber the years on the other, and that over so much longer a period of time there have been more variations in fortune than in a thirteen-year career?

(11) Why not compare men with a man, generals with a general, the fortune of one with that of the other?

(12) How many Roman generals I could name for whom fortune was never unfavourable in battle! In the annals and lists of magistrates you may run through pages of

consuls and dictators whose excellence and good fortune never gave the people of Rome a single day's regret

(13) and what makes them even more remarkable than Alexander or any other king is this: some were dictators for ten or twenty days, and none held the consulship for more than a year;

(14) their military levies were obstructed by the people's tribunes; they were delayed in going to war, and recalled early to hold elections;

(15) in the midst of their labours the year rolled on; sometimes the rashness, at other times the unreasonableness of their colleague was a hindrance or caused actual harm; they inherited situations mismanaged by their predecessors; they received an army of raw recruits, or one that was ill-disciplined and badly trained.

(16) How different things are for kings! Not only are they free from all hindrances, they are also masters of time and affairs and their decisions drive events rather than trailing in their wake.

(17) This means that an unconquered Alexander would have waged war against unconquered generals, bringing the same prior indications of fortune's favour to the contest;

(18) actually, his risk would have been greater than theirs because the Macedonians had only one Alexander, who over and above the many dangers he was exposed to, went out of his way to engage in them voluntarily,

(19) while there would have been many Romans who could have matched Alexander in glory or magnificence of achievement, of whom each could have lived and died as fate decreed without any danger to the state.

(8) Quantalibet magnitudo hominis concipiatur animo; unius tamen ea magnitudo hominis erit, collecta paulo plus decem annorum felicitate; (9) quam qui eo extollunt, quod populus Romanus, etsi nullo bello, multis tamen proeliis uictus sit, Alexandro nullius pugnae non secunda fortuna fuerit, non intellegunt se hominis res gestas, et eius iuuenis, cum populi iam quadringentesimum bellantis annum rebus conferre. (10) Miremur, si, cum ex hac parte saecula plura numerentur quam ex illa anni, plus in tam longo spatio quam in aetate tredecim annorum fortuna uariauerit? (11) Quin tu homines cum homine et duces cum duce, fortunam cum fortuna confers? (12) Quot Romanos duces

nominem, quibus numquam aduersa fortuna pugnae fuit! Paginas in annalibus magistratuum fastisque percurrere licet consulum dictatorumque, quorum nec uirtutis nec fortunae ullo die populum Romanum paenituit (13) et, quo sint mirabiliores quam Alexander aut quisquam rex, denos uicenosque dies quidam dictaturam, nemo plus quam annum consulatum gessit; (14) ab tribunis plebis dilecti impediti sunt; post tempus ad bella ierunt, ante tempus comitiorum causa reuocati sunt; (15) in ipso conatu rerum circumegit se annus; collegae nunc temeritas nunc prauitas impedimento aut damno fuit; male gestis rebus alterius successum est; tironem aut mala disciplina institutum exercitum acceperunt. (16) At hercule reges non liberi solum impedimentis omnibus sed domini rerum temporumque trahunt consiliis cuncta, non secuntur. (17) Inuictus ergo Alexander cum inuictis ducibus bella gessisset et eadem fortunae pignora in discrimen detulisset; (18) immo etiam eo plus periculi subisset, quod Macedones unum Alexandrum habuissent, multis casibus non solum obnoxium sed etiam offerentem se, (19) Romani multi fuissent Alexandro uel gloria uel rerum magnitudine pares, quorum suo quisque fato sine publico discrimine uiueret morereturque.

Reading Livy, we may be struck by the overwhelming emphasis on a comparison between the one (the king) and the many (the Roman Republic). Encapsulated in Livy's narrative is a textbook example of how a Roman can manipulate a potential conflict between Rome and *Greek* Macedon, *after* Rome's final demolition of Macedonian (and Greek) opposition. This means that Livy's disquisition opens up a forum in which discussion of this sort is both instantly relevant to Rome's imperial aspirations, and simultaneously 'safe' because relating to a battle already won. In this 'digression' on Alexander, Livy equates the potential for success of the two sides with the governmental forms they enjoy (9.18.13–16). The consul is far more effective than Alexander (or any other king), this passage argues, because the Roman magistracies are subject to strict temporal limitations, obstructive colleagues, and political expediency (9.18.13–15); hence everything that is achieved by the consul is achieved against the odds. There are benefits in a monarchy because kings can construct their own power structure rather than playing hostage to political circumstance; but as we shall see, Livy the narrator is less than convinced that this benefit outweighs the disadvantages. Livy is dealing initially with monarchy in general, but his rapid shift from thinking with Alexander, to thinking with a 'king' and back again, makes a degree of identification between the two unavoidable.[5] As a point of departure, this Livian salvo on kingship foregrounds the passive nature of the achievement and power of one born into and succeeding to a

hereditary monarchy.[6] Livy goes on to contrast this with the corresponding greatness achieved—*despite* obstacles—by Roman consuls.
So passive versus active, monarchy versus republic, offers one set of
parallels, but Livy was writing not just within a tradition of exemplary history, but also at a time when heredity versus an active
grasping of power was a potentially explosive topos. To what extent
is Augustus as *diui filius* a subtext here? Or might the reader perhaps
veer more towards a reading of Augustus the saviour who fought the
forces of despotism and snatched the Republic from danger, thereby
winning the right to act as its protector?

I have been describing this passage as a 'digression', and before we
think any further about what is actually going on, we should stop to
think about the way in which this narrative appears in Livy's history.
The section on Alexander was written into the narrative as an
aside, capping the story of Papirius Cursor, a late fourth-century BCE
Republican general, and a man whom Livy describes as having been
the most able and loyal Roman of his generation (9.16.19).[7] There are
a number of ways to interpret Livy's juxtaposition of Papirius Cursor
and Alexander. Livy was composing a history on annalistic principles,
and such histories are necessarily predicated upon at least lip service
towards a linear and developmental exposition of the past, so to find
synchronous parallels between a late fourth-century Roman general
and Alexander, who died in 323 BCE, would not necessarily be
surprising. Nevertheless, Papirius Cursor is, in the greater scheme of
things, a local hero, not a man who dominated the world stage, nor
even extended Rome's overseas territories. So why, apart from contemporaneity, should Livy single out Papirius Cursor for comparison
with Alexander? One reason is to be found in his characterization. In
Cursor, Livy has created an archetypal Roman, produced from the
clichés of opposition between the physical endurance and remarkable
self-discipline that were embedded in the Roman mythic national
consciousness, and the self-indulgence, weakness and corruptibility
that could be drawn upon as characteristic of an opposing and typically 'eastern' other. Perhaps the archetypal great Roman nobody. In
this context, we can read Papirius Cursor's concentration on solving
Roman problems in Italy as indicative of his good sense, while
Alexander's manic military expedition against the fleshpots of the East
becomes an indictment of everyone who tried to valorize Greek
achievements over Roman exploits. But there is, potentially, more to
it than that. Livy's narrative modelling of Rome's history actively
withholds all significant foreign involvement from the first ten books.
Even occasional moments of intersection between Rome and the East

(e.g. Brutus' visit to Delphi, 1.56–57) tend to emphasize an almost claustrophobic focus on Rome itself.[8]

Inbuilt in this rhetoric is an expectation that we are all in on the ironic end result of Alexander's story: he conquered an empire, but never ruled it. Livy's comparison evokes the brevity of Alexander's achievement and above all, its apparent insignificance. Unlike Alexander, sensible Romans dealt with unglamorous battles against Italian rivals in order to create a secure basis for lasting power, and because *Rome* rather than individual generals is the ostensible focus of the history, this heroic focus can persist. Rome itself becomes an embodiment of republican heroism. By highlighting Alexander's contemporaneity with Papirius Cursor, Livy is tacitly demanding that we acknowledge Rome's developing empire over a course of time that from the fourth century (then) to the narrative present would see Alexander's conquests split up between his generals, and eventually subsumed into other nations. This issue of succession continues to gnaw away at Livy's grand, republican scheme, as the comparison between Cursor and Camillus suggests. With this in mind, Livy's introduction of Camillus as 'successor' to Cursor (9.17.7–11) is particularly telling, given the almost symbiotic relationship between Rome and Camillus set up in Book 5, and then Camillus' Book 6 clash with that alternative Roman 'hero' (or perhaps super-villain) Manlius Capitolinus, saviour of the Capitoline.

If the sublimation of self and the surmounting of obstacles offers the only route to lasting greatness in Livy's scheme, we have to ask ourselves one very important question: how has *King* Alexander's memory remained such a potent force that it intrudes into Livy's history, given that the achievements of any king must pale in the recognition of his mortality? Clearly, there is something anomalous in Livy's syllogism. For a start, monarchy implies heredity, and although Alexander did succeed his father, his dynasty (if we can call the Successors that) was associative rather than hereditary in the first instance. If we compare this with Papirius Cursor, we find another peculiarity: his son, of the same name, continued his father's tradition of service to the Republic, serving as consul twice (293 and 272 BCE) and defeating the Samnites at Aquilonia, before helping to bring the Pyrrhic wars to an end.[9] In an ironic twist, this implicit nudge towards Cursor minor is already prefigured at 9.18.6–13 when Livy draws in Hannibal, which in turn could evoke Hannibal's alliance with Philip V of Macedon. Later, Livy mentions that other Alexander (of Epirus), who, fatally wounded, was still acknowledging the effeminacy of the East (19.19.11). The cluster of associations between Rome and

Alexander becomes ever more claustrophobic. So our comparison between king and citizen is already drawing out the instability of both models. Similarly, excess and the corrupting influence of absolute power ought to demand that Alexander's name be wiped from history, but as Livy's treatment of Manlius Capitolinus has already made clear (6.20.13–14), the act of excising someone from the national consciousness itself inevitably becomes a moment of historical significance. Notoriety and fame will be attached to 'great' bad deeds, and Alexander's excesses increase rather than obscure his claims to preeminence. The Great Alexander has to err on a grand scale. A nation obsessed with *libertas* and the avoidance of tyranny needs some model against which to measure its success. For Athens and the Greek states, Persia and at times Sparta could stand for tyranny in opposition to Athenian democracy. Roman imperial dreams could segue neatly from an abhorrence of monarchy to a demonstration of how the most famous warrior king of them all was outdone by a collective popular effort. But still Alexander persists, and Livy's textbook rebuttal of his claims only serves to enshrine his position at the heart of Roman history.

In an age of popular politics and personalities, it was unlikely that Livy's valorization of the collective over the individual would succeed; but does Livy actually set himself up to fail? The consequence of successfully promoting an annual consulship as the only means to ensure the triumphant progress of Roman *imperium* could well be a return to civil war from the precarious stability of the 20s BCE. For Livy to succeed, and to appear to want to succeed in these terms, places Alexander at the centre of a political and historical discourse that involves both Actian propaganda and traditional republican *bêtes noires*. Yet as I have suggested, Papirius Cursor is not an entirely straightforward character. His 'greatness' in Livy's scheme is developed only in contrast to Alexander. Without Alexander, here in Book 9, who would pause over Papirius Cursor? Without this rhetorical conflict between republican general and 'eastern' warlord, perhaps Papirius Cursor ceases, historiographically, to exist? This apparent contradiction touches upon a central Augustan paradox—the interdependence of peace and war, and the impossibility of renewal and restoration without destruction and bloodshed. Alexander represents a fascinating antithesis of a 'good' Roman leader's aspirations, but narratologically, the positioning of the digression (even allowing that it may have had its genesis in a rhetorical exercise) seems to be attempting to close off its potential as a device for contemporary speculation. Livy's editing of his material subtly demonstrates the fictitious nature of 'annalistic' records, and whether or not Livy drew this excursus from set-piece schoolroom rhetoric, consideration of his choice of context is vital. Even if the digression on Alexander was not composed as part of the *Ab Vrbe Condita*, its placement makes it a keynote statement on government and the nature of power within the second pentad of the text. This is particularly significant if Books 6–10 of the history were published before 23 BCE. This scheme complements the Alexander 'digression', which if positioned more prominently, might have jarred with a 'restored' Republic.[10] So even if a strictly annalistic chronology should exclude textual speculation as to how a young and ambitious Roman should direct his ambitions within a tottering republican framework, it still must spark conjecture concerning its author's intentions among its post-Actium audience. The affectation of 'set-piece' schoolroom rhetoric might in fact draw the reading present even more inevitably into the text.

Livy's 'digression' in Book 9 is inspired by a vision of an Alexander who can prove useful for Roman self-definition as a historical race, and as a people who, through good management of their 'Alexander-qualities', offer a new, improved model. Livy opens this excursus with a question and a claim—he tells us that he has often considered but never formulated the question of what the outcome of a war between Alexander and Rome, man versus state, would have been (9.17.2). This proposition structures the ideological debate that follows.[11] If we remember that this narrative of Livy's is designed to present the story of Rome from its foundation, then this digression on so splendidly individualistic an autocrat, a digression that never succeeds in entirely dimming his lustre, is particularly noteworthy. The tension set up by this rhetorical invasion of Rome's history by Alexander makes Livy's discussion particularly pointed. In such a monumental and potentially normative document of (re)foundation, and at a time when power and political structure at Rome were undergoing a period of intense renegotiation, Alexander's disruptive presence offers a self-conscious destabilization of both narrative history and the contemporary political situation.

Paradoxically, *Fortuna* handicaps Alexander and limits the state through its enhancement of his personal military prowess.[12] This echoes a changing perception of man's role in history as suggested in Chapter 1, diminishing the importance of personal (and perhaps inimitable) qualities in any story of Alexander. This 'limitation' is countered structurally by the 'digressive' technique by which Livy writes him into Rome. By making Alexander's Roman incursion into a declamatory invasion of 'historical' narrative, Livy implicitly invokes the paradigmatic pressures of persuasive declamatory rhetoric. The end result is that this apparent cul-de-sac may reinforce Alexander's centrality as an imitative model. We might speculate as to whether Livy considered it politically inexpedient to work through an argument entirely critical of Alexander's position because of the uncertainty surrounding the nature of Octavian's political settlement. As it was to transpire in the wake of Pompey and Caesar, the Augustan 'image factory' was to fall little short of the kind of media control established by Alexander's propagandist court. Perhaps it is even to be expected that the reader might be unconvinced by arguments playing down Alexander's greatness. Indeed Alexander's inclusion here offers an implicit, overarching, reason for his disastrous impact: he truly *is* 'great'. He is such a dynamic, all-conquering and charismatic figure that he eclipses all other potential candidates for greatness, making his empire over-dependent on him, and thereby attracting excessive and ultimately destructive favours from fortune. The distinguished nature (*egregius*) of Alexander's generalship is admitted (9.17.5), but only in terms of the factors that increased his celebrity (the solitary command and his youthful death in the midst of success). The greatness engendered by sole command is also, therefore, its limitation; no one else can approach Alexander's qualities, competition ceases, and the nation is diminished. The end of this version of the story is that Alexander's greatness cannot offer anything more than transient power, with the moral that playing the 'greatness' card ultimately leads to self-destruction, even on a national level.

If Alexander's brand of individual greatness is self-limiting and destructive for his empire, Livy can then argue with hindsight that this model is itself swamped by the collective greatness of Rome over the centuries. Self-limiting individual greatness cannot match the greatness of successive generations (9.18.9). This theme moves to its conclusion (9.18.18) with an evaluation of what would be at stake in a contest between Alexander and Rome: Macedon had to stand or fall dependent on the fate of *one* Alexander; Rome, improbably, has a multiplicity of successive Alexanders, but none of them ever really get to *be* him, despite the ambivalent overtones of Cicero's comments to Caesar on the interdependence of state and ruler (*Pro Marcello* 46). This development is mirrored in Curtius' representation of Macedonian demands that Alexander behave less rashly, and fears for their fate if he died or deserted them,[13] but another factor is also introduced, peculiar to Livy's textual scheme. To understand this, we must return to the positioning of this excursus on Alexander (9.16.19–17.2).

Livy has, he tells his audience, been prompted to write about Alexander because he has just been discussing the clemency, fairness and popularity of Papirius Cursor.[14] Tacitly, by admitting a validity for this comparison, Livy accepts that all these elements form part of Alexander's imagery. Livy then sets about his subversion of these associations. Could this Roman have defeated Alexander? And by extension: could Rome have defeated the Macedonian? These questions allow the introduction of a parade of potential Roman Alexanders (9.17.8–9), initiating a scheme for the text as a whole. Alexander is great, but his solitary splendour proves for Livy how much greater still is Rome, with a multiplicity of potential Alexanders. Yet in this model, with its myriad Alexanders, the very quality that defines Livy's dealings with him—his uniqueness—is dispersed. Further, if *one* Alexander was bad for all the stated reasons, how can so many prove better? What happens to one Alexander among many? What differentiates the model from the replicas? We might wonder whether a redrawing of Alexander could offer an alternative take on the realignment of the *res publica* under Augustus. Political conjecture along these lines would have been well suited to the transformative decade between Actium and the 'restoration' of the Republic.[15]

Plain Speaking: Autocracy and Freedom of Speech

Livy's musings on the nature and possibility of the triumph of an individual over a collective offer a version of the kinds of speculation that must have been rife in the years leading up to and after Actium, but although I have placed Livy first in this chapter, his is not the earliest text to introduce Alexander into the cultural history of Roman political speculation. The four following extracts are from letters written by Cicero to his friend Atticus in May and June of 45 BCE, less than a year before Caesar's assassination. These letters demonstrate the immediacy of Alexander as an obvious comparative for Caesar, and their easy introduction of the parallel suggests that it was one that already required no explanation.

READING 2.3
CICERO,
Letters to Atticus
12.40.1–2

9 May 45 BCE

Cicero to Atticus, greetings.

(1) I have seen what kind of form Caesar's tirade against my eulogy [of Cato] will take from that pamphlet which Hirtius sent me. He has gathered together all Cato's

faults, whilst at the same time offering me the greatest praise. So I have sent the book to Musca in order that he may give it to your copyists. I want it to be published, and in order to expedite this, perhaps you will instruct your people.

(2) I often make an attempt to write a 'letter of advice', but find nothing to say, even though I have here the letters of both Aristotle and Theopompus to Alexander. Where's the similarity? They could write what was both a credit to themselves and agreeable to Alexander. Can you come up with anything of that sort for this situation? Nothing along these lines comes to my mind.

vii Id. Mai. 45 BCE

CICERO ATTICO SAL.

(1) Qualis futura sit Caesaris uituperatio contra laudationem meam perspexi ex eo libro quem Hirtius ad me misit; in quo colligit uitia Catonis, sed cum maximis laudibus meis. Itaque misi librum ad Muscam ut tuis librariis daret. Volo enim eum diuulgari, quoque facilius fiat imperabis tuis. (2) Συμβουλευτικὸν saepe conor. Nihil reperio, et quidem mecum habeo et Ἀριστοτέλους et Θεοπόμπου πρὸς Ἀλέξανδρον. Sed quid simile? Illi et quae ipsis honesta essent scribebant et grata Alexandro. Ecquid tu eius modi reperis? Mihi quidem nihil in mentem uenit.

READING 2.4 14 May 45 BCE
CICERO,
Letters to   . . . It is really unbelievable how much writing I am getting
Atticus   done, particularly by night, when I am sleepless. Yesterday
13.26.2   I even composed a letter to Caesar, as you suggested. There
               was nothing wrong with writing it, just in case you
               thought it necessary, but as things stand now there is no
               need at all to send it. But it's up to you. I will send you a
               copy anyway, perhaps from Lanuvium if not from Rome.
               But you'll know tomorrow.

prid. Id. Mai. 45 BCE

. . . Equidem credibile non est quantum scribam, quin etiam noctibus; nihil enim somni. Heri etiam effeci epistulam ad Caesarem; tibi enim placebat. Quam non fuit malum scribi, si forte opus esse putares; ut quidem nunc est, nihil sane est necesse mittere. Sed id quidem ut tibi uidebitur. Mittam tamen ad te exemplum fortasse Lanuuio, nisi forte Romam. Sed cras scies.

READING 2.5
CICERO,
Letters to
Atticus
13.27.1

25 May 45 BCE

Cicero to Atticus, greetings.

On the subject of the letter to Caesar, it was always understood that your friends might read it in advance. If it had been otherwise, then I would have been failing in my duty to them and would also have run the risk of endangering myself, were I to displease him. But they have been open with me, and I am grateful that they did not hide their feelings. In fact what I consider best of all is that they wish to make so many changes that it would be pointless for me to attempt to redraft it. That said, what angle ought I to have taken on the Parthian War, if not the one I thought he wanted? Indeed, what other point was there for this letter other than flattery? If I had wanted to advise him in the way that I really thought best, do you imagine that words would have failed me? So the whole letter is pointless. For when it's impossible to score a great hit, and when even a minor miss would cause problems, why run the risk? Particularly when it occurs to me that since I haven't written to him in the past, he will think that I was going to write nothing unless the war was completely at an end. And furthermore, I fear that he may think that I wanted this to be a kind of concession for my *Cato*. What more do you want? I strongly regret it, nor could things have come about more to my wishes in this affair than that my effort should not be approved.

viii Kal. Iun. 45 BCE 13.27

CICERO ATTICO SAL.

De epistula ad Caesarem, nobis uero semper rectissime placuit ut isti ante legerent. Aliter enim fuissemus et in hos inofficiosi et in nosmet ipsos, si illum offensuri fuimus, paene periculosi. Isti autem ingenue, mihique gratum quod quid sentirent non reticuerunt; illud uero uel optime, quod ita multa mutari uolunt ut mihi de integro scribendi causa non sit. Quamquam de Parthico bello, quid spectare debui nisi quod illum uelle arbitrabar? quod enim aliud argumentum epistulae nostrae nisi κολακεία fuit? An, si ea quae optima putarem suadere uoluissem, oratio mihi defuisset? totis igitur litteris nihil opus est. ubi enim ἐπίτευγμα magnum nullum fieri possit, ἀπότευγμα uel non magnum molestum futurum sit, quid opus est παρακινδυνεύειν? praesertim cum illud occurrat, illum, cum antea nihil scripserim, existimaturum me nisi toto bello confecto nihil scripturum fuisse. Atque etiam uereor ne putet me hoc quasi Catonis μείλιγμα esse uoluisse. Quid quaeris? Valde me paenitebat, nec mihi in hac quidem re quicquam magis ut uellem accidere potuit quam quod σπουδὴ nostra non est probata.

26 May 45 BCE

Cicero to Atticus, greetings.

(1) Since you are going to have a look at the garden today, it will of course be tomorrow when I find out what you have seen. About Faberius also, when he has arrived.

(2) Regarding the letter to Caesar, believe me when I swear to you that I cannot do it; it is not the shame that deters me, even though that is what ought to be most off-putting. For when life itself is a disgrace, how shameful is flattery! But as I was beginning to say, it is not this shame that deters me (I only wish it were; for I would then be the man that I ought to be), but rather that nothing comes to mind. Think about the subjects with which the letters of advice written to Alexander by men of eloquence and learning were concerned. This was a young man who was burning with a desire for the truest glory, desiring to be advised so that he might be able to attain eternal renown, and they encourage him to choose honour. There is no lack of things to say on that topic; but what can *I* say? Nevertheless, I had managed to chisel out something, from tough material, that seemed to be along the right lines. Yet because there were some issues that I portrayed as slightly better than is actually the case, past or present, they are criticized; but I have no regrets. For if that letter *had* reached its addressee, believe me, I would have regretted it.

(3) You must see that even that pupil of Aristotle, with all his great intelligence and great discretion, became proud, cruel and excessive once he gained the title 'king'? What? Do you imagine that this fêted idol, this tent-companion of Quirinus, is likely to enjoy such moderate letters as mine? In fact it is preferable that he should long for letters unwritten than disapprove of ones received. In the long run, let it be as he pleases.

> What was spurring me on to action when I put the 'Archimedian Problem' to you has now gone. By Hercules I would now far rather—and even actively desire—that misfortune which I then feared.

vii Kal. Iun. 45 BCE

CICERO ATTICO SAL.

(1) Hortos quoniam hodie eras inspecturus, quid uisum tibi sit cras scilicet. De Faberio autem, cum uenerit. (2) De epistula ad Caesarem, iurato mihi crede, non possum; nec me turpitudo deterret, etsi maxime debebat. Quam enim turpis est adsentatio, cum uiuere ipsum turpe sit nobis! Sed ut coepi, non me hoc turpe deterret (ac uellem quidem; essem enim qui esse debebam), sed in mentem nihil uenit. Nam quae sunt ad Alexandrum hominum eloquentium et doctorum suasiones uides quibus in rebus uersentur. Adulescentem incensum cupiditate uerissimae gloriae, cupientem sibi aliquid consili dari quod ad laudem sempiternam ualeret, cohortantur ad decus. Non deest oratio. Ego quid possum? Tamen nescio quid e quercu exsculpseram quod uideretur simile simulacri. In eo quia non nulla erant paulo meliora quam ea quae fiunt et facta sunt, reprehenduntur; quod me minime paenitet. si enim peruenissent istae litterae, mihi crede, nos paeniteret. (3) Quid? Tu non uides ipsum illum Aristoteli discipulum, summo ingenio, summa modestia, postea quam rex appellatus sit, superbum, crudelem, immoderatum fuisse? Quid? Tu hunc de pompa, Quirini contubernalem, his nostris moderatis epistulis laetaturum putas? Ille uero potius non scripta desideret quam scripta non probet. Postremo ut uolet. Abiit illud quod tum me stimulabat cum tibi dabam πρόβλημα 'Αρχιμήδειον. Multo mehercule magis nunc opto casum illum quam tum timebam, uel quem libebit.

Reading this series of extracts from Cicero's correspondence takes us directly to the heart of the anxieties and political instabilities of the final years of Caesar's dictatorship. Livy, writing in the aftermath of Actium, was faced with a situation in which the ideological concerns of the republican system had been hi-jacked by the man whose presence as *primus inter pares* was the logical conclusion to the succession of increasingly autonomous military leaders who dominated Rome during the first century BCE. By feeding a warped version of the *res publica* back into the political framework, but on his own terms, Augustus succeeded where Caesar and previous aspirant Romans had failed. For Cicero, fourteen years before Actium, the negotiation of Caesar's power was still in the balance. This means that when Cicero tries (and fails) to construct an acceptable discourse for advising

Caesar, the introduction of kingship as a problematic governmental form is likely to have raised some extremely sensitive questions. A major element of the Roman Alexander discourse developed from the problem of negotiating an acceptable mode (in a monarchy-obsessed political forum) for the interaction between citizen and absolute ruler, and the issue of dealing with the inequality of the relationship between a king and a subject (even when the subject had a legitimate advisory role). This concern with how the state was governed, and the combined distaste and curiosity about monarchy, seems to have fed into a more generalized anxiety about how increasing levels of contact between Rome and the Hellenistic kingdoms would impact upon Roman power-figures and their relationship with the Senate. That this was perceived as an area of difficulty even in the last years of the Republic is borne out by these four letters from Cicero in which he attempts to negotiate his own potential role in the moulding of Caesar's *de facto* authority.

Writing to his friend Atticus on May 9 45 BCE, Cicero ruminates on Caesar's response to his own panegyric on Cato, which Hirtius has apparently foreshadowed in a preliminary pamphlet.[16] Cicero, although he only hints at it, is in an increasingly difficult position, and we can see how this tension functions if we consider these letters alongside another Ciceronian piece of rhetoric. During the previous year, 46 BCE, Caesar had been granted a ten-year dictatorship, and he had also mopped up the last of the Pompeian opposition at Thapsus in Africa, and more recently at Munda (March 45 BCE). In August and September 46 BCE he had celebrated lavish triumphs for his victories in Gaul, Egypt, Pontus and Africa. Meanwhile, Cicero had delivered in the Senate a conciliatory and overtly eulogistic speech addressed to Caesar on behalf of Marcellus.[17] This speech immediately problematizes all readings of the letters of the following year, because in this speech Cicero constructs a rhetorical discourse which appears to give us a sneak preview of what the abortive 'letter of advice' might have looked like. Addressing Caesar in gratitude for Marcellus' recall, granted in September 46 BCE, Cicero emphasizes that this speech breaks his self-imposed silence. The opening words are '*diuturni silentii*' and this emphasis is embedded in Cicero's analysis of his speech when writing to Servius Sulpicius Rufus in October of that year.[18] This speech, then, is one that we are being told to pay attention to. This is not 'just' Cicero the senator addressing the house; by stressing that it marks a distinct break with the public silence that precedes it, Cicero allows it to function as a model for how all similarly compromised senators can begin to enter into a dialogue with Caesar. Cicero *still* represents a traditional senatorial position, *princeps senatus*, however tarnished, and commands attention when he equates Caesar's restoration of Marcellus to the Republic with his own sudden recuperation of a public voice (*Pro Marc.* 2). What we find is that Caesar's power and authority now function as conduits for senatorial speech, even though without his anomalous presence, senatorial 'silence' might be assumed to be a non-issue. This is Caesar as cause and effect of silence and self-expression, but how 'free' is the new rhetorical outpouring?

Cicero's own position with Caesar was ambiguous. Like Marcellus, he had himself been in need of Caesar's clemency, and this knowledge has to underpin our understanding of all potential subtexts to this speech. When Cicero comments that for Marcellus to have received this favour from Caesar is glorious (*Pro Marc.* 3), and that Caesar's beneficence is therefore all the more magnificent, what we may be seeing is a key statement of a burgeoning discourse of how Romans should conduct themselves in relation to a king. Furthermore, as the following passage suggests, Cicero is also initiating a comparative model between Rome and monarchies that we have seen picked up by Livy with specific reference to Alexander and monarchy at Rome.

READING 2.7
CICERO, *On behalf of Marcellus 4–5*

(4) No one, Caesar, has such an innate flow of talent, such vigour and eloquence as an orator or author, as to be able to recount (I don't even say to extol) your achievements. Nevertheless I contend, and with your permission I maintain, that you gained greater glory through none of these deeds than you acquired on this day.

(5) I am often accustomed to keep this idea in view—and furthermore make use of it liberally in frequent conversations—namely that all the achievements of our own generals, all those of foreign states and of the most powerful peoples, all those of the most celebrated kings, are comparable neither with the greatness of your wars, nor the number of your battles, nor the variety of lands that you have conquered, nor the speed of your conquests, nor the difference of character that marked each of your wars. Assuredly, it would have been impossible for anyone to have journeyed over those countries, so remote from each other, more rapidly than they have been traversed by what I will term your victories, rather than your travels.

(4) Nullius tantum flumen est ingeni, nulla dicendi aut scribendi tanta
uis, tantaque copia quae non dicam exornare, sed enarrare, C. Caesar,
res tuas gestas possit. Tamen hoc adfirmo et pace dicam tua, nullam in
his esse laudem ampliorem quam eam quam hodierno die consecutus es.
(5) Soleo saepe ante oculos ponere idque libenter crebris usurpare
sermonibus, omnis nostrorum imperatorum, omnis exterarum gentium
potentissimorumque populorum, omnis regum clarissimorum res gestas
cum tuis nec contentionum magnitudine nec numero proeliorum nec
uarietate regionum nec celeritate conficiendi nec dissimilitudine
bellorum posse conferri, nec uero disiunctissimas terras citius passibus
cuiusquam potuisse peragrari quam tuis non dicam cursibus, sed
uictoriis lustratae sunt.

Delivered in September 46 BCE, this speech broke Cicero's political
silence in an atmosphere that must have been saturated with images
of the all-powerful and all-conquering dictator. Cicero's attempt to
articulate an appropriate comparative discourse for Caesar's achievements is made within a wider context in this speech: a context, which
from the speech's opening, emphasizes the importance of Cicero's
own rhetorical intervention in the powers that Caesar was accruing.
That this speech is less about Marcellus' recall than the government
of Rome is further highlighted when Cicero addresses the nature of
autocracy, commenting that even if military glory may be difficult to
apportion solely to the commander, the statesmanship, self-mastery
and clemency that Caesar has demonstrated give him a semblance of
the divine.[19] Even allowing for the potential exuberance of encomium,
the immediate context would suggest that in retrospect at least,
Cicero's words could be open to reinterpretation in the wake of his
letters of the following year. Presenting Caesar's clemency as the
attribute that has enabled Cicero to rediscover his public voice
imposes a paradoxical tension on the praise offered: this clemency has
caused Cicero to speak in the Senate—a key political duty for the
republican senator—yet in this speech Cicero is not advising the
consuls or deliberating on Roman policy, he is praising one man who
has gathered together a network of unconstitutional powers.
Furthermore, Cicero elsewhere tries to suggest that rather than being
prompted by Caesar's clemency, he was moved to speak by a sense of
senatorial duty.[20] The potential tension between these two explanations is rooted in the increasingly delicate balance of power between
Senate and Caesar. To have the ability to grant pardons, to permit
speech, is to have power over the recipient of these benefits, and these
two benefits cut to the heart of the identity of the aristocratic Roman
citizen within the republican system—presence in Rome (and atten-

dance at the Senate) and public, senatorial rhetoric. This implies that Caesar's power to trigger (or silence) senatorial speech may also be a function of his power over the Senate as a body, whilst his position as *euergetes* highlights his elevation. Once Cicero invokes a connexion between clemency, the power to authorize and reward, and Caesar's political role in Rome, all public speech needs to be defined in some way as either authorized (and subject to Caesar) or unauthorized.

Cicero's speech concerning Marcellus is clearly 'public' rhetoric, but when we consider his letters to Atticus (and others) we are to some extent reading over the shoulders of Cicero's model recipients, even allowing that Cicero wrote with an eye to eventual publication. This makes any comparison between the two modes of discourse problematic. Nonetheless, even if Cicero is constructing an entirely separate and epistolary discourse when he discusses (in a letter) how to go about writing a letter of advice *of the kind addressed to Alexander*, there are still important points of intersection. He comments (*ad Att.* 12.40.2) that he wishes he could perfect an appropriate essay of advice (and we may experience the doublethink here of his use of the Greek: a Greek term for a 'Greek' problem— Συμβουλευτικόν—with attendant distancing effect), but try as he might, he cannot think of anything 'appropriate' to say. In the wake of his own interpretation of his speech for Marcellus, we might argue that in autumn 46 BCE he still believed that Caesar might 'restore' republican government, but even this interpretation has inherent problems.[21] Could a *res publica* that was in the gift of one man conform to the kind of system that Cicero might aspire to? We might also question whether or not Cicero was unaware of the impossibility of turning back the clock to an idealized 'republican' past.[22] Unlike Caesar, Cicero suggests, Alexander provided a grateful prototype for openness to instruction, but when Cicero deals with Alexander he marks out two distinct phases: before and after he gained the title of 'king' (*ad Att.* 13.28.3). Returning to passage 2.3, a number of different nuances arise from this distinction. Cicero may have been hinting at possible imitation of Alexander by Caesar—and the comparison would not have been made lightly—which would forge a direct link between military victory and an ongoing validation of power.[23] Separating Alexander the amenable 'prince' from Alexander the proud, cruel and excessive king allows Cicero to suggest a sequence of cause and effect between obtaining autocratic power and losing the ability to take advice.[24] For the Senate, formally an advisory body, the presence of one man at the head of the Roman state, a man who by definition as a 'king' would be disinclined to take

their advice into consideration, offers a bleak outlook. Here, at the
end of the Republic, we find Alexander slap-bang in the middle of a
tentative discussion of the best way in which advisors can deal with
absolute power. Significantly, this letter also hammers home the vital
importance and influence of literary production and consumption in
Roman politics. Aristotle and Theopompus could write books of
advice to Alexander that were acceptable both to authors and to
recipient; Cicero, writing in praise of Cato, was also making a political statement, as was Caesar in his literary response. Rhetorical
ability, the skill to judge an audience, and a facility to engage in verbal
sparring were becoming increasingly important; after the victory of
Octavian, these literary skirmishes and paper victories were the only
triumphs available to the citizens of the new regime.

At the end of Cicero's letter of 14 May (passage 2.4) we find an
apparently throwaway remark that suggests that the idea of a 'letter
of advice' to Caesar has come from Atticus himself. This suggests that
the idea of writing has been under discussion for some time, and by
stating that the letter is entirely at Atticus' behest, Cicero disclaims all
responsibility for what happens to it once it reaches Atticus. Yet in the
earlier letter (passage 2.3), the 'letter of advice' seems to have been a
project of Cicero's that he was keen to undertake, even if it was
fraught with difficulty. In the final two letters concerning this point
(passages 2.5 and 2.6), following on almost two weeks later, Cicero's
tone has become defensive. The letter was only ever a draft, he claims,
and he intended that others among *them* (*isti*)—not *my* friends, Cicero
seems to suggest—should read it before it should be sent to Caesar. He
is indeed grateful that these people so *openly* (*ingenue*) expressed their
dissatisfaction with various points in the composition, saving him
from displeasing Caesar and endangering himself by that means.
Again the importance of the written word is emphasized: not only
might Cicero anger Caesar by ill-judged phrases, the very act of his
having written could alter the political balance. Cicero has not written
previously, so his choice of this moment now to write would have
added significance.[25] The period of composition for these letters, May
45 BCE, was during Caesar's third Dictatorship and fourth Consulship.
In 44 BCE Caesar was to receive a Dictatorship for life, and less than
a year after these letters were written, Caesar would be dead. As
Cicero comments to Atticus in passage 2.5, the final mopping up after
the war was still in progress. The Pompeians had been defeated at
Munda in Spain (March), and in early April, Pompey's son Gnaeus
was killed. Caesar spent two further months in Spain, parcelling out
rewards and punishments, and among his other acts he revisited the

temple of Hercules at Gades. There as a younger man (during his quaestorship in Hispania Ulterior in 69 BCE) he had exclaimed at the statue of Alexander that stood at the temple, wondering how he could have reached almost the same age as Alexander on his death, yet have failed to achieve such monumental feats.[26] We are bound to regard this story as apocryphal. Whether or not a link had been made between Caesar and Alexander at Gades in 69 BCE, his return in 45 must have triggered echoes.

When Cicero claims in this letter that the advice was only what he, Cicero, thought Caesar wanted to hear, the Greek word for fawning that he chooses (κολακεία) must highlight this nod towards the perilous descent of Alexander's court into sycophancy, so beloved of Roman authors. Why, Cicero asks, would he write anything about Caesar's proposed Parthian expedition (an expedition deep into Alexander-territory) that would give offence? Depending upon how seriously we take Cicero's self-representation as central to the power-struggle and Caesar's increasing hold on supreme authority—and on some level all Cicero's letters are as 'public' as his public oratory— Cicero's own input into the tricky political realignment during this period is bound to influence our reading of his comparison between Alexander and Caesar. Cicero's failure to construct an acceptable rhetoric of advice may in retrospect hint at the ultimate failure of 'peaceful' methods by those opposed to Caesar's control of the state, but it also foreshadows something of the new problem facing Rome, the problem of how to interact with, and to engage in a dialogue with, someone holding supreme power.[27] The final letter (passage 2.6), returns to the thorny question of advising Caesar. It places Alexander centre stage and reaffirms his significance for these tentative attempts to configure a new discourse of power. In this letter we find Cicero spelling out more clearly why he believes that he cannot amend his draft: the draft, he claims, was as full of fawning as he was morally capable without greater hope of its political value. The exercise is now pointless. Be aware of this important proviso slipped in by Cicero: he would not mind fawning, if the flattery were *to effect his political ends*. This marks a stark contrast to Cato's response to the possibility of a pardon from Caesar, and suggests that even at this stage, flexibility and adaptability had begun to play a pivotal role in the continuing reconfiguration of the Roman political status quo.

Cicero tries to negotiate a textualized way in which he can advise Caesar, whilst coming to terms with the problem of advising a ruler whose delimitation has freed him from the need to take counsel. The development of one-man rule posed a problem for a nation accustomed to dependence on *concilium*, and an elite expectation of conciliar power.[28] Two authors who are particularly important for the development of this ongoing discourse are the elder and younger Senecas. These authors deliberate on the problem of fostering self-discipline and self-judgement in an absolute ruler, working towards the development of a vocabulary of power and dependence acceptable in Rome. The following passages illustrate how thinking with Alexander might exemplify the difficulties inherent in any relationship between ruler and subject, difficulties that are ironized by an implicit acknowledgement that where Aristotle failed, could any successive 'adviser' hope to succeed?

READING 2.8
THE ELDER
SENECA,
Suasoria
1.5–6

(5) Division

Cestius used to say that this type of *suasoria* should be declaimed differently depending on the circumstances. An opinion should not be expressed in the same way in a free country as in a country ruled by kings; even advice which is beneficial to them needs to be given in such a way as will please them. And even amongst kings themselves there are distinctions: some are more tolerant of the truth than others. Out of this group we consider Alexander to be one of those who is particularly proud and puffed up beyond the norms of human behaviour. Finally, even with other proofs having been set to one side, the *suasoria* itself offers incontestable proof of his arrogance; his world cannot contain him. For that reason, he used to say that nothing should be said unless it showed the highest respect for the king, lest the same fate befall him as happened to Alexander's tutor, Aristotle's cousin, whom the king killed on account of an untimely and outspoken witticism. For Alexander wished to be regarded as a god, and when once he was wounded, at the sight of his blood this philosopher of his commented that he was surprised it was not the 'ichor, such as flows through the veins of the blessed gods'. Alexander punished this witticism with a spear. The point is made elegantly in a letter from Cassius to Cicero: after much joking at the expense of the stupidity of the young Pompey, who recruited an army in Spain and was defeated at the battle of Munda, he then said: 'Here we are mocking him, but I'm afraid lest he make his riposte to our mockery with his sword.'[29] In dealings with all kings one should be very wary of this kind of witticism.

(6) Accordingly, Cestius used to say that when in Alexander's presence it was necessary to give one's opinion in such a way that his feelings were soothed by lavish flattery, yet that with the requirement that a certain moderation be maintained lest it appear to be flattery rather than due respect, such as happened to the Athenians when their public blandishments were not only detected but punished. For at one time Antony wished to be spoken of as Father Liber and ordered that this name be inscribed on statues to him, and in his dress and his retinue he imitated Liber. So the Athenians, with their wives and children, met him on his arrival and hailed him as Dionysus. It would have turned out better for them if their Attic satire had stopped there. But they then said that they were offering their Minerva to him in marriage, and asked him to take her as his bride. Antony said that he would marry her, but that as a dowry he ordered that they hand over a thousand talents.

(5) Diuisio

Aiebat Cestius hoc genus suasoriarum aliter declamandum esse quam suadendum. Non eodem modo in libera ciuitate dicendam sententiam quo apud reges, quibus etiam quae prosunt ita tamen ut delectent suadenda sunt. Et inter reges ipsos esse discrimen: quosdam minus, alios magis ueritatem pati; Alexandrum ex iis esse quos superbissimos et supra mortalis animi modum inflatos accepimus. Denique, ut alia dimittantur argumenta, ipsa suasoria insolentiam eius coarguit; orbis illum suus non capit.

Itaque nihil dicendum aiebat nisi cum summa ueneratione regis, ne accideret idem quod praeceptori eius, amitino Aristotelis, accidit, quem occidit propter intempestiue liberos sales; nam cum se deum uellet uideri et uulneratus esset, uiso sanguine eius philosophus mirari se dixerat quod non esset ἰχώρ, οἷος πέρ τε ῥέει μακάρεσσι θεοῖσιν. Ille se ab hac urbanitate lancea uindicauit. Eleganter in C. Cassi epistula quadam ad M. Ciceronem missa positum: multum iocatur de stultitia Cn. Pompei adulescentis, qui in Hispania contraxit exercitum et ad Mundam acie uictus est; deinde ait: 'nos quidem illum deridemus, sed timeo ne ille nos gladio ἀντιμυκτηρίσῃ.' In omnibus regibus haec urbanitas extimescenda est. (6) Aiebat itaque apud Alexandrum esse dicendam sententiam ut multa adulatione animus eius permulceretur,

seruandum tamen aliquem modum, ne non ueneratio <uideretur sed
adulatio>, et accideret tale aliquid quale accidit Atheniensibus cum
publicae eorum blanditiae non tantum deprehensae sed castigatae sunt.
Nam cum Antonius uellet se Liberum patrem dici et hoc nomen statuis
<suis> subscribi iuberet, habitu quoque et comitatu Liberum imitaretur,
occurrerunt uenienti ei Athenienses cum coniugibus et liberis et
Διόνυσον salutauerunt. Belle illis cesserat si nasus Atticus ibi
substitisset. Dixerunt despondere ipsos in matrimonium illi Mineruam
suam et rogauerunt ut duceret; Antonius ait ducturum, sed dotis
nomine imperare se illis mille talenta.

The danger of over-close association with a ruler (and the perils of
giving advice) develops into a major element of the Roman Alexander
discourse. Cicero suggests (*pro Rab.*, delivered in court in 54 BCE) that
trusting oneself to a king in his kingdom is always unwise, prefiguring
(and perhaps reflecting) the rhetorical spectacle that the political
speech was to become. The *suasoria* tends to be overlooked as a
literary genre. It was a type of *declamatio*, and unlike the *controuersia*
(which tried 'fictitious' law cases) it was part of a tradition that
allowed for the showcasing of advisory skills. The speaker would
demonstrate how he might go about advising a historical or mythical
character on some apparently insoluble dilemma. Taken together,
Seneca's books of *suasoriae* and *controuersiae* read not just as a set
of imaginary rhetorical approaches to issues with broad cultural
significance. They are also part of a wider discourse that configures a
linear process of decline in Roman oratory. If we accept that these
works were composed towards the end of Seneca's life, possibly
during Tiberius' Principate, then a relationship between Seneca's
'books' of speeches and disputes, and the historical process as outlined
in Sallust (and indeed Livy), becomes part of a greater cultural
reflection on decline.

Thinking about this text puts us back amongst the kinds of
questions raised when reading Livy on Alexander. The *suasoria* is
sometimes thought of purely as an epideictic genre, divorced from any
immediate commentary on contemporary affairs, a schoolroom exercise for the education of prosperous young boys. But it is this intimate
connexion with the development of successive generations of politicians and orators that makes the *suasoria* such a central performative
genre during the late Republic. This was a period when individual
rhetorical brilliance and persuasive skills really could propel an aspiring autocrat into a position of power, and an ability to manipulate,
entertain and delight an audience was an indispensable feature in the
increasing popularization of power at Rome. These issues key directly

into some of the questions of genre and context that also cluster around Livy's use of Alexander. In collecting up these set-piece arguments and ascribing them to particular rhetoricians, Seneca is ostensibly constructing a reference work for future generations, preserving all that's best in Roman oratory to stand as an exemplar and source of rhetorical strategies for aspiring orators and politicians years hence. But this dialogic presentation, the spread of speaking parts involved, serves another purpose. For a start, it tacitly asserts that topics considered suitable for a *suasoria* are those which are well known not just amongst teachers and grammarians, but among their audience as a whole. And this audience can comprise anyone and everyone from schoolboys upwards. Furthermore, the typical *suasoria* took as its subject some topic or endeavour of uncertain outcome, or even practicability, making Alexander's quest not just into a Roman concern, but into a function of an ongoing discourse of destabilization and even failure.

Alexander's only quantifiable defeat is centred on this refusal by his troops to continue on to the Ocean, and maybe beyond, but how do we know that he wanted to push past this final boundary? Because texts such as this have turned it into a central topos—Alexander's one defeat is not at the hands of an enemy, or even an inability to push back the boundaries of nature, instead it strikes at the heart of the political changes taking place at Rome. The main theme of this *suasoria*—Alexander's desire to explore the Ocean—offers an oblique commentary on the relationship between ruler and subject. Alexander is forced to accept that he cannot function alone, without his citizen-army, yet ironically, as passage 2.8 sets up, those who however gingerly set themselves against an autocrat rarely have any success. Perhaps the mutineers' achievement is significant less because they stopped Alexander's previously meteoric eastward campaign than because it demonstrates the uneasy symbiosis between ruler and subjects, which in Alexander's case is destabilized even further by his death on the return leg of the trip. In purely narrative terms, one might argue that king and subjects were no longer capable of co-existing in a mutually beneficial manner *because* of the defeat they had inflicted.[30] Given that we always know, with hindsight, about Alexander's 'betrayal' of his troops through his death in Babylon, the relationship between men and leader is compromised before they set narrative foot in Asia. But there are further nuances to Seneca's modelling of Alexander's vanity. Although he requires flattery, it has to be subtle enough to appear to be no more than the respect that he deserved.[31] This is illustrated by a story about Antony and the

Athenians, and their derision at his desire to be known as Father
Liber. This juxtaposition of Antony, Alexander and puffed-up mortal
self-importance emphasizes a readily adaptable thesis: advice to kings
must be tempered by praise—the ruling monarch admits no jokes or
sarcasm concerning his person or pretensions, and anyone who fails
to humour them is likely to suffer fatal consequences.

There are five identifiable themes concerning theories of government and imperial behavioural models in this passage: (1) Alexander
the educated king (we have noted the reference to Aristotle) who, (2)
fails to listen to advice even though he consults philosophers (again
Aristotle, now joined by Callisthenes), and (3) still requires unos-
tentatious flattery; (4) he seeks counsel and praise, but (5) because of
his flawed nature heeds only the latter. These negative characteristics
are countered by representations of Alexander's acknowledged desire
to receive advice, and his patronage of philosophers. The two sets are
opposed, but this opposition is dictated by the uses to which the
speakers are putting Alexander's image; hence the same men can
propose contrary views without compromising their arguments. Here,
Seneca 'quotes' L. Cestius Pius (an Augustan rhetorician) to the effect
that opinions need to be voiced in different forms depending on
whether one spoke 'in a free country' (*in libera ciuitate*) or 'before
kings' (*apud reges*), who required their advice to be sugared. Yet even
among kings a further distinction might be made between those who
could tolerate truth reasonably well and those who could not;
Alexander, being according to tradition among the most haughty of
these kings (*superbissimus*), with a sense of self-importance puffed-up
beyond mortal standards, belonged to the latter sort. This discourse
involves a far more explicit guide to the potential modes of addressing
a *princeps* than Cicero could have considered, but the whole is couched
in terms of a rhetorical exercise of which Alexander is an important
contingent part. 'Cestius' accordingly says that if one was not sufficiently respectful towards Alexander one might meet with the fate of
Callisthenes (and the audience is reminded that he was a cousin of
Aristotle, to crank up the shock-value), whom Alexander killed because
of an untimely joke ('*quem occidit propter intempestiue liberos sales*').
We should be aware of the active and personal verb used here by
Seneca: 'killed', not 'put to death' or 'executed'. The implication of
tyranny and violent despotism is too good to pass up.[32] Free speech is
impossible when one man rules, this *suasoria* suggests, but it also
reinforces the relevance of Alexander in Rome. Not only was there no
need to apologize for or explain the use of Alexander as a set-piece
declamation, but a version of the deaths of Callisthenes/Clitus was

commonplace enough to be introduced into a rhetorical set-piece such as this.[33]

The themes foregrounded in these passages offer a template for thinking about Roman discourses of power at this transitional time, and for Seneca, Alexander can act as a type for the arguing of any case before *any* ruler. Yet behind the impeccable Roman rhetoric of freedom and tyranny we should be aware of the characters and author of this text. Born at Corduba in Spain *c*.50 BCE he died *c*.CE 40, and in addition to his rhetorical collections he also wrote a history of Rome from the civil wars until the 'present'. This historical venture is no longer extant, but the immediacy of his historical interests could suggest that the rhetorical distance and hackneyed subject characteristic not only of the *suasoriae* but of his collections of declamatory exercises generally, may well have had more political bite than is at first apparent. This sense is further reinforced when we consider that these rhetorical collections seem to have been put together towards the end of his life for the benefit of his sons, one of whom (M. Annaeus Mela) was the father of the disaffected poet Lucan, another, the younger Seneca to whom we turn now, was exiled by Claudius after his father's death, and went on to act as tutor and adviser to Nero.

READING 2.9
SENECA,
Epistle
94.60–67

(60) If you wish to exercise power that is profitable to yourself, but at the same time oppressive to nobody else, you must banish your own faults.

(61) Many can be discovered who set fire to cities, who storm fortresses that had been considered impregnable for generations and secure for some time, who raise mounds equalling the citadel under siege and break down walls raised to amazing heights with battering rams and siege engines. There are many who sending detachments on ahead can then harry the enemy's rearguard violently and arrive at the great sea drenched with the gore of nations; but even for these men, whilst they were conquering their enemies, they were themselves conquered by their greed. Nobody withstood their attack, but they themselves could not withstand the impulses of ambition and cruelty; so when they seemed to be hounding others, they were themselves being hounded.

(62) Some frenzy hounded Alexander into misfortune, and filling him with desire to lay waste to other's coun-

tries, it dispatched him to unknown lands. Do you consider the man sane, who could make a start by devastating Greece, the source of his education? Who snatched away that which is most valuable to each nation, ordering the Spartans to be slaves and the Athenians to keep silent? Not content with the destruction of the many states which Philip had either conquered or bribed, he overthrew other nations in a variety of places and carried his weapons throughout the whole world; though wearied, his cruelty did not ever reach a standstill. His was the cruelty of a wild beast, which devours more than its hunger demands.

(63) Already he has joined together many kingdoms into one; already Greeks and Persians fear the same man; already nations that under Darius were free accept the yoke of his authority; yet still he journeys beyond the Ocean and the sun, considering it a humiliation that his victorious progress should deviate from the paths of Hercules and Liber, and doing violence to the natural order. He does not wish to go on, but is incapable of standing still; just like a weight that falls headlong, for which the end of its momentum can only come when it lies still.

(64) Neither virtue nor reason persuaded Gnaeus Pompeius into foreign and civil wars; instead, it was an insane love of delusory grandeur. At one moment he was in arms against Spain and the supporters of Sertorius, at another he was advancing against the pirates in order to enchain them and to pacify the seas.

(65) These reasons were being used as pretexts for the extension of his power. What brought him to Africa, to the North, against Mithridates and Armenia and every corner of Asia? Undoubtedly it was his boundless desire to become great, even when it was only to himself that his greatness was insufficient. What incited Gaius Caesar onwards to what was equally a calamity for himself and for the state? Glory and ambition and the recognition of no limit to pre-eminence over other men.

(66) He could not permit a single person to outrank him, although the state placed two people at its head. Do you think that Gaius Marius, who was once a consul—

he received the consulship legitimately on one occasion, he stole it on all the others—was inspired by virtue when he sought out so many dangers, when he was slaughtering the Teutons and the Cimbri, and whilst chasing Jugurtha through the wastes of Africa? Marius commanded armies, but ambition commanded Marius.

(67) When men such as these were shaking up the world, they were themselves being shaken up, like cyclones which whirl together what they have seized, but which before this are whirled up themselves and for this reason rush onwards with greater force, because they have no control over themselves; therefore when they have brought disaster to others, they also feel in themselves that deadly force with which they have brought harm to so many. You should not believe that a man can become happy through the unhappiness of others.

(60) Si uis exercere tibi utile, nulli autem graue imperium, summoue uitia. (61) Multi inueniuntur qui ignem inferant urbibus, qui inexpugnabilia saeculis et per aliquot aetates tuta prosternant, qui aequum arcibus aggerem attollant et muros in miram altitudinem eductos arietibus ac machinis quassent. Multi sunt qui ante se agant agmina et tergis hostium [et] graues instent et ad mare magnum perfusi caede gentium ueniant, sed hi quoque, ut uincerent hostem, cupiditate uicti sunt. Nemo illis uenientibus restitit, sed nec ipsi ambitioni crudelitatique restiterant; tunc cum agere alios uisi sunt, agebantur. (62) Agebat infelicem Alexandrum furor aliena uastandi et ad ignota mittebat. An tu putas sanum qui a Graeciae primum cladibus, in qua eruditus est, incipit? Qui quod cuique optimum est eripit, Lacedaemona seruire iubet, Athenas tacere? Non contentus tot ciuitatium strage, quas aut uicerat Philippus aut emerat, alias alio loco proicit et toto orbe arma circumfert; nec subsistit usquam lassa crudelitas inmanium ferarum modo quae plus quam exigit fames mordent. (63) Iam in unum regnum multa regna coniecit, iam Graeci Persaeque eundem timent, iam etiam a Dareo liberae nationes iugum accipiunt; it tamen ultra oceanum solemque, indignatur ab Herculis Liberique uestigiis uictoriam flectere, ipsi naturae uim parat. Non ille ire uult, sed non potest stare, non aliter quam in praeceps deiecta pondera, quibus eundi finis est iacuisse. (64) Ne Gnaeo quidem Pompeio externa bella ac domestica uirtus aut ratio suadebat, sed insanus amor magnitudinis falsae. Modo in Hispaniam et Sertoriana arma, modo ad colligandos piratas ac maria pacanda uadebat: (65) hae praetexebantur causae ad continuandam potentiam. Quid illum in Africam, quid in septentrionem, quid in Mithridaten et

Armeniam et omnis Asiae angulos traxit? infinita scilicet cupido
crescendi, cum sibi uni parum magnus uideretur. Quid C. Caesarem in
sua fata pariter ac publica inmisit? gloria et ambitio et nullus supra
ceteros eminendi modus. (66) Unum ante se ferre non potuit, cum res
publica supra se duos ferret. Quid, tu C. Marium semel consulem
(unum enim consulatum accepit, ceteros rapuit), cum Teutonos
Cimbrosque concideret, cum Iugurtham per Africae deserta sequeretur,
tot pericula putas adpetisse uirtutis instinctu? Marius exercitus,
Marium ambitio ducebat. (67) Isti cum omnia concuterent, concutie-
bantur turbinum more, qui rapta conuoluunt sed ipsi ante uoluuntur et
ob hoc maiore impetu incurrunt quia nullum illis sui regimen est,
ideoque, cum multis fuerunt malo, pestiferam illam uim qua plerisque
nocuerunt ipsi quoque sentiunt. Non est quod credas quemquam fieri
aliena infelicitate felicem.

There is little sense that anyone seriously credited the notion of
Alexander as philosopher-king, and Aristotle was probably not hired
as his tutor to instruct him on the art of philosophical government.[34]
Nevertheless, the transference between tutor or adviser and pupil is
not necessarily one-way. Writing about four hundred years after
Alexander's death, Plutarch's discussion of the potentially corrupting
effects on a philosopher of a royal teaching appointment offers a
darker vision.[35] If the job itself can warp the philosopher's faculties to
such an extent that his powers of discrimination become clouded, his
role may be all the more dangerous to self and state. The danger to
the tutor from court corruption and his pupil's whims is effectively
illustrated in the younger Seneca's relationship with Nero.[36] When he
speaks of the madness of Alexander's destructive urges in the light of
his education, his own educative role is clearly called into question,
and in the context of his relationship with Nero, added zest is given
to his comment that only a madman would destroy the source of this
education. By robbing Athens (and Sparta) of their unfettered voice(s),
the pupil 'robs' his tutors of the freedom of speech which characterized his early education.[37] Education has failed Alexander,
Seneca suggests, because it has not imbued the pupil with any appreciation of how intellectual freedom is essential for its survival; but he
suggests elsewhere that it also fails by not providing Alexander with
any perspective on his place in the world.[38] Alexander's 'greatness',
and perhaps therefore all 'greatness', is fraudulent because of the
negligible size of the world. Some princes are incapable of benefiting
from the education lavished on them, but from a senatorial perspective, once one accepts that becoming a king is a function of
heredity rather than excellence, then tension surrounding the

diminishing role of the senate as an advisory body is joined by a parallel destabilization of the possibility of giving any advice at all. In the early Principate, it had seemed as if a new hierarchy of advice-giving might develop, with focus shifting away from the Senate and a movement towards a system whereby the *princeps* would choose his advisers from a less traditionally influential group, including freedmen and provincials. Yet if there is no guarantee that the ruler will be sufficiently mentally able even to construct a body of advisers, then no hope seems possible. For Nero and Seneca, Alexander becomes not only a potential model for a pupil-prince and his respected philosopher-tutor, but also a paradigm for a prince who is incapable of ruling according to the 'best' precepts *despite* the care taken with his education. Introduction of Alexander into an exploration of how Roman political models are coping with and adapting to this also invites speculation as to his suitability even as a cautionary model for a Roman Emperor.

READING
2.10
SENECA,
*Concerning
Benefits*
2.15.1–16.2

(1) Never let us grant benefits that could cause us shame in the giving. Since the sum total of friendship is to make a friend equal to oneself, the interests of both must be served at the same time. I shall give to him if he is in need, but not to the extent that it puts me in need myself. I shall help him if he is about to be ruined, but not to the extent of ruining myself, unless doing this buys the safety of a great man or a great cause.

(2) I will give no benefit which I would be ashamed to ask for. I shall neither inflate a small favour, nor allow a great favour to be regarded a minor one. For just as he who boasts about what he gives destroys the favour, in the same way he who makes clear the value of what he gives enhances his gift, rather than making it a matter of reproach.

(3) Everyone ought to consider their own means and resources, in order that we may not give either more that we can, or less. Also to be taken into account is the character of the recipient, for as some things are too small to be suitable gifts from a great man, some are too large for the recipient to accept. Therefore compare each of the people involved and in relation to these, consider the gift in order to decide whether it will be too weighty or too trivial, or whether in turn the recipient will either reject it as too mean, or find it too great.

(1) Alexander—madman as he was and incapable of conceiving anything but the grandiose—gave someone a whole city. When the man to whom it was presented took measure of it and shrank from the jealousy that so great a gift would provoke saying that it was inappropriate to his circumstances, Alexander said: 'I am not concerned with what it is appropriate for you to receive, but what is appropriate for me to give.' This seems a spirited and regal speech, but in fact it is extremely stupid. For nothing is in itself appropriate for anyone, it depends upon who gives it, to whom, when, why, where and so on, the issues without which one cannot evaluate the deed effectively.

(2) You swollen headed beast! If it is inappropriate for the man to receive the gift, it is also inappropriate for you to give it. The ratio of both in character and rank is taken into account, and since virtue is everywhere a mean, he who is excessive is equally in error as he who is mean. You certainly have the power and fortune has raised you to such a height that whole cities can be your largess (yet how much greater spirited it would have been not to capture them, than to squander them!); nevertheless there *are* those lesser men who cannot encompass a whole city in their grasp.

(1) Numquam in turpitudinem nostram reditura tribuamus. Cum summa amicitiae sit amicum sibi aequare, utrique simul consulendum est: dabo egenti, sed ut ipse non egeam; succurram perituro, sed ut ipse non peream, nisi si futurus ero magni hominis aut magnae rei merces. (2) Nullum beneficium dabo, quod turpiter peterem. Nec exiguum dilatabo nec magna pro paruis accipi patiar; nam ut qui, quod <dedit>, inputat, gratiam destruit, ita qui, quantum det, ostendit, munus suum conmendat, non exprobrat. (3) Respiciendae sunt cuique facultates suae uiresque, ne aut plus praestemus, quam possumus, aut minus. Aestimanda est eius persona, cui damus; quaedam enim minora sunt, quam ut exire a magnis uiris debeant, quaedam accipiente maiora sunt. Utriusque itaque personam confer et ipsum inter illas, quod donabis, examina, numquid aut danti graue sit aut parum, numquid rursus, qui accepturus est, aut fastidiat aut non capiat.

(1) Urbem cuidam Alexander donabat, uesanus et qui nihil animo nisi grande conciperet. Cum ille, cui donabatur, se ipse mensus tanti muneris inuidiam refugisset dicens non conuenire fortunae suae: 'Non quaero' inquit, 'quid te accipere deceat, sed quid me dare.' Animosa uox uidetur et regia, cum sit stultissima. Nihil enim per se quemquam

decet; refert, qui det, cui, quando, quare, ubi, et cetera, sine quibus facti
ratio non constabit. (2) Tumidissimum animal! si illum accipere hoc
non decet, nec te dare; habetur personarum ac dignitatium portio et,
cum sit ubique uirtus modus, aeque peccat, quod excedit, quam quod
deficit. Liceat istud sane tibi et te in tantum fortuna sustulerit, ut
congiaria tua urbes sint (quas quanto maioris animi fuit non capere
quam spargere!): est tamen aliquis minor, quam <ut> in sinu eius
condenda sit ciuitas.

In the story of Alexander, his eastward momentum and abandonment of Macedon results in his Macedonian subjects becoming
synonymous with his troops. His treatment of his 'subjects' (the
soldiers) is dependent on two factors: his own needs, and the self-
consciousness of his behaviour. The acceptance of a petition enforces
the superior power of the supplicated over the supplicant; but how
should a ruler deal blamelessly with gifts *to* 'inferiors'?[39] The act of
giving places the donor in a position of power, and the recipient in one
of subservience, reinforcing the authority of the ruler. Here,
Alexander is quoted as saying that it was not a question of what was
appropriate for the subject to receive, rather, what was fitting for
Alexander the King to give. *This* Alexander would have done well to
have used his power more magnanimously and judged people with
more care as to their requirements; but is Alexander the real subject
of this lesson?[40] The message outlines a code of behaviour where
judgement on the suitability of a gift must be focused on the recipient's needs. Can this assessment be taken one step further, applying it
to all dealings between people, but particularly to dealings between
those who are financially or socially unequal? In its most extreme case
this relationship is epitomized between Emperor and everyone else.[41]

READING
2.11
SENECA,
Concerning
Benefits
1.13.1–3

(1) To Alexander of Macedon the Corinthians sent an
embassy, congratulating the conqueror of the East when
he was elevating himself beyond mortal bounds, and
making him a grant of citizenship. When Alexander
had smiled at this kind of official courtesy, one of the
ambassadors said to him: 'We have never given citizenship to anyone other than you and Hercules.'

(2) Alexander gladly accepted so distinguished an honour
and provided hospitality and other courtesy for the
ambassadors; but his thoughts were not on those who
had given citizenship to him, rather on those to whom
they had given it. Since he was a man given over to the
pursuit of glory—even though he knew neither its true

nature nor its limitations and endeavoured to surpass the exploits of Hercules and Liber, not even halting where they made a stop—for this reason he turned his gaze to his companion in honour rather than to those giving it. It was as if heaven, to which in his enormous vanity he aspired, was his because he equalled Hercules in this honour!

(3) For what similarity to him had that mad young man, who in place of virtue was simply fortunate in his rashness? Hercules conquered nothing for himself; he travelled across the world not in a spirit of greed, but of judgement as to what he ought to conquer. He was an enemy of the wicked, defender of the good, peacemaker on land and sea. But this other man was, from his boyhood, a robber and despoiler of nations, destructive equally to his enemies and to his friends. He drew his greatest pleasure from terrorising all mankind, forgetting that it's not just the most ferocious but also the most cowardly creatures that are feared on account of their poisonous venom.

(1) Alexandro Macedoni, cum uictor Orientis animos supra humana tolleret, Corinthii per legatos gratulati sunt et ciuitate illum sua donauerunt. Cum risisset hoc Alexander officii genus, unus ex legatis: 'Nulli' inquit 'ciuitatem umquam dedimus alii quam tibi et Herculi.' (2) Libens accepti non dilutum honorem et legatos inuitatione aliaque humanitate prosecutus cogitauit, non qui sibi ciuitatem darent, sed cui dedissent; et homo gloriae deditus, cuius nec naturam nec modum nouerat, Herculis Liberique uestigia sequens ac ne ibi quidem resistens, ubi illa defecerant, ad socium honoris sui respexit a dantibus, tamquam caelum, quod mente uanissima conplectebatur, teneret, quia Herculi aequabatur. (3) Quid enim illi simile habebat uesanus adulescens, cui pro uirtute erat felix temeritas? Hercules nihil sibi uicit; orbem terrarum transiuit non concupiscendo, sed iudicando, quid uinceret, malorum hostis, bonorum uindex, terrarum marisque pacator; at hic a pueritia latro gentiumque uastator, tam hostium pernicies quam amicorum, qui summum bonum duceret terrori esse cunctis mortalibus, oblitus non ferocissima tantum, sed ignauissima quoque animalia timeri ob malum uirus.

Problems do not only arise when kings give inappropriate gifts. This story focuses on the modulations of what happens when subjects offer something to the king, and he responds badly. At issue here is whether or not this kind of response has any wider implications, and if so, how do they mesh with any subtext for his essay. Logically, if gift-giving places the recipient at a disadvantage, then finding that Alexander is incapable of accepting the grant of citizenship magnanimously is unsurprising. But before we assume that Seneca is entirely unfavourable towards Alexander, the details of the gift require further thought. In this instance, the gift is highly political, and indeed opens up all sorts of questions that could prove extremely problematic for any meditation on power and authority. For a start, we learn that when the Corinthians offer Alexander citizenship, rather than meditating on their kindness, he is puffed up with 'unnatural' pride that only Hercules shared the honour with him.[42] But this is no straightforward honour. We might want to read it as a simple rubber-stamping of the inevitable—the Corinthians offer the citizenship to Alexander because they are in his power, and they have chosen to give in gracefully. Alternatively, could this not also appear to be a covert and carefully thought out strategy of annexation on Corinth's part? After all, Alexander comes from imperializing but despised and culturally backward Macedon; by enfranchizing him, the Corinthians are spiking his guns. The implication is that although Alexander conquered the Greek states, it remains in their gift to withhold or offer the right to citizenship, and citizenship itself comes with an ideological baggage train. Citizenship involves duties as well as rights, and by implication at least, there must be a suspicion of a suggestion that Alexander will find membership of the Corinthian citizen body more attractive than his Macedonian, royal identity. Offering citizenship is politically charged in other ways. As a (or *the*) citizen of Corinth, it will be expected, notionally, that he will serve the interests of the state, and therefore that the gift itself is in the best interests of state rather than Alexander. Also, the dynamic of this gift suggests that the Corinthians have judged Alexander fit to receive citizenship, negating his right to ideological as well as civic conquest. Yet what else do the Corinthians have left to offer, when Alexander's power over them is complete? By gracefully offering to Alexander something over and above the land and buildings that make up their state, they are demonstrating their willingness to play the game of pan-Hellenic unity which Alexander badly needed to work if his campaign against Persia was to have any chance of success.

So how do we read Alexander's response? And why does Seneca choose this particular story for his essay? Hercules' presence in the anecdote is telling for a number of reasons. Alexander's fascination with outdoing Hercules and Dionysus is a popular theme in Roman Alexander-literature. Politically, Hercules had undergone a rehabilitation under Augustus after his contamination through association with Antony during the civil wars, and his qualities of endurance, and ability to withstand suffering, offer some attractive Stoic models. Yet in this context we find that his primary function is to be an inducement to Alexander to recognize the honour that the Corinthians are offering him. His Corinthian citizenship is the only element of his identity that the envoy explicitly invokes yet it is the introduction of Hercules as comparative that triggers the response that Seneca seems to be criticizing in Alexander. Alexander was amused (*'cum risisset...'*) when first offered the citizenship, but this is a fairly mild criticism. Perhaps levity is not the correct response to the gift, but its timing and studied nature within this anecdote suggest that we read the Corinthians as having a clear sense of political expediency, and offers us a colluding role with Alexander in his amusement. But the Corinthian pride in their citizenship only serves to destabilize the delicate balance between monarch and ambassadors. It is *their* pride in their gift, their civic identity, which leads the ambassador to make the comparison with Hercules and therefore another reading of Seneca's story could lead us to a slightly different conclusion. The ruler needs to beware the flattery of subjects who are trapped in a spiralling eulogistic discourse, inescapable, because only upward comparisons can be offered. And who ranks above a king except the gods?

Looking back to passage 2.10, what we have outlined is a critical model for considering how euergetism and benevolent autocracy collapse when brought up against the gulf that divides king from subject. It is difficult to see what solution, if any, Seneca has in mind. In both extracts the problems arise from a failure that is both linguistic and connotative. By commenting that at the heart of friendship lies a will to make one's friend equal to oneself, Seneca is affirming that there can be no friendship between the king and anyone else. The aporia and semiotic destabilization brought about by absolute power is made evident through Alexander's devastating effect on friends and enemies alike. It is impossible to distinguish any longer between the two. The impossibility of friendship between monarch and subject offers an extreme model for what may ultimately happen to a society in which the taxonomy of friendship and social relationships are under attack. All relationships within a monarchy are ultimately modulated with reference to the ruler, but the model of kingship represented by Alexander demands that we confront the possibility of societal meltdown.

This puts any putative king in an untenable position. Alexander perforce looms over all pretenders to autocracy as the primary, inescapable paradigm, yet rather than assimilating subjects and conquered alike into a cohesive and orderly society, he created a fractured and unstable unit in which identities were constantly contested, and which fragmented on his death. Both of these extracts offer Alexander as a disruptive model, but his use also tacitly acknowledges his inescapability when thinking about patterns of monarchical behaviour. But given the pessimism that runs through these stories, it is difficult to see how Seneca can hope to effect any positive political change within a monarchy. The only logical response—that with good advice, a king can hope to provide a beneficial civic ideology which combines the best interests of state and ruler—is flawed, as the authors from Cicero onwards have made plain. Advice is a powerful commodity and the provision of a framework for political tutoring undermines the autocratic dynamic. Without advice, there is the danger that all kings will appropriate models of power based on Alexander because just as a king stands as ultimate representative and embodiment of state and people, being Alexander is the inescapable subtext for all subsequent autocrats. The issues raised by the previous passages have been tending towards a closer focus on the relationship between ruler and ruled, exploring the extent to which it is possible for a mutually beneficial relationship to exist.

Flattery and Excess: The Collapse of Language

The final passage in this chapter picks up on the problem of flattery. Flattery tends to be depicted as the logical if not quite inevitable result of the disparity between ruler and subject, a form of excessive courtesy that corrupts on a very insidious level—it destabilizes language and loosens the semiotic connexion that ought to bind a community together.

READING
2.12
CURTIUS,
*History of
Alexander
the Great*
8.5.5–8

(5) And now with all ready, thinking that the time seemed right for what he had long considered in his perverse mind, he began to hunt for a way in which he might usurp divine honours. He wished not only to be called but also to be believed to be the son of Jupiter, as if he could govern minds as well as tongues.

(6) So he ordered the Macedonians to venerate him according to the Persian custom, saluting him by prostrating their bodies on the ground. Nor in his desire for such things did he lack pernicious flattery, the perpet-

ual evil of kings, whose power is more often overthrown by flattery than by enemies.

(7) And this was not the fault of the Macedonians—for
none of them could bear to fall away from any of their
native customs—but of the Greeks, who had debased
the profession of the liberal arts by their evil habits:

(8) Agis an Argive, the composer of the worst poems after
Choerilus, and the Sicilian Cleo, whose character as a
flatterer was as much a national as a personal defect,
and various other sweepings of their own cities. These
men were preferred by the king over his relatives and
the generals of his greatest armies. These were the men
who at that time were opening the road to heaven for
him, declaring that Hercules, Father Liber and Castor
and Pollux would yield before this new divinity!

(5) Iamque omnibus praeparatis <ratus>, quod olim praua mente
conceperat, tunc esse maturum, quonam modo caelestes honores
usurparet coepit agitare. Iouis filium non dici tantum se, sed etiam credi
uolebat, tamquam perinde animis imperare posset ac linguis, (6)
iussitque more Persarum Macedonas uenerabundos ipsum salutare
prosternentes humi corpora. Non deerat talia concupiscenti perniciosa
adulatio, perpetuum malum regum, quorum opes saepius adsentatio
quam hostis euertit. (7) Nec Macedonum haec erat culpa—nemo enim
illorum quicquam ex patrio more labare sustinuit—sed Graecorum, qui
professionem honestarum artium malis corruperant moribus. (8) Agis
quidam Argiuus, pessimorum carminum post Choerilum conditor, et ex
Sicilia Cleo, hic quidem non ingenii solum sed etiam nationis uitio
adulator, et cetera urbium suarum purgamenta [quae] propinquis etiam
maximorumque exercituum ducibus a rege <prae>ferebantur. Hi tum
caelum illi aperiebant Herculemque et Patrem Liberum et cum Polluce
Castorem nouo numini cessuros esse iactabant.

There is a great deal of uncertainty surrounding the author we
know as Quintus Curtius Rufus, who wrote the only surviving full-
length story of Alexander the Great in Latin. His identity is contested,
but Tacitus' reference to a Curtius Rufus who was renowned as a
flatterer—and therefore a political survivor (*Annals* 11.20–21)—and
Suetonius' inclusion of a Q. Curtius Rufus in the index to his work on
rhetoricians (*de Rhet.*) suggests that a mid to late first-century CE date
is at least plausible. And this would fit in with the intensely Roman
concerns with the nature of monarchy and power with which Curtius
fills his narrative.[43] Curtius' model of Alexander's citizen body is

interesting because he makes a careful distinction between the Macedonian people and those of the other Greek states. We also see a clear differentiation between the Persians and the Macedonians, the two extremes of monarchies, with the Greeks taking up an ignominious role somewhere in between. In fact this extract suggests that the presence of the Greeks, the enemy within, is as destructive to Alexander as the influence of Persian luxury. This concern with flattering advisors is likely to be intimately connected with the developments taking place in the bureaucratic structures and strategic alliances that accompanied successive emperors, as freedmen, family and 'courtiers' became increasingly influential in Roman politics. But there is more going on in this passage than a straightforward rant about court sycophants and career flatterers. What we are seeing is a further development in a complex process of rhetorical and political resignification. As the first century CE progressed, traditional meanings were becoming redundant and a new political vocabulary was being formulated, a vocabulary that needed to take account of increasing political centralization and a growing formalization of the detachment of power from the senatorial rank. When Curtius complains about Alexander's divine aspirations he is not just criticizing his requirement for deification, problematic though that is in itself. He is articulating a concern about an escalating need for ever-greater honours, and ever-more absolute control within a climate of political rhetoric that has so destabilized meaning that only the most extreme flattery can signify approval. It is no longer enough to be called *Iouis filius* (son of Jupiter), he also wants to regulate the innermost intellectual processes of his subjects—Alexander now wants them really to *believe* that he is Jupiter's son. Not just control of language, but thought control.

There are all sorts of reasons why anxiety about paternity and succession, and particularly divine heredity, were becoming increasingly important by the time of Nero's Principate. As the demands for intellectual conformity among the senators grew more onerous, acceptance of a dynastic right to succeed became less sustainable, leading eventually to the turbulence surrounding Nero's suicide. But this passage also picks up on the issue of divine comparison that we have already seen Seneca making use of. Curtius' ironic comment that Hercules, Father Liber and the Dioscuri will make way for Alexander in the scheme outlined by his court sycophants, subverts the notion of deification whilst also playing along with the rhetorical topos. The comparison is made between Alexander and four gods who have some human element in their background, but Jupiter as father. These are the only kinds of deity who will yield to him, not any of the traditional Olympian pantheon. We may wonder whether Alexander's inability to choose good poets is a function of a greater destabilization of value and judgement under the kind of rule that he has formulated.

Curtius' encapsulation of the instability of language (and therefore texts) within an autocracy provides an appropriate conclusion for this chapter. The slipperiness of his authorial identity and the impossibility of pinning down a definite context for his narrative mirrors that cycle of destruction and reconfiguration of identity that was such a feature of the Julio-Claudian period. Indeed, it is not until the Principate of Trajan that we begin to see a stabilization of language, as the vocabulary of monarchy gains acceptability.

At the heart of this chapter is an exploration of the relationship between individual and authority, but closely allied to that is an escalating imperative to negotiate an appropriate public voice for the private self, and vice versa. Increasingly, these texts have been focusing on the disastrous potential for seepage between private desire and public status, and its implications when centred on an autocratic ruler. This acceptance of the impossibility of divorcing the man from the person of the 'king' sets up a dramatic tension between national and individual identities and freedoms, a tension which crystallizes around Alexander's legendary excess, as the following chapter discusses.

3

Readings—Living Fast,
Dying Young . . .

Of course Alexander is far more than a model for thinking about the institution of monarchy, or even for exploring the nature of individual aspirations to power. These constructs only nibble away at the edges of some of the juicier worries raised by his story. Extremities of behaviour are essential to Roman concerns about autocracy, but they are also central to any ruler's mystique as a larger-than-life figure: the great bad man, akin in many ways to Sallust's Catiline.[1] This counter-cultural discourse of transgressive heroism runs in tandem with Roman anxieties about identity and empire, particularly during the second and first centuries BCE, when it increasingly seemed to be the case that Alexander's eastern conquests were ready to be overtaken by Roman success. The new-found availability of a world that was perceived to be decadent, luxurious and ripe for conquest segued into a growing sense of disquiet at the wealth that was flooding into Rome from the expanding Empire, and the levels of cultural appropriation that were taking place. This element of Alexander's story—his seduction by the luxury and decadence of the East—coupled with the political upheaval of the late Republic and early decades of the Principate, struck a chord with Roman authors such as Livy, the younger Seneca, Velleius, Curtius and Tacitus, yet a subversive subtext continues to lurk behind their rhetoric of criticism. As suggested by 'Longinus' in his treatise *On the Sublime*, might it not be inevitable that men of humble, mediocre natures remain safe, because of their lack of ambition, whilst true greatness is constantly testing the boundaries?[2] The shifting political parameters of these years may be responsible for the inconsistency with which this parallel is followed through. It may be the case that an uncomplimentary identification of Alexander with powerful politicians could have had serious reper-cussions, an issue that becomes particularly relevant when we read

3. Paolo Veronese, *The Family of Darius Before Alexander* (1565–1570) The ambiguity of the group dynamics in Fig. 2 is also evident in this picture; in fact, here, the possibility that Alexander may not be immediately recognizable as the great king is the whole point of the story. The Renaissance classicism, ermine and brocades that swathe the protagonists emphasise male power, and Sisygambis' uncertainty as to which of the two men is Alexander enhances his contemporaneity. If Darius' mother cannot instantly recognize Alexander, his mythical charisma is deconstructed and he can be assimilated into sixteenth century autocratic power games.

Seneca's comments on Alexander in the light of his own political experience.

When Alexander's murder of his companion Clitus—a result of a drunken argument at a late-night party—becomes central to certain strands of a Roman Alexander-discourse, we can see how there may be a multiplicity of readings through which the murderous king, morally and psychologically out of control, can function as a political paradigm for Rome. Death at Alexander's hands is the most potent of the images of Alexander subsumed by destructive passion, but the fate of another of his companions, Lysimachus, is also important to this ongoing rhetorical dialogue between then and now. As we shall see, Lysimachus survives Alexander's attack, but his inability to function honourably and moderately in turn as a king after Alexander's death, suggests that the destructive potential of Alexander's autocracy can have endless reverberations. Contemporary Roman concerns influence how the individual themes are structured and nuanced, but these stories of Alexander's increasing inability to function as a humane and moderate ruler also feed into the broader political concerns considered in Chapter 2. If one-man rule takes on a momentum of inevitability, and it becomes less the case that the death of each emperor triggers a serious call for a restoration of the Republic, then the focus shifts onto what kind of person should gain the top job. Inevitably, the suitability of the character of the emperor also becomes an increasing focus of concern.

The nine passages discussed in this chapter suggest ways in which the figure of Alexander could offer a binding link between the changing constructs of power in the century after the Battle of Actium, and how these constructs fared when imposed upon unstable, difficult, autocratic rulers. What gradually emerges is a sense of how senatorial satisfaction and dissatisfaction are increasingly concentrated on the person of the ruler rather than the institution itself. In turn, this may lead us to speculate as to whether the mainly senatorial authors were growing increasingly interested in personalities because by concentrating on negative character traits, one could construct a person-specific critique at one remove from the office of emperor. That this becomes more and more common after Tiberius, as succession and even sanity amongst the Julio-Claudians are increasingly up for grabs, is indicative of the changing political scene at Rome. Senatorial anxiety is increasingly centred upon the best kind of man to rule, rather than on the all-consuming evils of autocracy as a political reality. Once this intellectual shift has taken place, suddenly a weak emperor can become a focus for senatorial and military ambitions. Are successive Julio-

Claudians increasingly problematic because they simultaneously and sequentially reinforce the inevitability of succession, whilst stoking the ambitions of senatorial hopefuls?

Drinking-Up Time

The first passage, from Velleius Paterculus' history of Rome, takes us to the Principate of Tiberius, and locates us firmly in a discourse of excess. Here, Alexander's legendary alcoholism plays a key role in his integration into a world where alcoholic excess can be shorthand for a deeper, degenerative abscess at the heart of the body-politic.

READING 3.1 (1) Then followed the consulship of Gaius Caesar, who
VELLEIUS, takes hold of my hand as I write and—whatever my
Histories haste—compels me to linger on him. A member of the
2.41.1–2 Julii, that most noble family and—something that all
the ancients were in agreement upon—tracing his
descent from Anchises and Venus, his exceptional
appearance superseded that of all other citizens. In his
vigour of mind he was particularly keen, in his generosity he was lavish, and his spirit exceeded human nature
and even belief. In the magnitude of his plans, in the
speed of his military engagements, and in his endurance
of dangers he resembled Alexander the Great, but only
when Alexander was sober and not overcome by his
emotions.

(2) In short, Caesar only indulged in food and sleep when
it was necessary, never for pleasure.

(1) Secutus deinde est consulatus C. Caesaris qui scribenti manum
iniicit et quamlibet festinantem in se morari cogit. Hic nobilissima
Iuliorum genitus familia et, quod inter omnes antiquissimos constabat,
ab Anchise ac Venere deducens genus, forma omnium ciuium excel-
lentissimus, uigore animi acerrimus, munificentia effusissimus, animo
super humanam et naturam et fidem euectus, magnitudine cogita-
tionum, celeritate bellandi, patientia periculorum Magno illi Alexandro,
sed sobrio neque iracundo simillimus, (2) qui denique semper et cibo et
somno in uitam, non in uoluptatem uteretur.

Velleius' pro-Tiberius narrative stresses ancestry and heredity in a way that draws attention to the precarious nature of Tiberius' position. As successor to Augustus and like Augustus, Tiberius was an adopted son. Unlike Augustus, he was not forced to fight a civil war to achieve his 'inheritance'. In many respects, Tiberius was in a similar position to those successors of Alexander who needed to demonstrate their right to rule through military glory and conquest, *and* the proximity of their connexion with the glorious founder. Given that the years after Actium saw Caesar becoming less and less central to Augustan image-making, Tiberius seems to have been cast in the role of first 'successor'. This makes Velleius' emphasis on heredity particularly interesting. Augustus' familial links with Caesar make his use of the Julian divine genealogy plausible, over and above his adoption as Caesar's son. Tiberius' claims to the Julian heritage are based only on association and adoption. This focus on family *and* associative relationships makes Velleius' use of Caesar and Alexander especially striking. Ancestry and heredity are sandwiched between reference to the consulship of Caesar (and the inference is that it is this consulship which has triggered Velleius' narrative 'pause') and a trio of superlatives which emphasize both his place within the republic (*omnium ciuium*) and his exceptional status. The comparison works because there are other citizens against whom Caesar can be measured, but after this group of superlatives, things change.

From this point on, rather than emphasizing Caesar's excellence within the citizen unit, Velleius calls his spirit superhuman, unbelievable, before finally moving on to Alexander. In fact, all seven attributes might just as easily be assigned to Alexander, but only the final three are formally associated with him here. Furthermore, the way in which they are expressed signals the contextual shift from citizen body to autocratic monarch. The three positive qualities, expressed tersely in three pairs of words, place Alexander's sobriquet in direct conjunction with the ideas that they express—this is what greatness is all about. Alexander's name itself is separated from its adjective ('*Magno illo Alexandro*'), forcing the name away from the positive qualities and towards the intimations of excess: drunkenness and passion. Caesar was *simillimus* to Alexander (echoing the superlatives of the first set of comparisons) only when he was sober and calm, and he ate and slept only to sustain life.[3] Whereas Augustus' military prowess was open to contestation, Caesar's, like Alexander's (and perhaps Tiberius'?), was in no doubt. This suggests that one conceivable subtext for this passage is that military excellence can justify power. By comparing Caesar with Alexander but emphasizing the frugality of his approach to food, drink, sleep and anger, Velleius seems to be suggesting that some kind of compromise between autocracy and republicanism is possible; that an ideological connexion between great leaders can allow for a positive *associative* heredity in which the best elements may be carried forward, and the worst, abandoned.

Unlike Augustus, Tiberius did not manage to garner a favourable body of consensus literature about his regime, despite his military successes. Velleius had served as a cavalry commander under Tiberius in Germany and Pannonia, and he named him praetor for 15 CE. Velleius' *History* was dedicated to Marcus Vinicius for his consulship of 30 CE, so we know that Velleius intends the work to have up-to-the-minute contemporary significance. The focus for Velleius' *Histories* is contemporary and recent history. Notionally, this two-book work treats Roman history from the beginning, but the main focus is on the improvements that have been taking place under the two previous regimes, and their fruition under Tiberius. So emphasis is placed upon pacification, social and political benefits, and consolidation.[4]

In this version, Tiberius epitomizes wisdom and clemency, offering a stark contrast to the constructs canonized in senatorial histories. This is likely to be a function of close identification between Velleius and his commander, and the fact that although he came from a prosperous family, his political advancement was entirely dependent upon his connexion with Tiberius. Here, he offers us an alternative reading of the Principate in which we can see how prosperous military families might well choose loyalty and obedience in return for the kinds of opportunities for advancement that the emperor could offer.[5] Velleius' interests in the forces of cultural change and cultural history make his inclusion of Alexander particularly apt. Given that Alexander provides a starkly ambivalent model for the process of political change that has been exercising successive political and historical commentators, it is impossible that he could be unaware of the progression from Alexander as *ur*-king, through Caesar, then Augustus, to Tiberius. Velleius' historical programme suggests an evolutionary approach to literary, cultural and political issues on a grand scale. This model superimposes a new cultural and political ascent that takes Augustus' refoundation of Rome as a point in the historical progress of the state rather than as a new beginning in itself.[6] The two key figures at beginning and end, reading this model on to the extract above, are Alexander and Tiberius. Yet paradoxically, because the emphasis on Tiberius is cumulative and suggestive of completion, there is none of the sense of possible future progression that informs Augustan propagandist literature. This imposes a sense of dialogic tension in which Velleius' historical model seems to be at war with his Tiberian sympathies. Perhaps an end-stopping of imperial history with Tiberius would be the ultimate recuperative republican gesture?

All of Caesar's activities before his consulship (59 BCE) are completely absent from Velleius, so the section which this extract comes from takes us at a gallop through a laudatory potted history of Caesar's career and character.[7] That Velleius has chosen to introduce him in this digressive manner focuses our attention not just on to Caesar, but on to the kind of comparative that Velleius considers appropriate for him. It also offers itself as a semiotic key to Caesar's success—he strikes quickly, just as he has appeared suddenly, almost from nowhere, in this narrative. Velleius does not unduly emphasize Alexander's drinking, except insofar as his introduction alongside Caesar is striking in itself, but the throwaway nature of his comparison indicates that it needed no explanation to his audience. That this is the case is confirmed by Alexander's appearance in Seneca's epistle on drunkenness.

READING 3.2
SENECA,
Epistle
83.18–25

(18) Prolong the condition of drunkenness to several days, and will you have any doubt concerning his madness?

(19) Even as it is, the madness is no less, merely of shorter duration. Consider Alexander of Macedon, who stabbed Clitus, his dearest and most faithful friend at a banquet. With an understanding of the crime he had committed came a longing to die, which indeed he ought to have done.

Drunkenness kindles and discloses every kind of vice, and it removes the feeling of shame that restrains our evil undertakings. For more men refrain from forbidden behaviour as a result of the shame of doing wrong, rather than through good intentions.

(20) When too great a strength of wine takes control over the intellect, every lurking evil emerges. Drunkenness does not create vices, but it does draw them out; at such times the lustful man does not even wait to get to a bedroom, but without delay he allows free rein to the demands of his passions; similarly the shameless man openly confesses and publishes his disease; at such times the impudent man does not restrain his tongue or his hand. Pride increases in arrogance, cruelty in savagery, malice in envy.

(21) Every vice is allowed to roam free and thus makes itself evident. Take in addition that forgetfulness of one's own identity, the halting and scarcely intelligible words, indistinct vision, unsteady step, the dizziness, the ceiling itself moving about as if the whole house

was being whirled around by a cyclone; and when the wine froths up within, it distends the very bowels, causing torments to the stomach. Yet at the same time this can be endured as long as the man has his natural strength; but what can he do when this is diminished by sleep, and when what was drunkenness becomes gastric overload?

(22) Think what disasters that drunkenness on a public level has caused; it has betrayed the most brave and warlike peoples to their enemies; it has breached walls defended by the determined warfare of many years, it has brought peoples who were completely steadfast and defiant of the yoke under foreign control, it has conquered with wine those who were invincible in the field.

(23) Alexander, whom I have just now mentioned, passed through his many marches, his many battles, his many winter campaigns—through which he worked his way by overcoming the difficulties posed by time and place—the many rivers which flowed from unknown sources, and the many seas, all in safety; it was intemperance in drinking and that fatal drinking-bowl of Herculean proportions that sent him to his grave.[8]

(24) What glory is there in holding your liquor well? When the prize is yours and sprawling asleep or vomiting, the others refuse to join in your toasts, when you are the last man standing out of the whole party, when you have defeated everyone by your magnificent talent and there is no one with such a capacity for wine as yourself, still you are defeated by the wine-jar.

(25) What was it that ruined Mark Antony—a great man and one of distinguished ability—and drove him into foreign habits and un-Roman vices, if it was not a combination of drunkenness and love of Cleopatra? It was this that made him an enemy of the state, this which made him unequal to his enemies, this that made him cruel when, as he was dining, the heads of the leaders of the state were brought in, when, amidst the most elaborate feasts and regal luxury he would identify the faces and hands of those whom he had proscribed, when, though heavy with wine, he still thirsted for blood! If it was intolerable that he would

> do these things whilst getting drunk, how much more
> intolerable that he was doing them whilst actually
> drunk!

(18) Extende in plures dies illum ebrii habitum; numquid de furore
dubitabis? (19) Nunc quoque non est minor, sed breuior. Refer Alexandri
Macedonis exemplum, qui Clitum, carissimum sibi ac fidelissimum,
inter epulas transfodit et intellecto facinore mori uoluit, certe debuit.

Omne uitium ebrietas et incendit et detegit, obstantem malis
conatibus uerecundiam remouet; plures enim pudore peccandi quam
bona uoluntate prohibitis abstinent. (20) Ubi possedit animum nimia
uis uini, quidquid mali latebat emergit. Non facit ebrietas uitia sed
protrahit: tunc libidinosus ne cubiculum quidem expectat, sed cupid-
itatibus suis quantum petierunt sine dilatione permittit; tunc inpudicus
morbum profitetur ac publicat; tunc petulans non linguam, non manum
continet. Crescit insolenti superbia, crudelitas saeuo, malignitas liuido;
(21) omne uitium laxatur et prodit. Adice illam ignorationem sui, dubia
et parum explanata uerba, incertos oculos, gradum errantem,
uertiginem capitis, tecta ipsa mobilia uelut aliquo turbine circumagente
totam domum, stomachi tormenta cum efferuescit merum ac uiscera
ipsa distendit. Tunc tamen utcumque tolerabile est, dum illi uis sua est:
quid cum somno uitiatur et quae ebrietas fuit cruditas facta est? (22)
Cogita quas clades ediderit publica ebrietas: haec acerrimas gentes
bellicosasque hostibus tradidit, haec multorum annorum pertinaci bello
defensa moenia patefecit, haec contumacissimos et iugum recusantes
in alienum egit arbitrium, haec inuictos acie mero domuit. (23)
Alexandrum, cuius modo feci mentionem, tot itinera, tot proelia, tot
hiemes per quas uicta temporum locorumque difficultate transierat, tot
flumina ex ignoto cadentia, tot maria tutum dimiserunt: intemperantia
bibendi et ille Herculaneus ac fatalis scyphus condidit. (24) Quae gloria
est capere multum? Cum penes te palma fuerit et propinationes tuas
strati somno ac uomitantes recusauerint, cum superstes toti conuiuio
fueris, cum omnes uiceris uirtute magnifica et nemo uini tam capax
fuerit, uinceris a dolio. (25) M. Antonium, magnum uirum et ingeni
nobilis, quae alia res perdidit et in externos mores ac uitia non Romana
traiecit quam ebrietas nec minor uino Cleopatrae amor? Haec illum res
hostem rei publicae, haec hostibus suis inparem reddidit; haec crudelem
fecit, cum capita principum ciuitatis cenanti referrentur, cum inter
apparatissimas epulas luxusque regales ora ac manus proscriptorum
recognosceret, cum uino grauis sitiret tamen sanguinem. Intolerabile
erat quod ebrius fiebat cum haec faceret: quanto intolerabilius quod
haec in ipsa ebrietate faciebat!

When Seneca describes the depth and loyalty of Clitus' friendship
for Alexander, loyalty which was shattered on his brutal murder by a
drunken Alexander, we can sense the inevitability of the contemporary resonances. Encapsulated in Seneca's terse narrative of this

event is the enormous guilt and self-disgust felt by Alexander in its aftermath, and it is with this image of Alexander recovering from his drunken insanity and recognizing what he has done that Seneca concludes the first section of the extract.[9] The tripartite structure of the anecdote—the almost excessively faithful friend, killed at a banquet by the man to whom his loyalty has been given, and the subsequent recognition by both Alexander and Seneca that the king's death would have formed a fitting conclusion—focuses the reader's attention on the disparity of action and intent between the two characters, king and subject. Alexander has violated his position of responsibility as Clitus' commander (supposedly, he should be setting a good example), his duty of care and responsibility towards his subjects, and the reciprocity necessitated by the relationship between a host and his guest. Murder of a dinner guest must have had particular resonance for Seneca and his contemporaries, given the frequency with which poisoning and madness cropped up as motifs under the Julio-Claudians. The dining-room, arguably, was to become a key *locus* for the way in which inter-personal relationships and their attendant obligations were being warped by the political and intellectual changes necessary to accommodate this shuffling tyranny. By setting-up and narrating a collision between the obligations and possibilities opened up by autocracy, and by then locating this story of how the two unravel within the context of a banquet, a disastrous inevitability gathers around the disjunction between private and public, the hidden and the manner in which it is revealed. By infecting formal dining occasions with stories of betrayal and murder, the whole notion of communal consumption as an important performance of social cohesion becomes destabilized, and the reciprocity of the relationship between host and guest is dislocated.[10] Excessive drunkenness marks out a man who lacks self-control, and the condition of drunkenness makes this concrete through a graphic description of the abjection suffered by the drunkard who loses control of his bodily functions. The wine that he drinks becomes a poison for his body, perverting and corrupting rather than sustaining and nourishing, as food should. Thus Alexander's alcoholism can act as a model for a poisonous relationship between ruler and state, whilst his murder of a guest at his banquet functions as a warning to all those who enter into relationships with a solitary ruler. The difficulty is, of course, that in a *de facto* monarchy, all 'subjects' are forced to some extent into a relationship of subservience to the ruler, however dislocated or distant the relationship may be.

Seneca's contention that Alexander should have been allowed to die strikes a politically courageous and potentially controversial note.

Drunkenness, he states is a condition of *self-inflicted* insanity, suggesting that when a man engages in heavy drinking he is actively seeking out the condition of madness that excess produces, and also, that he is not averse to engaging in the exposure of self that drunkenness promotes. Drunkenness is a discloser of vice and a disperser of the shame that usually cloaks our wrongdoing, but it is the madness and loss of control of the sober, public self that causes the real dislocation, as the rest of the passage argues. Everything that should be controlled within the body spews out, yet paradoxically, this laying bare of the inner man could be construed as having a positive outcome: it allows us to gain a glimpse of his 'real' nature, and in Alexander's case, this provides his subjects with an important insight into his murderous urges. Ultimately, we may wish to return to the notion of drunkenness pervading an entire state, which in this context becomes interchangeable with the excessive alcoholic indulgence of a ruler. In Livy's scheme we saw how the Republic could be construed as the sum of its citizen parts, with each citizen-general representing the citizen body as a whole because each individual member of the state played a role in the governance of the state. When all of the various key political functions and powers are gathered together into the control of one man, then the body politic becomes a function of the ruler himself, and in this way, the abjection of one becomes the ruin of the other.[11] Seneca's interpretation of excessive behaviour of all kinds must be taken in the context of his experience of Caligula's madness. His behaviour—even if it owes more to later historical manipulation than to reality—seems to have tested the very limits of what would be acceptable to Rome from an emperor. Ultimately, the assassination of Caligula suggests that he tested the limits of his power unwisely, but this kind of behaviour—attempting to determine how far personal honours and caprice can be carried—is also characteristic of Roman manipulation of Alexander. Claudius' Principate, following after Caligula, is characterized by a distinct lack of anything that could be construed as Alexander-style personal excess, and it is certainly feasible that representation of Alexander as a positive comparative for Roman emperors was severely damaged by Caligula's admiration for Alexander.[12]

Excessive drinking is also, of course, a feature of late republican political polemic, and we can read remnants of this tradition in Seneca's concluding comments on Antony, but by the time we reach Seneca's *de Ira* (passage 3.6), written during his exile, direct connexions between Alexander and Romans suggest trouble. When criticizing Antony, there is an implicit understanding that the disgusting and un-Roman elements of Antony's behaviour are in some sense in direct opposition to the 'Romanness' laid claim to by Octavian, and developed through the political rhetoric of republican 'restoration' that became an important part of the Augustan settlement. Yet this directly inverted relationship between two opposing civil war factions becomes ever more murky and difficult to unpick during the successive Principates of Augustus, Tiberius, Caligula and Claudius. By the time of Nero's Principate, his descent from Antony has become a legitimizing factor rather than a potential taint in his ancestry. So when Seneca was writing the *de Ira*, probably during his eight-year exile on Corsica, it was in the wake of his experience of Rome and court life under Tiberius and then Caligula.[13]

Angry Young Man . . .

The final seven passages pick up on the connection between drunken excess and insane rage that Seneca explores in passage 3.2. Traced through these texts we see how models of excessive consumption and desires cluster around Alexander. Ultimately, they are bound into a process of intellectual and psychological collapse that has far-ranging consequences for all future political philosophy.

READING 3.3
CURTIUS,
History of Alexander the Great
6.2.1–5

[Referring to Alexander]

(1) But as soon as his spirit, which was better equipped to deal with military matters than with quiet and leisure, was freed from pressing worries, he gave himself up to pleasures. In this way, one whom the arms of the Persians had not conquered, their vices overcame:

(2) lengthy banquets, the mad delight of heavy drinking and late nights, the entertainments and crowds of prostitutes. In every respect there was a degeneration into foreign habits. By emulating these as if they were preferable to his native customs he so offended equally the minds and eyes of his fellow-countrymen, that he came to be regarded as an enemy by many of his friends.

(3) In fact he had driven men who held fast to their native discipline, and were accustomed to satisfy the demands of nature with frugal and easily obtainable food, to the bad habits of foreign and conquered nations.

(4) Hence the increase in frequency of plots against his

life, the mutiny of his troops, and greater freedom in expressing dissatisfaction amidst mutual complaints. Then on his part, now anger, now suspicions, which groundless fear aroused, and other similar problems, of which more later.

(5) Therefore whilst spending days and nights alike in lengthy banquets, Alexander used to break up the satiety of his feasts with entertainments, not content with the host of artists whom he had summoned from Greece: indeed captive women were ordered to sing a song in their native manner, which was discordant and hateful to foreign ears.

(1) Sed ut primum instantibus curis laxatus est animus militarium rerum quam quietis otiique patientior, excepere eum uoluptates, et quem arma Persarum non fregerant, uitia uicerunt: (2) tempestiua conuiuia et perpotandi peruigilandique insana dulcedo ludique et greges paelicum. Omnia in externum lapsa morem; quem aemulatus quasi potiorem suo ita popularium animos oculosque pariter offendit, ut a plerisque amicorum pro hoste haberetur. (3) Tenaces quippe disciplinae suae solitosque parco ac parabili uictu ad implenda naturae desideria defungi in peregrina et deuictarum gentium mala impulerat. (4) Hinc saepius comparatae in caput eius insidiae, secessio militum et liberior inter mutuas querelas dolor, ipsius deinde nunc ira nunc suspiciones, quas excitabat inconsultus pauor, ceteraque his similia, quae deinde dicentur. (5) Igitur cum tempestiuis conuiuiis dies pariter noctesque consumeret, satietatem epularum ludis interpellabat non contentus artificum, quos e Graecia exciuerat, turba: quippe captiuae iubebantur suo ritu canere inconditum et abhorrens peregrinis auribus carmen.

Drunkenness, as we have seen, was an important topos in Roman versions of Alexander, but the emphasis here is focused on Alexander's inability to maintain his normative Macedonian identity in a non-military context. Without discipline, hardship and warfare, Alexander's identity disintegrates, in what we might read as an ironic take on Horace's pithy 'Captured Greece captured its rough conqueror and brought the arts to uncivilized Latium.'[14] In this passage, Alexander can stand as a metaphor for the political and cultural changes that have been taking place in Rome, indeed the drastic effect of his behavioural change on his people is likely to have been read in this context. But the passage is not just a straightforward critique of contemporary Roman *mores*. In fact, as is the case with Seneca's use of Alexander, there is a multiplicity of possible nuances for this commentary on his degeneracy. For a start, the close connexion between thinking about Alexander and thinking about the political settlement at Rome would have forced all readers of Curtius' lengthy narrative of Alexander's campaigns to confront a potential for interpretative slippage. Furthermore, as aggressive imperialism was increasingly becoming a thing of the past, associations between pristine republican empire-building and Alexander *qua* effective, benevolent and self-possessed ruler and military commander would be unlikely to be overlooked. Moreover, authorial focus on the culpability of the ruler suggests that the role of the emperor and his direct responsibility for the moral and physical well being of his people is at stake.

Curtius proposes that Alexander gave himself up to pleasure, and thus was conquered by the vices of the subject people. This participation in his own downfall foregrounds the potential problems of over-dependence on one lone ruler that we noted in Livy, but it also suggests that when a state and a ruler become secure, and no longer need to perform and parade their identities in order to demonstrate their triumph over an external threat, then they are at their most vulnerable. The psychological disintegration that Alexander both participates in and suffers from is symptomatic of a wider distemper in the state whereby culpability (and responsibility) are avoided in favour of a pursuit of personal gratification. Alexander was responsible both for the glorification and invigoration of the Macedonians as a historical people, and simultaneously responsible—because of his hyper-efficiency as a leader—for depriving them of their ability to function independently. This reading suggests that Alexander's success as a leader is itself a function of his excessive character, and it also deprives the Persians—the nominal enemy—of any proactive role in proceedings. The focus of Curtius' critique is on the heavy drinking and prolonged nature of the banquets that Alexander indulged in; his drunkenness deadens his awareness of his behaviour, and dulls his perception of the passage of time. This sense of timelessness adds to the impression of decay and corruption that characterize the Persian court, a dislocation that is further emphasized by the comment that Alexander was eventually considered an enemy by those who had previously counted him as a friend. His identity within the state (and his troops and companions function narratologically as the Macedonian people) is itself under attack.[15]

Twice in the first sentence we find that Curtius sets out the rationale for the changes that overtook Alexander. First, we have a framing contrast between *curae* and *uoluptates*, and then an internal comparison between military affairs and quiet and leisure. Ostensibly this suggests a straightforward and mutually exclusive face-off between duty and pleasure, but this polarity is subverted very quickly, turning a mainstream topos of Alexander's psychological inability to deal with success into a subtle critique of the nebulous ways in which power, autonomy and identity are inextricably intertwined. Plots, treachery, mutiny and unrest are all functions of the dislocation of identity that is at the heart of this passage, and Alexander is responsible for them not simply because his own behaviour has become irreconcilable with traditional Macedonian practice. The key element here is that he had forced his companions to behave in like manner (*impulerat*). In this way we see played out a destructive symbiosis between ruler and subjects in which excess and idleness become the rule, yet paradoxically, the apparent inertia of luxury and idleness, when enforced, provokes subversive political action. Curtius' representation of plots and regicide is ambivalent. On the one hand he condemns the murderers of Darius, yet his narration of Alexander's torture and prosecution of Philotas for a suspected plot is more sympathetic than other versions of this episode.[16] Similarly on the Pages' conspiracy, Alexander's brush with death is subsumed in a greater critique of proskynesis, Lysimachus' ill-treatment, and Callisthenes' stance against flattery and deification.[17]

READING 3.4
SENECA,
Epistle
113.27–30

(27) Do not teach me whether bravery is a living being, rather, that nothing animate can be happy without bravery unless it is the case that it has gained strength in the face of random accidents, and has conquered all hazards by intercepting them in advance and planning a strategy. What is bravery? It is the unassailable bastion against human frailty, the place within which, when a man has secured himself, he can hold out in safety against life's siege; for he is using his own strength and his own weapons.

(28) At this point I would like to refer you to a saying of our philosopher Posidonius: 'you should never consider yourself to be safe when relying on the weapons of fortune: fight using your own! Fortune does not provide arms against herself, and so those who are equipped against their enemies are still unarmed against Fortune.'

(29) Granted, Alexander harassed and put to flight the Persians, the Hyrcanians, the Indians, and all the other races that the East lays out as far as the Ocean, but he himself, as he killed one friend or lost another, used to lie in darkness lamenting at one moment his

crime, and at another, his loss. Thus was the conqueror of so many kings and peoples laid low by anger and grief. For he had set about gaining control of everything save his emotions.

(30) O with what great errors are men preoccupied, who desire to push out the rule of their law across the seas, and who judge themselves luckiest when they occupy many provinces with their army and join new territory to the old, being ignorant of that kingdom that equals in greatness the kingdom of the gods. For self-control is the greatest power of all.

(27) Doce me non an fortitudo animal sit, sed nullum animal felix esse sine fortitudine, nisi contra fortuita conualuit et omnis casus antequam exciperet meditando praedomuit. Quid est fortitudo? Munimentum humanae imbecillitatis inexpugnabile, quod qui circumdedit sibi securus in hac uitae obsidione perdurat; utitur enim suis uiribus, suis telis. (28) Hoc loco tibi Posidonii nostri referre sententiam uolo: 'non est quod umquam fortunae armis putes esse te tutum: tuis pugna. Contra ipsam fortuna non armat; itaque contra hostes instructi, contra ipsam inermes sunt.' (29) Alexander Persas quidem et Hyrcanos et Indos et quidquid gentium usque in oceanum extendit oriens uastabat fugabatque, sed ipse modo occiso amico, modo amisso, iacebat in tenebris, alias scelus, alias desiderium suum maerens, uictor tot regum atque populorum irae tristitiaeque succumbens; id enim egerat ut omnia potius haberet in potestate quam adfectus. (30) O quam magnis homines tenentur erroribus qui ius dominandi trans maria cupiunt permittere felicissimosque se iudicant si multas [pro] milite prouincias obtinent et nouas ueteribus adiungunt, ignari quod sit illud ingens parque dis regnum: imperare sibi maximum imperium est.

READING 3.5
SENECA,
Concerning
Benefits
7.2.3–3.1

[what the philosopher must say to himself]

(3) ' . . . True pleasure, worthy of both man and hero, comes neither from filling or gorging the body, nor from exciting the lusts which are safest left undisturbed. Instead it derives from freedom from mental agitation, both that which is aroused by the ambition of men struggling amongst each other, and that which, intolerably, comes from on high when faith is put in rumours of the gods and we estimate them according to the standards of our own vices.'

(4) This pleasure, equitable and calm, and which will never leave him jaded, is what this man whom we are describing experiences to the highest degree; a man, so

READINGS—LIVING FAST, DYING YOUNG

to speak, steeped in divine and human law. This man rejoices in the present, he doesn't hang upon the future; for he who depends upon uncertainties has no concrete support. Having been freed, therefore, from great anxieties and mind-wracking cares there is nothing which he longs for or desires, and happy with his lot, he does not throw himself into doubtful concerns.

(5) And you should not suppose that this means he must be content with a little. All things are his, but not in the same way in which they were Alexander's who, although he stood on the shore of the Red Sea, still lacked more than the territory that he had traversed. Nor were those things which he held or had conquered even his, whilst Onesicritus, who he had sent ahead to explore, was wandering around and stirring up wars on unknown seas.

(6) Was it not abundantly clear that he was a man in need, who was extending his arms beyond the boundaries of nature? Who from blind greed threw himself headlong into the unexplored and vast ocean depths? What difference does it make, how many kingdoms he seized, how many he handed out, how much tribute he received from territories? For he still lacked as much as he coveted.

(1) Nor was this vice only Alexander's, whose fortunate rashness led him on in the footsteps of Liber and Hercules; it is the vice of all whom fortune has goaded on with rich rewards. Take, for example, Cyrus, Cambyses and the whole Persian royal line. Will you find any among them who was satisfied within the confines of his empire? Who did not end his life in some plan of advancing farther? Nor is it surprising. For whatever one acquires through greed is completely swallowed up and buried, and it makes no difference how much you pour into a bottomless pit.

(3) '. . . Illa est uoluptas et homine et uiro digna non inplere corpus nec saginare nec cupiditates inritare, quarum tutissima est quies, sed perturbatione carere et ea, quam hominum inter se rixantium ambitus concutit, et ea, quae intolerabilis ex alto uenit, ubi de dis famae creditum est uitiisque illos nostris aestimauimus.' (4) Hanc uoluptatem aequalem, intrepidam, numquam sensuram sui taedium percipit hic, quem deformamus quom maxime, ut ita dicam, diuini iuris atque humani peritus. Hic praesentibus gaudet, ex futuro non pendet; nihil enim firmi habet,

qui in incerta propensus est. Magnis itaque curis exemptus et distor-
quentibus mentem nihil sperat aut cupit nec se mittit in dubium suo
contentus. (5) Et ne illum existimes paruo esse contentum, omnia illius
sunt, non sic, quemadmodum Alexandri fuerunt, cui, quamquam in
litore rubri maris steterat, plus deerat, quam qua uenerat. Illius ne ea
quidem erant, quae tenebat aut uicerat, cum in oceano Onesicritus
praemissus explorator erraret et bella in ignoto mari quaereret. (6) Non
satis adparebat inopem esse, qui extra naturae terminos arma proferret,
qui se in profundum inexploratum et inmensum auiditate caeca prosus
inmitteret? Quid interest, quot eripuerit regna, quot dederit, quantum
terrarum tributo premat? tantum illi deest, quantum cupit.

(1) Nec hoc Alexandri tantum uitium fuit, quem per Liberi Herculisque
uestigia felix temeritas egit, sed omnium, quos fortuna inritauit
inplendo. Cyrum et Cambysen et totum regni Persici stemma percense:
quem inuenies, cui modum imperii satietas fecerit, qui non uitam in
aliqua ulterius procedendi cogitatione finierit? Nec id mirum est:
quidquid cupiditati contingit, penitus hauritur et conditur, nec interest,
quantum eo, quod inexplebile est, congeras.

The gory cruelty of Alexander's behaviour is used in this scheme to
teach that no good comes of excess (*Ep.* 113.29). Alexander retains no
pleasure in his victories, and unable to overcome the sorrow that
torments him, he kills his friends in an atmosphere of increasing
disease, in control of everything save his emotions. According to
Seneca, these 'obsessive conquerors' are unaware of the kingdom—
greater even than the heavens—that attends self-mastery. Alexander's
desire to lay waste others' countries was mad, and drove him to
misfortune. His weapons encircled the world, but he could not shift his
course of victory from the paths of Liber and Hercules, for shame at
not surpassing them. His wanton cruelty, like that of a wild beast
destroys more than it can consume.[18] Strong words, which may eventually have come back to haunt Seneca. That this moralizing imagery
is a commonplace of Alexander-literature, dealing with his descent into
the vices of the East, his love of excess, his uncontrollable anger, and
his pride, does not diminish its force in this context—Alexander is a
key character in the philosophical war against bad government at a
vital early stage in the transition between two rulers.[19]

READING 3.6
SENECA,
*Concerning
Anger*
3.17.1–4

(1) This savageness was characteristic of barbarian kings
when they were angry, men who were unaccustomed
to learning and literary culture. In contrast I shall
present you with Alexander, a king nurtured by the
care of Aristotle, yet who stabbed his dearest friend

with his own hand at a feast, a man with whom he had been brought up, just because he was sparing with his flattery and reluctant to transform himself from a Macedonian and a free man into a Persian slave.

(2) Similarly, he threw his friend Lysimachus to a lion. Even though Lysimachus managed by some good luck to escape from the lion's teeth, was he in consequence any more kindly when he himself was king?

(3) Not at all, for he then completely mutilated his own friend Telesphorus, the Rhodian, and when he had cut off his ears and his nose, he shut him in a cage as if he were some strange and unknown animal. For a long time he was in terror of him because the deformity of his maimed and mutilated face had banished all appearance of humanity. Added to this were hunger and squalor and the filth of a body left to wallow in its own excrement;

(4) furthermore, there were calluses on his hands and knees, which the narrowness of his quarters forced him to use in place of his feet, and his sides were ulcerated by rubbing. To those who saw him, his appearance was no less disgusting than terrible, and having been made into a monster by this punishment, he had forfeited even pity. Yet while the man who suffered these things was utterly unlike a human, the man who inflicted them was even less like one.

(1) Haec barbaris regibus feritas in ira fuit, quos nulla eruditio, nullus litterarum cultus inbuerat: dabo tibi ex Aristotelis sinu regem Alexandrum, qui Clitum carissimum sibi et una educatum inter epulas transfodit manu quidem sua, parum adulantem et pigre ex Macedone ac libero in Persicam seruitutem transeuntem. (2) Nam Lysimachum aeque familiarem sibi leoni obiecit. Numquid ergo hic Lysimachus felicitate quadam dentibus leonis elapsus ob hoc, cum ipse regnaret, mitior fuit? (3) Nam Telesphorum Rhodium amicum suum undique decurtatum, cum aures illi nasumque abscidisset, in cauea uelut nouum aliquod animal et inusitatum diu pauit, cum oris detruncati mutilatique deformitas humanam faciem perdidisset; accedebat fames et squalor et inluuies corporis in stercore suo destituti; (4) callosis super haec genibus manibusque, quas in usum pedum angustiae loci cogebant, lateribus uero adtritu exulceratis non minus foeda quam terribilis erat forma eius uisentibus, factusque poena sua monstrum misericordiam quoque amiserat. Tamen, cum dissimillimus esset homini qui illa patiebatur, dissimilior erat qui faciebat.

At the beginning of passage 3.6 Seneca makes a highly unfavourable comparison between the behaviour of Alexander, nurtured at Aristotle's breast, and that of barbarous alien kings, supposedly unlearned in the ways of civilization. This anecdote is clearly a popular one, but given that the essay may not have been complete at the time of his recall to Rome, and that it was through the influence of Agrippina that he gained his formal recall, issues of education and the relationship between a tutor and imperial tutee may well have informed his choice of anecdotes.[20] Nevertheless, the story of Alexander and Aristotle is only a precursor to the main point, a point that cuts directly to the heart of the problems of identity and Roman-ness that we saw beginning to be raised in Chapter 2, but which were gaining added urgency under Caligula. Any invocation of Alexander was bound to evoke concerns about the permanence of Roman iden-tity, given Macedon's inglorious history after Alexander. Here, Seneca taps into this model in ways that force the reader to confront the stability of his own sense of self as a Roman, and whether that sense of self must in turn be redefined within a political framework that makes each citizen subject to direct bodily harm at the hands of one man.[21] Seneca's own banishment could, as a result of Augustus' precedent, have taken on a more durable form if Claudius had not commuted the Senate's original death-sentence to exile.[22] In the wake of this experience, whereby the power of the ruler to determine legal precedent (in a manner that can have such a direct impact on the hold on life of each individual citizen) is made so directly manifest, Seneca's choice of these particular anecdotes cannot be uncomplicated. At the very least, the physical distancing of Seneca from Rome that Claudius effected suggests that the power of the emperor to remove a senator from Rome—and thus from the source of his public identity and civic power—would nudge the reader towards a comparison between the two situations. Furthermore, by identifying and reinvigorating the topos of Alexander's ability to maintain complete physical power over his men and to subsume their personal into their physical autonomies, Seneca may be intending his audience to contemplate not only his own exile (and death sentence), but also opening up the discourse to include other potential exile figures.[23]

This means that when we are confronted with a parade of increas-ing horrors, all triggered by the action of an apparently well-educated king, we need to think about the sequence of events as suggested by Seneca. Not only did Alexander stab his boyhood friend Clitus at a feast simply because he refused to flatter him in a 'slavish', 'Persian' fashion, Seneca complains, but he also threw his friend Lysimachus to a lion.[24] Alexander is to blame not only for his own behaviour, but also for the example that he sets for monarchs in general. If the essay was revised pre-publication, then this comment may tie in with Nero as a latter-day Alexander-follower, but where Lysimachus, thrown to a lion by Alexander, has the excuse of imitation from experience for his own bad behaviour as king, there is no justification for other potential Alexander-imitators.[25] At the very least, we can see echoes of Seneca's troubles under Caligula and Claudius showing through, but in a more general sense this essay is also engaging with some of the ways in which a monarchical system in one country can infect a whole succession of present and future national political organizations. Alexander's behaviour as monarch is both a function of his personal instability and his inability to cope with the Fortune which assists him in his meteoric conquests, and at the same time, is a result of the political system that allows him the power and scope for his megalomania to develop. His power is predicated on a Macedonian system of hereditary kingship, but in a broader sense, the intense personalization of his authority feeds into the future semiotics of what it will mean to be a king after his death. So an important part of his legacy to all future kings will be a requirement to respond in some way to the kingship model that he had established. When this kingship model becomes warped, reflecting worst rather than best practice, then all successive rulers become sucked into a destructive spiral of comparison with Alexander, as Seneca's story demonstrates.

With this in mind, we can choose to reread Seneca's story from a slightly different perspective. Clitus' death is horrific, certainly, and we must be intended to judge it as highly reprehensible on Alexander's part, both as man and as king, but Clitus' death is also on one level an end-stop within this narrative. We might suggest that the *Nachleben* for this murder affects Alexander's relationship with his companions, but within the context of *Seneca's* narrative, the negative effect is solely upon Alexander himself. The case of Lysimachus is strikingly different. Alexander throws Lysimachus to a lion, but by luck (*felicitate*), Lysimachus makes his escape. Seneca then asks his audience whether this fortuitous escape made any difference to his own behaviour when he became king, and illustrates his negative answer with a story about how the pattern of violence was replicated. Within this narrative framework Seneca is implicitly constructing a model of poisonous authority focused upon one-man rule, within which kingship in itself is a kind of hereditary virus which gains momentum as it passes and spreads out from one ruler to the next. Seneca presupposes that as king—and particularly as king in the aftermath of

Alexander—Lysimachus will be predisposed to rule harshly, otherwise why ask whether his escape from Alexander's violence will make him govern in a gentler manner?

This story illustrates a position whereby experiencing Alexander's personal authority becomes part of all successive monarchical packages; the survival of Lysimachus allows the contagion to spread, but his experience of violence at Alexander's hands is not simply replicated. Instead, the level of cruelty inflicted by Lysimachus on his victim (Telesphorus) exceeds that practised by Alexander. Alexander's violence towards his subjects is presented jointly as a function of his character and his role as king; but once Alexander has gained status as an archetype for monarchy, this problematic duality—the interplay and blurring of distinctions between public and private—becomes implicated in all future blueprints. As the pattern of rule set up by and for Alexander is replicated in an increasingly warped manner, Lysimachus' experience of violence is transformed from an immediate and impassioned desire to kill into an incremental process of dehumanization that contaminates both perpetrator and victim. The significance of this story for Seneca *and* Nero is potentially immense. It resonates through all successive models of solitary power and implicates all rulers who justify their right to rule through some pattern of inheritance. Furthermore, Seneca's narration of this story during the period immediately before his recall to Rome and his relationship with Nero suggests that in the increasing process of bodily degradation and physical humiliation that Lysimachus inflicts on Telesphorus, we may choose to read a connexion with the recent relationship between Tiberius and Sejanus.[26] Telesphorus is shut away in a cage, divorced from normal society physically and intellectually because his caged state, his suffering and squalor make it impossible for any communication between himself and his former fellow-subjects to take place. He loses the physical signifiers of humanity because he is treated first like a slave—when his nose and ears are cut off—and finally like a wild beast. His degradation is complete when he is no longer capable of walking upright. Yet although he can no longer function or communicate as a member of society, he still retains an important modal role. As Seneca explains, the excrement-surrounded inhuman body (*corpus*) that Telesphorus becomes retains its power to terrorize Lysimachus himself, and (as Seneca's use of the story demonstrates) to influence future judgement of his behaviour. This body can take on a metaphorical role representing both the dehumanization of any subject by a king, but also the way in which a state can similarly be afflicted. In this way, the two men are inextricably linked within a wider concern surrounding the potential for transformative and excessive behaviour to replicate itself through hereditary power structures, a concern that was becoming increasingly lively in the mid first century CE. This connexion with Roman politics, albeit tenuous, is reinforced in the next passage.

READING 3.7
SENECA,
Concerning
Anger
3.23.1–2,
4–8

(1) The grandson of this man was Alexander, who made a habit of hurling his spear at his dinner-guests, and who out of the two friends whom I mentioned a little earlier, he exposed one to a wild beast, the other to his own ferocity. Of these two, however, the one who was thrown to a lion survived.

(2) Alexander did not get this flaw from his grandfather, nor from his father either; for if Philip possessed any virtues, then one of them was an ability to endure insults, a great help in safeguarding sovereignty.

(4) The deified Augustus also did and said many memorable things, from which it can be seen that he was not governed by anger. The historian Timagenes commented unfavourably about Augustus himself, about his wife, and his whole family, and he didn't ensure that the comments were smothered; for indiscreet wit is all the more likely to remain in circulation and on everybody's lips.

(5) Caesar often warned him that he should keep his tongue in check; when Timagenes persisted, he barred him from his house. Afterwards, Timagenes lived to an old age in the house of Asinius Pollio, and he was struggled over by the whole city. No other door was barred to him, even though Caesar's house was forbidden.

(6) He gave readings of the history that he had written after this incident, and he put books containing the deeds of Caesar Augustus in the fire, and burned them. He continued in hostility towards Caesar, yet no one feared to be his friend, no one recoiled from him as if struck by lightening. Although he fell from such a height, there was someone ready to embrace him.

(7) As I said, Caesar endured this patiently, not even moved by the fact that Timagenes had attacked his glory and his achievements; he never complained about the host of his enemy.

(8) To Asinius Pollio he merely said, 'You're readying a beast for the arena.' Then when Pollio was contriving an excuse, he stopped him and said, 'Enjoy yourself, my dear Pollio, enjoy yourself!' and when Pollio commented: 'If you so order me, Caesar, I shall immediately deny my house to him,' he replied, 'Do you think that I would do this, when it was I who restored the friendship between you?' For it was the case that at one time Pollio had been angry with Timagenes, and he had no other reason for ceasing to be angry than that Caesar had now begun to be.

(1) Huius nepos fuit Alexander, qui lanceam in conuiuas suos torquebat, qui ex duobus amicis quos paulo ante rettuli alterum ferae obiecit, alterum sibi. Ex his duobus tamen qui leoni obiectus est uixit. (2) Non habuit hoc auitum ille uitium, ne paternum quidem; nam si qua alia in Philippo uirtus, fuit et contumeliarum patientia, ingens instrumentum ad tutelam regni.
(4) Multa et diuus Augustus digna memoria fecit dixitque ex quibus appareat iram illi non imperasse. Timagenes historiarum scriptor quaedam in ipsum, quaedam in uxorem eius et in totam domum dixerat, nec perdiderat dicta; magis enim circumfertur et in ore hominum est temeraria urbanitas. (5) Saepe illum Caesar monuit, moderatius lingua uteretur; perseueranti domo sua interdixit. Postea Timagenes in contubernio Pollionis Asini consenuit ac tota ciuitate direptus est: nullum illi limen praeclusa Caesaris domus abstulit. (6) Historias quas postea scripserat recitauit [et combussit] et libros acta Caesaris Augusti continentis in ignem inposuit; inimicitias gessit cum Caesare: nemo amicitiam eius extimuit, nemo quasi fulguritum refugit, fuit qui praeberet tam alte cadenti sinum. (7) Tulit hoc, ut dixi, Caesar patienter, ne eo quidem motus quod laudibus suis rebusque gestis manus attulerat; numquam cum hospite inimici sui questus est. (8) Hoc dumtaxat Pollioni Asinio dixit, yhriotrofe›w; paranti deinde excusationem obstitit et 'fruere,' inquit 'mi Pollio, fruere!' et cum Pollio diceret 'si iubes, Caesar, statim illi domo mea interdicam', 'hoc me' inquit 'putas facturum, cum ego uos in gratiam reduxerim?' Fuerat enim aliquando Timageni Pollio iratus nec ullam aliam habuerat causam desinendi quam quod Caesar coeperat.

In order to appreciate the interpretative fluidity available for users of Alexander, and the ways in which this can undermine apparently stable comparisons, we may want to start by looking at two words used by Seneca to describe Timagenes' fate after his 'banishment' from Augustus' house.[27] First of all, *consenesco*. Logic dictates that the primary meaning in this context must be 'grow old', but other, less palatable inferences are also potentially present. *Consenesco* can also mean 'to decay', or 'to grow weak and powerless', or even 'to lose respect'. This multiplicity of meanings immediately destabilizes any sense of security concerning Timagenes' fate in the aftermath of his quarrel with Augustus, and the second word used, *diripio*, further increases the potential for alternative readings. Particularly in conjunction with *ciuitas*, we might expect *diripio* to mean 'to plunder', 'to lay waste', 'to tear apart', yet post-Augustan usage allows a more positive sense to emerge, 'to struggle *for* something'. This association of two words with potential for both positive and negative interpretation allows for two opposite readings of Timagenes' fate. Perhaps Seneca is inviting us to play about with the semiotics of these at once contradictory and complementary renditions: either Timagenes lived to a ripe old age and was in constant demand from the Roman literati, or he grew feeble, lost the respect of his contemporaries, and was destroyed. The choice need not be uncomplicated, and both meanings are implicit in every reading. So when Seneca uses this example from Augustus' life as a contrast to the way in which Alexander was governed by anger, the way in which we interpret this contrast can depend heavily on our awareness of a pervasive sense of irony. Augustus' behaviour, so explicitly set against Alexander's example, may in fact offer a model for how anger can be deployed in very different but equally effective ways.

Seneca's essay is explicitly concerned with anger and its effects on the individual and society, and his choice of imagery to illustrate the way in which the intricate complex of relationships between Augustus, Timagenes, Pollio and Rome function suggests that Alexander may also play a greater role in this intersection than might at first seem likely. If we take Alexander's direct action, commented on so explicitly in passage 3.6, as a starting place, we can see how the political parameters for Alexander's monarchy are flexible enough to permit him to respond directly and openly to an insult. This narrative can accommodate his explosive and murderous rage without entirely breaking the illusion of government by consent because of the personality cult which forms an important part of his political authority and ideology of power. Alexander's acknowledged military autocracy, and the vital role he plays in keeping his citizen body (his soldiers) alive on campaign, makes it possible for his subjects to assimilate direct violent action of this kind into their relationship with him. As scripted in this passage, Lysimachus' behaviour strikes at the psychological and physical integrity of his subjects, but without the intense bond of dependence available for exploitation by Alexander. Augustus' 'clemency', if we accept the potential double meanings of *consenesco* and *diripio*, may suggest a further stage in the development of this theme. Rather than offering an uncomplicated demonstration of Augustus' ability to remain calm in the face of provocation, what we may be seeing is an example of how Seneca perceives Alexander's influence to have trickled down into the Roman political arena. Alexander's capacity for direct, violent action, which although excessive and destructive is also a predictable function of his charismatic military style, has gradually metamorphosed into an opaque behavioural model. Imperial clemency requires forethought rather than immediacy of action. It demands that the ruler take into consideration how his errant subject will react, but once pardoned, the subject loses all right to his own life, which in itself becomes a kind of death, or something held only on lease. Thus Augustus' apparent generosity towards Timagenes (and Pollio) can again admit two readings. Timagenes survived, and received no active injury from Augustus, but Augustus retained ultimate power over the situation: he could have chosen to demand Pollio's obedience, and as the concluding lines of this passage suggest, it was Augustus' anger that triggered Pollio's renewed friendship for the historian—the emperor was ultimately responsible even for this new relationship.[28] Furthermore, Seneca's positioning of the 'dialogue' between Augustus and Pollio at the end of this anecdote focuses the reader on Augustus' ultimate power to destroy Timagenes' relationship with Pollio, and also, potentially, to make his position in Rome untenable.[29]

The potential for alternative readings of this passage is emphasized if we read it in conjunction with another extract from the same essay (*de Ira* 2.23.2–3). This earlier reference, in contrast to the explicitly negative tone taken towards Alexander in the passages we have been discussing, suggests that Alexander was not always incapable of moderating his behaviour. Here, Seneca compares the behaviour of Alexander towards his doctor Philip with that of the sixth-century BCE Athenian tyrant Hippias. Alexander's mother Olympias wrote to him warning him against Philip, whilst Hippias tortured a would-be tyrannicide in order to make him reveal his accomplices. Through this behaviour, Hippias ended up executing all of his closest friends and supporters because they figured on a list given by the torture victim, with the result that Hippias' behaviour cost him all of those on whom he might have counted for protection. Alexander, we learn, was prepared to trust in his own judgement of his friend, and ignored his mother's warning. In itself, Seneca's use of this story demonstrates the flexibility of 'Alexander', who within one essay can represent impulsive anger and admirable restraint, but taken in conjunction with passage 3.4, it also offers a further gloss on how passage 3.5 can be read.

Perhaps with this very flexibility, the potential for both good and bad that must be allowed to exist within Alexander because of the diversity of available stories, Seneca may be commenting implicitly on the chancy instability of any monarchical system. When there is such clear potential for positive and negative within even one (arguably) archetypal ruler, there is bound to be a wide range of abilities and characters within a whole dynasty.[30]

Seneca was probably composing his essay on anger whilst in exile, during the period before his tutorship of Nero. The following passage, however, is from an essay on forbearance that was composed for and addressed to his tutee at the beginning of their relationship. Where the imperial and political subtext of the previous passages might be supposed to reflect an exile's view of a system that failed him, when writing explicitly for Nero on one of the key imperial virtues, then there should be a direct expectation of explicit political commentary.

READING 3.8
SENECA,
Concerning
Clemency
1.25.1

Cruelty is the least befitting human evil, and is unworthy of so gentle a spirit. It is the madness of a wild beast to delight in blood and wounds, and throwing off humanity, to change into a woodland animal. For what difference does it make, I beg of you Alexander, whether you throw Lysimachus to a lion or you yourself tear him to pieces with your teeth? One way or the other, the lion's mouth is yours, as is its savagery. How much greater would your delight have been had its claws been yours, yours the gaping jaws, big enough to devour men! We don't demand of you that that hand of yours, the most certain destruction of your friends, should actually save anyone! Nor that your savage spirit, that insatiable consumer of nations, should sate itself with less than blood and slaughter! Instead we have come to call it mercy if to kill a friend, the butcher is at least chosen from amongst the human race.

Crudelitas minime humanum malum est indignumque tam miti animo; ferina ista rabies est sanguine gaudere ac uolneribus et abiecto homine in siluestre animal transire. Quid enim interest, oro te, Alexander, leoni Lysimachum obicias an ipse laceres dentibus tuis? Tuum illud os est, tua illa feritas. O quam cuperes tibi potius ungues esse, tibi rictum illum edendorum hominum capacem! Non exigimus a te, ut manus ista, exitium familiarium certissimum, ulli salutaris sit, ut iste animus ferox, insatiabile gentium malum, citra sanguinem caedemque satietur; clementia iam uocatur, ad occidendum amicum <cum> carnifex inter homines eligitur.

Seneca's reinvigoration of this image of a man thrown to wild beasts is evidently intended to urge self-discipline and moderation on Nero, casting the Alexander of *de Clementia* as a direct model for the admonition of the young Roman 'prince'. In yet another take on this anecdote, we find that the focus shifts to the gory imagery of the Lysimachus episode. This emphasis on blood and guts transforms the story from one in which the future reverberations rather than the act itself are the key to understanding Alexander's importance, to one which demands us to confront the violence and brutality of his behaviour. Paradoxically, in the later version of this story, the man who suffers most is Lysimachus. Here we find that cruelty changes *whoever* enjoys it into a wild beast, hence to throw a man to the wild beasts is no different from rending him bloodily limb from limb oneself, perhaps also implicating everyone who is prepared to participate even voyeuristically in spectacles of cruelty. This shift suggests that Seneca is attempting to comment on the impossibility of distinguishing, however subtly, between active and passive emulation of Alexander. Anyone who enjoys or partakes of 'Alexander' is inescapably bound into the nexus of conflicting and (here) negative overtones of excess, just as anyone who relishes cruelty is, according to Seneca here, as culpable as the person who is inflicting it.

Taken in terms of Nero's admiration for Alexander, the potential for both positive and negative interpretations is overwhelming. On one level, we can read the comparison as overtly flattering; ostensibly, Alexander is being admonished and by implication we might expect that the (superior) Roman ruler will not be as deaf to his counsellor as Alexander proved. This allows the young Nero to bask in his improvement on his hero, as long as he heeds the warning, but also suggests that even if one understands the lessons to be learned from Alexander's behaviour, it is impossible to remain uncontaminated.[31] Thus by using Alexander in this way, both Nero and Seneca as author and addressee are similarly implicated in a paradigmatic performance of violence and power. Alexander's power over Lysimachus is embodied in his ability to throw him to a lion; that Lysimachus survives is, in this version of the story, almost irrelevant. If the ability to cause actual bodily harm is a key function of power, then Seneca's theoretical authority over Nero is always going to be undermined by the dynastic imperative that will grant imperial power to his tutee. So does Seneca hope to circumvent Alexander's instability as an example for Nero? Or is Nero's nominal role as addressee itself a function of a less than straightforward commentary on how one-man rule is changing Rome? Clearly, the idea of an essay of advice is a popular one, and we have already seen how Cicero plays around with the possibility of doing something perhaps less formal for Caesar, before discarding it. In this case, the 'public' nature of the advice on offer is even more explicit. Whilst Cicero's advisory discourse and his musings as to its feasibility were given an explicitly epistolary (and thus ostensibly private) framework, even taking an intent to publish into account, the duality of public and private context for this essay is highlighted by the relationship between Nero, Seneca and any possible senatorial audience.

Once we begin to explore this dual audience, the status of Nero and his relationship with Seneca as both senator and tutor become critical. By addressing this essay to Nero, Seneca is signalling his own role within the imperial court and is implicitly commenting on the constraints that bind all members of the imperial household. Just as much as Lysimachus, Seneca is risking the possibility of real physical harm befalling him. In the context of his commuted death sentence and exile subsequent to his previous brush with the imperial family, this subtext becomes particularly lively, but as I have been suggesting, the physical harm that the solitary ruler can inflict on his courtiers is functioning in microcosm as a model for the relationship between ruler and state. When the ruler is not subject to any external checks, the state as a whole is forced to depend upon his ability to check his own behaviour. In Alexander's case, this ability tends to be represented as diminishing as he progressed further east. Although the story of Alexander's trust in Philip the doctor suggests that he is capable of ignoring advice from his mother in favour of his own judgement, this kind of anecdote is essentially a topos which tends to become attached to rulers.[32] The danger in this usage is that although we are shown Alexander behaving violently and uncontrollably, we continue to acknowledge his 'greatness', not least because Seneca chooses to write about him and rulers continue to be fascinated by him. If we acknowledge that Seneca's use of Alexander as a comparative for Nero is part of a dangerous game, we are also forced into complicity (along with Seneca, Nero and the whole primary audience) in the memorialization, and implicit valorization, of Alexander that is being undertaken.

This anecdote focuses on Alexander and implicitly evokes Nero, but there is another interpretative level that also demands consideration: like the Romans, this Alexander indulges in wild-beast shows. The wild-beast show on offer here may differ from the games provided for the Roman public in that there is only one victim, and he has been put on display directly by the king, but the increasing imperial focus on the control and provision of games provides another possible connexion.[33] Yet here, by implication at least, Seneca suggests that this activity is in his terms, 'un-Roman'. A very fine distinction is

being made: on the one hand, wild-beast displays play a significant
and normative part in the Roman year, regulating and categorizing
imperial, political and religious events. On the other, these displays
were also a function of the expanding Empire and the political and
social changes that had already taken place. In this way, indulging in
these shows is both quintessentially Roman *and* 'other', and in
harking back to Alexander's violence as a prototype for Roman blood
lust Seneca is also referring to a degenerative historical model in
which progress is equated to an inevitable decline, and which may
even require a sense of the end-stopping of history.[34] Yet other, cyclical
models may offer a further gloss on Seneca's ideas: being 'Alexander'
may be evidence of a debased society, but for all peoples who have
fallen from the Golden state, perhaps being Alexander is a function of
an inevitable downward spiral of diminishing returns. We might want
to pick up on this as an ironic, intertextual reference to the foreign-
ness at the heart of the Roman worldview, whereby Seneca hints that
through similar behaviour—albeit on a voyeuristic level—a Roman
may become an Alexander through attendance at the arena. The only
potential hope on offer is a function of the genre itself; Seneca, Nero's
tutor, is attempting to advise him in such a way as to circumvent the
inevitability of this transformation. Maybe by abjuring the blood-fest
and slaughter of the arena, the first citizen (*princeps*) may exceed even
Alexander the Great, to be a true 'Roman'.

To be a Roman emperor was to be implicated in the accreted discourse of cruelty and excess that surrounded Alexander, but as we
have seen, there was also a sense of fascination with 'great' badness:
what we might even think of as a Byron-factor. If Alexander is 'mad,
bad and dangerous to know' he also demands admiration—only someone so wildly impetuous could have pulled off the feat of such
successful memorialization, could have gained such a potent immortality. It is this quality, the ability to demand and inspire an almost
grudging admiration, that informs Lucan's introduction of Alexander
into his narrative of the civil war between Caesar and Pompey.

READING 3.9   20   There lies the insane son of Pellaean Philip,
LUCAN,   a lucky pirate, his life cut short by a fate that avenged
Civil War   the world. His limbs that ought to have been scattered
10.20–52   across the whole globe
                         they laid in a sacred shrine; fortune spared
                         his corpse, and the destiny of his sovereignty remained
                            to the last.
               25   For if freedom had ever restored the world to them

he would have been preserved as a butt for mockery,
    not elevated as a useful
example for the world of how so many lands could
    be under the control
of one man. He abandoned his own obscure
    territory of
Macedon and scorned Athens, which had been
    conquered by his father,
30   and impelled by pressing fate, he rushed through the
    peoples of Asia
leaving human carnage in his wake, and plunged his
    sword into the heart
of every nation. He polluted far distant rivers,
the Euphrates and the Ganges, with Persian and
    Indian blood,
a fatal illness for the earth and a thunderbolt that
    struck
35   all peoples alike, a star of ill-omen
for mankind. He was preparing to launch his fleets
    upon the Ocean
via the outer sea. Neither the blazing heat nor the
    waves
nor arid Libya nor Syrtian Hammon halted him.
Following the curve of the earth he would have
    journeyed west
40   and would have circumnavigated the poles and drunk
    from the source of the Nile:
but the final day intervened, and nature alone
was able to bring this end to his mad reign.
The power by which he had captured the whole world
was vested only in him, through his jealousy, and
    with no successor left behind
45   for all his great destiny, he occasioned his cities to be
    torn apart.
But he died in conquered Babylon, and with the
    Parthians in fear of him.
For shame, that the peoples of the East feared the
    sarisa
more than they now fear the javelin. It's accepted that
    our power reaches as far as the Arctic
and the home of the west wind, and that we oppress
    the lands
50   beyond the burning south wind, yet in the East
    we yield

to the lord of the Parthians. Parthia, that was so ill-
   omened for the Crassi,
was a peaceful province of tiny Pella.

20   Illic Pellaei proles uaesana Philippi,
      felix praedo, iacet, terrarum uindice fato
      raptus: sacratis totum spargenda per orbem
      membra uiri posuere adytis; fortuna pepercit
      manibus, et regni durauit ad ultima fatum.
25   Nam sibi libertas umquam si redderet orbem
      ludibrio seruatus erat, non utile mundo
      editus exemplum, terras tot posse sub uno
      esse uiro. Macetum fines latebrasque suorum
      deseruit uictasque patri despexit Athenas,
30   perque Asiae populos fatis urguentibus actus
      humana cum strage ruit gladiumque per omnis
      exegit gentes, ignotos miscuit amnes
      Persarum Euphraten, Indorum sanguine Gangen,
      terrarum fatale malum fulmenque quod omnis
35   percuteret pariter populos et sidus iniquum
      gentibus. Oceano classes inferre parabat
      exteriore mari. Non illi flamma nec undae
      nec sterilis Libye nec Syrticus obstitit Hammon.
      Isset in occasus mundi deuexa secutus
40   ambissetque polos Nilumque a fonte bibisset:
      occurrit suprema dies, naturaque solum
      hunc potuit finem uaesano ponere regi;
      qui secum inuidia, quo totum ceperat orbem,
      abstulit imperium, nulloque herede relicto
45   totius fati lacerandas praebuit urbes.
      Sed cecidit Babylone sua Parthoque uerendus.
      Pro pudor, Eoi propius timuere sarisas
      quam nunc pila timent populi. Licet usque sub Arcton
      regnemus Zephyrique domos terrasque premamus
50   flagrantis post terga Noti, cedemus in ortus
      Arsacidum domino. Non felix Parthia Crassis
      exiguae secura fuit prouincia Pellae.

The immediacy of anger displayed by Lucan—Seneca's nephew—
corresponds with the pungent force of the epithets that characterize
Alexander in default of any mention of his name.[35] Instead of using
his name, Lucan makes destructive deployment of the adjective
Pellaeus, diminishing Alexander by forcing him not just back to
Macedon, but to the city of his birth. The small-town boy from
nowhere replaces Alexander the conqueror of Persia. As I suggest in

Chapter 1, the implications of naming, and how names and nomenclature influence our perception of the significance of 'Alexander' are
vitally important. For this reason, his namelessness in this passage
should immediately demand our attention, particularly given Lucan's
use of Pella in the poem as a whole; Pella is not the only 'nowhere' to
take centre stage. As the first line of the epic suggests, topographical
defamiliarization is a key element in Lucan's technique of cultural
alienation. Lucan plucks Pharsalus from relative obscurity and places
it centre stage in a manner comparable to the valorization of Actium
in Augustan literature, but with very different results. Whereas Actium
became a symbolic focal point around which Augustan victory ideology could be constructed, providing a setting for the physical memorialization of the triumph of Rome over the foreign enemy, the significance of Pharsalus is far darker. Like Actium, Pharsalus provides a
non-Roman *locus* for civil war, but unlike Actium, there was no
effective way in which the victory at Pharsalus could be construed as
anything other than Roman fighting and defeating Roman—a constant bloody reminder of disease at the heart of the State.[36] At Actium,
Cleopatra could function as a non-Roman enemy and object of
vilification, but sorting out 'us' from 'them' at Pharsalus was a very
different proposition. By calling Alexander 'the Pellaean' Lucan may be
hinting at this fundamental problem, and suggesting how the positive
discourse of reconciliation that followed on from Caesar's victory
over Pompey might be subverted. Here we have a scenario in which
'Alexander' disappears, to be replaced by a generic representative—
surely a joke—of civic Macedon, who at one and the same time is
narratologically directly comparable to the victor of Pharsalus, yet
also has close ideological links with the doomed Pompey. Alexander's
integral role in the conflict, because nameless, gains an overarching
significance; in other words, because nameless, he becomes omni-
present. But 'Pella' and 'Pharsalus' are not the only examples of Lucan
playing fast and loose with our cultural topographies. If we examine
his use of yet another loaded *locus*, Emathia, we find him indulging in
a dialogue of potentiality that later authors (e.g. Statius, Silius Italicus
and Juvenal) would be all too happy to pick up. If the ubiquity of
derivatives of Pella situates Alexander the eternal home-boy throughout the landscape of civil war, then where does the even greater
frequency of 'Emathia' fit in?[37] A landscape saturated with echoes
of Alexander swings us back and forth from his birth-city (and
Macedon's capital) to a greater sense of poetic pervasiveness for
Macedon and Thessaly as a whole. Emathia was a region poetically
inclusive of Macedon and Thessaly. That Pharsalus—Lucan's poetic

hub for the demise of the Republic—was also in Thessaly gives the doublethink its bite.[38]

Alexander figures in this epic poem in terms of insanity, excess and decomposition, and as a disturbing symbol of ultimate destruction (e.g. 3.233–34). Alexander is noteworthy because of his vast capacity for magnificent devastation, and like Sallust's almost-fascination with his awesome Catiline, Lucan has Caesar as his ultimate target. Lucan launches into a stream of invective at the 'Emathian', where Emathian means *both* Caesar (Caesar the catalyst for Pharsalus) *and* Alexander. Lucan characterizes Alexander as the fortunate plunderer (*felix praedo*), he is deranged, a man of insatiable greed and rapacity; carnage rather than civilization follows in his wake. The rule embodied in such a man is a curse, striking with thunderbolt-like indiscriminateness, echoing the earlier, similar comparison involving Caesar (1.151–57).

Lucan's realignment of the battle at Pharsalus (where Pompey the Great suffered a final defeat by Caesar) transforms it into the death of the Republic. With Pompey out of the way, this precipitates a final ideological clash between Caesar and state, which Caesar must ultimately win. Where most authors (modern and ancient) focus on tracing the development of the Empire from Actium and the defeat of Antony by Octavian, Lucan forces us back in time to consider when the Republic collapsed, and in his scheme, Caesar's victory over Pompey and Pompey's ignominious end are the key factors. This model allows Lucan to suggest that the destruction of the Republic was attributable to Caesar, and to construct this political shift in negative terms, whilst omitting direct criticism of the line of emperors commencing with Augustus. The poem offers a tripartite analysis of the forces and ideologies at work, and none prove completely satisfactory. Pompey, the *ur*-hero, becomes trapped in a web of self-reflection and dreams; he becomes a passive rather than an active participant in his own downfall (and that of the Republic). Cato, the pure and ascetic idealist, offers little in the way of admirable human characteristics, despite his putative role as prototype for the Pisonian conspiracy in which Lucan took part. Indeed Lucan goes some way towards undermining Cato's viability as a Stoic hero through his desert interlude and encounter with the snakes. Caesar, the mad, vigorous, destructive force, is both fascinating and horrifying. Take your pick.

Lucan was an oddity, born into a senatorial family, he combined literature and politics rather than soberly waiting until his 'maturity' to begin his historical epic, and this was not his only unusual characteristic. Unlike the vast majority of whingeing senators, bewailing the Senate's powerlessness and their own toothless role in Roman government, Lucan combined literature, politics and insurrection! Who knows, he may even have unwillingly seen something of his own choice of action rather than acceptance in his portrait of Caesar, and ultimately Alexander. In this way, Alexander's namelessness takes on yet another possible significatory layer, allowing audience and author alike to collude in a game of self-identification with Alexander, Caesar, Pompey and Cato: role-playing with an added bite.

The passions invoked by these passages are almost completely negative (only Lucan shows an awareness of a potential for grandeur in Alexander's desires). Authors using Alexander in this context include him because of the negative connotations of excess and lack of limits, and this theme is closely tied to the problem of power without defined parameters. Indulgence in one area of life can flow over into others; but representations of Alexander's sexuality generally retain a certain asceticism: as we have noted, there is no strong tradition of a sexually indulgent (or deviant) Alexander. Hephaestion (his boyhood companion and closest friend) and Bagoas (a Persian eunuch whose 'enslavement' of Alexander only Curtius seems to have been interested in) aside, homosexuality was not an issue in the Latin interpretations. Instead, these authors highlight Alexander's inability to profit from his excessive behaviour, his destructive rather than constructive effect, and the lack of success attributable to all his imitators. His incapacity to practise self-control informs his continuing (textual) search for the 'limits' of the earth, a search for boundaries that were absent in his rule and demeanour.

Considering the Latin tradition of sexual invective in political criticism, it is surprising that Alexander's Persian odyssey has attached so little sensuality to his imagery. He indulges in drink and violence, but is strangely indifferent when it comes to sex. One reason might be that this is a result of the different traditions conflated in the various references and extended comments we have been considering. There was no systematic tradition of Stoic hostility to Alexander in antiquity; generally, Seneca's hostility to Alexander (as self-centred and insatiable for victory) is most apparent in his later works. This connexion with the political situation (rather than Stoic values) may be the guiding factor behind Cicero's criticism in the *De Officiis*.[39] Sexual continence seems to have become part of Alexander's imagery at an early stage, particularly if we accept that Arrian follows Ptolemy's narrative, and that Ptolemy would have been likely to have reproduced the prevailing positive spin of the official history. Overwhelmingly,

military conquest, with its attendant problems (Orientalism) and
bonuses (wealth and glory), dominates. A vocabulary for discussing a
sexually voracious or unacceptably passive Alexander does not seem
to have filtered into Roman political invective. Even Curtius' comments
on Bagoas' undue influence are slanted toward political rather than
sexual corruption.

   What marks this strand of stories of Alexander as semiotically
distinct from those we read in Chapter 2 is the chronological spread,
or rather bunching. Why do we have so few anecdotes linking
Alexander the drunkard with Antony? Linking Alexander the
luxurious debauchee with Pompey? The simple answer would be that
once clemency and reconciliation became enshrined in the imagery of
the newly developing political framework, first under Caesar, then
more coherently under Augustus, it became imperative to incorporate
'Alexander' into successive victorious ideologies, sweeping his potential association with defeated enemies out of sight. This would call for
a general suppression of comparisons between Alexander and defeated
enemies and I will be discussing this in more detail in Chapter 5, but
there are also other possibilities. From the elder Seneca's 'reconstruc-
tion' of a rhetorical tradition embracing Alexander, and indeed from
Livy's almost casual insertion of a critical excursus on Alexander, we
can see traces of an earlier negative exemplary tradition. But as far as
we can tell, this negative Roman tradition concentrates on Alexander
the king and conqueror, it does not engage publicly with his excessive
consumption or emotions. Perhaps this tacitly mirrors and comments
upon the changing political climate—as the focus of political power is
increasingly centred upon the person and personality of the Emperor,
so personal characteristics become more and more fundamental to
any kind of political theorizing. Furthermore, as the rhetoric of
criticism of emperors focuses increasingly on excess and immorality,
Alexander's character flaws and a discourse of degeneracy take centre
stage. Of course, as we saw in Chapter 2, positive and negative anecdotes of Alexander were in common currency simultaneously, and as
suggested by Lucan's fascination with Alexander *and* Caesar, abhorrence and allure can coexist even within one narrative. In fact, what
the extracts in this chapter make most evident is the ongoing seduc-
tiveness of excess, of cruelty, of desire and madness and ultimate
conquest.

4

Readings—Imaging Alexander

Image, reality and their potential for manipulation play a central role in all Roman discourses of Alexander. The polyvalence of 'Alexander' within Roman political and cultural discourse means that there is no one stable and internally consistent figure who can be defined as 'the Roman Alexander', and this built-in fluidity means that all use of Alexander as a figure to conjure with must take the role of textual and visual manipulation very seriously. I started out, in Chapter 1, by looking at the different ways in which the title 'Alexander the Great' could be written and read, and suggested some ways in which texts both construct and presuppose model readers, all equipped with a variety of cultural competences. In this chapter, the emphasis is on how these textualizations offer a commentary on Alexander as a proto-type for engaged political self-reflexivity for successive audiences. An awareness of the power of media representation, both visual and literary, plays an important part in the way in which Alexander's style of leadership is constructed. This self-consciousness on his part, coupled with the tight control that he maintained over the dissemi-nation of his image and the narrative of his campaigns, has a direct impact upon his use in Rome. It allows the authors considered in this chapter to offer 'Alexander' as a highly nuanced model for some of the key ideological changes taking place in Roman politics. There are two ways of approaching this theme; the first interrogates Alexander in a culture increasingly aware of the political significance of informa-tion management and increasing centralization of authority. The second considers how Alexander's eastward imperialising feeds into Roman concepts of empire, and suggests that the ways in which Alexander's campaigns came to be constructed were to have a significant impact on the Roman worldview. This gives us two further angles on how Alexander functions: we find both self-conscious models of Alexander

119

4. Charles Le Brun, *The Entry of Alexander into Babylon* (1665) The classical credentials of this scene contrast strongly with the visual rhetoric of Figures 1 to 3. Here, Alexander rather than Darius occupies the chariot, whilst the richly caparisoned elephant further complicates Le Brun's message. *This* Alexander is the conquering hero: tripods billow smoke to the heavens, and the flower-strewn route and passive spectators suggest order rather than the chaos of war. But this is a strangely subdued triumph: no one smiles, Alexander's gaze out towards the viewer is pensive, and the mounted soldier on the right of the scene is positively downcast. Perhaps these undercurrents nod towards Alexander's problematic translation from military genius to mighty emperor?

the king, holder of a one-way ticket east and enveloped in an aura of reckless youth and divinity, *and* Alexander the conqueror, bringer of civilization and archetype for the whirlwind military campaign. Combining the two offers us ways of understanding the inescapability of Alexander as a motif for self-evaluation in Roman political thought.

Words, Memory and Myth: The Making of Kings

To begin with a question: is there a sense of ambivalence in Roman representations of power, namely that those who actively seek it are automatically considered to be unfit to rule? This question is intrinsic to the nature of the rule embarked upon by Augustus, and his need to control its imagery in order to make it acceptable. For our purposes we may consider the Principate as essentially a continuation of the republican power structure, sufficiently republican to validate Augustus' claim to have restored the Republic, but made flexible enough to tolerate an exalted *princeps* at its head.[1] This suggests that rather than there being a hidden meaning behind the official image, the image was the meaning. If Augustus wished to create a myth for the identity of the Roman state rather than a personal ruler-myth, then contemporary comparisons with Alexander work in two ways. They hark back to republican usage (in which he can have a positive role), and also offer a commentary on his political manoeuvrings.[2]

Although not strictly part of the geographical east defined by Asia and Parthia, Egypt still functions on an intellectual and cultural level as part of the East from a Roman perspective. It was still closely identified with Alexander's conquest and the legacy of his successors. Rome versus Egypt, versus Antony, versus Alexander (and tyranny) creates a model in which the Republic and Rome triumph. Curtius Rufus narrates a change in Alexander's sensibilities as he moves east, losing an initial gloss of Greek and Macedonian nationalism and becoming increasingly orientalized and self-serving.[3] If Alexander commences this major Roman narrative as a promoter of nationalism, but lapses into advocacy of 'Alexandrianism', how does this affect his representation within a politicized narrative? In fact, the Alexander story has tremendous potential as a positive example of a monarch who refrained from creating a position of pre-eminence for himself, but this possibility was not given any sustained development in the early years of the Principate.[4] Once granted that the Principate represented a compromise between continuing republican tradition and autocratic government, it becomes clear that it was defined by the honours, titles and subsidiary powers that were *refused* (a *recusatio*). This model makes Alexander's gradual assumption of greater powers and increasing departure from Macedonian tradition particularly resonant.

If monarchy (and Alexander's in particular) carries with it this cultural baggage in Latin sources, then Alexander's Roman role demands that we should examine how, from a Roman perspective, image and propaganda were already highly strategic weapons. We can also consider whether our sources show any awareness of the wider implications of their role in the continuation of Alexander's legend. But over and above this, we should keep in mind our complicity in the continuing enhancement of his mythic status. Is Alexander famous for being memorable, or memorable for his fame? The passages in this chapter offer an effective illustration of Alexander as a media-conscious monarch, and his role for Roman imperial self-definition. An awareness of the potential benefits of image control is made explicit in all of these examples, but Alexander's faculties of discernment are given mixed praise, calling later governmental models into question.

READING 4.1   How many historians of his achievements are Alexander
CICERO,   said to have had with him! And still, when he stood at the
On behalf   tomb of Achilles on Cape Sigeum he said: 'O happy youth,
of Archias,   who acquired Homer as the herald of your excellence!'
the Poet 24   And he spoke the truth. For, if the *Iliad* had not existed, the
                same tomb which covered over his body would have also
                consigned his reputation to oblivion. Was it not the case
                that our own 'Great,' whose courage equalled his excel-
                lence, gave citizenship to Theophanes of Mytilene, a histo-
                rian of his exploits, at an assembly of soldiers? And those
                brave men of ours, though country born and soldiers,
                moved by the sweetness of glory as if they themselves were
                partaking of the same renown, did they not approve the
                act with a great shout?

Quam multos scriptores rerum suarum magnus ille Alexander secum habuisse dicitur! Atque is tamen, cum in Sigeo ad Achillis tumulum astitisset: 'o fortunate,' inquit, 'adulescens, qui tuae uirtutis Homerum praeconem inueneris!' Et uere. Nam, nisi Ilias illa exstitisset, idem tumulus qui corpus eius contexerat nomen etiam obruisset. Quid? Noster hic Magnus qui cum uirtute fortunam adaequauit, nonne Theophanem Mytilenaeum, scriptorem rerum suarum, in contione militum ciuitate donauit, et nostri illi fortes uiri, sed rustici ac milites, dulcedine quadam gloriae commoti quasi participes eiusdem laudis magno illud clamore approbauerunt?

Our discussion so far assumes a connexion between Alexander's control of his own imagery and Roman versions of personal propaganda. This connexion is made evident in Cicero's speech for Archias, where his appeal to a Roman audience familiar with the idea of Alexander leads into an exploration of ideas of self-definition or mythologization.[5] Alexander is portrayed as understanding (and exclaiming) that the magnificence of Achilles' exploits did not, in itself, guarantee immortality to his memory; only Homer could achieve that.[6] Cicero's choice of phrase to express this idea is significant: he says that Achilles 'acquired' (*inuenio*) Homer, rather than vice versa, suggesting that Achilles was the active party in forging the relationship between author and subject. This interpretation sets up a pattern of interaction which Cicero traces through Alexander and his historians in a direct line to Pompey and Theophanes, and sets up an interesting connexion with Cicero's subsequent re-use of the motif in a letter to Lucceius seven years later (passage 4.2). On his arrival in Rome (*c*.102 BCE), the poet Archias had celebrated the victories of C. Marius and L. Licinius Lucullus, and given the way in which Cicero deals with the themes of memorialization and the essential role played by the chronicler of greatness, we may suspect that some expectation of reciprocity was in his mind. In fact, no poem of praise of Cicero was forthcoming from Archias.[7] This speech also emphasizes, albeit contextually, an acceptance of a clear connexion between Alexander and Pompey, a connexion that has taken on wider dimensions than purely military success. By implication at least, Cicero suggests that his audience will understand and appreciate how such an alignment can function within Roman politics, but from this overtly positive comparison we can also gain a further sense of some of the ramifications of Alexander's reputation for media manipulation.

We have already seen that Cicero was prepared to implicate Alexander in both positive and negative comparisons involving Romans, but the structuring of this excerpt may raise the possibility of the presence of a certain playful irony. To begin with, Alexander's poetic discrimination was not uncomplicated in itself, despite general acceptance of his success as a patron of the visual arts.[8] For this reason, Alexander's recognition of Achilles' good fortune in acquiring Homer—praise of Achilles rather than direct praise of Homer—may suggest he is less awestruck by Homer's literary talents than by his successful construction and furtherance of Achilles' glory. Perhaps an implicit subtext might hint that the relationship is not entirely one-way: without Achilles as subject, would the *Iliad* still be admired? Similarly, Theophanes' fame was, in Rome at least, dependent upon the achievements of Pompey.[9] This complements Curtius' emphasis on Alexander's acceptance that fame and renown are more fearsome weapons than great deeds and armies, but also focuses our attention on the role of the biographer as benevolent parasite.[10] Mention of Pompey and Theophanes is relevant to Archias' case, and sets up a model for a non-Roman whose services to Rome were held in such regard that the honour of citizenship was bestowed on him. Yet Theophanes' services were for Pompey, not Rome; by merging the two, Theophanes' conflation of Alexander and Pompey was, ironically, to gain a Roman identity for the historian himself. With the implication that Pompey's good and the good of Rome were to be inseparably intertwined, Cicero's emphasis on the public and military ratification of Pompey's gift highlights the civic implications, and stresses the need for collusion between 'people' and leader for any such construction of 'glory' to function. For this reason, we should think carefully about the rationale for the soldiers' affirmation of Theophanes' right to be Roman. Through his textual memorialization of Pompey's magnificent achievements, Theophanes was able to manipulate their understanding of their own feats so that Pompey's glory became their own. Once the historian could appear to be chronicling not just the individual glory of Pompey, but the collective attainments of the army (or even the citizen body) as a whole, then the transference of military allegiance from state to individual leader makes the symbiosis complete.

Through whatever literary-historical quirk, it remains Cicero rather than Archias whose fame persists. This adds complexity to the following extracts from Cicero's begging-letter to Lucceius.

READING 4.2
CICERO,
Letters to his Friends.
5.12.1, 2–3, 6–7

(1) I am inflamed with an incredible desire, of which, I think, I have no cause to be ashamed, to wit, that my name should be advanced and praised in your writings.

(1) Ardeo cupiditate incredibili, neque, ut ego arbitror, reprehendenda, nomen ut nostrum scriptis illustretur et celebretur tuis.

(2) What if those actions do not seem to you to be particularly worthy of commendation?

(3) Yet after all, it's only right that a man who has once crossed the boundary of modesty should do the thing properly and be completely shameless. And so again

and again I ask you openly that you both praise my actions with more warmth than perhaps you feel, and in that respect that you disregard the laws of history. And to remind you of that partiality you have shown me. . . if it commends me strongly to you, don't cast doubt upon it, and add a little extra to our friendship than truth may strictly allow.

(2) Quid, si illa tibi non tanto opere uidentur ornanda? (3) Sed tamen, qui semel uerecundiae fines transierit, eum bene et nauiter oportet esse impudentem. Itaque te plane etiam atque etiam rogo, ut et ornes ea uehementius etiam, quam fortasse sentis, et in eo leges historiae neglegas, gratiamque illam . . . si me tibi uehementius commendabit, ne aspernere, amorique nostro plusculum etiam, quam concedat ueritas, largiare.

(6) For that reason it will fall in more closely with my wishes if you come to the conclusion that you should separate what might be termed the drama of my actions and experiences, from the main body of your composition in which you embrace a continuous history of events. For it includes varied acts and many shifts both in policy and circumstance. Nor am I afraid that I shall appear to be hunting down your favour with petty flattery when I point out that I want to be honoured and praised by you above all others. For you are not one who is unaware of his own worth, or who does not recognize that those who do not admire you are more jealous of you than those who praise you are to be counted as flatterers. Nor, again, am I so senseless that I wish to be consigned to everlasting glory by one who in consigning me does not also himself gain the glory that is rightly attendant upon genius.

(7) For it was not merely as a personal favour that Alexander himself did not wish to be painted by anyone but Apelles, nor to be sculpted by anyone but Lysippus. Instead, he considered that their art would glorify both artists and subject; and those artists used to make images of his person that were known to those unknown to him. Yet even if these examples didn't exist, famous men would still not be uncelebrated. No less deserving of mention than those who have taken pains over such things is the Spartan Agesilaus, who would allow neither a portrait nor a sculpture of himself to be made. For just one pamphlet of Xenophon's

in praise of that king has easily surpassed all the portraits and statues of all of them. And it will have been
more demonstrably to the credit of my present happiness and the excellence of my reputation that I should
have gained a place in your history than if I had done
so in that of others, in that not only would your genius
have been lavished on me—as was the case for Timoleon
from Timaeus, from Herodotus for Themistocles—but
also the authority of a most illustrious and respected
man, well-known and of the first repute in the most
important and weightiest affairs of state. Thus it shall
seem that I have gained not only the renown which
Alexander, when he visited Sigeum, said had been
bestowed upon Achilles by Homer, but also the weighty
testimony of an illustrious and great man.

(6) Quo mihi acciderit optatius si in hac sententia fueris, ut a conti-
nentibus tuis scriptis, in quibus perpetuam rerum gestarum historiam
complecteris, secernas hanc quasi fabulam rerum euentorumque
nostrorum. habet enim uarios actus multasque <mut>ationes et
consiliorum et temporum. ac non uereor ne adsentatiuncula quadam
aucupari tuam gratiam uidear cum hoc demonstrem, me a te potissimum ornari celebrarique uelle. neque enim tu is es qui quid sis nescias
et qui non eos magis qui te non admirentur inuidos quam eos qui
laudent adsentatores arbitrere; neque autem ego sum ita demens ut me
sempiternae gloriae per eum commendari uelim qui non ipse quoque in
me commendando propriam ingeni gloriam consequatur. (7) neque enim
Alexander ille gratiae causa ab Apelle potissimum pingi et a Lysippo
fingi uolebat, sed quod illorum artem cum ipsis tum etiam sibi gloriae
fore putabat. atque illi artifices corporis simulacra ignotis nota
faciebant, quae uel si nulla sint, nihilo sint tamen obscuriores clari uiri.
nec minus est Spa<r>tiates Agesilaus ille perhibendus, qui neque pictam
neque fictam [tam] imaginem suam passus est esse, quam qui in eo
genere laborarunt. unus enim Xenophontis libellus in eo rege laudando
facile omnis imagines omnium statuasque superauit. Atque hoc
praestantius mihi fuerit et ad laetitiam animi et ad memoriae dignitatem
si in tua scripta peruenero quam si in ceterorum quod non ingenium
mihi solum suppeditatum fuerit tuum, sicut Timoleonti a Timaeo aut ab
Herodoto Themistocli, sed etiam auctoritas clarissimi et spectatissimi
uiri et in rei publicae maximis grauissimisque causis cogniti atque in
primis probati, ut mihi non solum praeconium, quod, cum in Sigeum
uenisset, Alexander ab Homero Achilli tributum esse dixit, sed etiam
graue testimonium impertitum clari hominis magnique uideatur.

With this letter from Cicero to Lucceius (April 55 BCE[11]) we move
towards a position whereby greatness is explicitly defined in terms of

representational semblance rather than actuality. Cicero clearly con-
strues his historical role—his consulship, and treatment of the
Catilinarian conspiracy—as being worthy of expansive treatment in
Lucceius' history, but as he also admits, this assessment may not be
one that ties in with the historian's own conception of the sweep of
history. Actions demand controlled representation to evolve into defin-
itive greatness, and Cicero's letter promotes a self-conscious inclusion
of his own actions into this tradition. Cicero wants a favourable
record of his consulship and dissolution of the Catilinarian conspiracy,
and he wants to ensure that the history being written by the addressee
fulfils his requirements. He speaks of Alexander's desire to be represented in painting and sculpture only by Apelles and Lysippus, and of
his tribute to Achilles (Achilles, remembered through Homer's mediation) at Sigeum;[12] but what form does the letter take? Alexander provides a mimetic exemplar through which Lucceius may be flattered,
and Cicero grovel within a familiar and recognizable tradition of such
bargains between author and subject.[13] Achilles had his Homer,
Alexander, his Callisthenes, and Cicero hopes to insert Lucceius'
account of his achievements into this tradition, but as tends to be the
case when Alexander is invoked, there is a catch.

This passage uses Alexander in three ways: first, as someone who
understood the importance of visual self-commemoration, controlling
the identity of his image-makers and choosing the best exponent of
each art form. Second, as someone who was influenced by, and appre-
ciated, literary characterisations. Third, as an example of how self-
publicity and awareness of the power of image and text are integral
functions of the great leader (as also exemplified by Agesilaus).
Implicit in Cicero's scheme—and exemplified by his comment that
even without visual representation, the text still has the power to
immortalize—is the notion that 'greatness' does have some basis in
achievement, that there is more than hot air involved in a 'great'
reputation, but that it requires some literary catalyst in order to be
displayed to best and most durable advantage. We may note, however,
that great Alexandrian deeds are not enumerated. His greatness, for
the purposes of this account, is restricted to his ability to choose the
best artists to represent him. Cicero keeps silence, in this letter, on
Alexander's potential literary shortcomings, but they must surely be
implicit: Cicero chooses Lucceius, Homer influenced Alexander, but
he could find no Homer of his own. It is arguable whether Cicero
is suggesting that Alexander's monopolization of his image was
statesmanlike, or that this aggrandizement was in doubtful taste;
perhaps Cicero's own approach, the (unsubtle) hint, the 'published'

letter, is the 'right' strategy for such a tender subject, if dangerous
monarchical overtones are not to be suspected.

From this letter it can be argued that Cicero's definition of stature
rests on an ability to manipulate one's image as a calculated reflection
of 'great' predecessors. Cicero has constructed a circular argument
defining the needs of the statesman, but shying away from an overt
insistence on their fulfilment.[14] Cicero, as we continue to be made
aware in these references, is concerned that he be intrinsically tied up
with Alexander and his Roman afterlife. Cicero the Consul's greatest
moment of triumph comes with his defeat of Catiline, Catiline who
will later find echoes in Lucan's Caesar/Alexander. Yet for Cicero, the
execution of Roman citizens, Catiline's partisans, without trial was
also to prove his downfall (despite the *senatus consultum ultimum*
and the immunity decreed by the Senate). Under pressure from the
tribune P. Clodius, he went into exile in 58 BCE. Perhaps in evoking
Alexander's success in controlling his visual imagery, and keeping
silent on the fate of Callisthenes, the 'official' campaign historian,
Cicero hopes to avoid the uncomfortable issue of what happens when
image-making gets out of control. Callisthenes had to be removed
because his interpretation of Alexander was no longer what was
required. Similarly, the backlash against Cicero proves the dangers of
losing control of how events are interpreted and reported. Cicero's
exile, a kind of Roman death, particularly given its use as a punishment for his execution of citizens, may also remind the reader of
tangled connexions surrounding Alexander's treatment of Clitus.
Cicero returned in 57 BCE, but was essentially a spent force in the
ensuing civil war politics. Caesar himself, a new Alexander, would
seize victory, and Cicero was not included in the conspiracy to assas-
sinate the Dictator. Cicero died early in the proscriptions of 43–42 BCE
at the beginning of the second triumvirate; Antony, yet another
Alexander, had demanded his death, and paradoxically, in his dis-
memberment we can see a foreshadowing of the dehumanizing process
set in motion by Seneca's Alexander in passage 3.6. This 'echo' of
Alexander, Lysimachus and Telesphorus reverberates through the
relationship between Caesar and Antony, Caesar and Augustus, and
all successive emperors.

READING 4.3
HORACE,
Epistle
2.1.232–44

Choerilus, who could thank his ill considered and
    misbegotten
verses for the Philips—good royal coin—he received,
found favour with great King Alexander
235 but just as ink when handled leaves mark and

stain, so often with foul verse poets besmirch
bright exploits. That same king,
who lavishly paid so dearly for so risible a verse,
by an edict forbade any save Apelles to paint him
240 or any other than Lysippus to model in bronze
the likeness of brave Alexander. But if you
call his judgement—so keen when viewing works of
art—to bear upon books and the gifts of the Muses,
you'd swear that he'd been born in Boeotia's
     leaden air.

Gratus Alexandro regi magno fuit ille
Choerilus, incultis qui uersibus et male natis
rettulit acceptos, regale nomisma, Philippos.
235 Sed ueluti tractata notam labemque remittent
atramenta, fere scriptores carmine foedo
splendida facta linunt. Idem rex ille, poema
qui tam ridiculum tam care prodigus emit,
edicto uetuit, nequis se praeter Apellen
240 pingeret aut alius Lysippo duceret aera
fortis Alexandri uoltum simulantia. Quodsi
iudicium subtile uidendis artibus illud
ad libros et ad haec Musarum dona uocares,
Boeotum in crasso iurares aere natum.

This excerpt from Horace *Epistle* 2.1 (addressed to Augustus) demonstrates how Cicero's usage can be adapted to suit a changed political structure. Formally, the poem's frame presents the reader with an address to Augustus which develops into a discourse on his role as literary patron and subject. The body of the poem appears to digress into an examination of the development of literature in Rome, but I suggest that the explicit presence of Augustus—as subject and addressee—in this poem sets it apart from other texts on a similar theme. The 'intrusion' of Augustus, coupled with a parallel discourse of artistic immortality into which Horace weaves both Alexander and his own authorial persona, demands that we question how available Horace may have been making this poem to a politically engaged reading. To begin with, Augustus' 'framing' role, and his position as addressee, combine to suggest that he has a position of complete control over Roman cultural and political norms. For (any?) literary endeavour, the author is (here explicitly) in the position of beginning and ending with Augustus. The emperor promotes literary 'talent', but through his patronage he inserts himself either causally or tacitly, as patron, subject or addressee, into the production of the authors he promotes. And in such a climate, even silence on Augustus becomes voluble.[15] The central artistic and literary discussion interweaves the relationship between Greece and Rome with the changes taking place in the contemporary literary scene.[16] Horace's diatribe against the current state of literary culture is problematic for various reasons; suggesting that all is not well with Roman literature is at least a tacit comment on Augustus as super-patron, that much is clear, but there is also a suggestion of a greater malaise affecting Rome, perhaps embodied in the stagnation of artistic development. Rome worships what is old and unintelligible; yet the political settlement after Actium was a striking new departure for Roman politics. So huge change *has* been taking place, change focused on Augustus. Taking this full circle, the political changes that had dramatically altered the political framework of Roman society were programmatically configured by Augustus as the inauguration of a *return* to traditional Roman values—regression rather than progression.

In such a cultural climate, looking to the past becomes, in artistic and literary terms, an implicit statement of political conformity. But if we return to thinking about how Alexander fits into this poem we may find that an alternative reading becomes available. Like the literary achievements of Greece, achievements which have come to dominate the Roman scene, Alexander could be construed as a figure from the past, and specifically from a foreign, 'Greek' past. In this context, we might think about the determinedly backward-looking iconography of the Forum of Augustus, in which its 'audience'—or even those 'participating' in its spectacle, its consumers—were firmly directed to keep their minds focused on Rome's mythic past, despite Augustus' inescapable presence. The whole scene was constructed upon his private property, so as landlord, if nothing else, all visitors were there on his terms and as his guests. Almost a grand exposition of the patron–client relationship. Alexander's presence in the Forum—as actor, illustrious precursor, and even *doppelgänger*—is difficult to pin down. Pliny (*NH* 35.27, 93–94) describes the images of Alexander by Apelles that Augustus had placed in his Forum. There were also two statues described as having been from Alexander's own tent in Alexandria (Pliny *NH* 34.48). Another potential connexion comes from the date of the dedication of the Forum: according to Dio (60.5.3) it was August 1st, commemorating the anniversary of Augustus' conquest of Alexandria, but other sources (e.g. Ovid *Fasti* 5.545–98) cite May 12th. A final twist comes from the story that Claudius had the face of Alexander replaced by that of Augustus in the Apelles images, and also on what may have been a colossal statue of

Alexander.[17] It is arguable how schizophrenic the Roman attitude to hellenisation was, since wealthy and educated Romans had certainly embraced Greek literature, philosophy and art during the third, second and first centuries BCE. Yet as is so often the case when a conquered— or perceivedly 'inferior'—people comes to exert a dynamic cultural influence over an apparently dominant nation, a cross-referential undertone of anxiety is also present. If political syncretism is added to an already existing cultural disquiet concerning the integrity of a discrete Roman 'identity', then Alexander's role in this poem becomes even more uncomfortable: another example of how, at least in some strong sense, Greece had regained ascendancy.

Horace's introduction of Alexander into this poem presents him in the role of grand arbitrator of commemorative art and poetry; this Alexander may be 'great' (*magnus*), but his success as a judge of art is equalled only by his failure of discrimination with regard to Choerilus' poetry. Cicero's treatment of the historical manipulation that he pro- poses to impose upon Lucceius was apologetic, emphasizing the posi- tive aspects of the symbiotic relationship between author and subject. Yet despite Cicero's rhetoric of immodest modesty, his request that Lucceius foreground his role as consul places him on a par with men such as Pompey (and Caesar) whose role within a 'traditional' repub- lican government was becoming ever more difficult to sustain. This suggests that in the middle years of the century, Alexander could still, just about, function as a 'safe'—if tacitly Pompeian—model for the consideration of textual immortality. Yet as the introduction of Pompey and Theophanes in the earlier *On Behalf of Archias* suggests, Alexander's successful control of his own memorialization had already cut him temporally adrift. Even by the mid 50s BCE, Scipionic and Pompeian usage had cloaked Alexander in an increasingly ideologi- cally dangerous Roman garb. The tension between self-promotion and republican ideology that informs and contextualies Cicero's letter had lost its bite by the time Horace was composing his verse-epistle to Augustus. Here, the expediency of royal media control is not openly questioned, and given Horace's privileged (if equivocal) position with Augustus, this is not surprising; instead, Horace's discussion centres on who does it best. It comes as no surprise to discover that unlike Alexander, Augustus possesses excellent poetic discrimination (2.1.245).

Reading this passage demands that we consider whether any ruler who engages in self-definition and association with the arts is on some level also dabbling with playing 'Alexander'. Reading the previous passages suggested ways of modelling literary and visual comparisons between Alexander and Roman power figures, but the pre-existence of such flattering comparisons is not uncomplicated. The forty-odd years between Cicero's conquest of his modesty and Horace's introduction of Alexander into a poem to Augustus had seen radical changes taking place in Roman politics, and in the wake of Antony's appropriation of Alexander—and despite post-Actium revision—this was to effect a more sinister reconfiguration of Alexander. Despite this, it could still plausibly be argued that use of Alexander as a comparative might still appear to be flattering and even potentially desirable, if constructed as a recuperative model for an Augustan ideological hegemony. Furthermore, the subject proposed by Horace is art and literature— no matters of state are explicitly in the balance, and the parallel is itself an artistic conceit, a topos familiar to Augustus and any wider audience. Alexander is the 'great king' whose flaw in a poet's eyes is an inability to discriminate poetically; but does the 'great' statesman and leader automatically fail, if he fails as a literary judge? Alexander's memory and story have survived the three hundred years after his death, but poetic patronage has not featured as a highlight of his career. Augustus' posthumous fame as a poetic subject can only be the subject of speculation, but Horace may be suggesting that judging from Alexander's literary ineptitude (and often negative reputation), Augustus must ensure that *he* patronizes the best poets. The public inscription of the *Res Gestae* demonstrates Augustus' awareness of the power of the monumental word to influence posterity.

The nature of all comparisons between Alexander and Augustus is complex; overtly at least, taking this passage at what we might try to think of as face value, the lines have a complimentary veneer: Alexander the Great failed, Augustus 'the Greater' does not; yet Horace makes no move to demote Alexander for his indiscriminate behaviour.[18] Alexander the failure, duped by a flatterer, undercuts the heroic image that provides Augustus with his reason for identification. Such a reading could suggest that Horace subverts the whole notion of emulation as a fit subject for an emperor through this parodic treatment, but at the same time contributes to the mystification and mythologization of Alexander's continuing image. He both is and is not a parallel Augustus, and vice versa. But if we return to Cicero's rhetoric in passages 4.1 and 4.2, a further question needs to be posed: what kind of role is Horace seeking for himself in this comparison? Within the internal logic of the text, Horace is the author of the comparison— he has decided to set Alexander up as a prototype for Augustus—but by writing in a part for Alexander he has also positioned himself within a long-tailed tradition of Roman use of Alexander. Even the most naïve of model readers would be unlikely to miss the frisson that

such an apparently banal comparison of literary and artistic judgement would evoke. If we take at face value Suetonius' comments that
this poem was written to order, there must also be a level on which
Horace's sub-ironic use of Alexander functions as part of an admission of his collusion in a literary production line.[19] Yet despite the
possibility of authorial (and maybe audience) complicity in acknowledging Augustus as primary 'author' for all textual production, we
still have to examine the possibility that Horace is involving us in a
potentially dangerous double bluff.

References to Alexander's image as infantile madman, as hubristic
tyrant, as corrupter, or the seeker after the impossible are absent, but
by excluding these characteristics, Horace does not deny their existence, nor, indeed, would that be possible. If we return to my construction of Alexander as a highly potent and polyvalent cultural
myth, firmly embedded in the political consciousness of the Mediterranean world as a whole, then we must accept that Horatian silence
on some aspects of his character could in itself serve to highlight them.
A large proportion of Horace's readership would have been induced
to recall multiple negative stories concerning Alexander (alongside the
potentially positive elements) as soon as his name was mentioned.
Augustus' political capitalization on Alexander motifs was firmly
rooted in a cultural context of widespread awareness of Alexander.
This epistle, with its complex rhetoric of direct address from poet to
patron, subject to ruler, mortal to god, has become part of our awareness of Alexander's place in Rome. Through his self-conscious 'annota-
tion' of the laureate role, Horace is implicitly exploring the availability
of myths for authors by royal appointment, a relationship that takes
in not just Alexander, but also Ptolemaic sponsorship of the library
at Alexandria, a cultural allusion that Horace draws out through his
commentary on Augustus' Palatine 'canon' (*Ep.* 2.1.216–17). This
makes the introduction of an Alexander who has been shorn of his
political authority and military glamour subversive on two counts.
First, it demarcates an explicit distinction between the kinds of
'Alexander' available for comparison with Augustus—once a Roman
really has the political and military authority to perform every aspect
of 'Alexander', those aspects of his myth may become too unstable for
official consumption. Second, given the suspicion that Augustus was
lacking in spectacular personal military leadership quality, there must
have been a lurking sense of the send-up in Horace's introduction.
Cicero seems to have had some sense of the ridiculousness of military
comparisons between himself and Alexander, even if in a tongue-in-
cheek manner.[20] I suspect that Augustus' rumoured dependence upon

Agrippa's military nous—and the gradual closing down of options for triumphs for non-members of the imperial family—would have given these undertones a shrewdly subversive edge.

READING 4.4
CURTIUS,
*History of
Alexander
the Great*
8.8.10–17

(10) 'Indeed it should be noted that the Persians, whom we have conquered, are held high in my honour! In itself the surest indication of my moderation is that I do not rule even the vanquished tyrannically. For I came into Asia not in order that I might overthrow nations and lay waste to half the world, but so that those whom I had subdued in war might not regret my victory.

(11) Therefore there are those fighting alongside you and shedding blood for your empire who, if treated tyrannically, might have rebelled. Possession that is gained by the sword does not endure for long; gratitude for acts of kindness is everlasting.

(12) If we wish to hold Asia rather than to pass through it, our clemency must be shared with its people; their faith in us will make a stable and lasting empire. And really, we have more spoils than we can carry, yet insatiable avarice keeps us filling an already overflowing vessel.

(13) Then he [Hermolaus] accuses me of enforcing Persian customs amongst the Macedonians, and it's the truth! For I can see things in many nations that we should not blush to imitate; and so great an empire cannot be ruled appropriately without a process of mutual education.

(14) It was almost laughable when Hermolaus demanded that I should oppose Jupiter, whose oracle acknowledged me as his son. Are even the oracles of the gods in my power?

(15) He offered the title of son to me, and to accept it is hardly disadvantageous to the plans which we are undertaking. How useful it would be if the people of India would also believe that I am a god! For the outcomes of wars hang upon reputation, and it's often the case that a fallacy, widely believed, has accomplished as much as the truth.

(16) Do you think that it was as a gratification for my luxury that I embellished your arms with gold and silver? I wished to demonstrate to those who are accustomed to nothing cheaper than those metals that the Macedonians, invincible in other things, cannot even be outdone with gold.

(17) Therefore I will first arrest the eyes of those who are expecting a completely sordid and humble force, and I shall show them that we do not come lusting after gold or silver, but in order to subjugate the entire world. It was this glory, you traitor, which you wished to put an end to, and by killing their king, to hand over the Macedonians to the races they had conquered.'

(10) 'At enim Persae, quos uicimus, in magno honore sunt apud me! <Id> quidem moderationis meae certissimum indicium est, quod ne uictis quidem superbe impero. Veni enim in Asiam, non ut funditus euerterem gentes nec ut dimidia parte terrarum solitudinem facerem, sed ut illos, quos bello subegissem, uictoriae meae non paeniteret. (11) Itaque militant uobiscum, pro imperio uestro sanguinem fundunt, qui superbe habiti rebellassent. Non est diuturna possessio, in quam gladio inducimur; beneficiorum gratia sempiterna est. (12) Si habere Asiam, non transire uolumus, cum his communicanda est nostra clementia: horum fides stabile et aeternum faciet imperium. Et sane plus habemus quam capimus. Insatiabilis autem auaritiae est adhuc implere uelle, quod iam circumfluit. (13) Verumtamen eorum <mores> in Macedonas transfundo! In multis enim gentibus esse uideo, quae non erubescamus imitari; nec aliter tantum imperium apte regi potest, quam ut quaedam et tradamus illis et ab isdem discamus. (14) Illud paene dignum risu fuit, quod Hermolaus postulabat a me, ut auersarer Iouem, cuius oraculo adgnoscor. An etiam, quid di respondeant, in mea potestate est? (15) Obtulit nomen filii mihi: recipere ipsis rebus, quas agimus, haud alienum fuit. Utinam Indi quoque deum esse me credant! Fama enim bella constant, et saepe etiam, quod falso creditum est, ueri uicem obtinuit. (16) An me luxuriae indulgentem putatis arma uestra auro argentoque adornasse? Adsuetis nihil uilius hac uidere materia uolui ostendere Macedonas inuictos ceteris ne auro quidem uinci. (17) Oculos ergo primum eorum sordida omnia et humilia expectantium capiam et docebo nos non auri aut argenti cupidos, sed orbem terrarum subacturos uenire. Quam gloriam tu, parricida, intercipere uoluisti et Macedonas rege adempto deuictis gentibus dedere.'

This speech articulates a series of recurring themes in my discussion of how Alexander's 'presence' in Rome was becoming increasingly

problematic in the second part of the first century CE. Reading
Horace's epistle to Augustus, I suggested that his take on the role of
the littérateur in the developing political accommodation could still be
interpreted as making a claim for authorial autonomy. Perhaps, given
Horace's relationship with Augustus and his public involvement in the
refocusing of Roman myth—epitomised in the *Carmen Saeculare*—
this suggestive assertiveness is unsurprising. Curtius poses different
interpretative problems. His historical insubstantiality, the difficulty
in pinning him down to a fixed name or date, make it impossible to
construct one settled reading of his narrative. Yet we can see in this
speech a sense of how explicitly self-reflexive image-control has lost
some of its gloss as a battleground for contesting models of authority.
In fact, textual context can provide another way of reading this
speech as a tacit intervention into developments in Roman autocracy.
Alexander makes this speech in response to accusations brought
against him by one of his pages, Hermolaus, who was being tried for
attempted regicide.[21] It immediately follows Curtius' treatment of
what is usually termed 'the Proskynesis affair' in which the historian
Callisthenes speaks out strongly against the introduction of the
practice.[22] This means that when Alexander talks loosely about the
need to ensure 'correct' dissemination of his image, the need to enforce
(if possible) an authorised version, it is within a wider context of a
problematisation of how to map political necessity onto narrative
history. Callisthenes may have been taken along to provide an 'official'
history, but we do not know how willingly, or even how fully, he was
complicit in this project. Clearly, changes in Alexander's political
rapprochement with the Persians and his decision to attempt to provide equality of treatment between the Greek and Macedonian troops
have slipped out of synch with the political and psychological aspirations of his army.

Curtius has Alexander suggest that his honourable treatment of the
conquered Persians is a sign of his moderation, but this rhetoric seems
to plug into a discourse of anxiety centring on Greek influence in
Rome that was already well-developed by the mid-first century.[23]
Instead of reassuring his textual audience, Alexander's sarcasm and
the subsequent torture and death of the conspirators and Callisthenes,
caused him to become an object of resentment among the Greeks.
According to Curtius (8.6.24) Callisthenes was never named as one of
the conspirators, but suffered guilt by association. Curtius' attitude to
Callisthenes is tricky. As one historian to another, we might presuppose some fellow-feeling, as is suggested by Curtius' comments
that Callisthenes had been a fine fellow of unsullied character, a good

friend to Alexander, and simply unsuited to the increasing sycophancy of court life (8.8.21–23). This ties in with an authorial gloss on Callisthenes' part in the proskynesis affair, proposing that he was perceived as a champion of public liberty (8.5.20). This positive portrait takes a knock when we read an exchange between Hermolaus and Callisthenes after the page had been flogged by Alexander (8.6.25). But it is important to be alert to the nuances of authorial 'voice' within a text; what we get here is a series of destabilizing comments that may actually serve to highlight the need for alert and questioning approach to historical texts. We're told that 'some people' tell a story of how Hermolaus' complaints about the flogging drew from Callisthenes the response that they ought to remember that they were men.[24] But not only is the story itself distanced from the main—and therefore implicitly authoritative—narratorial voice through the indefinite pronominal phrase *'quidam adiciunt'* (some say. . .), the suspicious reader may also find problematic echoes in Callisthenes' gnomic response.

For a start, this response is again destabilised by our author, who refuses to provide an authoritative interpretation of what Callisthenes may have meant. Instead, he tells us (quoting his 'sources'?) that it was hard to know whether Callisthenes was trying to console the pages, or to incite them.[25] It is impossible to recover what Curtius' anonymous 'sources' made of this but the choices on offer are awkwardly expressed: would it really be considered a 'consolation' to be told that one was a 'man' and should therefore grin and bear it?[26] Might it not rather seem a rebuke for having complained and whinged like a child? To all practical purposes, the position of Royal Page transformed groups of aristocratic boys into slaves, susceptible to floggings at the order of the king, but with the attractive promise of preferment once they had reached an age for command and responsibility. The lacerations meted out to Hermolaus inscribed Alexander's authority on his body, making the penetration of his flesh a visual testament to his subservient position, and forming a secondary narrative of events (Curtius 8.6.8). That the comments ascribed to Callisthenes might inflame the young men further seems more likely, particularly if the reader is alert to his comments to Cleo during the proskynesis affair. Cleo had just been characterized by Curtius as one of Alexander's chief flatterers, and on Alexander's orders at a luxurious banquet, he gives a speech telling the Macedonians that it is their duty to follow Persian custom and worship Alexander as a god, prostrating themselves before him. Callisthenes' response concludes with the words:

I am not ashamed of my fatherland, nor do I desire to learn
how I ought to honour my king from the vanquished. As
far as I'm concerned I must acknowledge them to be the
victors, if we have to accept from them the laws by which
we live.

Non pudet patriae, nec desidero ad quem modum rex mihi colendus sit
discere a uictis. Quos equidem uictores esse confiteor, si ab illis leges
quis uiuamus accipimus. (Curtius 8.5.19)

Both Cicero and Horace suggest versions of how the artist or author
can become part of a popular account of famed figures. These excerpts
intimate how the closer the controlling relationship between artist and
patron, the more authorized the 'text' will become. But the underlying
assumption, made explicit in Curtius' story, is that behind the mystique of a ruler, there may be more manipulation than action.

Frontiers, Limits and a Rhetoric of Conquest: Acknowledging the Power of Words

There may be an element of subterfuge behind any choice of Alexander
as a subject: playing the 'other' offers a myriad roles, and much of the
fascination of 'Alexander' clusters around the diversity of narrative
possibilities that his name opens up. This in turn is bound up in the
multiplicity of roles that can be constructed around him, and the
guises that he can adopt. These guises are both a function of his
control over the dissemination of his image—and the subsequent
importance of 'image-making' for later Alexanders—and also indicative of the motif of the death-dealing quest for world's end, the strange
new worlds, and the fatal, and fatally open-ended, mission. The fascination with limits, definition and circumscription that clusters around
Alexander is intimately connected to the questions of representation
and manipulation that I have been discussing. In this section, however, I want to focus on how the actual physical limits to Alexander's
eastward trajectory function within Roman reworkings of his campaign. I will be suggesting ways in which we can read these attempts
to map Alexander's empire—mythic and territorial—as both an integral
part of his fascination, and as a persuasive intellectual model for
Roman imperialism. Limits are the defining factor of Alexander's
expansion: not only is his life circumscribed by early death, he travels
east to find the world's boundaries, and he conquers so that this aim
can be accomplished. The prevalence of this topos in narratives of

Alexander hammers out its significance for understanding Alexander in Rome, whilst also prompting a reassessment of the relative instability and fluidity of the geo-political frontiers of Roman control. For Alexander, retreat and withdrawal from an expansive model signal the approach of his death; a similar anxiety informs the ongoing renegotiation of the relationship between *auctoritas* and *imperium* in the first century CE.

READING 4.5
THE ELDER
SENECA,
Suasoria
1.9, 14

(9) The philosopher Fabianus made the same point his first: even if the Ocean could be sailed, it ought not to be. But his primary reason—that a limit must be set to prosperity—was different. At this point, he introduced the following epigram: 'great happiness is only that which has self-determination as its basis.' He then offered the commonplace on the variability of fortune, describing how nothing is stable, everything is fluid: now raised up and now depressed in unpredictable change; lands are submerged, seas drained, and mountains subside. He then gave examples of kings who have been overthrown at the height of their power, and added: 'it's better that nature rather than fortune should run out.'

(9) Fabianus philosophus primam fecit quaestionem eandem: etiamsi nauigari posset Oceanus, nauigandum non esse. At rationem aliam primam fecit: modum imponendum esse rebus secundis. Hic dixit sententiam: illa demum est magna felicitas quae arbitrio suo constitit. Dixit deinde locum de uarietate fortunae et, cum descripsisset nihil esse stabile, omnia fluitare et incertis motibus modo attolli, modo deprimi, absorberi terras et maria siccari, montes subsidere, deinde exempla regum ex fastigio suo deuolutorum, adiecit: 'sine potius rerum naturam quam fortunam tuam deficere.'

(14) Arellius Fuscus said: 'I swear that your world deserts you sooner than your soldiers.
   Latro, seated, spoke thus; he did not excuse the soldiers, but said: 'Lead, and I follow. Who presents me with an enemy, with land, daylight or sea? Give me somewhere to pitch camp and fight a battle. I have parents and children at home. I want some furlough; is this untimely, right at the very Ocean?

(14) Fuscus Arellius dixit: testor ante orbem tibi tuum deesse quam militem.

> Latro sedens hanc dixit; non excusauit militem, sed dixit: Duc, sequor; quis mihi promittit hostem, quis terram, quis diem, quis mare? Da ubi castra ponam, ubi signa inferam. Reliqui parentes, reliqui liberos, commeatum peto; numquid immature ab Oceano?

Earlier in this *suasoria* (1.4) Seneca reminds us that although Alexander conquered the world, it was not pacified—no guarantees could be given of the security of what lay behind him. The empire that he created was unstable and ephemeral (surely a nod to the instability of the Roman government of the recent past). This *suasoria* has already figured as a potent and culturally loaded model for Alexander's role in late republican Rome. We have thought about Alexander as a governmental model, as an excessive and degenerate figure, but perhaps it is here in this section on the empire of the mind, an *imperium* that will always exist, irrespective of its actual collapse, that we get closest to the heart of what Alexander was really doing in Rome. This is a discourse of boundaries, of what and who can exist on the extreme edges of the world, and the extent to which these people who can inhabit the boundaries become so representative of all perceptual and behavioural limits that their liminality, ironically, drags them into the mainstream of popular consciousness. To some extent at least, this is the story of Alexander at Rome. A man who so exemplified extremity of conquest, of political identity, of personal magnetism that he was bound to become a paradigm *ne plus ultra* for an increasingly individualistic political system. The *suasoria* format is ideally situated, culturally and intellectually, to home in on highly charged contemporary topics within a non-specific and at least overtly unthreatening framework. Given the 'impossibility' of the proposed conquest of the Ocean, this inclusion of Alexander's one significant failure—and the emphasis on his troops' role in turning his course away from this final frontier—pushes him back from divinity and invulnerability towards the achievable and (relatively) available realms of the nearer east. It opens Alexander up for conquest.

The dialogue presented in this *suasoria* suggests some of the ways in which we might want to think about Alexander and the limits to conquest imposed by the Ocean stream that bounded the world. Variations on a theme are ascribed to Cestius and Fabianus.[27] Cestius' argument focuses on consolidation, the duty of care owed to his troops by a ruler, and to his mother by a son. Alexander had enough glory; he should take care of the lands already won, and set them in order; he should have some thought for his troops, worn out by the victories achieved, and for his mother, Olympias (the Ocean, anyway, being unsailable). This last tag, the impossibility of Alexander's plan to 'conquer' the Ocean, even though it is included in an almost throw-away manner, gets to the heart of the dilemma. To what extent can greatness succeed when pitted against the forces of nature and even the fabric of the world itself? Clearly, the dynamics of how empire and *imperium* could stretch the boundaries of the physical world were particularly important in the late first century BCE. If this limit to expansion could be elastic, could be surmounted, then Alexander's 'failure' could impact upon Roman eastern conquests in a variety of ways. Did Alexander fail *because* it was impossible, or because of character defects, or because the nature of his rule over his people was essentially flawed? Or could it even be read as a warning—by attempting the impossible he set up a cause-and-effect chain of events that lead ultimately to mutiny and death? Or might the pushing back of this final eastern frontier stand as a warning, prefiguring a negative discourse equating Roman expansive imperialism with luxury, degen-eracy and loss of identity? This opens up a potentially terrifying scenario in which Rome is spatially and culturally decentred, whereby the empire becomes not *the* cosmos, but one cosmos among many. It suggests, implicitly at least, that we have to re-examine our whole notion of what the 'end' (*finis*) signifies within a world where even the physical landscape is in a constant state of flux (1.9).

These teleological questions demand that we contemplate how explicitly, and even how intentionally, this rhetorical discourse was seeking to map Roman imperialistic ambitions on to Alexander. Certainly, it feeds into and out of a tradition of paradigmatic usage of Alexander as a model for thinking with, but it also denotes a high level of popular currency for 'Alexander' as a suitable topic for young Roman senators-in-waiting. Fabianus' 'comments' suggest similar con-cerns, but approached from an angle that highlights a liminal space within which fortune and nature intersect. Self-control *ought* to have a limiting function on excessive prosperity because fortune is variable and unpredictable; for this reason, nature rather than fortune ought to be allowed run out (1.9). We then find echoes of Cestius' final point in Fabianus' argument that, although there were no habitable lands in or beyond the Ocean, were they to exist they would prove unreach-able, and if reached, they would certainly not be worth the trouble. Could this be a warning to eager young Romans that doing Alexander is not just (potentially) un-Roman, it's also an activity that ultimately can offer no serious hope of advantage? Not just 'Alexander tried and

failed, so why should you succeed?', but a programmatic statement of
the pointless emptiness of that kind of endeavour—even if the unthinkable can happen and the Ocean could be crossed, nothing could
possibly exist there that would provide any justification for the effort
expended.

Latro's arguments are supposed to represent those that might have
been offered to Alexander by the Macedonian troops when they
refused to accompany him to the edge of the world, and the Ocean
(1.14).[28] These proposals are essentially about taxonomy (as, perhaps, are all the propositions contained in this *suasoria*). They address
ways in which Romans could categorize and conceptualize appropriate modes of imperializing behaviour, and they provide us with a
way of accessing some of the popular representational models that
were available. This allows access to Alexander from a variety of
angles. From the perspective of the 'citizen' soldier whose stake in the
scope and aims of the campaign might approximate to that of the
Roman soldier; from a senatorial perspective; or from a familial perspective. If we take the family as the primary social and public civic
unit, we can read this final Alexander as disrupting and disregarding
the most basic building blocks of society.[29] The main focus of this
argument is that the Ocean is not the province of the soldier, who
requires an enemy, land, or even sea (not *Ocean*, something entirely
different and 'other') to practise his trade. In these terms, 'Ocean'
seems to have taken on a very explicit sense of 'otherness' whereby it
cannot function as an appropriate (or even a feasible) *locus* for
military activity. His other argument is a reworking of the theme that
family awaits Alexander at home and that surely the attainment of the
very boundaries of the world makes the time ripe for furlough. These
emphases represent Alexander as one who ought to have had more
care for *patria*, for his troops as its representatives, for family, and the
(un)acceptability of a quest for Ocean. Whether or not the quest can
reach its goal, it is not a suitable effort for him to contemplate.[30] The
final, and self-conscious, sentiment of the *Suasoria* (1.16), that the
author wanted to offer both sound and corrupt speeches without
editorial censorship, has a close link with other narrators' claim
that they transcribe more than they believe, but this is not the only
level of similarity between Curtius' and Seneca's narratives.[31] Much
of the argument for returning home (both from Latro and before
the *diuisio* from Argentarius, Pompeius Silo, Moschus, Albucius Silus,
Marullus and Fabianus [1.1–4]) is analogous to Curtius' presentation
of the Macedonian troops' complaints in his *History of Alexander*.

So what we find in this thematic relationship between textbook rhetoric and historical narrative is located in a point of intersection between different but complementary expressions of popular consciousness.

The *suasoria* was a literary form that required subjects of uncertain practicality for discussion. This kind of rhetorical set piece was intended as a student exercise, a testing ground for hopeful orators' skills rather than a forum for serious debate on political hot topics. In a discussion of this type of public-speaking exercise, Quintilian presents four examples of suitable topics: whether the Isthmus can be cut through; the Pomptine marshes drained; a harbour constructed at Ostia; or Alexander find land beyond the Ocean.[32] Overtly, this is more concerned with how we are intended to receive Alexander as a theme for *suasoriae* than how Quintilian regards Alexander, but it does confirm that his search for a land at the edge of the world was a well-known topos, as was a negative judgement of his success. The dilemmas facing the army offer archetypes for any Roman general setting out for the resonant eastern frontier. Thus in his record of common rhetorical deliberations on Alexander, Seneca is engaging in a dialectic that not only displays the rhetorical use of the unanswerable Alexander-debate, but also links him to an ongoing idea of Romans (authors, politicians and generals alike) contemplating the Macedonian king. In this scheme, Alexander stands as the forerunner of Roman expansion eastward, a 'Greek', a king and commander, a victim of mutiny, and a sacrifice to oriental degeneracy.

A role for Rome in Alexander's conquistadorial story depends on how the author and audience collude in interpreting oriental ambitions, and the extent to which talking of Alexander means thinking about Rome. Livy notes Alexander's metamorphosis into a quasi-Darius figure when he becomes conqueror, explicitly contrasting the different styles of government so that any consideration of one extreme demands the existence of its opposite.[33] In this way, Livy's dismissal of the value of Persian and Indian troops as new recruits for Alexander's army, together with his report that Alexander of Epirus claimed that Alexander of Macedon had made war only against women, sets up an implicit polarity between 'them' and 'us'.[34] This creates a paradoxical situation in which Rome simultaneously claims the potential to master the East, while denying the worth of the endeavour. This rhetoric is already familiar, and Seneca foreshadows its reappearance in Curtius. What we are seeing is a developing discourse of empire and identity whereby narrative reconfiguration of the defeats of Macedon and Greece, provides an important mode of Roman self-conceptualization as conquerors not just of the Greek world, but also of the Far East. Despite Roman emphasis on the transience of Alexander's empire and the long-term insubstantiality of his achievement, we still find that his defeat of Darius and Persia allows Roman conquest of Greece to function as a synecdoche for Roman victory over the whole eastern world. Rome's victory over Alexander's former kingdom is a key point in Livy's disparagement of his posthumous reputation, but there are more subtle modulations of the motif. The significance of the *name* Alexander, particularly given the resurgence of a threatening 'Alexander' from the East, in Alexander of Epirus, focuses our attention on the problems of intense identification between man and cause, and particularly when national *locus* and identity are closely defined by the imperializing ability of one man. In the following passage, again from Curtius, we can see some of the ways in which a dangerous and potentially mutually destructive interdependence can develop. This Alexander is inconceivable without his victories and his eastward momentum, and his people's desire to secure his longevity for the greater long-term good subverts the duties of care and allegiance between monarch and subjects. When the king ceases to serve the common good, then he has already caused the relationship to break down.

READING 4.6
CURTIUS,
*History of
Alexander
the Great*
9.6.18–22

(18) 'But the thoughts of those people who wish to die in my place are not the same as my own; in fact I believe that it was through my courage that I earned this goodwill of yours. For whilst you may wish to enjoy long-term, perhaps even perpetual success through me, I judge myself not on the length of my life, but on my glory.

(19) I could have been content with my father's power and within Macedonia's boundaries have anticipated a life of leisure leading to an obscure and undistinguished old age (although not even indolent men can control their own destiny, and those who reckon that the only good thing about life is its duration are often overtaken by a premature death). No, *I* count not my years but my victories, and if I reckon up fortune's favours to me accurately, then I have lived a long life.

(20) From my beginnings in Macedonia I now have control over Greece; I have conquered Thrace and the Illyrians; and I rule over the Triballi and the Maedi. I

have Asia from the Hellespont as far as shores of the Red Sea in my possession. Now I am not far from the world's end, and once having passed beyond this I have resolved to open up for myself a second realm of nature, another world.

(21) From Asia I crossed to the boundaries of Europe in a single hour. I am the conqueror of both continents after the ninth year of my rule and the twenty-eighth year of my life. So does it seem likely to you that I can give up on this pursuit of glory to which I have so single-mindedly devoted myself? No, I at least shall not fail in my duty, and wherever I shall fight, I shall believe myself to be on stage for the whole world.

(22) I shall give distinction to unknown places, I shall open to all the peoples of the world those lands which nature had set far away. That I should die in the midst of these exploits, if chance so wills it, would be a fine thing. I am born from such a line that I must choose a full life over a long one.'

(18) 'Ceterum non eadem est cogitatio eorum, qui pro me mori optant, et mea, qui quidem hanc beneuolentiam uestram uirtute meruisse me iudico. Vos enim diuturnum fructum ex me, forsitan etiam perpetuum percipere cupiatis: ego me metior non aetatis spatio, sed gloriae. (19) Licuit paternis opibus contento intra Macedoniae terminos per otium corporis expectare obscuram et ignobilem senectutem; quamquam ne pigri quidem sibi fata disponunt, sed unicum bonum diuturnam uitam existimantes saepe acerba mors occupat. Verum ego, qui non annos meos, sed uictorias numero, si munera fortunae bene computo, diu uixi. (20) Orsus a Macedonia imperium Graeciae teneo, Thraciam et Illyrios subegi, Triballis Maedisque imperito, Asiam, qua Hellesponto, qua Rubro mari subluitur, possideo. Iamque haud procul absum fine mundi, quem egressus aliam naturam, alium orbem aperire mihi statui. (21) Ex Asia in Europae terminos momento unius horae transiui. Victor utriusque regionis post nonum regni mei, post uicesimum atque octauum annum <uitae> uideorne uobis in excolenda gloria, cui me uni deuoui, posse cessare? Ego uero non deero et, ubicumque pugnabo, in theatro terrarum orbis esse me credam. (22) Dabo nobilitatem ignobilibus locis, aperiam cunctis gentibus terras, quas natura longe submouerat. In his operibus extingui mihi, si fors ita feret, pulchrum est: ea stirpe sum genitus, ut multam prius quam longam uitam debeam optare.'

The overwhelming impression here is of polarization and opposition. This Alexander is intent on setting out the difference between himself and his troops, between himself and his father, between Macedonia, Greece and Asia, between security and glory. Ironically, the outward movement from Macedonia to Greece and then Asia culminates in a breaking-down of boundaries rather than the creation of a discrete new empire; the confines of *this* world are to be transgressed and Alexander will open up a new stage on which his achievements can be acted out for the peoples of the whole world. From the catalogue of names we can almost construct a genealogy for Alexander's empire, delineating its beginnings and its middle, and speculating on its end. This is echoed in Alexander's emphasis on his destiny to prefer glory to longevity because of his bloodline—perhaps an implicit reference to divine ancestry, but certainly a nod to the choice of Achilles. The new world order which Alexander envisages is wholly performative—all the peoples of the world will be united in their role as audience for the drama of Alexander that will be enacted for them. *Desum* (9.6.21), the verb used to express Alexander's determination to carry through his destiny, is an interesting choice; it can mean to fail in one's duty, to neglect, desert, be absent, or simply to fail. Yet Alexander in some sense *will* be absent for the very reason outlined in the final clause of the sentence: Alexander will be absent from his people because he will be performing the role of 'Alexander' for the world at large.

So what exactly is Alexander not going to fail his people in? A mutually responsible relationship between ruler and subjects must be impossible when the king places his own future glory above the security and well-being of his people. But this interpretation is based on a reading that has little place in the Roman Alexander discourse; for these Roman authors, the whole point of 'Alexander' was that through his reputation, through the stories that clustered around him and the tradition of the glory-crazed individualist, he did succeed in conquering a boundless empire, an *imperium sine fine* both spatially and chronologically. And it is this boundlessness against which Roman authors constantly struggle whilst they continue to reconfigure and commemorate it. In this way, Curtius' Alexander is central to Roman interest in Alexander because his lengthy narrative has the scope to mimic—almost to scale—the scope of Alexander's empire. Most readers will expect Curtius to interlink and conflate all the available Alexanders in what amounts to an aetiology of Roman autocracy. Through successive literary reinventions of Alexander's story his actual relationship with his troops (and the real scope of his victories) becomes immaterial. The emphasis placed here on display and performance is mirrored in Alexander's claim that he is going to alter the taxonomy of the natural world: it is through *his* activities that previously unknown places will become renowned, and furthermore, he is going to ensure that places which nature had ordained to be far away—far away, we assume, from a centre that could as easily be Rome as Macedon—will be opened up and made available to the whole world.

This suggests that the meteoric passage of Alexander across the world will cause some kind of geo-cultural shift, but is that in fact what happens? Far from making the whole world 'home' to all peoples, stories of Alexander actually serve to reinforce a distinction between 'us' and 'them' and to highlight the otherness of the lands and peoples that he conquered. That Alexander alone could achieve these victories emphasizes the immensity of his achievement, but also demands that all future imperializers develop some way of quantifying their own victories. To acknowledge that Alexander did, in fact, do it all already would be counter-productive, leading to a sense of parallel operative discourses. On the one hand, Alexander is the man to match or outdo, and everyone who sets their sights on eastern conquest is inevitably sucked into some kind of comparison, but on the other hand, it is impossible to allow the grandiosity of his claims, or all subsequent conquest would be ruled out. This is to some extent solved by the very fact of the unknowable strangeness of the storied East as it stands; clearly, Alexander's achievements have not lasted, however successful he may have been at the time. The tradition of reception of Alexander as *ur* warrior-king and conqueror of the East has a built-in self-destruct. This is how Livy's scheme functions, and it offers a seductive and practicable model: Alexander conquered the known world and would have extended his empire into the unknowable had he not been let down by the mortal concerns of his soldiers and companions, and because the whole edifice of empire was closely predicated upon identification with Alexander as glorious leader, without him the glory, and the empire, was doomed to fade. We can see echoes of this kind of story in the legends surrounding Camelot and King Arthur, but whereas Arthur himself was said to be waiting for his country's time of ultimate need, when he would return, Alexander seems to have inspired a different kind of immortality. As I will be discussing in more detail in Chapter 5, rather than Alexander himself having the capability to return in person, what we get is a succession of Alexander wannabes.

The following extract, from Statius' *Siluae* (4.6.43–74), purports to offer a poetic genealogy and provenance for a statue of Hercules said to have belonged to Alexander, but now in the possession of Nouius

Vindex, a wealthy Roman poet-patron and art connoisseur.[35] This emphatic location of Alexander as entrenched at the heart of Roman society in the late first century CE develops the issues raised by passage 4.6 a stage further, confronting its audience with an Alexander who does achieve the end that Curtius' Alexander longs for, but fails to accomplish: a death in the midst of great exploits. Here, again, Alexander is referred to simply as from Pella, but the tone is strikingly different to that taken by Juvenal (passage 4.8) or Lucan (passage 4.9), with an emphasis on glory and greatness shrouded in an inevitably mysterious death.

READING 4.7 **STATIUS**, *Siluae* 1.1.1–2, 8–21; and 4.6.43–74	What immense mass, doubled in size by the colossus atop it, stands holding the Latian forum in its embrace? Quae superimposito moles geminata colosso stat Latium complexa forum?

Come now, let former fame marvel at the long-
    renowned
Dardanian horse, for whom Dindymon bowed his
    sacred peak
10 and Ida was shorn of her groves.
This horse would never have been contained by
    Pergamum, with its walls sundered,
nor could the flock of mingled boys and unmarried
    girls
nor Aeneas himself nor Hector the great, have
    pulled it!
Furthermore, that horse was harmful, and gathered
    in its embrace savage Achaeans;
15 this horse, its gentle rider commends. It's a pleasure
    to gaze upon that face
on which are mingled the marks of war and signs of
    undisturbed peace.
And do not think that this exceeds the truth: equal in
    beauty and grace,
equal in dignity. Not more loftily does the Bistonian
    steed carry Mars
when the fighting is at an end, and revels in his great
20 weight; without delay, having snatched him quickly,
    on he goes at full steam
up the river, and with his vast puffing he parts the
    Strymon

Nunc age Fama prior notum per saecula nomen
Dardanii miretur equi, cui uertice sacro
10 Dindymon et caesis decreuit frondibus Ide:
hunc neque discissis cepissent Pergama muris
nec grege permixto pueri innuptaeque puellae
ipse nec Aeneas nec magnus duceret Hector!
Adde, quod ille nocens saeuosque amplexus Achiuos,
15 hunc mitis commendat eques: iuuat ora tueri
mixta notis belli placidamque gerentia pacem.
Nec ueris maiora putes: par forma decorque,
par honor. Exhaustis Martem non altius armis
Bistonius portat sonipes magnoque superbit
20 pondere nec tardo raptus prope flumina cursu
fumat et ingenti propellit Strymona flatu

. . . so compressed a form yet such a great deception!
What technical skill, what enterprise in the skilled
45 craftsman at one and the same time to strive to
        fashion a table ornament
and to turn over in his mind a mighty colossus!
Such a *jeu d'esprit* neither the Telchines in their
        Idaean caves
nor stolid Brontes nor the Lemnian who polishes the
        armour of
the gods could have made out of such a small lump
        of metal.
50 No stern likeness was this, a stranger to an indulgent
        banquet,
but just as he was when thrifty Molorchus'
        household was amazed by him
or as the Tegean priestess saw him in the groves of
        Alea;
just as when, sent up to the stars from Oeta's ashes
he joyfully drank the nectar, despite Juno's frown:
55 with so gentle a countenance, as if rejoicing from his
        heart
he cheers on the feast. One hand holds his brother's
        indolent
cup, but the other remembers his club: a rough seat
supports him, and a stone draped with the Nemean
        decoration.
There was a worthy fate for so divine a work. The
        Pellaean king
60 held this deity in awe at his joyous banquets,
and west and east alike he kept it close by him;

and gladly he set it before him, with the right hand
    that had
both seized and proffered crowns, and had razed
    great cities.
Always he sought from it courage for tomorrow's
    battle,
65 to it, as victor, he always related the glorious fight,
whether he had stolen the shackled Indians away
    from Bromius
or broken open beleaguered Babylon with his mighty
    spear
or obliterated the lands of Pelops and the freedom of
    the Greeks
in war. Out of this great train of glorious deeds
70 he is said only to have apologized for his triumph
    over Thebes.
And when fate broke off his great deeds
and when he was drinking the fatal wine, already in
    the dark cloud
of harsh death, he felt fear at the altered countenance
    of his beloved deity
and at its sweating bronze at that last banquet

. . . tam magna breui: mendacia formae!
Quis modus in dextra, quanta experientia dati
45 artifices, curis pariter gestamina mensae
fingere et ingentes animo uersare colossos!
Tale nec Idaeis quicquam Telchines in antris
nec stolides Brontes nec, qui polit arma deorum,
Lemnius exigua potuisset ludere massa.
50 Nec torua effigies epulisque aliena remissis,
sed qualem parci domus admirata Molorchi
aut Aleae lucis uidit Tegeaea sacerdos;
quails et Oetaeis emissus in astra fauillis
nectar adhuc torua laetus Iunone bibebat:
55 sic mitis ultus, ueluti de pectore gaudens,
hortatur mensas. Tenet haec marcentia fratris
pocula, at haec clauae meminit manus; aspera sedis
sustinet et cultum Nemeaeo tegmine saxum.
Digna operi fortuna sacro. Pellaeus habebat
60 regnator laetis numen uenerabile mensis
et comitem occasus secum portabat et ortus,
praestabatque libens modo qua diademate dextra
abstulerat dederatque et magnas uerterat urbes.
Semper ab hos animos in crastina bella petebat,

65 huic acies semper uictor narrabat opimas,
   siue catenatos Bromio detraxerat Indos
   seu clusam magna Babylona refregerat hasta
   seu pelopis terras libertatemque Pelasgam
   obruerat bello; magnoque ex agmine laudum
70 fertur Thebanos tantum excussasse triumphos.
   Ille etiam, magnos Fatis rumpentibus actus,
   cum traheret letale merum, iam mortis opaca
   nube grauis uultus alios in numine caro
   aeraque supremis timuit sudantia mensis.

Siluae 4.6 is a poem about relationships in the broadest sense, a poem about how ancestry and inheritance define the state of Rome in the late first century CE. Moreover, in its literary nod to the *ekphrasis*, it becomes an investigation into the artifice of individual greatness in imperial Rome. Statius locates himself firmly within the public contemporary city when he introduces his narrative persona at the beginning of the poem, wandering in the Saepta Julia. Apparently, the poet is strolling at leisure, unoccupied by poetry, yet the composition of this poem undermines any temptation to take this detachment from verse at face value. In the opening lines of this poem Statius characterizes himself as having a heart lightened of Apollo ('*Phoeboque leuatum / pectora*' 4.6.1–2), but Apollo is not, typically, associated with the kind of occasional poetry that the *Siluae* would seem to identify itself with. So immediately we are engaged upon a dialogue between public duty and private concerns, a dialogue reinforced by the history of the poetic *locus*. In the poem's narrative present, the Saepta Julia formed a huge covered market in the Campus Martius, between the Pantheon and the Temple of Isis. But its history was not commercial. Originally the Saepta had been voting enclosures, and as such, a highly visible and physical manifestation of the public workings of the Republic. During the early Empire they were used for games and gladiatorial contests, as entertainment rather than political responsibility gradually became the dominant mode of public engagement for the citizen body as a whole. They were replaced as an entertainment complex by the Colosseum in CE 80, when they were damaged by fire, and then rebuilt as a vast market, with commerce finally displacing spectacle when the imperially sponsored amphitheatre took over that role. This means that from the first lines of this poem we are plunged into a world where literature and city are immediately subjected to a process of enquiry, a process that demands that we look beneath the surface to the archaeology of knowledge that lies submerged. Neither public nor private existence will be uncomplicated, and the rest of the poem bears this out.

Kindly Vindex seizes Statius and carries him off to dinner (*'rapuit me cena benigni / Vindicis'* 4.6.3–4), but the juxtaposition of *benignus* and *rapio* again undermines our ability to gain a firm hold on what is going on. Is Vindex simply generous and friendly? Or should we be alert to some of the other implications of *benignus*? Is Vindex prodigal and lavish? Or wealthy? Or is this a reference to his role as patron, a role that Statius cannot ignore? We do not have to force these meanings apart, and it is likely that all are implicit, but in conjunction with *rapio* we may wonder whether the more sinister overtones might not have gained the upper hand? Furthermore, given Statius' choice of the Saepta for his stroll, his knowledgeable (if allusive) dissociation of Vindex's dinner-party from those where luxuries are consumed could seem ironic.[36] This emphasis on frugality of consumption is tacitly picked up when we learn that the statue of Hercules that forms the main subject of the poem is by Lysippus, Alexander's official sculptor, and this Hercules captured the heart which at the poem's opening we learned had been lightened of Apollo—one god's control replaces that of another.[37] Alexander's legendary descent into fatal over-consumption is glossed teasingly in our final glimpse of the statue in Alexander's company: its liquefaction and mysterious 'changed countenance' mirrors his own incapability of remaining impervious to the temptations of Persian luxury, and increasingly heavy bouts of drinking.

Alexander's function in this poem, I suggest, is directly keyed into his role as an easily recognizable signal that we be on the alert for the significance of genealogies and deification. Alexander operates as an archetype for men who claim divine descent not just in the distant past, but right here in the immediate and knowable past and present. When Caesar promoted his descent from Venus, the links with Alexander remained submerged, despite Livy's highlighting of a connexion between Alexander and Scipio as subjects of miraculous conception (26.19.5–7). With Alexander and Augustus, both claiming direct descent from a god, the connexion reasserts its claims on our attention. The lengthy frame on Vindex (opening) on Vindex's authorial gaze (4.6.17–31) is succeeded by a description of the statue (4.6.32–58). Alexander follows (4.6.59–74) and then in quick succession Hannibal (4.6.75–84) and Sulla (4.6.85–88): the closer we get to the present, the more elusive these models of ownership become. If we read the description of the statue of Hercules at 4.6.43–49 in conjunction with *Siluae* 1.1.8–21, we may begin to wonder if the hyperbole followed by increasing uncertainty is not sending us back in a subversive loop to *Siluae* 1.1.1–2? After all it is impossible not to feel nudged to a rereading of the first *colossus* in the light of the second, compressed version. Similarly, the duality of Vindex's Hercules expressed at 4.6.56–58 neatly invokes the comparison of horses and warlike peace of Domitian's face at 1.1.14–18. The reappearance of *mitis* (1.1.15 and 4.6.55) surely signals the existence of this allusive dialogue between the two poems.

The final connexion between the rhetoric of this poem and earlier imperial comparisons is perhaps the most obvious, if also particularly elusive. The main concern of this chapter has been to investigate ways in which the rhetoric of conquest, and a tradition of reworking and reimagining Alexander's story, create a flexible archetype of an Alexander imbued with trans-historical significance. The story becomes more important than the 'facts' it was originally designed to memorialize. In Horace's epistle to Augustus (passage 4.3) we noticed how artistic and political judgement could, in the highly politicised atmosphere of the Augustan principate, merge; I suggest that a similar symbiosis is taking place here. Eleven lines of the (110-line) poem are given over to elaborate praise of Vindex's taste (4.6.20–31), but tellingly, whereas Augustus was praised for his literary discernment, and Alexander for his artistic taste, Vindex apparently combines the best of both: he is knowledgeable and appreciative of art *and* composes his own lyric verse. Yet despite the purity of the intellectual sustenance on offer at Vindex's table (4.6.4–7, 32; tacitly prefiguring the drunken feasting of Alexander which follows), the statue of Hercules not only captures Statius' heart, it also leaves him unsatisfied (4.6.34). Just as this passage closes with Alexander's final confusion and fear, the lack of the closure that a full life would have brought, so Statius' desires for the unattainable have been stimulated and then disappointed.

This reading suggests that Statius is subverting the kind of intellectual soirée that Vindex apparently favours, but his echo of Horace's epistle can make an even more biting comment on the conscious disengagement from politics practised by Vindex. Statius may claim that Vindex's critical faculties are second to none, but he does so in terms that leave us wondering what exactly it is that we are supposed to admire about him. For a start, the catalogue of wonders to be found at Vindex's house reads like a standard roll-call of 'great' art, with all the big, obvious names represented—Myron, Praxiteles, Pheidias, Polycleitus, Apelles—yet amongst this unexceptionable list, Statius comments on wax statues that are so lifelike that they deceive the eye (4.6.21–22). These deceptive wax images foreshadow the treachery with which the Hercules statue finally betrays Alexander, but the very substance from which they are made also makes a difference.[38] Wax was on occasion used for art works in its own right (as against simply being part of the process of casting bronze), but it would be surprising, given the genealogical concerns of this poem, if Statius was unaware that his description might invoke the *imagines* (ancestor masks) traditionally displayed in the homes of wealthy and prominent families. This ties in neatly with the notion of genealogy/provenance, constructing Vindex as the ultimate self-made man, whose 'ancestors' are bought in by the crate. But that's not all; focusing specifically on the material itself, fluidity, erasability and transience are its characteristics, and its role as a writing surface makes it particularly evocative here. These deceptive wax images, like words written on wax, can melt or be scratched out on successive occasions, reformed and refashioned into something new. In this way, Statius' poem operates not just as a pretty and complimentary occasional piece, but within its generic parameters it also underscores the transience of stories, of history and reputation, and the way in which successive generations rewrite and reconfigure each layer of the past.

Africa Dreaming. . .

Boundaries (and their transgression) are at the heart of all stories of Alexander, but within these broad limits lie an intriguing subset. The final three passages of this chapter explore Rome's often elegiac and always larger than life bogeyman Hannibal, Alexander's equally doomed alter ego. Conceptually, these texts tell a story whereby Hannibal's Carthage and Alexander's Macedon are fused in the mythic landscape that maps out Roman fascination with an exotic and mysterious African never-never land.

READING 4.8
JUVENAL,
Satires 10.
133–73

Spoils of war—a breastplate fixed as a trophy
to a bare trunk, a cheek piece hanging from smashed
    helmet
135 a yoke broken off from a chariot's shaft, a pennanted
    prow
of a conquered trireme, a dispirited prisoner atop an
    arch—
these are believed to be the greatest assets for
    mankind. For these
things a general, whether Greek, Roman or foreign,
    rouses himself

to excitement, considering that these justify the
    danger and
140 struggle: so much the greater is the thirst for renown
    rather than
virtue. For who embraces virtue
if you take away the rewards? Still, at times, the
    desire of a few men for glory
and for praise, and titles to be carved into the stones
    that guard their ashes, has destroyed countries,
145 stones which the destructive force of the barren fig-
    tree succeeds in shattering;
since even to sepulchres themselves, an allotted span
    is given.
Weigh Hannibal up: how many pounds will you find
    in that mighty
commander? This is the man whom Africa can't
    contain, Africa,
pounded by the Moorish ocean and stretching out
    from the steaming Nile
150 as far as the Ethiopian peoples and their alien
    elephants.
Spain is added to his empire, he traverses the
Pyrenees. Then nature sets both Alps and snow
    against him:
he splits the rocks and shatters the mountains using
    vinegar.
Now he holds Italy in his palm, yet still he pushes
    ahead, pressing his march onwards.
155 'Nothing is gained,' he declares, 'if with my Punic
    troops I have not smashed
the gates and raised our banner in the heart of the
    Subura!'
O what a sight and what a fitting image:
the Gaetulian beast carrying the one-eyed
    commander!
So how does it end? O the glory of it! As we all
    know, that same man
160 is beaten and flees, headlong, into exile; there, as a
    great
and surprising client, he sits in the palace of the king,
until it pleases the Bithynian despot to awaken.
What shall make an end to that spirit, which once
    threw all human affairs into turmoil,
will be neither swords nor stones nor spears, but that

165 champion of Cannae, that avenger of so much
      bloodshed—
    a ring. Go, madman, and race across the cruel Alps
    only so that you may entertain young boys and end
      up as a topic for declamation!
    Just one world is not enough for the Pellan youth,
    miserable, he rages against the narrow limits of the
      world
170 as though confined on Gyara's rocks or tiny Seriphos.
    Yet when he enters the city fortified by its potters,
    he must rest content with a coffin. Only death makes
      plain
    how trifling human bodies really are.

          bellorum exuuiae, truncis adfixa tropaeis
          lorica et fracta de casside buccula pendens
135 et curtum temone iugum uictaeque triremis
      aplustre et summo tristis captiuos in arcu
      humanis maiora bonis creduntur. Ad hoc se
      Romanus Graiusque et barbarus induperator
      erexit, causas discriminis atque laboris
140 inde habuit: tanto maior famae sitis est quam
      uirtutis. Quis enim uirtutem amplectitur ipsam,
      praemia si tollas? Patriam tamen obruit olim
      gloria paucorum et laudis titulique cupido
      haesuri saxis cinerum custodibus, ad quae
145 discutienda ualent sterilis mala robora fici,
      quandoquidem data sunt ipsis quoque fata sepulcris.
      Expende Hannibalem: quot libras in duce summo
      inuenies? Hic est quem non capit Africa Mauro
      percussa oceano Niloque admota tepenti
150 rursus ad Aethiopum populos aliosque elephantos.
      Additur imperiis Hispania, Pyrenaeum
      transilit. Opposuit natura Alpemque niuemque:
      diducit scopulos et montem rumpit aceto.
      Iam tenet Italiam, tamen ultra pergere tendit.
155 'Acti' inquit 'nihil est, nisi Poeno milite portas
      frangimus et media uexillum pono Subura.'
      O qualis facies et quali digna tabella,
      cum Gaetula ducem portaret belua luscum!
      Exitus ergo quis est? O gloria! Vincitur idem
160 nempe et in exilium praeceps fugit atque ibi magnus
      mirandusque cliens sedet ad praetoria regis,
      donec Bithyno libeat uigilare tyranno.
      Finem animae, quae res humanas miscuit olim,
      non gladii, non saxa dabunt nec tela, sed ille

165 Cannarum uindex et tanti sanguinis ultor
    anulus. I, demens, et saeuas curre per Alpes
    ut pueris placeas et declamatio fias.
    Unus Pellaeo iuueni non sufficit orbis,
    aestuat infelix angusto limite mundi
170 ut Gyarae clausus scopulis paruaque Seripho;
    cum tamen a figulis munitam intrauerit urbem,
    sarcophago contentus erit. Mors sola fatetur
    quantula sint hominum corpuscula.

Juvenal's irony (cutting Alexander down to size with the smallest
possible geographical signifier 'a Pellaean. . .' [168]) is reminiscent of
Lucan's Alexander, but this reimagination also offers us a re-take on
Lucan's Caesar (and Statius' Lucan).[39] Where Caesar was the man
'whom the whole Roman world fails to suffice' (10.456), Juvenal's
Alexander 'rages against the narrow limits of the world'. This theme
provides a consistent thread throughout Roman usage of Alexander,
from the late Republican rhetorical acrobatics reimagined by the elder
Seneca, through to the younger Seneca's investigation into the definition and limits of power and onwards.[40] But there is a lot more at
stake here than one author picking up on a hackneyed and stereotypical theme, and going through the well-trodden satirical motions.
This use of Alexander as a comparative for Hannibal takes us back to
some of the issues raised by Livy that are so central to our understanding of what the principate is, and is becoming. The huge defeat
inflicted on Rome at the Battle of Cannae scarred the Roman psyche
in a way that was still reverberating centuries later. The Punic wars
themselves, as discussed in Chapter 1, triggered a flowering of historical epic, interweaving Roman and Greek myth into an aetiology for
the inevitability of this clash between the two great Mediterranean
empires, one apparently at its peak, the other rising. With Livy's
iconic treatment of Hannibal's seemingly inexorable advance and then
defeat, and Virgil's canonization of the fate that brought Rome and
Carthage into a violent clash, Hannibal's place as the evil genius of
Roman history was secure. But it remains difficult to decide where
Alexander intersects with this nexus.

The earliest reference to Alexander's potential as a threat to Rome
comes from Livy, in other words relatively late. But as discussed in
Chapter 2, the positioning of Livy's excursus provides us with a plausi-
ble link to Hannibal, which would make sense of the echoes between
Lucan, Silius Italicus and Juvenal. If so, then what we have is
Alexander the Great being juxtaposed with his alter ego Pyrrhus of
Epirus, who allied himself with Hannibal and, abortively, attacked

Italy. This suggests a strong associative connexion between Hannibal and Alexander, and specifically a threat that almost, but does not quite succeed; it sets up a dynamic whereby the speed and surprise tactics of Hannibal in crossing the Alps, and the strangeness of his war elephants (along with their ultimate failure) become inextricably bound up in Alexander, and a more generalized topos whereby threats to Rome come from the 'East'.[41] So if it is possible for Alexander to morph into Hannibal, and vice versa, we can read this whole extract as being intimately concerned with both, drawing a relationship between Alexander and Rome through Hannibal, and building on the narrative connexions already set up by Livy, but where does Caesar fit in?

Juvenal's compression of Hannibal's war against Rome keeps silent on his fatal hesitation, nor does it articulate that it was his hesitation, his hanging back from taking Rome when he had the opportunity, that allowed Rome the chance to regroup and eventually to defeat him. Instead, implicit within this story is a sense of blazing compulsion and onward racing towards an inevitable end that becomes explicit only once, at line 166. Perhaps the sense of inevitability is a function of the centrality of this story to Roman history—Hannibal must have been great, even to have teetered on the brink of conquering Rome, but his momentum must also have been impelling him headlong towards self-destruction. But Juvenal's language, and the allusive way in which he recounts the story, suggest that Hannibal's speed is meant to be noted. As we race through the gasping momentum of the catalogue of names that signify his conquests and his destruction (*rumpit*) of the mountains, still the very allusiveness emphasizes that it is not until he is on the cusp of taking Italy that anything significant has been achieved ('*iam tenet Italiam*'—suddenly the narrative becomes more descriptive) and we get a piece of direct speech from Hannibal. His speedy onslaught halted, his destruction is inevitable. Cannae itself is displaced from history, and mentioned only after Hannibal's ignominious fate has been related. Then Juvenal rewrites his almost miraculous dash across the Alps as an ironic order to a madman that he should race across the cruel Alps only to end up as a children's story, and a subject for declamation, and material for Juvenal's parody-factory. Juvenal is not just parodying declamation; he is writing a parody-declamation, recycling the rhetorical clichés and caricatures that provide an interpretative generic framework.

If we map this back onto Lucan's Caesar, we find that his famous *celeritas bellandi* and its destructive effects offer an important model for what Juvenal is doing. After all, it surely cannot be coincidence that in the lines dealing with Hannibal's fate (*'vincitur . . . tyranno'* 159–162) Juvenal chooses to emphasize *magnus* (end line, juxtaposed with *'mirandusque cliens'*) *regis* and *tyranno* (the three line ends). Furthermore, the three verbs associated with Hannibal (*uincitur, fugit,* and *sedet*) focus on his defeat, flight and final grind to a halt, where he must hang around waiting on the pleasure of a drowsing king of Bithynia. This last, the *'libeat uigilare'* used to define the relationship between the two men, focuses our attention on Hannibal's loss of status. He no longer has a public role or military power, and is forced to attend upon a king's whim. But there may be more going on than this, an added layer that cements his relationship with Caesar. What we may be seeing is a sly reference to some of the more scurrilous stories circulating about Caesar's sexuality and early youth, and specifically his time at the court of King Nicomedes of Bithynia. Accusations of effeminacy and passive homosexuality centring on the idea of young Caesar as the sexual plaything of an eastern potentate were common currency, and it is almost impossible that these connexions would not have been prompted by this passage.[42] If all this seems to be taking us rather far from Alexander, then this is the moment for tying up some of the trailing ends. Hannibal, from Africa and therefore already tainted with Alexander's negative traits, almost takes Rome, but is forced to flee east, where he degenerates and grows soft. Bithynia, the narrative locus for his downfall (interestingly, Juvenal downplays Rome's military defeat of Hannibal), would later be a site for Caesar's orientalization, and Caesar functions teleologically both as successor and forerunner to this Hannibal. Whereas Lucan pairs Caesar and Alexander explicitly, with Pompey and Cato functioning as additional adjuncts to the sinews that bind Alexander into all Roman stories of power, here the explicit comparison is with Hannibal. Both men are uncontainable, yet both, and particularly Alexander, are ultimately constrained by the limits of their mortality. This is a defiantly anti-mystical conceptualization of Alexander, but it is also striking in the syncretism that it makes available for successive different experiences of Africa. All these experiences, as I discuss in Chapter 5, ultimately need to be read in terms of the relationship between Antony and Cleopatra, and the epoch-making battle of Actium that set it firmly within the Roman historical consciousness.

If we look backwards to Lucan's version of Alexander in Africa, his Cato in the desert, and also read in Silius Italicus' epic narrative of Hannibal's conflict with Rome (passage 4.10), then we see the development of a Roman fixation on Egypt that allows 'Egypt' to become the conquered other, a stage where Roman identity can be played out.

READING 4.9
LUCAN,
Civil War
10.272–283

Alexander, the most exalted of kings, envied the Nile
which Memphis worships, and he sent a chosen band
        out through
the furthest reaches of Ethiopia, where they were
        stopped by the blazing
275 zone of the scorched heavens. There they saw the
        steaming Nile.
Sesostris came west to the furthest limits of the world
and powered his Pharaonic chariot with the bowed
        necks of kings;
but he drank of your rivers—the Rhone and the Po—
        before
he drank from the source of the Nile. Crazy
        Cambyses penetrated
280 the east as far as the land of the long-lived people;
then the banquets ran out and he feasted on his own
        slaughtered men,
and returned, O Nile, with no knowledge of you.
        Not even untrustworthy legend
has dared to speak of your source.

Summus Alexander regum, quem Memphis adorat,
inuidit Nilo, misitque per ultima terrae
Aethiopum lectos: illos rubicunda perusti
275 zona poli tenuit; Nilum uidere calentem.
Venit ad occasus mundique extrema Sesostris
et Pharios currus regum ceruicibus egit;
ante tamen uestros amnes, Rhodanumque Padumque,
quam Nilum de fonte bibit. Vaesanus in ortus
280 Cambyses longi populos peruenit ad aeui,
defectusque epulis et pastus caede suorum
ignoto te, Nile, redit. Non fabula mendax
ausa loqui de fonte tuo est.

Lucan emphasizes Alexander's desire to know the source of the Nile,
whilst also introducing the theme of deification. These topics continued
to tempt emperors, but are particularly relevant to the Egyptism pro-
fessed by Nero after CE 60, which menaced the stability of the Empire
much as Antony's had done until Actium.[43] The search for the Nile's
source was to prove unsuccessful for Alexander, but Lucan edits this
from his version of events (cf. passage 3.9 and Lucan *BC* 10.40). For
Lucan, Alexander's exploratory bug is a lone positive characteristic,
Caesar would like to emulate his questing spirit, but his lack of
hunger for the unknown (mirrored, perhaps, in his concentration on

victory over his homeland, while Alexander ranges far and wide) holds him back. There is a connexion here between Alexander's geographical (and military) exploits and his desire to engage with the 'other' of divinity at Ammon,[44] and significantly, Lucan's Cato backs away from the questioning, exploratory Alexander image, turning down the chance to hear his destiny at the temple of Ammon.[45] Thinking about Alexander's quest for acknowledgement as the son of Jupiter might seem to demand inclusion in visions of Alexander's excess and mental instability, but there are at least two reasons why this topos is less explicitly criticized than we could expect. We have already seen that Curtius was scathing less about the will to be honoured as divine than about what he portrays as Alexander's desire to control his subjects' belief-system. Intellectual and moral freedom is at issue, rather than the rights or wrongs of ruler-deification. And this pinpoints a key issue for the early development of the Principate, a species of doublethink that allowed for the construction of a revised republicanism which could accommodate both a discourse of collective power *and* individual authority. Once the outward forms were preserved and stability maintained, that was enough and there appears to have been a tolerance of intellectual subversion based on an understanding that myth and belief are impossible to fix without atrophy setting in.[46]

READING 4.10 SILIUS ITALICUS, Punica 13.762–776

After this the priestess, pointing to a young man,
    spoke thus:
'This is that man who wandered the world as a
    conqueror,
bearing his standards in every direction. This is he
    who forged a way through Bactra and the Dahae,
765 who drank from the Ganges, and with Pellaean
    bridge bound up
the Niphates; he whose eponymous walls stand on
    the sacred Nile.'
So the son of Aeneas began: 'O true-born son of
    Libyan
Ammon, since your undisputed glory eclipses that of
    all other commanders and my own heart burns
770 with desire for the same things, tell me the path you
    followed that led you to your proud
glory and the highest pinacle of renown.'
He answered in this way: 'Hesitation and ingenuity
    bring dishonour in warfare.
With audacity you will win wars. Sluggish bravery
    scarcely ever of itself

overcomes strategy. When you have great deeds to be
   done
775 make haste to do them: black death overhangs your
   every act.'
Having spoken thus, he departed.

Post haec ostendens iuuenem sic uirgo profatur:
'Hic ille est, tellure uagus qui uictor in omni
cursu signa tulit, cui peruia Bactra Dahaeque,
765 qui Gangen bibit et Pellaeo ponte Niphaten
astrinxit, cui stant sacro sua moenia Nilo.'
incipit Aeneades: 'Libyci certissima proles
Hammonis, quando exuperat tua gloria cunctos
indubitata duces similique cupidine rerum
770 pectora nostra calent, quae te uia, fare, superbum
ad decus et summas laudum perduxerit arces.'
ille sub haec: 'Turpis lenti sollertia Martis.
Audendo bella expedias. Pigra extulit artis
haud umquam sese uirtus. Tu magna gerendi
775 praecipita tempus: mors atra impendet agenti.'
Haec effatus abit.

This extract relocates us in the republican heartland of the Punic
Wars, but what is it doing here? If we are thinking about liminality,
then here at the end of these text-focused chapters it is as well to
return to one of the key enticements of Alexander that I signalled
in the Introduction: the impact of potentiality on posthumous fame.
Alexander died young, sealing his mythic status and ironically, guar-
anteeing his immortality. The constant sense of geo-temporal restraint
that colours so much of Alexander's reception is a function of his
limitless availability. Because he was forced to accept a limit to his
eastward campaign, he turned for home. Because he turned back, he
died. Because he died, he gained a plasticity that would ultimately
result in his credibility as a cast member of Silius' neo-Virgilian, post-
Homeric underworld. Livy's canonization of a Scipionic Alexander
initiates a loop that Silius closes in this epic poem. Returning to the
themes that kick-started Roman literary production, Silius asserts
Alexander's centrality to Scipio's quest for (Roman) glory, but he
denies him the ability to communicate freely. Alexander is still the
young man, debarred from maturity and trapped in an endless phase
of reckless youth, offering advice that rings hollow in its gnomic
brevity and Alexander's own impotence. The ultimate limitation, as
Cicero understood when writing to Lucceius (passage 4.2) is that

imposed by the authors who construct your posterity, and with Silius, Alexander becomes a pathetic and rootless figure, a shadow to be invoked at will.

Silius' redrawing of Alexander suggests a gradual easing of the anxieties associated with his reinvention. He retains his cultural interest but this text suggests that his political unruliness has begun to be tamed. Alexander may not have been erased by death, but he has been circumscribed by the sheer familiarity and sense of *déjà vu* that Roman audiences must have experienced on hearing his name. By the time Silius came to write *his* Alexander into Roman history it was *almost* 'safe' to present him as a neutered and strangely pathetic figure. Returning to Livy (passage 2.1), when limitations of any kind are imposed upon a king it is the semiotic tension between omnipotence and *termini* that make this act so ideologically charged. The king's potential *imperium sine fine* has been denied by the fixed boundaries to the world, and then to life. Alexander had to die *because* he was great, when greatness is defined against limits that have to be transgressed; without the limits, greatness is unquantifiable and therefore impossible. Parameters for Alexander are among the most debated aspects of his fame; no wonder that the retreat from 'the Ocean' is problematic for the posthumous tradition—the transgressor ought not retreat. Seneca discusses terms of geographical conquest (*de Ben.* 7.2.5–3.1 passage 3.5), proposing that Alexander could never have stopped conquering, because anything that was conquerable became valueless, lost in the vastness of his exploits.[47] Hence he had to plunge on into boundless, unknown territories, because the more he had the greater his need became. Seneca suggests that this vice is common to all those who are goaded on (*irritauit*) by the gifts of fortune.[48] These examples strengthen the idea of Alexander as a functional character with whom the impossible or unthinkable can be debated in politically unthreatening terms,[49] and they emphasize the nagging problem of limits that dogged the early years of the Principate: what kind of power was a limitless power, and how could it coexist with traditional modes of behaviour, and what kind of empire exists only to swamp everything that had once given it shape?

5. **Charles Le Brun, *The Battle of Arbela* (1668)** Although Alexander dazzles beneath his hovering eagle, Darius de-centred and high above the *melée*, is locked into the action through the eye-contact that appears to unite the two kings. The twisted muscles and distorted postures of men and horses further highlight the pool of light and space that surrounds Alexander, whose own pose is uncomplicated.

5

Autocracy—The Roman Alexander Complex

TRANIO: 'They say the great Alexander and Agathocles
            were a pair who did mighty big things: how about
                myself for a third,
            given the immortal deeds I'm doing single handed?'

            'Alexandrum magnum atque Agathoclem aiunt maximas
            duo res gessisse: quid mihi fiet tertio,
            qui solus facio facinora immortalia?'[1]

                            (Plautus, *Mostellaria* 775–77)

The composite Alexander that we have seen emerging over the past three chapters provides an impression of how he could be appropriated to Roman political theorizing. But it also offers an ever-lengthening list of derivative leadership figures, associated (by themselves or by others) with a general consciousness of Alexander. What I am suggesting in this chapter is that we return to the Livian model set up in Chapter 2, and think about how his version of Roman history, as being populated by a set of super-Alexanders, becomes a normative model for Roman leadership, focusing on the generalissimos and autocrats themselves.

With this in mind, we might still speculate as to the extent that Livy was reflecting a cultural perception that already located Alexander at the heart of Roman political ideology. Given the centrality of Alexander to Cicero's engagement with Caesar, and indeed his canonical status as a topic for trainee Roman orators, he becomes an extremely attractive marker for ongoing political redefinition during the first centuries BCE and CE. There is a mutuality, indeed an almost parasitic relationship between Alexander and the development of a Roman discourse of empire, which involves us in thinking about how these Roman super-heroes are bound together by their connexion to Alexander.

The reception of these figures—we might almost call them characters in an ongoing drama—provides a tradition of engagement with Alexander's image that could be revitalized and developed across successive generations. Despite the brush with failure encapsulated in Pompey's overt *aemulatio*, the name and reputation denoted by 'Alexander' retained enough flexibility to continue to shift between positive and negative assessments.[2] As we have seen in a succession of authors from Cicero to Juvenal, spanning over 150 years, the use of a name (and its omission) can encapsulate a variety of intentions and ideological contexts.[3] There is, however, one defining factor for all Roman Alexanders: power—whether the search for power, its retention, or its increase. And this power is linked to popularity and image-control as political tools in their own right, as much as it is to military success.

It is hardly surprising that 'Great deeds' (whether duelling or single-combat in battle) became unavailable to Roman emperors, who were left only with the more nebulous attribute of greatness for greatness's sake, much like today's cannibalistic concern with self-perpetuating 'celebrity'. This dynamic is one that mirrors some of the problems that we have with Alexander. We only ever see Alexander winning an empire; just as it looks as if he may have to start consolidating, governing and planning for the future, he conveniently dies. From Augustus through to Nero no Roman emperor actually leads his troops into battle, either to win the right to rule or to increase the size of the Empire. Within a culture that still defined itself through imperialism and military supremacy, the development of an increasingly incestuous and centralized court bureaucracy demanded an ever-closer relationship between Rome and emperor. Taking control of Rome itself had been vital to the successes of Caesar and Augustus, and loss of Rome, underestimation of its tactical, political significance had put an end to Pompey and Antony much as banishment from Rome had earlier marked the end of Scipio. The negative propaganda that blankets our knowledge of Nero makes it difficult to decide how strategic his attempts to breathe new life into dreams of Parthian conquest really were, but as the fate of his general, Corbulo, makes clear, sending out a plenipotentiary only exacerbates the problem. In Book 9 of his history, Livy explores the dynamics of group and individual leadership, trying to turn this to Rome's conglomerate advantage, and illustrating the tension that exists between the emperor and a potential successful rival when solitary endeavour, even on the *princeps*' part, becomes inappropriate. The validity of fears arising from this tension become concrete with the confusion surrounding the death of Nero, and the succession of military coups that followed. As in previous chapters, I shall take a thematic approach, looking first of all at style of command, then thinking about how going east functions in Roman politics, and finally discussing military success. Informing all three sections is a concern with Alexander's existence in a 'Roman consciousness', beyond the separate recorded instances (and his congeniality to the Julio-Claudians in particular).[4] Over and above this, as a persisting context, lies Roman ambivalence to Greek power figures and towards a nebulous orientalizing threat from the Greek East and Asia.[5] These tensions, set up by the eventual integration of the Hellenistic world into the Roman Empire, are reflected in the focus and fusion of Roman Alexanders, and the lack of ultimate oriental success that attends their endeavours.[6]

Style of Command

To compare someone to Alexander can have a range of implications. It may be impossible to reconstruct their full force, but what remains is the symbolic importance attached to Alexander's image in association with figures of contemporary power, eventually centred on the emperor and his family.[7] Judgements on Alexander by Roman authors can imply that a literary 'refraction' of the Roman internal political situation is taking place. Emphasis on *limits* for Alexander and his dominion may encourage not a pacifist stance, but one which engages with the Roman debate heralded by Augustus' 'limits', and counterpoints the possibility of a limitless Orient for conquest in Alexander's mould.[8] Limits to power are important not just in the physical context of a geographical empire, but also in the idea of command created by a leader whose power steps outside previously accepted delimitation. As the texts discussed in the previous three chapters make clear, there is no single, monolithic and internally consistent 'Roman Alexander'; instead, what we find is that the vitality of 'Alexander' is in his fluidity and flexibility, in the multiplicity of potential ways of reading more into his story. This polyvalence is exemplified in the shifting patterns of use of Alexander from the late Republic to the early Empire, which is why I have split this into a series of linked discussions that explore how clemency, image-making, dynasticism and deification dominate and control our reading of Alexander's autocracy.

Alexander and Pre-Augustan Rome

Scipio, Pompey, Caesar, Antony: the generalissimos of the late Republic offer a procession of potential Alexanders and these four characters provide the focal points for this section.[9] Scipio, the earliest of the big Roman names linked to Alexander, shares the epithet *inuictus* (unconquered) with Pompey. This tag was also applied to Alexander and Hercules, and to Lucan's Cato (Lucan *BC* 9.18), fitting in with a greater nexus of associations tying Alexander separately to Cato and Caesar; but as quickly becomes clear, there is nothing straightforward about the comparisons or connexions.[10] For a start, we have no contemporary texts chronicling links between Alexander and our earliest Roman model, Scipio, and this means that not only can we not assume that the connexion was commonplace during his lifetime, we do not know to what extent, if any, he may have encouraged or instigated the comparison himself. This can be a recurring problem for all our Roman Alexanders to a greater or lesser extent, but only if we allow it to be one. What I have been arguing throughout this book is that rather than becoming obsessed with historical recovery, we ought instead to be focusing on the texts that provide us with our information, thinking about how and why these authors have chosen to tell particular stories in particular ways at any given time. In fact, Scipio offers an excellent example of how particular topoi gain a life of their own, attaching themselves to different Roman figures depending on context.

Livy tells a story of a meeting between Scipio Africanus and Hannibal, which seems to provide a direct echo of a similar story told by Cicero. In Cicero's version, however, the Roman commander is Lucullus rather than Scipio, and the foreign enemy is Mithridates, not Hannibal. Written earlier than Livy's history, Cicero's story is also set in the more recent past, challenging its audience to evaluate how a comparison of this nature plunges the 'historical' Alexander into the immediacy of the 'present' eastern struggle. Cicero's *Academica* tells how Lucullus' magnificent factual memory (2.2) and his natural talent forced Mithridates to admit him better than any storybook general. In this scenario, Mithridates ranks second only to Alexander, who is himself then outclassed by Lucullus. Lucullus being a good Roman citizen, is instantly set apart from the kings in this story, both of whom, ironically, he supersedes. Cicero presents us with a Mithridates who is the greatest king since Alexander, so in Mithridates we find that the modern Roman 'really' can now defeat a king who could well stand as yet another version of the Macedonian; citizen beats king.

The political comparison that remains implicit in Cicero's version is available to Livy, and as we read in Chapter 2, Livy devotes a whole excursus to developing the contrast between republic and monarchy, but twenty-six books further on from that excursus Livy's reinvigoration of Cicero's story continues an ongoing exploration of this theme. During Livy's account of this fantasy summit meeting, an account which surely demands that we read in it a dialogic reassessment of Cicero's anecdote, Scipio takes the opportunity to ask Hannibal for his greatest all-time military commander. Hannibal's reply places Alexander first (stressing his exploration beyond the bounds of human knowledge), with Pyrrhus and himself second and third.[11] Scipio 'laughingly' asks where Hannibal would have positioned himself had he actually defeated Rome, and the Carthaginian general's reply offers a carefully shaded evaluation of Roman interest in Alexander's military status as a comparative. He states that in those circumstances, he would have placed himself before Alexander and all other commanders (Livy 35.14.11). The East is the realm of the Alexander imitator, and in these terms Livy shows how even the foreigners against whom the Macedonian had such success consider the 'great' Roman commander a worthier enemy than Alexander. After all, in Carthage, Rome and Alexander shared a foe, as well as sharing dreams of empire, whilst as we have seen, Hannibal himself is saturated with Alexandrian overtones.

Lucan makes Alexander a *doppelgänger* for Caesar, a highly charged, negative political figure, but is Caesar portrayed as an equivalent (but Roman) Alexander, or as a Roman with the negative traits of an Alexander? Does Lucan assimilate Alexander into his version of Roman history or does he remain outside it? And finally, is there an evaluative sense: is there some judgement as to whether Caesar or Alexander is 'worse'? Military success defines the rights and wrongs of Lucan's Caesar, but it is military success in which such close identification exists between cause and leader that the basis for this sort of rule is itself challenged. Alexander likewise provides an example of the unification of man and cause, and the dark and depressing picture of his aftermath tolls a note of doom for the consequences of Caesar's victory. The barren tomb, not the living city of Alexandria, interests Caesar, and this sterility is what *his* world leads to.[12] Caesar's predilection for mythology and self-association with Troy and Venus through Aeneas is an important strand in the poem as a whole. This characteristic ties together Achilles, Dionysus, Hercules and Alexander, providing a point of intersection with Caesar's ambitions. In quick succession Caesar visits Troy (in Alexander's footsteps), is presented with Pompey's head, and then determines to make for no other site in

Alexandria than the Macedonian's tomb.[13] In contrast, Lucan edits
out Pompey's glorious Alexander-potential; his poetic character seeks
only popularity, comfort and calm, lacking the demonic energy allotted to Caesar and the puritanical mania that Cato acquires. In the
shadows of advancing age with which Lucan swathes him, his absence
from military duties has robbed him of that one attribute that guar-
anteed his fame and success: his military mastery.[14]

A comparison between Caesar and Alexander is at once so obvious
as to need no explanation, and also surprisingly difficult to analyse.[15]
The incident at Gades when Caesar admired a statue of Alexander at
the temple of Hercules and supposedly mourned his own puny achievements at a similar age, is apparently an obvious example of self-comparison.[16] Strabo, writing under Augustus, tells us that Caesar was an
Alexandrophile (φιλαλέξανδρος), and recreated Alexander's ceremonies at Troy when he visited the site; Lucan takes up this theme in
his epic of civil war. Caesar's unfulfilled eastern plans suggest that his
ambitions were leading him towards the realm where imitation/
emulation of Alexander becomes paramount, and comparison likely.[17]
The Ciceronian letters (discussed in Chapter 3) concerning ability to
receive advice willingly and wisely, also indicate contemporary links.
Even Alexander's attempts to enforce *proskynesis* have a rhetorical
resonance in Caesar's efforts to secure an offer of the kingship.[18]
Whilst we might initially wonder at Caesar growing into Pompey's
Alexander imitation, perhaps believing (as some do) that Pompey had
already contaminated the comparison beyond redemption with his
'excessive' imitation and dazzling military successes, coupled with
vanity and lack of political acumen, I suggest an alternative progression. In the post-Pharsalus world, Pompey's unsuccessful Alexandrianism may have seemed to die with him: he had tried to go down that
route and failed. With Pompey dead, Caesar could take tentative steps
towards manifesting *himself* as the true heir of Alexander, exceeding
both model and previous emulators.[19]

Clementia: *The Power of Forgiveness*

Through his enemies, Lucan's Caesar gains a justification for his
actions: if his enemies accept the pardon that he offers then they are
also acknowledging his authority to grant pardons, and in a round-
about way, this means that the reciprocity engendered by the offering
and acceptance of clemency validates Caesar's right to rule.[20] *Clementia*
(clemency) becomes a major feature of the Augustan settlement, of the

re-ordering of the political sphere after Actium, and the public personae of future *principes*; that this element is also a major factor in the story of Alexander at Rome brings this behavioural pattern full-circle.[21] Leading figures in republican times gained praise by practising 'clemency' (e.g. Sallust, *The Conspiracy of Catiline* 54.2–4), and it was later integrated into the image-factory of the Principate.[22] We could argue that true *philanthropia-clementia* can only exist when the absolute power of the ruler allows him to stand above the capabilities of human institutions to punish him; in other words, without a figure of proto-imperial power—whether republican generalissimo or *princeps*—the concept would be redundant. This is not a new topic, and some of the same issues have already arisen in Chapter 2, looking at the power to accept or deny a petition. Here again, power is defined through a reciprocal relationship between ruler and subjects, each being defined by the other. But strangely enough, taking this analysis to its extreme, we end up with a situation whereby the ruler's identity depends more intrinsically upon his acceptance by his subjects than vice versa.[23] The ruler may have the power to punish, the power to give life or death to his people, but over-use of this power would leave him without any subjects to rule. 'Friends' or 'enemies', tyrannicides or power-mongers, one of the key features of those who plot against Caesar is that chief amongst them are men whom he has previously pardoned, and who have reason to be grateful for advancement under his clemency. If we go on to draw a comparison between records of Caesar's assassination and Alexander's death (not necessarily assassination, though rumours of foul play abound), again we find intimations of treachery. The unrest that Alexander's death sparked off implicates all his generals in the fragile hold he had on unity towards the end of his life. In his *History of Alexander*, Curtius presents these factors in the context of Alexander's increasing fears of treason, and his defeat by his own men at the mutiny of the Hyphasis when he was forced to turn homewards because nobody would accompany him further east.

These authorial emphases could figure in an argument that pressed Curtius' text into an analogy with Caesar's fate, but might it not also be the case that rather than Caesar slipping into the role of Roman Alexander, what we are actually seeing is a process whereby Alexander becomes successively Romanized? If this is the case, then what we have been witnessing all along is the development of a symbiotic relationship between Alexander and Rome, in which both undergo a transformation. Caesar's clemency towards his enemies picks up on a discourse that acknowledges and modulates the delicate—and ideally,

mutually beneficial—interplay between ruler and ruled, and all subsequent discussions of clemency are always informed by Caesar's
pardons and his betrayal. But if a connexion between Caesar and
Alexander based on a common association with the pardoning of
enemies seems too loose, we could return to Livy's Scipio for an earlier
example of how this theme can work (Livy 26.50). In his narrative of
the war against Hannibal, Livy recounts Scipio's treatment of the
family of Indibilis, a local chief, and the exceptionally beautiful fiancée
of another local chief, Allucius. He ordered that Indibilis' mother and
daughters be accorded the same dignity that would be offered to a
Roman matron and her family, whilst Allucius' fiancée was returned
to him, with the comment that she had been treated as carefully as if
she had been at home with her parents. The gold brought to Scipio by
her grateful parents was then given to Allucius by Scipio as a wedding
gift, who in turn went home singing the praises of the godlike young
warrior.[24] In Alexander's story, after the battle of Issus Darius' beautiful wife, their two daughters and son, and her mother, were all captured. In order to soothe their distress, Alexander announced that he
would be treating them as their status befitted, and when Alexander
visited them, all narratives agree that he ensured that they understood
that they were to be treated as queens and princesses.[25] Interestingly,
Arrian casts doubt on the story of Alexander's personal visit to Darius'
family (2.12.6–8), but does believe that he granted them royal honours.
This distances Alexander from the Scipionic echo, and it is difficult to
know why Arrian chose to doubt the personal contact between the
two groups. It may be a result of his tendency to make explicit distinctions between himself and other authors on the grounds of scholarly
methodology.[26] It may also be a function of his position as a Greek
living within the Roman Empire.

   Curtius and Arrian may be the two authors giving us the most
extended narratives of Alexander, but another author who recounts
this story in Latin provides a useful comparison. In Aulus Gellius'
Attic Nights we have a compendium of popular stories from the
second century CE, much later than the majority of the texts we have
been reading, but significant because it ties us back to the complex of
popular comparisons with Alexander accessed through the elder
Seneca's *suasoria*. It is unlikely that Gellius was writing in ignorance
of Livy's version, but it is not Livy that he cites (7.8.1–6). Instead, he
introduces this anecdote with the comment that a Greek author called
Apion 'the Quarrelsome' had written up the story of Alexander's treatment of Darius' wife as a testament to his magnificence. Without any
explanatory preamble, Gellius comments that this would naturally

suggest a comparison between the sexual restraint of Alexander and Scipio. The latter had looked over a beautiful girl taken prisoner at (New) Carthage, and then handed her over to her parents; Alexander had refused even to look upon Darius' wife. This, he says, seems to offer an excellent topic for a pair of declamations on the subject of Alexander and Scipio (7.8.4). But whilst Gellius thinks that these speechlets would be a wonderful idea, and (perhaps) the obvious response to Apion's story by any talented, idle orator, that is not what his readers are going to get from *him*. Instead, he will be telling us a story of Scipio that has been passed down through the 'historical' tradition ('*historia*' 7.8.5). Yet immediately he backtracks, telling us that he does not know whether or not the story is true, and now calls it '*fama*' (hearsay). According to Gellius, Scipio had a racy youth very different from the usual portrait of him as an extremely virtuous young man, and one Valerius Antias writes that far from giving the girl back unharmed to her father, in fact he kept her as his mistress (7.6.8).

The lack of justification for Scipio's appearance in this anecdote, the way in which his role as Roman Alexander is tacitly affirmed by the decision not to explain why this comparison should spring to mind, suggests that a tradition of introducing Alexander into comparisons even with Republican hero figures, is still alive and kicking. The comparison is straightforward enough to require no further contextualization. In fact, what we might think that Gellius is doing is presenting a somewhat shamefaced self-justification for producing another angle on such a hackneyed theme. In telling us that he is *not* going to perform another declamation on Alexander and Scipio, the inclusive first person plural of '*nos satis habebimus, quod ex historia est, id dicere*' ('we shall be satisfied with relating that which comes from history' 7.8.5) suggests that both he and his audience are interested in more concrete evidence, and then introduces his uncomplimentary variant on the tradition of Scipio's legendary chastity. This historical variant cuts through the ambiguity of Gellius' question as to which commander was the more praiseworthy. Is it better to remove oneself entirely from contaminative temptation, like Alexander, who did not even want Darius' wife to be touched by his gaze, or to face up to the temptation, like Scipio, and overcome it? Whilst we might have decided that Scipio's victory over temptation was the greater, the lone, contradictory voice of Valerius Antias, using language more familiar from erotic neoteric poetry, conjures up a portrait of Scipio that is directly—and anachronistically—at odds with our expectations:

I myself think that it was on account of these verses that
Valerius Antias was brought into opposition with all other
writers on Scipio's character, and came to write, contrary
to what we agreed above, that the captured girl was not
returned to her father but was kept hold of by Scipio, and
wrongfully possessed by him as an erotic plaything.

His ego uersibus credo adductum Valerium Antiatem aduersus ceteros
omnis scriptores de Scipionis moribus sensisse et eam puellam captiuam
non redditam patri scripsisse, contra quam nos supra diximus, sed
retentam a Scipione atque in *deliciis amoribus*que ab eo *usurpatam*.
(Aulus Gellius, N.A. 7.8.6)

The implications of '*in deliciis amoribusque*' could hardly be further
from the matrimonial assistance provided by Livy's Scipio, but even
the narrative context demonstrates a different slant. In Gellius' 'authorized' tradition, far from bringing about the happy reunion of local
worthy and his captured fiancée, Scipio is simply returning the girl to
her parents; she has no prior attachment. And in these terms we might
wonder whether the message being given out by Gellius is not rather
mixed. Certainly the anecdote seems to be all about valorizing sexual
continence, but Alexander's complete lack of sexual engagement, his
refusal even to allow Darius' wife to be caressed by his gaze, is part
of a larger picture.

We know that sex does not form a part of the composite Alexander
who has been transmitted to us, and that his excess and degeneration
are predicated upon a tradition of gradual 'orientalization' of his
power, drunkenness and emotional volatility. When Curtius tells the
story of Alexander and Darius' family he includes the episode of
Alexander's patience when Darius' mother misidentifies Hephaestion
for him, and immediately follows this with an authorial aside commenting that if this kind of moderation had continued to characterize
Alexander, then his fortune would have been all the greater (3.12.18).
None of the examples of Alexander's fall have anything to do with
sexuality; in fact, they are all connected with his relations with his
soldiers and his reinvention of the monarchy. This more 'canonical'
Alexander has no qualms about looking upon Darius' wife, perhaps
precisely because there was no popular tradition of him exercising
a predatory sexuality. Yet that Alexander's chastity remains noteworthy, and Scipio's also becomes an important function of his
imagery, suggests that there was something quirky, and perhaps
almost deviant, in their admirable restraint. In this context, Gellius'
closing word (*usurpatam*) takes on added significance. It could pro-

vide an implicit allusion to the reading that what we are *also* seeing is one tradition on Scipio apparently trying to *usurp* the dominant version, and this alternate history presents not just a different Scipio, but a differently genred, and sexualized figure. From history into verse, from chaste to sensuous.

Succession and Dynastic Ambitions

Ironically, one of the key moments in any reign is the transition from one ruler to another. If power is successfully transferred from parent to child, or at least to a nominated heir, then closure is complete. Republican Rome was no less concerned with family prestige and succession than Rome under the Principate. The key difference was that a group of families could legitimately hope to monopolize power between them, based upon a system of alliances and shared interests. It is for this reason that once he had managed to gain acceptance for his position, Augustus' next major task was to accustom the senatorial class, and Rome as a whole, to the idea of a seamless transfer of his power to his heir. But this concern with the transmission and retention of power within one family was already developing into an issue with Octavianic monopolization of Caesar's memory and assimilation of his increasingly mythic role into his own propaganda, and Sextus Pompey's cashing in on the mystique of his father. It is difficult to know the extent to which Caesar perceived himself as founding a ruling dynasty; his adoption of Octavian suggests that he was conscious of the need for an heir, but this strategy of adoption if no suitable son were living was a traditional method of acquiring an heir and consolidating alliances. What we do have for comparison, however, are two significant, and significantly later narratives dealing with Caesar, Alexander and posterity, and these two texts, Plutarch's *Lives* of Alexander and Caesar and Suetonius' *Julius Caesar*, are the focus of this section.

Extended biographies of Alexander have not been the focus of this study, and up to now I have only been referring to Plutarch in endnotes, but Plutarch's decision to pair Caesar with Alexander in his series of biographies of Greeks and Romans makes this a significant text for looking at the intersection between the two leaders. Plutarch's pairing of Alexander and Caesar would originally, according to the scheme for the *Lives* as a whole, have been linked by a comparative discussion dealing with similarities and differences between them and providing a rationale, or authorial gloss for Plutarch's narratives. The comparison is missing in this case, and perhaps it might have provided an explanation for a notable omission in Plutarch's treatment: both men die without defined programmes for succession, or even any emphasis on this element of the consolidation of power. A two-dimensional reading, taking Plutarch's comments on genre at the beginning of his *Alexander* at face value, could suggest that since he claims only to be interested in the illumination of character, the aftermath of a life has no concern for him. In fact, this is not the case. Another possible contributory factor could be that by Plutarch's time the concept of hereditary power was so well fixed in Roman politics that an awareness of the importance of dynasticism would go without saying. In fact, the turbulent years after Nero made it all the more evident that an emperor's duty was to ensure a smooth and peaceful transmission of power. One final, possibly additional explanation that we might consider draws upon Plutarch's own ambivalent position as Greek in a Roman world, a world where Roman colonialism and appropriation of Hellenism made definitions of Greekness—and there-fore Greek leadership and self-determination—particularly tricky. This could suggest that Plutarch ends his life of Alexander one chapter after Alexander's death, specifically in order to focus our attention on the void that followed him, emphasized by the fact that in that chapter (77) he describes a calculated, though delayed, retribution falling on those who could be implicated in treachery to the late Great. He focuses on the mayhem of civil war that more immediately tore the Empire, and on the propping up of the mentally feeble Arrhidaeus on the throne. He offers no suggestion of a possibility of a valid, viable successor except allusively, through the intertextual dialogue set up by the pairing with the *Caesar*. Similarly, of Plutarch's three chapters covering the aftermath of Caesar's death (*Caesar* 67–69), none offers any suggestion of dynastic concerns (the life ends with another ghostly visitation for Brutus, and his suicide in defeat). What this might suggest is that such a reading offers a fundamental if implicit parallel between the lives: both accounts conclude with death to those impli-cated in the murders of the 'heroes'; in both cases retribution is slow, and in both cases civil wars follow to determine the succession.

Alexander's heritage will be in his personal fame, and perhaps Caesar's posterity is similarly enshrined. Nevertheless, to take this at face value requires us to erase the troubled and stuttering pattern of succession of the first century BCE. By the time Plutarch was writing his *Parallel Lives*, the Julio-Claudians had been replaced first by a succession of stopgaps (the so-called year of the four emperors, 69 CE), then by the Flavians, who managed only two generations before being succeeded by the Ulpians. This central instability makes the negotiation of a coherent dynasty particularly important, and given Plutarch's decision to favour the tradition that Alexander was surrounded by treachery at his death, it is unlikely that this endgame would have gone unnoticed. From a Greek perspective, even that of a Romanized Greek, one lesson to be learned might well be that if Caesar's death finds echoes of Alexander's, then Greeks would be wise to be wary of the kinds of political behaviour that an increasingly Romanized Alexander was being drawn into. It might appear to be a good thing to have a Greek culture hero on a Roman pedestal, but if dissolution of identity and death were all that awaited, Greeks might do well to think twice. If even a watered-down version of this reading is accepted, then Plutarch is creating an extremely different focus from that suggested by Suetonius, who places Caesar at the head of a unitary group of 'Caesars', a group whose common denominator is the shared name. Julius Caesar becomes the first of a chronological succession; the father of an 'imperial house', rather than an inspirational maverick.[27] The difference in emphasis between the lives is immediately apparent; where Plutarch's opening links Caesar with his rival Pompey, and contextuality ties him to Alexander, Suetonius instead works to situate Caesar within a familial and social framework (*Iulius* 1, as the manuscript stands; the introductory paragraphs are missing).[28] This trend is reinforced in the closing chapters where it is first stressed that Caesar altered his will in favour of Octavian from Pompey (83), then that the comet which appeared shortly after his death did so on the first day of the Games given by his *successor* (*heres*) Augustus (88), and finally that his assassination was parricide. The senate would never meet on the Ides of March again, and his assassins all came to bad—and unnatural—ends (88–89). No suggestion of ensuing civil turmoil is given, save for Caesar's own prophecy that his life is the only guarantee of peace for Rome (86), perhaps alluding, in retrospect, to the message of the *Carmen Saeculare*.

Neither of these authors offers an explicit commentary on the nature of dynastic power, nevertheless their texts offer us a striking pair of implicit narratives. We may speculate on the possible influence of Trajan's exploits and Alexandrian comparisons on Plutarch's *Lives*, and we may wonder whether Trajan's focus on the ideology of the soldier-emperor coloured both Plutarch's Alexander and his Caesar. Perhaps they offer oblique commentaries on the perils and glories of overwhelming success? Perhaps a reading of Caesar's lack of eastern success would be subtly modified by Trajan's Parthian campaigns? Certainly Trajan's title of *Optimus* (CE 114) offers a gentle nudge towards Alexander's mere *Magnus*. Trajan's deathbed provision of an heir—the adoption of Hadrian, according to the official version— pushes our twenty-first century reading towards this comparison. Suetonius, who published his *Lives* early in Hadrian's Principate (CE 120), may well have been influenced by Hadrian's resemblance to Octavian in the pattern of succession. Hadrian's position as Trajan's great-nephew, and lately adopted son, begs us to recall the similarity with Octavian's relationship with Caesar. Renowned for his philhellenism, Hadrian was also an emperor who was forced into the position of conceding the abandonment of the untenable provinces conquered by Trajan (particularly Armenia, Assyria and Mesopotamia). His journeys throughout the provinces occupied half his Principate, and he oversaw a real political integration of Greek-speaking elites into the Empire. Whatever the extent to which Suetonius intended his audience to identify his work with contemporary and past political activity, it is inevitable that successive audiences would find political resonance in the activities of the emperors under which both Plutarch and Suetonius lived and worked.

Divinity

In the terms set up by Roman treatments of the Alexander-motif, an aspiration to divinity, coupled with enforced observance by subordinates, becomes central to the negative effects his despotism embodies. A *princeps* cannot remain a citizen-emperor, *primus inter pares*, if he is raised far above them by divine status. Roman sources stress an opposition between the *proskynesis* and adoration of the monarchy that Alexander demands, and a Macedonian desire for liberty. For the conservative senatorial group at Rome, Macedonian stalwartness in the face of demands for worship could provide a point of identification for Roman senatorial opposition within the story of Alexander.[29] Like the Macedonian nobles, the senators could oppose (unsuccessfully) the promotion of their ruler as (living) god, but for the divine aspirants themselves, his example is vital. Alexander's birth is associated in Roman references with the appearance of a star, and this motif is also reflected in the comet that was interpreted as marking the apotheosis of Caesar.[30] Returning briefly to Scipio, it has been argued that Ennius made an attempt (in the poem *Scipio*) to promote a myth of deification for Africanus, creating a pantheon of demi-gods for later Roman writers.[31] We might see in this an early intimation of deification for great Romans into which (ready-made) tradition Horace and Virgil could step when linking Augustus to this company.

Livy's description of Scipio characterizes the newly elected Spanish commander (211 BCE) as remarkable not only for his ability, but for his skill in self-representation and public display. Livy enforces a potential connexion with Alexander in this context, recounting the 'commonly circulated view' (either contrived or by chance) that Scipio was of divine race, which was made more plausible by his daily secluded visits to the Capitol temple and his public demeanour as if his actions were prompted by visions or the gods (26.19.3–6).[32] This gamesman-like attitude—and Livy's stress on the public nature of the behaviour—corresponds to similar characteristics in the Alexander-tradition, but it is almost impossible to disentangle the intricate network of allusion and memory that ensures its continuing vitality. The creation of a thematic Alexander-link in public perception is emphasized by what follows. The rumour is said by Livy to have revived the tale told of Alexander the Great, that his conception was the result of his mother's visitation by an immense serpent, demonstrating how the interactive potential of these myths continuously reinvigorates a potential dialogue between the older and the contemporary.[33]

Caesar's much vaunted descent from Venus is highlighted by Velleius with a description of Pompey and his greatness (passage 3.1; cf. 2.40.1–5). Velleius states that Caesar's claim was allowed by all, while his beauty, generosity and intellectual qualities, and greater than natural spirit, all gave him resemblance to Alexander at his best. Again divinity is an issue when working within an Alexandrian schema, and here once again we find that the Roman is an improved model.[34] In this case, Caesar's divine ancestry can parallel Alexander's claims to descent from Jupiter-Ammon, but whereas Alexander's claims to divinity tend to be mocked by Roman writers, Caesar's deification gets a serious treatment. Hardly surprising, given the political climate, but still requiring a capacity for doublethink that seems unlikely to have produced a seamless recuperative history. If claims to divinity are open to question in one case (and we must remember that Velleius is writing in the wake of Livy's doubts about Scipio), then all such claims are problematized. We might suggest that Velleius' reaffirmation of the truth of Caesar's deification is part of a programme of reclamation of a Roman right to transfiguration. This would place Suetonius' association of Augustus with 'Alexandrian' prodigies in a wider tradition of national self-assertion, for example the story of Octavian's conception as a result of a visit to his mother by Apollo in the guise of a serpent, which feeds into an ongoing rhetorical dialogue between the divine and the mortal. Similarly, Octavian was supposed to have been 'recognized at birth' as the future world-ruler; when his father Octavius consulted the priests of Father Liber about his son's destiny, the wine they poured over the altar rose up as a pillar of flame into the sky in a sign granted to none other than Alexander when sacrificing at that altar (Suetonius, *Aug.* 94).

What we find in this consideration of divinity is that when talking about (potential) early Roman Alexanders, divine explanations and justifications for their power and success are usually offered, and the role of omens is clearly important. Authors attempting to come to terms with the destiny of men of power can offer the connexion with Alexander either as a sobering reference, or as a glorification of the new Roman version. Potentially divine ancestry is a plus, and particularly relevant for our investigation, but we should be aware that a strong cultural association between Alexander and these kinds of legends must have existed for authors to have dropped them without explanation into their narratives. That the imperial cult should eventually have offered a solution to the problem of deification for subjects and rulers alike would no doubt have been part of a discourse that would eventually demand that Rome should improve on Alexander in all respects.

Uncharted Waters: Alexander in the Principate

It is a vast over-simplification, when Andrew Anderson writes that:

> The Roman empire was in essence the realization of the ideal of Alexander. The Romans knew well that they were his political and cultural heirs, even though they did not specifically say so.
>
> (1928:55)

Nevertheless, it may be a helpful opening premise. If 'the Romans' were so completely aware of their status, why need Alexander be mentioned at all? Will any comparison not appear laborious? On the other hand, the wealth of extant images and references is doubtless only the tip of an iceberg encompassing written and other reflections. Drawing on an observable pattern of Roman republican usage of Alexander, it is clear that the far-reaching changes to the state that the Principate entailed will significantly alter the kinds of models of power available (and acceptable) for imperial usage. Where once Alexander's attributes as commander and conqueror were paramount, the media war between Octavian and Antony in particular crystallized a highly polarized opposition in which Alexander came to represent the decadent, the un-Roman, and the dangerous. Yet his conquests could not entirely be overlooked in a world where less far-reaching conquests had to be represented as magnificent, and thus an uneasy truce seems to have developed. As a king (maybe even because a king), Alexander was a failure; as a general his success in its own terms was praiseworthy, but then he had never been faced with a western enemy: *he* only fought and conquered orientals. Under Augustus, Rome self-consciously turned its back on monarchy in favour of a 'restoration' of republican ideals, providing a compromise stabilized government, and avoiding the ostensible danger of tyranny. With this (in itself a simplification of a simplification) in mind, we can move on to a consideration of how and why Romans and emperors found in Alexander a useful comparative for negotiating the realities of imperial government.

Augustus is the first of the Roman Alexanders to leave a successful image in both military and political spheres, and ultimately, this may be his 'greatest' achievement. In the role of improved Alexander it becomes particularly appropriate for him to spare Alexandria on the grounds of its founder's fame, making a distinction between great monarch and mere rulers.[35] Claudius later had the features of two paintings of Alexander, triumphant, replaced with portraits of Augustus (Pliny, *NH* 35.93–94). Augustus' use of Alexander on his second seal ring, and the sequence of the seal images—sphinx, Alexander, then his own features—could be over-emphasized, but the progression from Alexander to Augustus as official model demonstrates one version of Augustus' conception of the progression of his own rule.[36] Opinions differ concerning Octavian/Augustus' 'official' appropriation of Alexander-imagery. We might argue that Actium is the pivotal point, after which Octavian relinquished dreams of universal monarchy, in exchange for the reality of realizable power as *princeps* in Rome (with Alexander as an admirable precursor rather than a subject for personal imitation).[37] Yet an alternative interpretation could suggest that Augustus' parallels with Alexander were a matter of political reality rather than chimerical dreams, particularly in the wake of Cicero's comparison of Octavian with Alexander.[38] Octavian's position as a potential Alexander echoes that of Caesar in Pompey's shadow; the difference is that while Caesar defeated Pompey/Alexander, he did not make use of the kind of anti-Alexander propaganda against Pompey that characterized Octavian's battle of words against Antony at Rome.

It might seem to be the case that the Roman world after 27 BCE would lose the need for an Alexandrian gloss. Augustus (rather than Octavian), secure in his power and in the increasing formalization of his role as *imperator*, was gradually developing other, more nation-alistic and overtly Roman ways of presenting his authority. We have already discovered the extreme malleability of Alexander as a model, capable of slipping in and out of political imagery as suits the con-ditions of the time, but this makes too little of the difficulties that must have been inherent in the shift from negative propaganda to assumption of an Alexander-role.[39] The demise of Pompey and the civil wars that tore the Republic apart mark not only the end of a transitional phase of government, they also bring about a redefinition of how Alexander comes to be used in political terms. Scipio and Pompey are shown imitating, and to some extent trying to *be* Alexander, but Caesar is shown seeking to outdo the Macedonian, outside the republican system.[40] This shift of identification, whereby Alexander becomes for a time the model of choice for self-seeking opponents of the status quo, temporarily puts his role as an imperial model on ice, but under Nero his imagery sugars Seneca's pill for his pupil, paving the way for the rehabilitation of his imagery after the Julio-Claudians.

Image and Identity: Velleius and Statius

(2) For the praetor Quintus Metellus, who on account of his valour received the name Macedonicus, defeated the Macedonians—under the leadership of a pretender to the throne who called himself Phillip—in an out-standing victory. He also vanquished the Achaeans, who were beginning to rebel against Roman rule, in a great battle.

(3) This is the Metellus Macedonicus who had built the portico which enclosed the two temples without inscrip-tions, the ones which are now surrounded by the portico of Octavia, and who brought from Macedonia that group of equestrian statues which face the front of the temples, and remain the greatest ornament of that spot even today.

(4) The story of the origin of this group is as follows: that Alexander the Great persuaded Lysippus—a sculptor

unparalleled at works of this sort—to make statues of those horsemen of his own squadron who had fallen at the river Granicus, and to place his own likeness amongst them.

(5) This same Metellus was the first Roman to erect a temple built of marble, which he placed amongst these monuments, which made him the foremost author of this kind of munificence, or perhaps we should say extravagance.

(2) Quippe Q. Metellus praetor, cui ex uirtute Macedonici nomen inditum erat, praeclara uictoria ipsum gentemque superauit et immani etiam Achaeos rebellare incipientes fudit acie. (3) Hic est Metellus Macedonicus qui porticus, quae fuerunt circumdatae duabus aedibus sine inscriptione positis, quae nunc Octauiae porticibus ambiuntur, fecerat, quique hanc turmam statuarum equestrium quae frontem aedium spectant, hodieque maximum ornamentum eius loci, ex Macedonia detulit. (4) Cuius turmae hanc causam referunt Magnum Alexandrum impetrasse a Lysippo, singulari talium auctore operum, ut eorum equitum, qui ex ipsius turma apud Granicum flumen ceciderant, expressa similitudine figurarum faceret statuas et ipsius quoque iis interponeret. (5) Hic idem primus omnium Romae aedem ex marmore in iis ipsis monumentis molitus uel magnificentiae uel luxuriae princeps fuit.

(Velleius Paterculus 1.11.2–5)

A comparison between equestrian statues of Domitian and of Caesar:

Let that horse give way, which, from opposite Dione's temple
85 holds sway over Caesar's Forum. That one which you, Lysippus, dared to
undertake for the Pellaean commander; not long after, it was Caesar's face
that it carried on its amazed back. Scarcely could your weary gaze
discover how far was the downward prospect necessary from this monarch to that!
Who would be so unsophisticated that he could deny, once he had seen both,
90 that the differences between the horses are matched by those between the rulers?

> Cedat equus Latiae qui contra templa Diones
> 85   Caesari stat sede fori; quem traderis ausus
>   Pellaeo, Lysippe, duci; mox Caesaris ora
>   mirata ceruice tulit: uix lumine fesso
>   explores quam longus in hunc despectus ab illo.
>   Quis rudis usque adeo qui non, ut uiderit ambos,
> 90   tantum dicat equos quantum distare regentis.

                                        (Statius, *Siluae* 1.1.84–90)

What we find in these two texts is an example of how closely
Alexander has been integrated into both intellectual and physical
topographies of Rome. A comparison between Caesar and Alexander
may have become (almost) straightforward, but as Livy's comparison
with Papirius Cursor suggests, other less obvious elements in this
allusive dialogue can also be drawn out. The unexpectedness of the
connexions foregrounded in these two texts focuses audience attention on the episodes in a way that might be elided by more readily
expected comparisons. So what is going on? For a start, *we* know that
Velleius will go on to compare Alexander unfavourably with Caesar,
giving Caesar all of Alexander's positive qualities, and none of his
negative ones. This passage deals with Roman history roughly a century
before Caesar's Dictatorship, and is set at the time when Rome was in
the process of completing the integration of the Hellenic world into
the Empire. Velleius describes the defeat of Achaea and Macedon (148
BCE) by Q. Caecilius Metellus Macedonicus, and continues with a
description of a group of equestrian statues brought back from
Macedon, and placed facing the two temples he had previously built
a portico around. The work is said to have been commissioned by
Alexander from Lysippus, and to have included his own likeness
among the cavalry who had fallen at the Granicus. So far, so clear:
Alexander's first great victory in the East is appropriated to the
Roman scheme, but also takes over the Roman site of its new
location, 'even now' providing the chief ornament to the place.[41] But
we can tighten the nexus of connexions binding Alexander to Rome
still further.

Over the past chapters I have been emphasizing the importance of
language and naming, stressing that it really does make a difference
when particular words and names are constantly, or even surprisingly
linked. Alexander's 'Great' got its first known Roman outing in the
play quoted at the beginning of this chapter, and Pompey's 'Great' is
its direct descendant, but there are other, more subtle variations, that
suggest themselves. The Roman tradition of adding a cognomen that

indicated a particular triumph to a successful commander's name may well have provided a home-grown rationale for the adoption of an Alexander-style *magnus*, and we have already been thinking about ways in which Scipio *Africanus* played up to and upon potentials for comparison. But in Scipio's case it was his achievement in defeating the new Alexander of Hannibal rather than explicit nuances associated with his name that triggered our interest. 'Africanus' may potentially evoke Alexander via his defeat of Tyre (mother-city of Carthage) and of Egypt, ruled by the descendants of his successor Ptolemy, but Metellus' 'Macedonicus' sets us right in the centre of the tussle for Alexander's identity. Metellus' successes in Achaea and Macedon were only moderate personal triumphs, but his explicit association with Alexander makes this excerpt particularly teasing. Surely it is ironic that Africanus and Macedonicus—two generals who score notable overseas victories for Rome—are both successively de-Romanized by their new names: Scipio becomes the African, Metellus becomes the Macedonian. And it is as the Macedonian that Metellus integrates Alexander inextricably into the fabric of Roman public space. His victories in Macedon and Achaea can function as a microcosmic story of Rome defeating Alexander, where Rome is represented by one man, and Alexander by two nations. Yet the defining characteristic of this conquest is the integration of Alexander, victorious, right into the heart of the city, and the language used by Velleius to characterize Metellus' reshaping of the urban landscape. They are the greatest (*maximum*) ornament of the space even in Velleius' time; yet the statue group is a monument to death, to the dark side of victory, and Alexander himself prefigures his own early death by having himself included amongst those who fell at the Granicus. This subversion of triumph might, one could argue, stand as a great public *memento mori*, reminding Rome not just of the transience of the individual life, but of the impermanence of power. Alexander's empire disintegrated on his death, but his memory continued to play a powerful, formative role in the political and military development of the Mediterranean world. Velleius' characterization of Metellus' reshaping of the city is suspiciously close to the kind of language of excess and degeneracy that we see associated with Alexander, and Antony: '*uel magnificentiae uel luxuriae princeps fuit.*'

Statius' poem on equestrian statues opens his collection, and is also closely concerned with public space and the role of visual signifiers in its interpretation. Just as Alexander's presence makes a huge difference to the portico of Octavia, facing it in a cultural standoff that highlights the changes taking place to the experience of being Roman, this pecu-

liarly unstable equestrian statue of Alexander/Caesar is set against that
of the new monument in town, Domitian. The poem is introduced in
the dedicatory address to Stella as having been a piece commissioned by
Domitian himself and written—we are informed—overnight following
the day of its public dedication.[42] Statius' characterization of Domitian
as *indulgentissimus imperator*, followed by a passive comment that he,
the poet, has been *ordered* to come up with this poem overnight, draws
us back into a world of benefits and clemency whereby the emperor's
overarching authority is reinforced by a recognition that his indulgence
is predicated on obedience. Intriguingly, Statius then further subverts
the integrity of the poem by suggesting that some may claim that he
could never have been so fired by inspiration as to have been able to
compose this poem overnight, that he must have had an advance viewing of the statue. He retorts to these imaginary interlocutors that Stella
will vouch for his ability to compose poems at speed—referring to
Siluae 1.2. Another name-drop brings in Manilius Vopiscus, who
without prompting (*ultro*) makes much of Statius' ability to versify at
speed: here the reference is to *Siluae* 1.3. Is Statius protesting too much?
Is attack the best form of defence, or is this symptomatic of a subtle
process of destabilization of the integrity of *Siluae* 1.1, through which
his own authorial integrity may be reasserted? If we read the collection
as a whole with this in mind, it raises the question of whether or not
Statius is tacitly suggesting that all commissioned poetry is tainted in
one way or another. Whether the addressee is Domitian, a patron, a
friend, or a public worthy, poetic integrity is inevitably compromised.
And a larger issue associated with this is whether Statius may not, in
fact, be questioning the whole notion of poetic or even authorial
integrity within the power dynamic of an imperial system where everything, ultimately, reflects back on the emperor. Ironically, this statement
of authorial impotence may stand as a subversive (if covert) reassertion
of the power of the author's voice. By acknowledging his impotence he
reaffirms a warped interpretative dominance whereby annotated or
exaggerated compliance becomes resistance.[43]

In this context, Statius' closing sentiments on the statue are
particularly interesting. He presents us with a brief catalogue of natural and divine phenomena that it will be impervious to (1.1.91–93),
and equates its immortality with that of the city of Rome itself: '*stabit,
dum terra polusque, / dum Romana dies.*' (1.1.93–94) In other words,
the statue is as invulnerable to destruction (and change?) as is the city
in which it is located. And in that analogy, Statius instantly undermines the premise of imperviability which the preceding ninety-two
lines have apparently been building towards a climax. The horse may

be huge, and its rider mightier yet, but as successive lines demonstrate, the spatial rhetoric and its public, monumental expression are very much up for grabs.[44] The Trojan horse provides an archetype for dangerous equine infiltrators, making it difficult to think of colossal public horses without a subversive subtext. But the allusion to Arion (1.1.52) might recall that he bore two riders (Polyneices and Adrastus), whilst Castor's Cyllarus (like the horses of Alexander and Caesar) would only allow one rider.[45] But despite Pliny's assertion of Bucephalus' fanatical 'loyalty' (*NH* 8.154–155), *this* 'Bucephalus' has had to adapt to survive. Reading Statius' poem is akin to reading the monument itself, converted from cold bronze to words, but demonstrating in its textualization that both words and images are equally contestable. As sophisticated readers of monuments and space, whether textual or concrete, we are aware of the intrinsic instability of both.

We already know that horses inserted into public spaces have a problematic Homeric past, but what about the emperor who sits astride? If the horse can symbolize an insidious threat to the state, the rider poses a rather different question to the alert reader. Statius compares this statue to the similar but smaller equestrian statue of Caesar, which we already know has had a previous incarnation before beheading transformed it—neck upwards—from Alexander. Riders, unlike their mounts, are subject to summary reconfiguration to suit the prevailing political climate. The once deified Alexander became the posthumously exalted Caesar, but even Caesar's divinity is now under threat, and he is forced to give way to Domitian. The point of transformation, the *locus* for this divine and imperial instability, is the neck. Where once we would have seen Alexander's distinctive upturned head, instead we find Caesar's. Where Caesar once held power, we find Domitian. Becoming the new Alexander (which surely is what is happening to Domitian) tacitly admits that one is part of an ongoing line of new pretenders, each destined to be supplanted. Statius' focus on heads and necks in this context is surely ironic: '*una locum ceruix dabit omnibus astris*' ('your neck alone, will provide a place for all the stars' 1.1.98), particularly given the foretaste at 1.1.55: '*uni seruiet astro*'. *This* horse's claims to serve only one master are just as brittle, presumably, as the neck around which the stars cluster. Furthermore, if we reread Statius' dedicatory address to Stella in this context, his comment that his verses are on the Great Horse (*equus maximus*) is particularly biting. At the end of the day, the horses retain their identity and integrity, when the riders they carry have been reshaped and reinvented.

A fitting afterword to these unstable Alexanders can be found in a rather different text: the so-called *Alexander Mosaic* (Frontispiece) from the House of the Faun at Pompeii.[46] This mosaic is usually described as being a copy of a 'lost' Hellenistic original, and has been variously identified as *The Battle of Issus* and *The Battle of Alexander against Darius*. In the wake of the Granicus sculpture group described by Velleius and the obsessive intrusion of Alexander motifs into Augustus' forum, we can see that Alexander was not solely the preserve of the Roman literati. He also carpeted the lives of prosperous Roman society. It is unlikely that we will ever be certain whether this mosaic was imported, plundered, a copy, or even a variation on a theme. We do know, however, that its presence in this huge and lavishly decorated Pompeian mansion stakes out a role for Alexander in the complicated process of public display and social standing that such houses were designed to complement. The mosaic is relatively intact, but signs of repair during the lifetime of the house suggest that it retained an ongoing importance right up to the time of the eruption of Vesuvius (79 CE). Perhaps the key mystery of the devastating yet strangely elegiac scene depicted in this mosaic is the prominence given to Darius rather than to Alexander. Darius' elevated figure, the whites of his eyes gleaming, above a huge chariot wheel and the prominent hindquarters of a riderless horse are what immediately draws our attention. The only similarly emphatic compositional element on the left of the mosaic is a dead tree, rising above the soldiers, and towards which all the raised spears seem to point.

From the layout of the room in which the mosaic was set, we gain a sense of theatricality: two columns allowed the 'audience' to gaze in upon this 'floor', whilst a 'reverse' view was allowed through a window in the wall behind. So this Alexander is also 'unstable', but for rather different reasons to those other images we have read about. For a start, defeat and the inevitability of decline and change are the hallmarks of an image that highlights the pathos rather than the glory of victory, but Alexander's own inability to found a dynasty and the collapse of his empire upon his death, may also be hinted at. Furthermore, the dramatization of this critical moment, a moment which the artist has chosen to portray as the turning point in Alexander's career, saturates it with a wide mythic symbolism for all successive empires. This is a tragedy that is being played out here, and even in his moment of victory we are forced to confront defeat and death as inevitable consequences for Alexander. But finally, the most fundamental instability for this mosaic is its openness to a multiplicity of angles of gaze. It is on the floor, beneath the feet of any who enter the room from the peristyle from which it opened. This vast mosaic provides an Alexander who can be trampled upon, turned on his head or sideways, who can be a decorative addendum to a garden, or its focal point, all at the whim of the course strolled by the viewer. One could even, potentially, excise Alexander altogether and gaze from one garden to the next without dropping one's eyes to the floor.

We do not know why, or even when, this scene was originally installed here in Pompeii, but I think we can hazard a guess that even if it dates back to the second century BCE (the completion of the house), it would still have had an immediate and topical impact on its audience. The wider significances of what the scene might have 'meant' would undoubtedly have continued to shift, particularly if the mosaic was *in situ* when Pompeii was forcibly settled by Sullan veterans. Under Sulla, Pompey, Caesar and Augustus we might expect that the bloodshed of civil war and ultimately, the defeat of Antony, would have made Darius' poignant gaze all the more meaningful. Like Darius, and indeed Alexander himself, the Pompeians were also 'outsiders', Roman allies from the early third century BCE, but only gaining citizenship (and adopting the Latin language) in the early first century BCE. As so many of the later first century CE versions of Alexander that we have read have suggested, it was to be the inevitability of defeat as the flip-side of victory that came to dominate his Roman role.

Eastward Ambitions: The Politics of Victory

Macedon and Rome both mastered vast territories—what happens next? Discussion of Alexander in Rome commenced at a time of crisis in the Republic, when growing interest in eastward expansion was proving an ongoing fascination. Two strands of Roman engagement with Alexander are evident: the civilizing force, and the mad tyrant, slave to his passions.[47] Rather than receiving Alexander as a Hellenic or civilizing king, Alexander became a Persianized degenerate, and this conversion to barbarism is central to an understanding of the link between eastern ambitions and emulation of Alexander.[48]

What happens when a Roman goes East?

Roman conquests in the East proved the main factor in shaping Roman generals in Alexander's image. Monarchy was incompatible with Greco-Roman ideals of freedom, and nations that were subjected to the name and trappings of monarchy were perceived to exist in a state of bondage. One important element of monarchy that made it unacceptable was its disenfranchisement of elite aspirations to power, and its emasculation of a typical elite conciliar body. Alexander, at the centre of a court of flatterers and enemies, could embody the result of this fear: he required counsel and needed to delegate his authority, but because he was the ultimate and continuous arbiter of power, no counsel that he received would be unequivocally motivated. We could interpret this to suggest that in his new-style monarchy, he carried the seeds of his own personal destruction with him. Taking it a step further, his monarchical position and his isolation (both physical, and increasingly intellectual) from his Macedonian origins can act as a model for future rulers who drastically shift the power-balance in their states. Remember that Roman narratives of Alexander tend to emphasize the changes that he imposed upon traditional Macedonian 'democratic' practice.

Whilst he remained in the East, Pompey's assault on Roman political orthodoxy appears to have been (relatively) acceptable. He almost escaped the doom that this scheme of 'being' Alexander suggests was inevitable, but in being drawn back to Rome, just as Alexander was forced to turn back towards Macedon, he embraced his fate.[49] Perhaps for a Roman to play Alexander in the East was still to play safe. Developing this scheme, emphasis is focused less on *where* the Roman Alexander goes and *what* he does there, than on how his travels and power-aspirations affect his behaviour back home. In other words, what authors are interested in is not the personalities themselves, but how they impact upon 'us'. This reading suggests that when Plutarch highlights the corrupting ties of society and politics in his *Lives* of *Pompey* (46), *Caesar* (57, 60–62), and *Alexander* (45, 50, 53, 74) in a combination that demonstrates how intimate circles can corrupt, wherever the action takes place, his interests are firmly on their relevance for the here and now. That stories of Pompey's eastern exploits are in themselves (without any explicit gloss) immediately comparable to Alexander's achievements, only goes to show how far a slippage between then and now had progressed. Just by narrating Pompey's exploits, one was also tacitly invoking Alexander.[50] Lucan emphasizes Roman inability to conquer Pella's 'province', Parthia, and coupled with his moral drift in Book 10, we see Caesar overcome by an increasing inability to take control of his own story, enmeshed by Egypt/Cleopatra and a web of palace machinations. These versions contribute to a growing sense of Alexander's increasing ambivalence in the late Republic, and foreground his destructive potential in the reign of Nero.[51] But that is not all. They also reinforce the allusive qualities of the ongoing dialogue between Alexander and Rome. To talk of one demands that one thinks about the other.

For the ruler to send a deputy East (as Augustus sent first Tiberius, who remained on Rhodes, then Gaius, his own grandson) displayed confidence that the representative would not exploit the potential of the power entrusted. The gesture could be read as a designation of official status as heir, and Gaius' potential supremacy in the East could shift the Alexandrian-mantle from Augustus to the next generation, making this young man symbolic of Rome's championship of the Greeks against 'the old enemy' (the Persians). That there were elements of this kind of imagery floating around for association with a 'new' Caesar is evident from the celebrations surrounding the dedication of the temple of Mars Ultor in 2 BCE.[52] Tacitus' highly polarized portrait of the young Germanicus, the favoured successor after the deaths that robbed Augustus of his first choices of heir, has traditionally been interpreted as entirely favourable to him, and opposed to his adoptive father, Tiberius. This view can be countered with the suggestion that a far less favourable estimate of Germanicus may emerge from between the lines, one in which he can come to play a sinister part in Tacitus' overall scheme of historical realignment.[53] Tacitus' juxtaposition of Tiberius and Germanicus is echoed in the later parallel between Nero and Corbulo, but no Alexander-aspirations are attributed to Tiberius. Tiberius' mistrust of Germanicus, emphasized by Tacitus (e.g. *Ann.* 1.7.9, 11.4, 33.2–4), is increased when the younger man is transferred to the East, a move that Tacitus (*Ann.* 2.41.5, 42.1), Suetonius (*Tib.* 52), and Velleius (2.129) all represent as pivotal.

Tacitus' report of the journey eastwards is characterized by criticism for Germanicus' dropping of 'Caesarian dignity' (in Athens and Alexandria), and for his acceptance of a Parthian crown. These cavils, and the Alexandrian edict made by Germanicus (CE 19), lead inevitably (it seems to me) to the Tacitean eulogy of comparison with Alexander.[54] Unauthorized arrival by Germanicus in Egypt could *still* have overtones of Antony's attempt to create a power base there, and the province itself was one that only he seems to have regarded as within his remit.[55] By tracing the scheme of narrative references made by Tacitus we can see a link created between Germanicus and Antony, and thereafter a narration of Germanicus' move to Athens (*Ann.* 2.53); links are sequentially created with Augustus (1.33.1), Antony (2.43.5), and Caesar (at the Nile, 2.60.1).[56] Tacitus presents Germanicus' entry into Egypt as particularly galling for Tiberius (*Ann.* 2.59.3): not only did his adopted son issue decrees, making a reverent reference to

Alexander as founder of the city (implying that he and this heroic founder shared the same aspirations [P.Oxy. 2435 v18–21]), but reading between the lines, we can also see him being greeted with divine honours. Of course his recorded refusal of divine honours could be read in a number of ways. For a start, it could be a conscious echo of the topos of Caesar refusing the diadem at the Lupercalia, shortly before his assassination; it could also be a literary double bluff of the kind epitomized by the archetypal no-news, newspaper headline 'Man doesn't die.' Just because Germanicus may have refused to be treated as a god does not have to mean that anyone suggested that he should be, it simply *implies* that the honours were offered for the refusal to make logical sense. But whether or not deification was in the air, this connexion between Germanicus and Alexander is further reinforced by Tacitus' comment (*Ann.* 2.59.3) that Tiberius was displeased by Germanicus' adoption of Greek clothes and imitation of Scipio Africanus—going native (going 'Alexander'?). Again, the comment is interesting as a function of what could be read into a change of dress, whatever the historical reality of Germanicus' behaviour. In the end, from the perspective of a developing tradition of appropriation of Alexander, Tacitus' assumption that his audience will understand the implications of this concatenation of hints and allusive references is unavoidable. The popular reaction to Germanicus' death in Rome marks a final link, connecting with the frenzied grief on Alexander's death in Babylon, and characterized by similar bewildering and emotive rumour (*Ann.* 2.82–83); the political manoeuvring on his family's part matches descriptions of the power play on Alexander's death.[57]

How does Tacitus use Germanicus? Is Tacitus the sole author of this allusive and referential nexus of association between Germanicus and Alexander? Did Germanicus himself play any active role in the association? Or should we conclude that Germanicus had no part in the correspondence? There is no glaring narrative of Alexander-*imitatio* in Tacitus' version of Germanicus.[58] Nevertheless, it would be a mistake to assume that just because Tacitus does not propose Germanicus as the author of this comparison with Alexander, that Tacitus himself is solely responsible. Based on the ubiquity of Alexander as a comparative for Roman power figures, it is far more likely that Tacitus is picking up on a comparison that if it had not already been explicitly articulated, had at least been in the air. So why might Tacitus have chosen to emphasize a link between Germanicus and Alexander when such a suggestion of interdependence between the two could work to Germanicus' disadvantage? One explanation could be that Tacitus uses this comparison to provide a prelude to the beginning 'proper' of the Annals, marking an end to the Augustan era in his creation of a 'perfect' prince both in terms of his almost excessive legitimacy of descent (from both Antony and Caesar [*Ann.* 2.53.1–3]), and in his idealized qualities.[59] By setting Germanicus up as a super-Alexander (much as we have already seen Velleius reconstruct Caesar) Tacitus may be playing ironically on audience knowledge of the outcome. We know that Germanicus will die therefore we know that his paradigmatic status as perfect prince is compromised from the start, and that if imperial perfection is only possible through him, then the perfect ruler can never exist. Alexander may provide the archetype, but Alexander's monarchy was flawed, and successive Roman Alexanders have demonstrated that the flaws are so deeply built into the model that they prove inescapable; early death is the only way of avoiding the fate of a Scipio or a Pompey, or even an Antony. If Germanicus represents the death of idealized imperial power, how does Alexander affect the composition? The comparison made by Tacitus appears stylized and rhetorical, and its terms allow qualities to Germanicus that are not features of Alexander-representation,[60] yet the variety and scope of available parallels with Alexander suggest that comparisons would readily be attached to 'potential' Alexander-situations. Perhaps we should understand that Tacitus' Germanicus is not only a Tiberian foil, but also a warning that such 'Alexandrian' style is no longer possible (or desirable?).[61] Whether Tacitus contrived the parallel or not, it is unlikely that he would have been unaware of the resonances that he was setting in motion, and this is fully played out in his later account of the fate of Nero's general, Corbulo.

Degeneracy

Going east means travelling into a world defined as much by myth and fiction as by hard fact. To journey eastwards is to take a trip into a region dominated by stories of excessive consumption, of luxury and wantonness, of sexual profligacy, and decadent refinement. A place where men are made effeminate and gender roles are turned upside down, where kings rule as despots over their people, and magic and superstition are rife. This is the kind of world that Roman Alexander narratives invoke, and the seductive, aggressively degenerative characteristics of this storied East are apparent throughout all of the versions of 'Alexander'. Suetonius represents Antony degenerating in Alexandrian terms: he fails to conduct himself as befits a

Roman (for which we might read in 'Macedonian'; *Aug.* 17.1), and his adoption of the roles of new-Dionysus, new-Helios, and descendant of Hercules bolster the comparison with Alexander and its increasingly problematic overtones. Curtius' use of the slogan *'uindex publicae libertatis'* (defender of public freedom; 8.5.20, 10.2.6–7), in conjunction with a growing, though ineffectual series of challenges to Alexander's authority transforms this changed, orientalized Alexander into an enemy within. Curtius' emphasis on the Macedonian inability to shake off Alexander's increasing orientalism is comparable to popular distaste for Antony's supposed enslavement by the 'barbarian Queen', Cleopatra.[62] A connexion between the above slogan and the motif of *dominatio* (essentially an expression of tyranny: government by a Lord and Master) in propaganda against Antony is evident in the particular hostility shown by Augustus to the term.[63] The negative implications of the word make it easy to see how a contemporary inference could be drawn from the use of *uindex publicae libertatis* as an epithet for an opponent of Alexander's orientalization.[64] Plutarch describes how Antony sought to play up through his dress a supposed likeness to Hercules in features, but in the end, subdued by the spells of Cleopatra, his similarity was more akin to Hercules disarmed by Omphale.[65] Imitation of Hercules and Dionysus leads to Alexander, a line traced directly by Plutarch in his 'Life of Antony' (*Ant.* 4, 24, 54, 60). If Antony was descended from Hercules and became a new Dionysus in life, then his *imperium* still had aspirations to Alexander's universal empire, with its centre at the symbolic capital of Alexandria. Buying into this imagery, Antony opened himself to charges of luxury, orientalism and *dominatio* from Octavian, who had no difficulty in convincing the Senate of the dangers of such an orientalizing course. The convergence of terms applied to Antony and Alexander encompass not only these 'dangers', but also the 'threat' of enchantment by a barbarian wife.[66]

The role of Dionysus gave Antony a further identification, tying him to ideas of world-conquest and civilizing forces; but conjoined with the role of Osiris in Egypt, it had the effect of opening the way for a war of words and myth to accompany the looming battle. Plutarch probably reflects part of a concerted campaign to show that Antony was spiritually inferior to Octavian, but even after his death, the idea of *being* a successful Antony figure (much as Caesar tried to be the Alexander that Pompey failed to achieve), would still have had potency as a motif.[67] This is exemplified by the rumour that Dionysus left Alexandria the night before its capture—propaganda tailored to feed Roman fears, and to convince Rome that not only was Octavian/

Apollo stronger than Antony/Dionysus, but that the gods of the West in general were more powerful than those of the East.[68] On a 'divine' level, the East/West clash had its basis in the political reality of Roman nationalism. If Antony likens himself to the Egyptian Osiris, Antony can be portrayed at Rome as enslaved to the barbarism of Egypt and its queen; as slave to Cleopatra, how can Antony be anything other than a man, and one whose only resemblances to divinity are sottishness and revelry?[69]

Any consideration of the verbal war between Antony and Octavian must take into account the factors that may have influenced Octavian; Antony's desertion of Octavia for Cleopatra was one element in the strategic conflict, an East/West opposition was another, but perhaps most important was that whoever won would need, in the aftermath, to combine mastery of East and West.[70] For this reason Octavian began to take steps in Greece to place *himself* as heir to Alexander post-Actium, with the foundation of the nearby Nicopolis, described by Suetonius immediately after the episode concerning his visit to Alexander's tomb.[71] Caesar had already demonstrated tactical clemency, and the most efficient way for the new victor to erase his rival was to take on board those features of his image that were beneficial to ruler imagery (Alexander's military successes, divine favour, charisma) and could be redefined for appropriation for his own mythology. Superiority in the East as a joint Alexandrian and Augustan attribute is heralded 'officially' by Virgil,[72] and the claim there that Augustus spread his *imperium* beyond the stars, outstripping the annual paths of the year and the sun ('*extra sidera, extra anni solisque uias*') is echoed by Tiberius' oration on Augustus.[73] These explorations give us some idea of the complexity of the situation we address. By necessity a *princeps* needs to be able to adapt equally to the mentalities of his fellow citizens in Rome and to his subjects in the provinces, but despite the multiplicity of available Alexanders for deconstruction as imperial models, it may have been the case that 'Alexander' was a double-edged sword. As the texts of Chapters 2 to 4 suggest, redrawing Alexander as a propagandist device has a tendency to backfire because of the very polyvalence that makes him a ubiquitous model in the first place.[74]

Fortunes of War

The charismatic military brilliance that characterized the succession of late republican Alexanders underwent a shift in focus after Antony's defeat. Before Actium, it had been Antony who pushed the boundaries of empire, whilst Octavian consolidated his control of the centre, and this dynamic was to become the norm for the next century, until the Principate of Trajan. The political balance of the Principate involved a constant renegotiation of the balance between personal military success and the difficulties involved in leaving the central power base on campaign. Octavian's one personal, glamorous military victory (Egypt) was complicated by the implicit role of Antony and therefore its civil war connotations. Augustus' subsequent decision to set boundaries to Roman expansive imperialism offers a tacit admission of the problems involved in rewriting 'Alexander' as a statesman. One possible model for the pattern of dynastic succession set up by Octavian after Caesar's assassination has been termed a 'theology of victory' (a charismatic ruler who owed his status to divinely granted victories). If Caesar, with his divine ancestry, descent from Aeneas and military genius could be marketed as the founder of an imperial family, then once power had been secured by his successor, dynastic ideology could begin to supplement such a theology of victory as a means of legitimizing power.[75] We see the beginnings of this in Caesar's attempts to create a rationale for kingship based on descent from Venus through Aeneas, on links with traditional Alban kingship models, and on his position as the divinely favoured Roman who could outdo Alexander, but the scene had already been set by the legends surrounding Scipio Africanus and Pompey. In the *de Lege Manilia* (10.28; 66 BCE), Cicero states that a great general characteristically possesses military know-how (*scientia rei militaris*), courage and manliness (*uirtus*), power (*auctoritas*) and good luck (*felicitas*). Pompey was well equipped with all four, but whilst others had received divine *fortuna*, only Pompey had *felicitas* (16.47). Cicero's vision of a Roman saviour owes more to politics and wishful thinking than to reality, but in his creation of the creature, he opens the way for another to try his luck in the role.

Just how clear the way was for eastern Alexander-games is evident from the wry overtones of Cicero's letters from Cilicia of 51 BCE (*ad Fam.* 2.10.3, November, and *ad Att.* 5.20, December). The first letter is addressed to M. Caelius Rufus, the Curule Aedile designate, and written during the siege of Pindenissus, conducted by Cicero. He recounts how his army's renown was well served by his own prestige amongst 'foreigners' (2.10.2), and that in the wake of the glory of his victory at Amanus, he was rightly acclaimed *imperator* at Issus: 'Thus after an overwhelming victory I was acclaimed *imperator*' (2.10.3). But Cicero makes certain that the potential comparison with Alexander is hammered home; there is nothing left to the chance interpretation of his addressee when he states that Issus was the site, Caelius Rufus has often told him, of Alexander's defeat of Darius. This emphatic statement rules out any possibility that Caelius might forget his comment, but it also sets up a suspicion that by reminding Caelius so explicitly of his interest in Alexander, Cicero is also writing for a wider audience. It is possible that Cicero is overstating Caelius' references to Alexander, but one way or the other, in this comment we can read on-going evidence of the potential for positive late republican Alexanders, and a widespread appreciation of his usefulness as a shorthand for military glory.

The joke must be that whereas Alexander defeated Darius, the Persian Great King, Cicero only has a victory at unknown Amanus to celebrate. Underscoring his awareness of the irony embedded in drawing a comparison between his exploits in Asia and those of Alexander, Cicero mocks the inglorious status of the Pindenissitae only when he has defeated them, writing this time to his friend Atticus (*ad Att.* 5.20). In expansive manner he redraws his campaign in the epistolary wake of this victory—the quasi-regal progress from Ephesus to Laodicea, the great welcome afforded him by towns along the way, and his settlement of grievances for these peoples. News of Parthian trouble brought him to Amanus; there he routed the enemy, and declares: 'I was hailed as *imperator*.' Cicero's itinerary places him inexorably in Alexander's shadow, but he gives his story of Issus a slightly different slant for Atticus: 'We made camp for a couple of days there', he comments, 'where Alexander (a general who was not a little greater than you or me) fought Darius.' Is the reader being dared to agree that, yes, Alexander is a far better general than the author, whose progress and success have been so carefully described?

We already know how consciously Cicero attempted to model his image, and these letters offer another angle on his strategy for memorialization. What we are seeing, in effect, is a continuation of the discourse of Alexander's fame as a function of the stories written about him, a discourse that is elegantly exploited by Horace almost thirty years later when he describes his first three books of *Odes* as a '*monumentum aere perennius*' (monument more lasting than bronze; *Odes* 3.30.1). Cicero's self-deprecation reads as arch rather than humble, particularly in the wake of his acclamation as *imperator*. Either Cicero is saying that this Roman honour is negligible in comparison with Alexander's achievements, or the apparent humility is intended to enhance the aura of greatness that Cicero has so carefully constructed. The immediacy and explicit nature of the comparison involved in these letters makes them particularly relevant at this moment in Roman history—in his eastern progress, Cicero plays Alexander, and he reinvents Alexander's triumph in the language of Roman imperialism. But Alexander's is not the only shadow looming over Cicero's adventure. Pompey, a far more recent and perhaps even more problematic Roman Alexander, had already staked out the east as his own, whilst Caesar's proposed Parthian campaign, into the heart of Alexander's territory, was one of the motives for his assassins. Perhaps this undercurrent of danger surrounding someone who is *too* successful in the East is behind Cicero's revised (and maybe more considered) account as delivered to Atticus. We might also, of course, read these letters in conjunction with the later correspondence between Cicero and Atticus, discussed in Chapter 2, where Cicero aligns himself with Alexander against Caesar.

There is no evidence to suggest that Caesar actively copied any aspect of Alexander's military strategy, even if, as suggested by Plutarch, he did study Alexander's campaigns (*Caesar* 11). Nevertheless, if we compare Cicero's bold self-comparison with Alexander with the Caesarian narratives of Velleius and Appian, we see a rather different picture of Roman appropriation evolving. For a start, Caesar, like Cicero was engaged both implicitly and explicitly, in a programme of literary self-historicization. But whereas Cicero is happy to make a direct comparison between himself and Alexander, comparisons between Caesar and Alexander are made by other people, or attributed to Caesar by later authors. Not surprisingly, Caesar's commentaries are never so unsubtle as to draw a clear analogy between the two men. Despite this, roughly a century apart, we find in the Caesars of both Velleius and Appian a soldier in the mould of Alexander. Velleius compares Alexander and Caesar in their great ambition, speed of military operation and willingness to endure danger; but unlike Alexander, Caesar did not put himself in a position of instability through excessive indulgence in alcohol (passage 3.1). Appian also highlights the lightning warfare (*celeritas bellandi*) for which both were famed (and which forms an important part of Curtius' narrative technique [Curtius 4.4.1–2; 5.1.36]), and he concentrates on the same comparative qualities of ambition, recklessness and capability to endure hardship. Both men owe much of their success to luck or fortune, both are inquisitive, good looking, generous in victory and of divine ancestry. Both were followed with keen personal loyalty by their troops (despite mutinies), and both were to die unexpectedly, in the throes of planning fresh campaigns (Appian 2.21.149–154). Caesar may not have planned his Parthian expedition for any reasons other than national security and rational frontier policy, but having once embarked on such a plan, it becomes obvious that a comparison with Alexander, one that may or may not have driven Caesar, must take on an overarching significance.[76]

A shift in focus of loyalty from state to commander defines the careers of the late republican Alexanders, and Caesar's appeal is based on a combination of personality and his attention to the practicalities of the soldier's life. The problems experienced by veterans (settlement, and disinheritance by the state) are addressed by Lucan's Caesar, and echoing Aeneas' pleas to Apollo gives the poet an opportunity to show how Caesar regards himself as another Aeneas.[77] Developing this theme locates Alexander as part of a greater anxiety surrounding the potential for loss of empire. In yielding the East—a nebulous, unconquerable concept as much as a real topography of mud and rocks and cities—as Aeneas has had to do, Rome could lose definition and 'die', and Caesar's triumph over Pompey is overshadowed by the ever-present knowledge that his death also put a stop to Roman expansion in the East until Nero tried again, abortively, with Corbulo, a campaign that ended in the mock triumph of Tiridates' submission (66 CE). In this sense by writing a narrative of these civil wars, Lucan is defining (and creating) an inbuilt end-stop to Roman expansion— every story has to have a conclusion. When a story is told, even of Roman greatness, some sort of 'conclusion' has to be negotiated.[78] Rome did not face a Persian horde, as had fifth-century Greece, instead the enemy (the *felix praedo*) came from within, destroying Rome through the military success that had defined Roman understanding of 'greatness' and empire (Lucan 8.494–95). As alert and sophisticated members of Lucan's audience, we know that what followed on from Caesar's death was the fiasco of Antony's attempt on Parthia. The defeat at Actium put a stop, temporarily at least, to expansive Roman dreams of eastern glory.

In Nero, however, that was to change, and it may also have been with this in mind that Lucan chose to highlight Caesar's double connexion with Alexander, both in style of leadership and through Caesar's liaison with Cleopatra and Egypt. When Nero determined to make attack the best form of defence on the eastern frontier, he did not lead the legions into battle in person. Instead, he sent a general, Corbulo, whose experiences in Alexander's old domain (and their consequences for his fate at home) are evidence of the continued potency of the fear of a threat from the East—home-grown or external.[79] The key narrative for Corbulo's campaign on Nero's behalf is contained in Tacitus' *Annals*. His account commences with a sequence that mirrors Curtius' Alexander spying on the *proskynesis* discussion

(*Ann.* 13.5–6; Curtius 8.5.21), and this atmosphere sets a tone which suggests that Corbulo's final downfall has less to do with the success of his own actions than with their imperial consequences. The problem is presented as one in which the appearance of 'holding' territory, of being seen to have appointed a charismatic commander, is of the utmost importance for the prestige of the emperor himself, but the danger of appointing a general who is too charismatic and successful is obvious.[80] Nero's reaction to Corbulo's military success is closely linked to the ambivalent status of a general acting as imperial proxy, on a campaign that takes him directly in Alexander's footsteps. Tacitus focuses the opening stages of his account on Corbulo's need to undertake rigorous training of his troops. The hardship that he endures on equal terms with them echoes this motif in Alexander's behaviour.[81] A link between Alexander and the Parthian king Tiridates is also suggested, when the latter is described achieving his victories through reputation, and the terror inspired by his name;[82] Rome is notably absent from the initial focus on the bond between Corbulo and his troops, but is reintroduced tactically when describing the capture of the city of Artaxata (*Ann.* 13.41.2). If the city was not *seen* to be held and garrisoned, then all the glory of its taking would be lost. This emphasis on perception as the key to the ultimate reality-effect is a topos familiar from the Alexander tradition, and if—as seems likely— Curtius was writing in the first century CE then we can trace a familial connexion from Lucan's characterization of Pompey, Caesar and Cato, through Curtius' Alexander, to Tacitus' multiplicity of Roman Alexanders. The main focus of the seizure of Tigranocerta is its propaganda value: to inspire terror and help acquire a reputation for clemency, and the flexibility of action displayed in the aftermath shows marked similarities with Alexander's treatment of his adversaries.[83] The sense of continuity that Tacitus constructs between the 'great' generals of Rome's eastern campaigns (*Ann.* 13.34.2), is echoed in Paetus' attempt two books later to introduce Rome's past victories as a bargaining chip (*Ann.* 15.14.2). Tacitus resurrects this sense of continuum in turn, in his comparison of Nero's powers to those of Pompey (15.25.3). Whether this is panegyric, or simply statement of military scope is debatable but the parallel is drawn.[84] It is difficult, with the hindsight that Tacitus must have relied on his audience deploying, not to see Nero's ignominious death prefigured in this too defiantly innocuous comparison. And in the sour taste that this death foretold leaves behind may be the key to Tacitus' deliberate playing-out of such a multiplicity of tangled strands of the Alexander-tradition in his account of the end of the Julio-Claudian dynasty.

Mutiny!

Having spent some time trying to tease out possible ways in which military parallels might exist between Alexander and Roman wannabes, it is ironic that one key point of intersection is the topos of how to deal with mutinous troops. This kind of situation, where a general is forced to confront the national psyche rather than an external enemy, forms an increasingly important strand in narratives of the latter stages of Alexander's campaign. It also provides an alternative military focus for the playing-out of Roman concerns about the changing nature of political power and the increasing dominance of autocracy within the Republic. We can see this in action when Lucan uses mutiny as a model for political debate about the nature of Roman national identity in his narrative of the civil war between Pompey and Caesar, which on another level might be re-examined as a conflict between old and new models of appropriation of Alexander. Lucan's Caesarian soldiers claim that they have come as far as they had ever planned or bargained for—all the way to now-Roman, once-Macedonian Epirus, in fact—and they cannot understand what more Caesar seeks (5.261–95). Caesar responds contemptuously, defying the troops to kill him (5.317–18). This scenario is mirrored in Curtius' treatment of the Hyphasis and Opis/Susa mutinies. At the Hyphasis Alexander whinges, pleads and loses; the troops have the same grievances as Lucan's Caesarians. At Opis, Alexander, fury personified, dares the troops to manage without him, and carries all before him.[85] At the Hyphasis Alexander suffers a breakdown in ability to judge his power over his troops, and in defeating him, the troops also detract from his ability to lead them. Curtius implies that this leads Alexander to turn ever more to the Persians for companionship (10.2); this broken relationship also, probably, ensures the development of further problems at Opis. At Opis, the vital factor in Alexander's victory over his troops is his confidence in his own right to wield authority.[86] In Brundisium and Campania the threat of exile (from Caesar, not state) is effective; at Opis, the taunt *'ingratissimi ciues'* helps quell the Macedonians.[87] What we find in these post-republican Roman stories of Alexander is that his victories over the Persians and other eastern peoples become increasingly marginal to the main narrative thrust. Instead, emphasis is placed upon the growing sense of internal conflict focused on the changes taking place in the way Alexander governs his people.

In the light of this shifting emphasis, it is unsurprising that when we look forwards to the Principate, mutiny retains its importance. The mutinies faced by Caesar at Placentia, in Rome (the tenth legion), and at Dyrrhachium figure variously in a variety of narrative accounts from Caesar himself onwards.[88] Characteristically, Caesar's own account of his relationship with his troops during the civil war offers a rhetorical negotiation of a balance between his ability to inspire devotion and obedience and their willingness to endure privations for him.[89] When Caesar fails, his third person singular persona ascribes it to fortune, or excessive enthusiasm on the part of his troops; even in defeat this rhetorical tactic strengthens Caesar's political and military self-definition.[90] In the same vein, Caesar also minimizes Pompey's victory at Dyrrhachium (*BC* 3.41–75), demonstrating the complexity of representation that makes up our perceptions of historical events. Representation can almost obscure 'fact', but by a sleight of hand, events at Dyrrhachium are slanted to foreground Caesar's 'achievement' rather than Pompey's victory. The power of perspective in modelling and re-envisaging history is echoed by Lucan's decision (we assume it was a decision) not to represent Caesar engaged in the typical epic-heroic *aristeia*. In fact in Lucan, Caesar's destructive military brilliance is entirely focused upon his own people.[91] About half a century after Lucan, we find Tacitus engaged in a process of acculturation that refocuses our attention on the internal dynamics of a mutiny and its implications for Rome as a whole. After Augustus' death, the Rhine legions engaged in a quasi-mutiny with the aim of forcing Germanicus to make a bid for the succession (Tacitus, *Ann.* 1.34–35). Given the ambivalence surrounding Tacitus' representation of Germanicus, we know we are intended to read this episode with difficulty. Germanicus' first speech to the soldiers has little effect, and in the wake of this psychological defeat his reaction is to leap down amongst the troops as if to leave. When they try to force him to remain, at point of sword, he swears that death is better than dishonour, holding his sword to his chest. This extremely physical threat to a reluctant leader demonstrates the danger of taking on mutineers on their own terms—a physical context pitting one man against many has only one result outside the realm of folk-tale, and Tacitus makes no attempt to mythologize Germanicus' physical prowess. His threat to kill himself is swiftly followed by cries from the troops that he ought to be allowed to complete his suicide. Only the ironic pause offered when one soldier offers his sharper blade as a weapon, allows Germanicus' friends to hurry him away. Tacitus' emphatic presentation of this episode sets up a highly dramatic parallel with both Caesar and Alexander, the ambivalence of which adds to the disquiet surrounding the Tacitean Germanicus.[92] As with Alexander at the

Hyphasis, the leader's bluff is called and he has nothing to offer when the threat of withdrawing his person (whether through death, or as with Alexander, by going on alone) has no effect.

The end of this chapter is also the formal end of this book about the Roman Alexander, but as with the story of Alexander, closure is not that simple. Going on remains the only option, and that process of ongoing reinvention and revitalization of Alexander, and indeed Classics, is at least part of why I have written and you are reading these words. As I commenced by saying (pp. xiii–xix), our Alexander today is a product of the story of Roman cultural appropriation that this book has explored, and this means that every successive modern Alexander is rooted in an ongoing process of reimagining and reconfiguring what 'Alexander' can and might mean. And so in turning the page to the final chapter of *this* text, what you will find is an open-ended story of what happens next.

6. Albrecht Altdorfer, *Battle of Alexander and Darius on the Issus* (1529) The fairy-tale spires and candy-coloured tents that melt into the far away crags and peaks set this battle firmly in Northern Europe. Although we still have a battle *melée* (as in the Frontispiece and Fig. 5), here the human skirmish is entirely overshadowed by the brooding forces of nature which mirror the conflict below. Darius' flight (and Alexander's pursuit) are made evident only by a gap in the fighting; the visual dynamic of this moment forces the eye to struggle to focus on the narrative significance.

6

Alexander *after* Alexander

Alexander's potency as an intellectual paradigm has persisted to the present day, and, drawing this book to a conclusion, it seems logical to trace some of the routes by which *Alexander* has arrived in the twenty-first century. Alexander continues to inform all modern perceptions of heroism, masculinity and individuality, and permeates our perceptions of how we deal with fame, notoriety, power and success.[1] In the developing story of Alexander we find that the flexibility displayed in ancient sources becomes even more marked through time, but that within a given period, there tends to be greater homogeneity of interpretation. Key features of Alexander's story that retain a high level of significance through this development are: self-destruction and excess; youth and beauty; the semi-mystical quest for the 'other' at the edges of the world; and the problem of how to represent his cultural fluidity, either a 'degeneration' into barbarian luxury, or a vision of a world brotherhood and empire.[2]

One of the most pervasive elements in narratives of Alexander in the Orient is a fascination with boundaries and limits (*termini*), whether boundaries of character, politics, culture or geography. In the modern world, this interest in the nature of frontiers and liminality has gained increasing prominence in popular and critical thought.[3] To the east, explorers and conquerors sought the earth-girdling Ocean, and in the east, Alexander has continuously been redrawn. When geographical world-limits were unforthcoming in Asia, this region came to be defined by what was mythic and unknowable, hence the importance of strange portents, monstrous creatures and barbarous peoples.[4] Alexander-legends and the Romance tradition develop this mode of engagement to its extreme conclusion, taking us from Alexander's 'Roman' incarnation through to the developments of the

Middle Ages. For a time, Alexander is lost to the practical, political and military world of the West, having been subsumed into an oriental idyll where he experiences fabulous adventures, miraculous occurrences and mystical experiences. This world is simultaneously both of the West (the western conception of the East) and a function of an eastern adoption of Alexander as a kind of cult hero. His eventual return to the 'western' world is only accomplished with the growth of humanistic studies and renewed interest in contemporary relevance for a classical past.[5]

The text known to us as the *Alexander Romance* (erroneously ascribed to Alexander's historian Callisthenes) may have been composed as early as the third century BCE, but survives in its earliest version from the third century CE. This highly influential and extremely popular narrative was a fictive and fantastic account of Alexander's life and travels which mingled 'credible' historical narrative with stories of magic and marvels, one of the most famous examples being Alexander's visit to the heavens in an eagle-drawn chariot. The *Alexander Romance* was widely known throughout medieval Europe, and forms the main basis for the widespread dissemination of the legendary adventures that remained popular until the fifteenth and sixteenth centuries.[6] A second important narrative, one that has figured in previous chapters, is that of Quintus Curtius Rufus, probably dating to the first century CE.[7] Curtius' history of Alexander was broadly 'historical', but told in a highly rhetorical manner, with much Roman colour. This narrative was immensely popular throughout the medieval period and after, influencing Chaucer, Gower and Walter of Châtillon. These texts, coupled with the multiple shorter stories and dialogues that also abounded, meant that in the late Roman period and early Middle Ages two distinct but interrelated traditions of 'Alexander' gradually evolved: extended narratives (mainly romances), and a tradition based on the recounting of anecdotes. The two strands probably shared common assumptions and sources, but it seems most likely that it was from the latter that any popular conception of Alexander would have been derived.[8]

It might at first seem difficult to understand how Alexander could have become a significant figure in the developing rhetoric of Christianity, but in the Alexander of the moralizing works of Cicero, Seneca and Valerius Maximus the early Church Fathers had found a useful figure. This Alexander was at once flexible enough to bear the pressure of adaptation to Christian moralizing, and also deeply embedded in the pre-Christian rhetoric and worldview. In this way, he was instantly accessible as a model for a religion still developing out of a culture in which literary and artistic 'culture' was a non-Christian preserve. The new religion of Christianity did not have a monopoly on the developments taking place in the narrative of Alexander, and a secular tradition was simultaneously developing, which encompassed ancient fascination with the eastward aspirations of the narrative tradition. Knowledge and stories concerning Alexander's time in India were heavily informed by Ctesias of Cnidus (who wrote on Persia and India in the fifth century BCE, and whose work survives in Photius' ninth-century CE summary) and Herodotus. This limited information evolved into an important adjunct to the Christian ascetic tradition and the Cynic/Stoic strand of the early Christian Church.[9] These two avenues of approach to Alexander and the East—the Herodotean/ Ctesian miraculous events and fabulous beasts, and the Cynic/Stoic philosophical and moral ideas—gave rise to two main types of narrative: secular and religio-philosophical, informed by the idea of reaching beyond what was known and catalogued, seeking the 'other' of ocean, and world's end.[10] These narratives were very popular in the Middle Ages, but as the way in which emphasis has shifted from the political and national imperialist focus of early Roman engagement should be making clear, this popularity was based on changing patterns of requirement. Classical texts were being reinterpreted and integrated into the growing *Christian* canon, as part of a conscious intellectual expression of the new order.[11] In this new world order, moralizing ethical and 'fantasy' texts such as the 'Letter to Aristotle' and 'Wonders of the East' were to become useful geographical sources,[12] providing a valuable rhetoric of western engagement with the East in which a Westerner had a starring role. As such, these narratives coexisted happily with European attempts at eastward expansion.[13] Alexander's 'moral standing' gradually improved, and by the fourteenth century, almost all negative aspects had been filtered out.[14]

Corresponding to this progression runs the evolution of a courtly Alexander, representative of the flower of chivalry.[15] Although this usage tended to decline in Europe in the late medieval period, we can see echoes of Alexander's mystical quest for the eastern Ocean in narratives such as the Arthurian Grail-quest, and the mythical landscape through which the Round Table knights journeyed. Furthermore, in the idea of a select band of knights, flower of their age, a faint echo survives of the idea of Alexander's band of 'Companions', his contemporaries with whom he was educated, and who formed his core support when he embarked on his great adventure.[16] Although there are clear thematic links between the Alexandrian and the Arthurian material, we do not have to depend solely on the thematic similarities. The fourteenth-century French romance *Perceforest* tells how Alexander visited Britain and established the monarchies of England and Scotland when he had been swept off course after his conquest of India. This directly positioned Alexander as an early ancestor of Arthur himself. Apart from the specifically Arthurian links, Alexander was also a significant figure in the medieval courtly tradition. The twelfth-century French *Roman d'Alexandre* was highly influential on both German and English chivalric traditions, whereby Alexander becomes a Crusader king, fighting the Saracens in a landscape of courtly pageantry. It was partly from this discourse that Renaissance imagery would eventually develop.

One of the main factors affecting the growth of classical humanism during the Renaissance was the increased availability of classical texts, many which were brought west by refugees after the fall of Constantinople (1453). Combined with the growth of a wealthy, leisured, consumer class, and sparked by the opening-up of trade routes with the east, a shift away from feudal practice and unquestioning religious submissiveness led to a rapid expansion in the range of literary and iconographical possibilities available. This situation is analogous to the period of redefinition in Rome, which, as I suggested in Chapter 1, carried with it an increased consciousness of the potential uses of Alexander-imagery. Medieval western interpretations emphasize Alexander as a type; in the Renaissance, politically and artistically we find a shift towards emphasis on redefining the role of the individual in society, and as the visual rhetoric of Figure 1 makes clear, 'Alexander' continues to reflect these changes.[17]

Renaissance portraiture of Alexander makes his importance in this cultural realignment particularly clear, as images such as Pietro della Vecchia's *Timoclea Brought Before Alexander* and Veronese's *Family of Darius Before Alexander* demonstrate.[18] In della Vecchia and Veronese we find a 'modern' Alexander, acting out scenes from his life in pseudo-classical settings that blend the contemporary with contemporary versions of how the past might have been. This Alexander stands in for the aspirant nobles who are beginning to take on greater importance in the power struggles of the post-feudal world. These men who commissioned and enjoyed images of Alexander espoused the renewed interest in classicism and increasingly took Alexander as an effective model in a changing world where the traditional authority of Pope and Holy Roman Emperor was being undermined by growing humanism, religious reform and gradual secularization of society. Exploration and imperial conquest, and the opening-up of the East and the Americas shattered traditional medieval perceptions in the same manner as visually, the development of perspective in art had transformed the figurative landscape. The questing Alexander began simultaneously to gain in real political and military stature. Secular interest in Alexander was matched by Papal recognition of his importance for negotiating how power and authority could be enforced and invigorated through propagandist imagery. This is made evident through Pope Paul III's redecoration of the Sala Paolina in the Castel Sant'Angelo at Rome.[19] The rooms featured a series of murals based on the life of Alexander, emphasizing, by association, the way in which secular and spiritual authority could be combined in one ultimate, victorious package. A hundred years later we find an even more grandiose proposal re-emerging. Alexander's architect Deinocrates had, apparently, proposed to remodel Mount Athos into a monumental image of the recumbent Alexander. Pietro da Cortona reinvented this scheme in homage to Pope Alexander VII (1655–67), and had himself depicted (*c*.1655) kneeling to the Pope, presenting the scheme.[20]

An alternative vision of Alexander emerges in Altdorfer's massive *Battle of Alexander and Darius on the Issus* (1529) (Figure 6), commissioned by William IV, Duke of Burgundy.[21] Unlike Le Brun's *Battle of Arbela* (Figure 5), this is a vision that prefigures the focus on man's relationship with the elements and the natural world that would form such a significant element in the Romantic tradition. Again, this is an image created for a monarch, and again we can see how contemporary concerns and modern imagery take precedence over any sense of the visualized action as *of* the past. The landscape overpowers the diminutive actors, crammed together in the lower portion of the scene; the sky is turbulent, and the setting is a fairy-tale version of the landscape that the audience would recognize as representative of an idealized Germanic world, William's own. Yet this image is not all about the glorification of a William-Alexander composite. The majesty and brooding vigour of the landscape makes the human conflict almost incidental to the scene, destabilizing Alexander's importance, and problematizing visual focus on the ostensible (and titular) subjects of the painting: Alexander and Darius. When the centre of the human action does come into focus, a minuscule mounted Alexander pursues Darius, fleeing in a chariot. The 'insignificance' of these human players in comparison to their setting may recall some of the ambiguities of the *Alexander Mosaic* in Pompeii (Frontispiece). Above the actors and cast of thousands, a 'wooden' inscription plate hovers in the stormy sky, interpreting the action for the viewer. This 'interpretative' panel and the majestic clash of the elements are the primary visual focus, and this decentralization of the human participants and the foregrounding instead of the relationship between man and nature, artifice and elements, and the artist and his audience prefigure the struggles of the Romantic era.

The mountains that play such a key role in Altdorfer's vision of Alexander and Darius symbolize on one level the realms of the unobtainable and the dangers attached to the quest undertaken by the Macedonian, and the mountain had an important role not just as a point of contact with the unknown, but also as a warning against hubris. A combination of these nuances can be seen in the emerging neo-classical movement that transformed Europe in the eighteenth century. In conjunction with a developing nineteenth-century Romantic sensibility, this led to a revitalization of the mystical, questing Alexander-experience, echoes of which can be seen in a Romantic idealization of incompleteness and ruin. Furthermore, in this Romantic reworking of some of the key elements of Alexander-mythology we find a renewed interest in the glorification of the impossible quest.[22] Canonical examples include Byron's 'Childe Harold', and Coleridge's 'Kubla Khan' and 'The Ancient Mariner', poems which focus on wandering, unfulfilled journeys, and mystical realms.[23] With hindsight, these young-dying artists embody one other key sense of Alexander's mythology: dying young. The idea of self-destructive obsession and parallel melancholy reflected in unfulfilled promise makes the early deaths of Romantic heroes such as Keats (25), and Schubert (30) fundamental to our engagement with and interpretation of 'Hyperion' and the 'Unfinished Symphony', while Shelley's 'romantic' end and Byron's 'heroic' death have become key features of the Romantic movement. [24] The nineteenth century was also an era of idealistic as well as capitalistic imperialism, and British involvement in India and European expansion into Africa places these powers firmly in the middle of Alexander's storied campaigns. Napoleon was famously a keen admirer of Alexander, but in general, less direct use of Alexander was made during this period than might have been expected.[25] For the British Empire, it was the cultural model of Greece, but the military and political model of Rome that would find most favour. Alexander could not offer an ideal example for the economic and political concerns of the British Empire, and the maverick figure who most closely recalls the difficulties of the Alexandrian model is T.E. Lawrence: Lawrence of Arabia.[26] One text that is not usually cited as specifically concerned with Alexander, yet which combines many of these nineteenth-century obsessions (the Romantic quest, exploration, increasing commercialization) with explicit comparisons between its 'hero' and Alexander, is Hermann Melville's

Moby Dick. In this narrative of obsession we can see how Ahab and the whalers become quasi-Alexanders, each engaged in personal quests that will bring them into contact with 'greatness'.[27]

Twentieth-century western versions of Alexander have been dominated by two texts: Mary Renault's *Alexander Trilogy*—dealing with his youth (*Fire From Heaven*), the eastern campaign as recounted by a young Persian eunuch, Bagoas (*The Persian Boy*), and the civil wars that followed Alexander's death (*Funeral Games*)—and Robert Rossen's 1956 film *Alexander the Great*. Both texts reflect key twentieth-century concerns with the figure of Alexander: the idea of an individual struggling with personal and public responsibilities and ultimately cracking under the strain of negotiating a course between the two, a vital and ever-present longing for a hero to worship, and a sense of an intimate connexion between mysticism, nationalism and imperialism sought through a persistent parallelism between classical past and 'present' (whenever that may be).[28] These two texts straddle the century, and seem to have had a formative influence on (at least) two generations. For some, Alexander is forever a golden-haired Richard Burton, tainted inextricably by Burton's off-screen parallels, his drinking, his sex-life, his glamour and his slide from golden boy to old age. Even Burton's liminal status as a Celt, the man from the edges of Union who conquered the centre but was incapable of dealing with his success, echoes Alexander's marginal status as the Macedonian king who could not quite hold the world together. For others, Alexander is Renault's sensitive and tortured soul, misunderstood by his comrades, and burdened by the fate of his people, his mission and his dream. These contrasting versions and agenda embrace the different ways in which the discipline of Classics as a whole has been undergoing a period of renewed change during the twentieth century, and how, increasingly, the study of Classics is becoming associated with a popular valorization of individuality and of difference.[29] Paradoxically there has been a concomitant realignment of twentieth-century heroism along classical lines, as can be seen in David Lean's characterization of Lawrence in *Lawrence of Arabia* (1962). This plays on the familiar motifs of individual glamour and solitary adventure, introspection, military success and death.

Recent years have seen a rash of abortive or stalled projects to make a new Alexander movie. At present, three films seem to be in the pipeline, one with Martin Scorsese as director (and Leonardo di Caprio as Alexander) a second, directed by Ridley Scott, and the other (and now more permanently stalled) directed by Oliver Stone and starring Tom Cruise; their tortuous progress means that we probably should not hold our breath.[30] Nevertheless, this resurgence for interest in Alexander demonstrates a renewed popularity for historical epic stories that is evidenced in films such as Ridley Scott's *Gladiator* and Julie Taymor's *Titus*, proving that although, more recently, grand epic scenarios have tended to be reserved for narratives such as the *Star Wars* sequence, the ongoing vitality of the ancient world to provide ways of commenting on ourselves is regaining a voice.

Working out parameters and criteria for reading and discussing historical fiction raises problems of 'accuracy', and opens up a debate about the nature of historical 'truth' and 'fiction' within primary and secondary sources. Why, we may ask, should some of Renault's stories be judged fiction, and others biography? Why should *The Alexander Trilogy* sit on a fiction shelf at the bookshop, while Arrian or Curtius on Alexander can be found in the ancient history section?[31] The slippage between the genres of fiction and history when ancient sources are at issue is a particularly difficult area, and debate about the subject tends to assume that 'fiction' and 'history' are terms that can be accorded a trans-historical meaning. What must be kept in mind is that although Renault has garnered much praise for her historical skills and her ability to combine accuracy with psychological insight into her characters, the degree to which she has become entangled with her version of Alexander, and her own role in his creation is in many ways equivalent to the kinds of rationale and methodology that her ancient counterparts were using.[32] The relationship between author, authorial persona and reader is one that much self-conscious modern fiction emphasizes, allotting a direct role in the textualized narrative to a distinct authorial voice.

In the ancient sources on Alexander we tend to focus on the various snatches of authorial commentary or editorializing, and there is a tendency to require these snippets to tell us something meaningful and 'true' about the way in which author and material are connected. For historical fiction of the kind composed by Renault, there has been a tendency to divorce her narrative from the printed text as a whole and thereby to elide any engagement with her paratextual apparatus, the self-conscious 'concluding notes'.[33] A comment typical of the way in which Renault's apparent status as 'serious' historian comes into direct conflict with her role as novelist is her judgement on the Alexander conjured up by Curtius Rufus:

> **Muddled sensationalism** is typical of Curtius, an unbearably **silly** man with access to **priceless** sources now lost to us, which he **frittered away** in the cause of a **tedious** literary concept. . . . Alexander's story is bent

that way by recourse to Athenian anti-Macedonian **agitprop**, written by
men who never set eyes on him, and bearing as much relation to
objective truth as one would expect to find in a *History of the Jewish
People* commissioned by Adolf Hitler.

(RENAULT, *The Persian Boy*, 412–13 (my emphases))[34]

The rhetoric employed by Renault makes her position particularly
tricky. On the one hand, she is writing fiction, and acknowledges this
as a different project to that taken on in her historical narrative, *The
Nature of Alexander*. On the other hand, what is it that makes one
fiction and one history? Why should ancient sources be judged for
their factual 'accuracy', and Renault's fictions for their ability to
provide a sense of psychological truth?[35] Ultimately, Renault is faced
with a familiar problem: she finds it impossible to accept intentional
distortion of the story that has evolved as a result of her research, but
the multiplicity of available interpretations of Alexander and the
shifting definition of history over the centuries have made the lack of
a single, consistent reality the one constant in the field.[36] Other fiction-
alizations of Alexander have appeared during the past century, and
Helga Moray's *Roxana* trilogy and David Gemmell's fantasy novels
(*Lion of Macedon* and *Prince of Darkness*) offer some examples of
narrative angles that never gained a widespread popularity. More
interestingly, Tom Holt's *Alexander at the World's End* reconfigured
Alexander as a bit-player in another (fictional) character's life, whilst
Valerio Massimo Manfredi's earnest (if emotionally charged) trilogy is
set to become the basis for the de Laurentiis/Scott film. A fascinating
interview with Manfredi in *The Bookseller* (17/8/2001:38) concludes:

> 'I created the trilogy like a crescendo,' the author declares. 'I swear to
> you, I finished this book with tears in my eyes, crying and writing at the
> same time.'

This evidence for an ongoing revitalization of Alexander suggests that
his story retains much of the potency that attracted Roman authors,
but as the cycle of interest continues to shift its interpretative emphasis, we can see that Alexander has, for the West at least, lost some of
his immediacy as a gloss on contemporary events, the role that he
fulfilled so successfully at Rome. Instead, we see a shift in the politicization of Alexander, as recent political developments in the Balkans,
particularly concerning the creation of the Former Yugoslav Republic
of Macedonia (FYROM), have given added piquancy to the role that

has been an integral part of Alexander since his own lifetime: his status as a figurehead for nationalistic aspirations.

This potential may first have come to the world stage in the 1980–82 exhibition, *The Search for Alexander*.[37] The timing of this event implicitly demands two questions of its audience: why is a search for Alexander necessary now, and what kind of Alexander will emerge at the end of the twentieth century? This exhibition, in many ways, used its title as an attractive lure: the majority of the material on show had less to do with Alexander than with Macedonia and the ruling family in general. The rationale behind the high profile, Alexander focused title is clear: 'Alexander' sells, and the idea of a quest—that highly Alexandrian endeavour—simultaneously promised mystery but no ultimate fulfilment.[38] What does emerge as a significant concern from the exhibition is a renewed sense of Alexander's nationalistic importance for Greece and the Balkans. In a world where borders and allegiances undergo rapid redefinition and where national aspirations have had a chequered history, reclaiming Alexander offered a link to an ancient past within which blueprints (and excuses) for the present might be discovered. Many exhibits had only the most tangential connexion with Alexander, but Yalouris' article in the catalogue amply demonstrates a Greek political need for a *Greek* Alexander to work with.[39] He emphasizes the persistence of a legendary Alexander in 'Greek' lands, his symbolic role embodying the desire for a national uprising (shortly before the Greek war of independence), and the representation of Alexander on a proclamation circulated by the poet and Greek nationalist martyr, Rhigias Pheraios, in 1797. In this way a 'Greek' heritage is traced for the hero, demonstrating his centrality to a symbolic and geographical entity, and a Greek people who can be presented as his symbolic and actual heirs. Alexander the Greek nationalist is still a problematic figure, even as he was in Roman times. Alexander's 'Greece' was a collection of antagonistic city states, held together briefly by threat, with promise of revenge on the Persians and the lure of booty. These states were disinclined to admit Macedon to their number, and for many of these fourth-century Greeks, particularly the Athenians, Macedon was not part of the club. The problematic nature of Macedon's relationship with the Greek states can be seen in Herodotus' comment that Alexander I of Macedon was apparently forced to resort to using a genealogical argument to prove an ethnic right to enter the Olympic games (Herodotus 5.22). The Macedonian question simmers along, outgunned by the more ferocious nationalistic conflicts that have swept through the Yugoslav republics, but for Greece (and the Greek province of Macedonia) and the state with the compromise title (FYROM) strong ideological antagonism still exists.[40]

Elements of the appeal of Alexander as a popular iconic figure persist in patterns of youthful death, self-destruction and glamour.[41] This is played out most fully in the lifestyle and glamour associated with the Kennedy presidency in America, with its sense of economic prosperity and world leadership. The young, glamorous President, who faced down the evil 'eastern' empire during the Cuban Missiles Crisis (1962), and greater sense of American involvement on a world stage allows analogies with Alexander imagery to surface.[42] The primary metaphorical reading of the Kennedy presidency draws upon Arthurian Camelot imagery, but as we have already seen, this is itself steeped in the ideology of the courtly questing Alexander. With the death of John F. Kennedy Junior, there was a resurgence of an idealizing, melancholy rhetoric, focused on a perceived sense of loss associated with the dissolution of the ideal. The immediate ascription of a 'curse' reflects ancient ideas of a Fate or '*Fortuna*' that dogged Alexander, forcing him inexorably into a path that would lead to his destruction.

On television, after a long break following the epic film, Alexander has started to creep back more directly into the popular consciousness.[43] This exposure re-emphasizes a potentially wide receptivity for material concerning Alexander, highlighted by recent television exploitation: in the 'quasi-serious' role of 'great commander' in the Channel 4 series of that name, he is the first in a line that stretches forward through Caesar (the other 'ancient' figure) and Napoleon to Georgi Zhukov.[44] Similarly, though more tangentially, he acts as a hook for programming in another Channel 4 series—John Romer's *The Seven Wonders*. The series of super-Alexanders that *The Great Commanders* proposed echoes the passage from Livy Book 9, discussed in Chapter 2. By leading off with Alexander, the series demands that each successive general-of-the-week is following literally and temporally in his footsteps. A similar effect is achieved by Brian Walden in his series *Walden on Heroes*, a curiously old-fashioned lecture to camera in which a conscious effort seems to have been made to avoid anything which might suggest technological wizardry or media manipulation. Naturally, the demands of to-camera speaking on film do require an artificial situation, but the series' presentation was sternly anti-innovatory.[45] More recently, Michael Wood's *In the Footsteps of Alexander the Great* (BBC 1997) has reinvented Alexander-as-Michael-Wood (or perhaps vice versa), complete with flowing locks and a visionary 'campaign'. How much more Alexander-

in-waiting can one get, than to retrace his footsteps? It is interesting
that Wood presents the contrast between the civilizing Alexander of
the 'West' and the destructive war-monger of 'Eastern' myth. This
compromises and complicates Wood's role as latter-day Alexander,
particularly given his self-construction as super-Alexander for 'our'
intellectually imperializing reconquest of the East. [46]

Three last examples return us to the kind of anecdotes with which
I commenced, and which form the most common popular currency
for Alexander, but they also demonstrate the continuing validity of
Alexander as a 'thought-model', whether through versions of his story
or as a reflection of the fascinations of his exploratory, questing pattern. Early in 1995, reports began to emerge of a dig at Siwah in
Egypt, purporting to have discovered the long-lost tomb of Alexander.
Sufficient interest emerged for *Hello!* magazine to consider the topic a
popular preoccupation, because the event was given a full colour
spread: 'The Tomb of Alexander the Great: Affirmed by some, denied
by others, the mystery remains unsolved'.[47] Cultural icons are not the
only potential Alexanders of the modern world, and while references
to the Gordian Knot for gardeners may seem trivial,[48] the serious
debate on homosexuality in the armed forces has been enlivened by
comparison with Alexander's prowess.[49] These 'references' resurface
in many guises, but continue the tradition commenced in the ancient
sources; that Alexander imagery recurs consistently is less surprising
than the lack of investigation it attracts.

This book focuses on the literary issues and cultural conditions that
may have affected our record of Alexander, and an awareness of these
contexts is vital for reading the texts, but over and above the political
conditions affecting the authors who chose to write 'Alexander',
another element should not be forgotten: Alexander's story is exciting.
His life spans two continents, it fuses mass action and violence, court
intrigue, sex, decadence, doomed youth, glamour, gluttony and death.
The sheer scale and variety of Alexander's recorded and legendary
exploits make his story one that continues to fascinate today. For
quick and punchy stories and images of power, intrigue, civilization
and degeneracy, all still pertinent contemporary issues, Alexander
makes them all available for comment. Many of the works dealt with
in this study are not histories, but in their reference to Alexander they
draw upon and partake of both history and cultural myth, demonstrating his popular availability as a character with which to think
about the first centuries BCE and CE. In the light of his mass popularity,
both as an exemplum and as the ultimate hero we can deduce the
existence of a ready-primed audience for Alexander stories.

Conjuring with Alexander

Having reached the end of this investigation, what have we discovered? Alexander's appeal as an exciting hero coexists with his
despotism and excess, and there is no need to reconcile the two. This
flexibility in his imagery is the first factor for consideration: he is a
casting agent's dream. The existence and vigour of disparate interpretative traditions demonstrates both the liveliness of his afterlife
and his varied potential as a referential figure. The division between
literary and political analysis in this book mirrors this diversity, whilst
at the same time downplaying the ubiquitous emphasis of so many
stories of Alexander: peeling back the layers to reach the 'real'
Alexander beneath the myth. The focus in the four central chapters
has been on the story inscribed and excluded from the layers themselves.

Roman narratives of Alexander can be interpreted simultaneously
as histories of Alexander's campaign *and* an appeal to Roman political conditions. No rigid definition of Roman popular attitudes can
succeed, but the collation of a wide variety of sources (covering anecdotes, history, epistles, rhetoric, school-texts, philosophy and poetry)
attests a broad appreciation of Alexander as a suitable, sometimes
dangerous, but always significant figure for contemporary parallel.
Alexander remains greater and more ubiquitous than the sum of the
individual stock Alexanders of rhetoric and history might suggest, and
the readings in this book explore some of the ways in which cumulative references can take on such a pervasive stranglehold on notions
of heroism, power, excess, beauty and death for successive eras. Yet,
ultimately, the question remains: why use Alexander, an equivocal
foreigner, for Roman identity debates? This question has not hitherto
been addressed head-on; debate has previously focused on *whether*,
rather than *why*, Alexander figures prominently in Roman political
considerations. This book offers a selection of possible reasons, ranging from a growing need to redefine one-man rule in terms of imperial
expansion and Roman monarchical fears, to implicit critique of
government; from personal gain, to a desire to harness Alexandrian
charisma as a justification for moving outside the 'system'. That these
themes connect up is fundamental not just to the developing imagery
of the early Principate, but also has wide-ranging implications for all
readings of contemporary culture and literature. I have suggested
some of the ways in which a Roman might have perceived versions of
Alexander: a dispersed character in his eastward, one-way quest, in
the fragmentation that his death precipitated, and in the seemingly

disintegrated contexts for his usage. It is in this last that the potency of Alexander ultimately resides. From a bundle of anecdotes, 'quotations', comparisons and character-sketches emerges an Alexander whose immortality and ongoing relevance is rooted in his reflective opacity. Each Alexander reflects a figure that answers us in our own idiom.

Modern Alexanders

I have listed the works about which I have full bibliographical details, and which concentrate on Alexander rather than sources. Investigating any of the websites at the end of this section may suggest various other titles and authors, but as is so often the case with web-based information, *caueat emptor*! The selection of websites was chosen on the basis of their content providing more than simply a narrative 'history' of Alexander, of which, of course, there are many more out there.

Fiction

Mary Renault *Fire From Heaven* (London: Longman, 1970), *The Persian Boy* (London: Longman, 1972), *Funeral Games* (London: Peter Murray, 1981); I refer to the Penguin editions of 1972, 1980, 1983.

Other examples of narratives of Alexander include: Jakob Wassermann *Alexander in Babylon* (Ziff-Davis: 1949; originally published in 1905); Louis Couperus *Iskander, de roman van Alexander de Grote* (Rotterdam: 1920); Konrad Bercovici *Alexander: A Romantic Biography* (J.J. Little and Ives: 1928); Klaus Mann *Alexander: A Novel of Utopia* (Brewer and Warren, 1930); Mary Butts *The Macedonian* (London: Heinemann, 1933); Nicholas Kazantzakis *Alexander the Great: A Novel*, originally published in serial form in early 1940, and intended for 'young adults', it was reissued posthumously in 1979 as a novel, to coincide with the discoveries at Vergina; Robert Payne *Alexander the God* (A.A. Wyn, 1954); Karl V. Eiker *Star of Macedon* (G.P. Putnam, 1957); Edison Marshall *The Conqueror* (Doubleday, 1962); Aubrey Menen *A Conspiracy of Women* (Random House, 1965); Helga Moray's 'Roxana' trilogy (London: Robert Hale,

1971), covering Alexander's married life, and its aftermath, and providing an interesting structural counterpoint to Renault's work; Melissa Scott *A Choice of Destinies* (Baen, 1986); David Gemmell *Lion of Macedon* and *Prince of Darkness* (London: Century, 1990/ 1991) which give a fantasy setting to the reigns of Philip (focusing on his commander, Parmenion) and Alexander; Judith Tarr *Lord of the Two Lands* (Tor, 1993); Ben Bova *Orion and the Conqueror* (Tor, 1994); Anna Apostolou *A Murder in Macedon* and *A Murder in Thebes* (St Martin's Press, 1997, 1998; Anna Apostolou is P[aul].C. Doherty writing under a *nom de plume*); Valerio Massimo Manfredi's Alexander trilogy: *Alexander: Child of a Dream*; *Alexander: The Sands of Ammon*; *Alexander: The Ends of the Earth* (Pan London: Macmillan, 2001; originally published in 1998 in Italian); Tom Holt *Alexander at the World's End* (Little, Brown & Co., 1999).

There are two particularly useful online lists of Alexander-fiction. One (with reviews) can be found at http://home.earthlink.net/ ~mathetria/Beyond_Renault/list.html; the second forms a subsection of Nick Lowe's excellent and extensive pages on classical historical fiction http://www2.rhbnc.ac.uk/Classics/NJL/novels.html#24.

Faction

Harold Lamb *Alexander of Macedon: the Journey to World's End* (London: Robert Hale, 1946).

Biography/history

Ulrich Wilcken *Alexander the Great*, tr. G.C. Richards (New York: Norton, 1967 [1st ed. 1931]); Arthur Weigall *Alexander the Great* (London: Thornton Butterworth, 1933); W.W. Tarn *Alexander the Great* 2 volumes (Oxford, 1948); Fritz Schachermeyr *Alexander der Grosse: Ingenium und Macht* (Graz: A. Pust, 1949); E. Badian *Alexander the Great and the Unity of Mankind* (Wiesbaden, 1958), *Some Recent Interpretations of Alexander* (Geneva, 1975); Robin Lane Fox *Alexander the Great* (London: Allen Lane, 1973); Peter Green *Alexander the Great* (Harmondsworth: Penguin, 1974); Mary Renault *The Nature of Alexander* (London: Allen Lane, 1975); A.B. Bosworth (ed.) *Alexandre le Grand, image et réalité* (Geneva: Fondation Hardt, 1976), *Conquest and Empire: the Reign of Alexander the Great* (Cambridge: CUP, 1988) and *Alexander and* the East: *The Tragedy of Triumph* (Oxford: OUP, 1996); N.G.L. Hammond *Alexander the Great: King, Commander and Statesman*, (Bristol: University of Bristol Press, 1989) and *The Genius of Alexander the Great* (London: Duckworth, 1997); John Maxwell O'Brien *Alexander the Great: The Invisible Enemy* (London: Routledge, 1992); Jesper Carlsen (ed.) *Alexander the Great: Reality and Myth* (Rome: L'Erma di Bretschneider, 1993); Richard Stoneman *Alexander the Great* (London: Routledge, 1997); E.E. Rice *Alexander the Great* (Stroud: Sutton Publishing, 1997); A.B. Bosworth and E.J. Baynham (eds) *Alexander the Great in Fact and Fiction* (Oxford, 2000); Alan Fildes and Joann Fletcher *Alexander the Great: Son of the Gods* (London: Duncan Baird, 2001).

Web pages (live in Spring 2002)

http://www.isidore-of-seville.com/Alexanderama.html
http://www.pothos.co.uk/
http://www.bbk.ac.uk/hca/classics/alexander.htm
http://1stmuse.com/frames/index.html
http://www.royalty.nu/Europe/Balkan/Alexander.html
http://www.itihaas.com/ancient/1.html
http://www.acs.ohio-state.edu/history/isthmia/teg/Hist111H/issues/
   alex1.html
http://wso.williams.edu/~junterek/index.html
http://www.gayheroes.com/alex.htm
http://www.pbs.org/mpt/alexander/
http://www.greece.org/alexandria/alexander/Pages/alexandros.html
http://www.hackneys.com/alex_web/siteinfo.htm
http://www.sangha.net/messengers/alex.htm
http://www.triv.net/html/History/alex1.htm
http://www.geocities.com/WestHollywood/Heights/8255/alexander.
   html

Notes

Introduction: The Empty Bottle

1 Wilcken 1967: xxix (first published 1931). See also Badian 1976: 280.
2 See Baynham 1998:63.
3 Readers unfamiliar with Alexander's career may turn to the chronology at pp. 22–4f. For Alexander's life and campaigns, try Green 1974, Hammond 1989 and Bosworth 1988, for useful, fairly sober accounts.
4 See Beard 1993.
5 I have provided translations for all the texts discussed. The translations are not always elegant, but attempt to capture the flavour of each author's words whilst remaining (reasonably) literal.

1   History into Story

1 See Plautus, *Mostellaria*, 775 (early second century BCE) and Fraenkel 1960:14
2 As the titles of Bosworth (1988a) and Hammond (1989) suggest, these roles tend to be highlighted by a 'serious' biographer/historian.
3 See Cowan 2000, Karakasidou 1997 and Shea 1996.
4 The terms 'Greece' and 'Greek' are themselves problematic. I use them, in this instance, to provide a cultural shorthand for Athens and its allies, but during the Hellenistic period and under the Roman empire 'Greece' was once again a politically loaded concept.
5 Not only the republican Romans had a problem with monarchy, for the democratic Athenians, kings also represented tyranny. For a history of Macedon, see Hammond et al. 1972–88.
6 After the Persian Wars of 490 and 480/79 BCE; the treaty of Miletus (412 BCE) began a period of co-operation between Sparta and Persia that seems to have lasted until about 405 BCE, and brought about the decline of Athens as an imperial power.

7   E.g. passages 3.9 and 4.8.

8   The discussion that follows assumes a basic familiarity with Roman history. Useful introductory volumes are Beard and Crawford 1999[2], Alston 1998 and Scullard 1991[5].

9   Even the name given to those who carved up Alexander's empire (Successors: οἱ διάδοχοι), and which came to define the kingdoms that they founded, keeps them firmly in Alexander's shadow; they are defined only in relation to him. See Diodorus 17.4.1.

10 The loss of the contemporary 'official' versions seems to have taken place at a relatively early date. We can only speculate as to whether this was solely down to chance, or whether 'unofficial' versions were more enticing. Official sanction for visual representations of Alexander went to Lysippus (sculpture) and Apelles (painting).

11 Of course Alexander also 'believed' his family to be descended from Heracles, and he went on to give support to the idea that his father was Zeus. The more impressive genealogies, the better.

12 Compare e.g. Stadter 1980: 60–80, 164–69, and Bosworth 1995:5–7.

13 See Hammond 1983:160–69.

14 Callisthenes of Olynthus was a historian and nephew of Aristotle. Before joining up with Alexander he had co-operated with Aristotle on an official list of the victors at the Pythian Games. Independently, he had written on the third Sacred War, and composed a history of Greece from 386–356 BCE. It is likely that his account of Alexander's campaigns was extremely positive. On the *Ephemerides*, see Hammond 1983:5–11, Robinson 1932, and Hammond 1988.

15 For Roman developments of this 'theology' of victory, see Fears 1977.

16 For discursive introductions to 'orientalism' ancient and modern, see Hartog 1988, Said 1991 and Romm 1992.

17 By the time of the *Aeneid*, Carthage had long since ceased to have enemy status, but Carthage's origins as a Near-Eastern colony could tie the city to the 'new' eastern enemy, Parthia.

18 Naevius' epic predecessor at Rome was Livius Andronicus, a Tarentine Greek, who was said to have been brought to Rome as a slave after the surrender of Tarentum to Rome in 272 BCE (two years before Rome finally gained control of all peninsular Italy). We know very little about his life; he may have taken his owner's name on manumission. He staged the first Latin tragedy in 240 BCE, and apparently wrote many works, but all we have left are some fragments of his *Odyssia*. He seems to have attempted to reinterpret Greek themes and stories in Latin and in a manner that would give them relevance in Rome. He also seems to have set a standard that would continue to inform much Roman epic, whereby a solemn tone and serious treatment of subject matter was favoured.

19 The poem seems to have treated more recent history more expansively, though with less attention played to the first Punic war than to the

second. The scope of the poem seems to have reached as far as the end of the Istrian War (171 BCE), having dealt with the war against Philip of Macedon (201–196 BCE), and against Antiochus III of Syria, an ally of Hannibal, who was defeated at Magnesia by Scipio Asiaticus (190 BCE).

20 Ennius may have been a Pythagorean, and a believer in metempsychosis (this would tie in with the 'dream sequence'), but whether or not it was the case, his theme was to be picked up by Virgil in *Aeneid* 6, Ovid (more playfully) in *Met.* 15, and Valerius Flaccus (*Argonautica* 1.531–60).

21 When 'reading' any of these characters it is vital to be aware of the potential for historical bias that may colour their representation. Marius makes a wonderful foil for Sulla, but the bluff soldier versus political and strategic supremo contrast does not have to be swallowed whole.

22 Sulla had negotiated the hand-over of Jugurtha. He also forged a peace with Parthia and dealt extensively with Mithridates of Pontus when proconsul of Cilicia in 96 BCE.

23 For this Sullan spin, we are dependent mainly on much later testimony. Plutarch gives a full account (*Sulla* 34), and is open about his general indebtedness to Sulla's own memoirs, but it is difficult not to suspect that Sulla's 'divine' self-fashioning owes something to hindsight.

24 On the developing iconography of Alexander in the Hellenistic period, see Stewart 1993.

25 Caesar was born around 101 BCE, into an old patrician family allied with Marius, and he established links with the *populares* early on.

26 Horace *Odes* 3.5. Even after the return of the standards, and their eventual resting place in the new Temple of Mars Ultor (2 BCE), Parthia continues to disturb. See pp. 195–200 for the ongoing significance of Parthia.

27 For a detailed summary of Caesar's changing image, with full references to ancient sources, see Gelzer 1969:278–79, 308–9, 315–23.

28 Nicolaus of Damascus *Caes.* 26.95. Nicolaus was a philosopher and historian, who wrote a universal history in 144 books. He tutored the children of Antony and Cleopatra (probably in the late 30s BCE) and went on to become a friend and advisor of Herod the Great, in whose service he came into contact with Augustus. After Herod's death he spent some time in Rome, according to his own testimony, and gained Augustus' favour. As we shall see, not all comparisons between Caesar and Alexander are posthumous. Green 1989b rounds up most of the comparisons, but ascribes too little weight to Cicero's testimony.

29 E.g. Virgil *Aeneid* 8.680ff. Cf. Dio 49.4.1–4. Yet as Dio recounts, Agrippa did receive a golden crown in recognition of Naulochus (49.14.3), and a dark blue flag for Actium (51.21.3).

30 See Livy, 1.10 and 4.20; cf. Propertius 4.10.

31 Perhaps Augustus' emphatic assertion that he was hailed *imperator* twenty-one times (*Res Gestae* 3–4) may evoke an undercurrent of comparison with Caesar's highly personal style of military command in the field.

32   On these honours see Zanker 1988:221–23. Zanker also examines the 'problem' of repackaging Tiberius (1988:227–30)

33   See Chapter 5 (pp. 191–3 and 202–3) where this discussion is picked up.

34   On the rise of the slogan '*uindicatio libertatis*' in the late republic see Wirszubski 1960:52, 103–5, and *Res Gestae* 1.1–2. Compare with Curtius 4.12.14–17; 5.10.2, 9.14; 8.5.20; 9.4.22; 10.2.15, 7.11, 9.2–3.

35   After the turbulence surrounding the Gracchi and Marius, the development of a professional army and increasingly populist politics heightened a perceived threat of autocracy. The terms used in criticism of powerful leaders express fear and hatred of this development. Tiberius Gracchus was accused of aiming at *regnum*, as was Saturninus; Cinna's regime was branded *dominatus* and *tyrannis*; Sulla's dictatorship was considered *dominatio, tyrannis, seruitium* and *regnum*. See Wirszubski 1960:62; Dempsie 1991:135 on Curtius 10.5.9.

36   Harris 1989 allows little, but for alternative views see Beard et al. (1991).

37   See Walbank 1970, 1979.

38   Cf. Fears 1977; Murray 1972:200–13.

39   Marincola 1997.25.

40   For a different emphasis, see Wirszubski 1960:95–99. His suggestion that there would have been a 'majority', oblivious to the political developments, is implausible.

41   *Brutus* 81.262. For further discussion cf. Ceauşescu 1974, Kienast 1969, Wirth 1976, Heuß 1954, Weippert 1972 and Treves 1953. M. Crassus the triumuir had clear Alexander-potential. There is surely irony in Cicero's comparison of P. Crassus to Alexander, when his father's is the stronger claim.

42   This is reflected in Claudius' triumph *de Britannis*, where military *res gestae* are accomplished under imperial auspices. This *auctoritas* is comparable with the fluid nature of Alexander's kingship; the self-creation of role that he undertakes is matched by the necessity for his generals to accept his authority because of the distance from Macedon, and their own inability to engage confidently with the leadership of the army so far from home.

43   Naevius' *Bellum Punicum* (late third century BCE) is the first recorded piece of Roman historiography, and it is in the form of an epic poem.

44   E.g. Cassius Hemina, Calpurnius Piso, Cn. Gellius. C. Quadrigarius, Valerius Antias and Licinius Macer continued this in the first century BCE.

45   On the 'dumbing-down' of late republican historiography, see Marincola 1997:28–29.

46   E.g. Plutarch's life of Alexander, and Arrian's *Anabasis*. Cf. Dio's orations on kingship, starring Alexander. These can be read in conjunction with Pliny's *Panegyric*. Useful introductions to Plutarch and Alexander can be found at Placido 1995 and Prandi 2000, but Zecchini 1984 is also worth pursuing.

47 A good introduction to the ethos and cultural movements of this period can be found in Swain 1996. On biography, see Edwards and Swain 1997.
48 Arrian's dates are *c*.86–160 CE. Swain 2000 is a welcome addition to scholarship on Dio, whilst Goldhill 2001 provides a series of explorations of the artistic and cultural tensions involved in 'being' Greek in a Roman world. Of particular interest are Goldhill's introduction (1–28) and Henderson (2001).

2 Readings—Alexander *Rex*

1 Bosworth 1996 explores (idiosyncratically) some of the ideas raised by this vocal 'silence'.
2 It was also during this period that the rumbling threat from Gaul was neutralized, so that in the activities of the developing Roman state we can see a (potential) parallel for the Macedonian hegemony of Greece, and perhaps a hint towards the imperializing activities to come.
3 Developing Kennedy 1992:27, where he states that the 'politics of Latin poetry is inextricably linked with the politics of talking about it', we can read this meta-literary discourse on to all modes of verbal expression. This becomes particularly relevant when reading Cicero (passages 2.3–2.7).
4 For other examples of the popular *topos* of Alexander the irascible drunkard see e.g. Velleius (passage 3.1); Seneca, *Concerning Anger* (*De Ira*) 2.23.3; passages 3.2 and 3.3; *Ep.* 94.62.
5 This is particularly interesting in the context of Cicero, *Concerning Duties* (*de Off.*) 2.16, where he quotes Panaetius to the effect that Alexander is one of those who only accomplished great things for the state because he had the co-operation of others to draw upon.
6 In Livy's ideal situation he makes no allowance for any power-struggle necessary to ensure succession, potential rivals and factions, and strong opposition to weak monarchs.
7 The 'digression' as a whole takes up a significant chunk of text: 9.17.1–19.7. L. Papirius Cursor is best known as a hero of the Second Samnite War. He held the consulship five times between 326 and 313 BCE, and was—at least—twice dictator (325, 310 BCE). After the Roman disaster at the Caudine Forks (321 BCE) he took command of the war, and had successes at Luceria (320 BCE) and Satricum (319 BCE).
8 Christina Kraus perceptively drew my attention to this paradoxical sense of a narrowing of Roman horizons associated with contact between Rome and the East in Livy's first decade. The Brutus episode is particularly significant, of course, because it introduces the rape of Lucretia and the fall of the Tarquins, ending Rome's monarchy and foreshadowing Brutus' role as first consul.
9 Like his uncle, Alexander I of Epirus, Pyrrhus responded to a call for help against Rome. In coming to Tarentum's aid he seems to have had designs

on carving out a new kingdom in a unified Magna Graecia, and had some initial successes. He was finally defeated in 275 BCE.

10 See Kraus 1994:5.

11 See Kraus 1994:13–14 for the best introduction to Livy's narratological style. Livy makes the popular claim that he records only what historians cast no doubts upon (9.18.5). Instead of suggesting to the reader that he presents *all* possible information, Livy reports that he has already digested the material and filtered out erroneous versions; we must now accept what he tells us.

12 *Fortuna* appears eight times: 9.17.3, 6; 18.2, 9, 10, 11, 12, 17. Particularly interesting is Livy's ascription of the benefits brought to Rome by fortune, an attribute not only of the city, but also of individual commanders.

13 Curtius 3.5.4–8; 9.6.15; Alexander's replies: 3.5.13–14, 6.6; 9.6.18–24. Cf. Lucan *Civil War* (*BC*) 5.682–689.

14 On Papirius: '*Et uis erat in eo uiro imperii ingens pariter in socios ciuesque*' (9.16.16).

15 Embedded somewhere in this set piece is the idea that as Rome towers over Alexander, so Livy towers over earlier, Greek, historians. Cf. Marincola 1997:224. Fox 2000:280 discusses Scipio's perhaps similar role in Cicero's *Concerning the Republic* (*de Rep.*).

16 M. Porcius Cato seems to have taken over the leadership of the politically influential grouping that had been centred on Q. Catulus, Q. Hortensius and L. Lucullus in the 70s and 60s BCE. He was firmly opposed to both Caesar and Pompey, and came to be viewed as something of a republican hero (and Stoic 'saint') after his protest-suicide at Utica in 46 BCE. On the political network surrounding Cato, see Gruen 1974:52–58, and 1993:52–83, for a useful overview of how Cato's 'republicanism' fitted into a general concern with the influence of Hellenism in Rome. Hirtius' response to Cicero's *Cato* may have been intended to act as an introduction for Caesar's own more lengthy response.

17 *Pro Marcello* (*On behalf of Marcellus*). The speech was in gratitude for Caesar's clemency towards his opponent, M. Claudius Marcellus (consul 51 BCE), whom he had been persuaded to recall. Its delivery (46 BCE) broke Cicero's political silence. Cicero refers to this speech in a letter to Servius Sulpicius Rufus (*ad Fam.* 4.4.3–4; probably from October 46 BCE). We can compare this with a rather formal and stilted letter to Cicero from M. Claudius Marcellus himself, written from Mytilene in November 46 BCE (*ad Fam.* 4.11) and Cicero's response (*ad Fam.* 4.10; December 46 BCE).

18 '*ego rogatus mutaui meum consilium; nam statueram, non mehercule inertia sed desiderio pristinae dignitatis, in perpetuum tacere. . . . Sed tamen, quoniam effugi eius offensionem, qui fortasse arbitraretur me hanc rem publicam non putare si perpetuo taceram, modice hoc faciam*' (*ad Fam.* 4.4.4); ' I was called upon to speak and I changed my decision. I had determined—not, by Hercules out of laziness but because I was conscious of my former position—to keep silent forever. . . . But since I

have now escaped giving him offence (he might well have interpreted my eternal silence as distaste for the present political regime) I shall now continue my participation, but in moderation.'

19 *Pro Marcello* 6–8; cf. '*paene diuinam*' *Pro Marcello* 1. This comparison with a god is likely to have been figurative (cf. *Milo.* 91; *Verr.* 2.5.41), nevertheless the eulogistic tone plugs into a Hellenistic rhetoric of royal panegyric in which deified rulers played an important part. In the wake of Caesar's triumphs there was a cluster of significant changes in his imagery, as will be discussed in Chapter 5. Caesar's emphasis on speed of conquest and action may suggest more specific echoes of Alexander, but these nuances remain implicit within the wider consideration of Caesar's role.

20 *Ad Fam.* 4.4.4. The issue of *clementia* as a Roman political concept was beginning to become particularly important in the wake of its 'adoption' by Caesar, and it was eventually to become one of the paradigmatic imperial 'virtues'. See Fears 1981. As early as 49 BCE Cicero makes epistolary reference to a 'policy' of conquering using mercy (*misericordia*) and generosity (*liberalitas*), *ad Att.* 9.7C.1; so the concept, which had previously been attributed to Scipio, Sulla and Pompey (perhaps picking up in turn on its association with Alexander) was clearly one that was familiar in connexion with Caesar. In general, *mansuetudo* and *clementia* were noted as forming an accepted part of Roman foreign policy towards conquered nations (e.g. *Verr.* 2.5.115).

21 *Ad Fam.* 4.4.3–4

22 See Fox 2000:270–83, whose elegant observations on Scipio in the *de Rep.* have important implications for the study of Roman Alexanders.

23 Weinstock 1971:188 (also Green 1989b:205) raises the idea that Caesar himself introduced Cicero to such a Caesar/Alexander parallel; Green, however, raises the idea only to dismiss it as implausible.

24 Cf. Cicero's use of '*summa potestas*' to describe Caesar's political position, *Pro Marcello* 1. *Potestas* could refer to power wielded by republican magistrates, but could also denote sovereignty. On Roman hatred of the term 'king', see Livy's Scipio (27.19.4) and Cicero, *de Rep.* 2.30.52. Cf. Serres 1991:99–114, 123–25; Barton 2001:101.

25 Admittedly we have the verdict of a confirmed letter-writer for this significance, but taken in terms, for example, of Sallust's record of the use made against Catiline of incriminating letters (e.g. *The Conspiracy of Catiline* [*Bell. Cat.*] 44.1–6; 47.1–2), Catiline's use of letters in his defence (e.g. 34.2), and the importance accorded to a letter written in Catiline's name (34.3–35.6), we must give some credence to Cicero's claims. Particularly given his chagrin when his composition is vetoed. We should also refer this emphasis on the breaking of (epistolary) silence back to the similar focus on Cicero's decision to break his silence in the senate at the beginning of the *Pro Marcello*.

26 Suetonius *Iulius* 7.1.

27 Cicero's realization that all dialogue between autocrat and subject is inevitably compromised is further evidenced in his claim that it was only his death that saved Hortensius from the rhetorical silence that Caesar's dictatorship would have forced upon him (*Brutus* 6). Only a well-ordered and peaceful republic could allow oratory to flourish. Without freedom of speech, oratory swings between criticism and flattery, finding a none-too-safe middle ground only in allusion. On what she terms this 'oppositional innuendo' see Bartsch 1994:63–97. Cicero himself discusses the possibilities of innuendo in his speech for Sestius (cf. Quintilian, *Inst. Or.* 9.2.66–69; Demetrius, *On Style* 289, 294; Pliny, *Paneg.* 3.4; Plutarch, *De Adulatore et Amico* 56 E-F, 58A, E-F).

28 Cf. MacMullen 1967, Griffin 1989, and Rawson 1989, on philosophy and Roman politics. Millar 1977: 465–77 discusses imperial attitudes to learned counsellors.

29 Cicero *ad Fam.* 15.19.4.

30 See Chapter 4 for further discussion of this text (passage 4.5).

31 Cf. Plutarch *Mor.* 58F, 60B-C, 65C-F, 124C-D, 471E, 472D.

32 Callisthenes was put to death for his alleged part in the Pages' conspiracy (cf. Curtius 8.8.21), but it was Clitus who was personally killed by Alexander for a snide remark at a drunken banquet (8.1.45). The remark about *ichor*, here attributed to Callisthenes, is made by Alexander in Plutarch (*Alex.* 28), and by Anaxarchus in Diog. Laert. (9.60). Cf. Plutarch (*Mor.* 71C, 449E, 458B-C, 781A-B). Arrian offers a different angle on Callisthenes (4.12.6–7): he was arrogant and foolish to refuse to exalt Alexander when in his service. Clitus, similarly gets little sympathy from Arrian (4.9.1–2).

33 Seneca (*Suas.* 1.5) quotes Cicero (*ad Fam.* 15.19.4) on Cassius' quip about Pompey's defeat at Munda; yet another link in the web.

34 *Despite* Plutarch's comments at *Alex.* 7.2–8.4. Aristotle is said to have reshaped his educative ideas in response to Isocrates (Cicero *de Or.* 2.58; 3.141). Quintilian recorded that Philip wanted the best philosopher of the age to undertake his son's education, and Aristotle was happy to oblige (*Inst. Or.* 1.1.23). See also Valerius Maximus 3.3 ext. 4.

35 *Mor.* 1043D. Plutarch lived from before 50 CE until after 120 CE. It is difficult to establish a relative chronology for his works, and Jones 1966: 71–74 offers a helpful discussion.

36 Seneca was born at Corduba in Spain between 4 BCE and 1 CE, and was forced to commit suicide by Nero in 65 CE. He had previously been banished by Claudius for adultery with Gaius (Caligula)'s sister, Julia Livilla (Cassius Dio 60.8.4–5; 41 CE). He was recalled in 49 CE through the influence of the younger Agrippina, made praetor, and appointed tutor to the young Nero. In 39 CE, according to Cassius Dio (59.19.7–8), his oratorical skills nearly cost him his life at Caligula's hands. Seneca's 'official' position as tutor (and the split between Nero and Seneca in 60 CE) personalizes his interest. We may speculate as to how genuine these

Senecan 'letters' are as correspondence; no evidence exists to doubt their origin as 'real' letters, but we might want to consider whether the whole body of epistles offers an intact record. Some of the longer may have been worked up, or even interpolated at a later point.

37 This behaviour on the pupil's part is then compared with Pompey, Caesar and Marius. Nero's admiration for Greece is also, of course, a form of orientalism, mirroring Alexander's adoption of eastern mores. Alcock 1994:104–7 argues that Nero's Hellenism had a practical political motive, but still admits a role for Alexander. Cf. Cassius Dio (c.164 to after 229 CE) 78.7, on the long afterlife of Alexander's uneasy relationship with philosophy: Caracalla went so far as to penalise the latter-day followers of Aristotle because of the latter's supposed role in Alexander's death. Dio's history of Rome was highly positive towards the shift from Republic to Empire.

38 Seneca *Ep.* 91.17

39 Cicero (*de Off.* 2.53–54) has Alexander criticized for corrupting the Macedonians with wealth, but reading Seneca's essay is like reading a gloss on the *de Off.* for a whole new world. For thematic similarities, see 1.42–43 (you should not harm the object of your benefaction), 1.42–44, 2.55, 1.45–60 (the gift should be in proportion to the means of the donor and the merits of the recipient), 3.118, 2.32 (one should be wary of one's motives). Cf. Atkinson 1980:223 on Curtius 6.8.7. Greek versions can work from two angles: Alexander as a 'positive' figure, representing Hellenism and a prototype for a successful Greek leader; or as a 'negative' model (the cynic/stoic tradition); not a programmatic hostility; cf. Fears 1974:113, 130. Millar 1977:135–9, 465–77, 491–506 discusses the emperor and attitudes to benevolence. Cf. Plutarch *Mor.* 818B. See Wallace-Hadrill 1982.35.

40 Cf. Cicero (*Tusc. Disp.* 5.91–92); Valerius Maximus (4.3 ext.3, 4); Seneca (*de Ben.* 5.4.3–4, 6.1); Juvenal (14.308–16); Plutarch (*Mor.* 179F-180A; 188C-D) (on Alexander and Diogenes/Anaxarchus). Cf. Plutarch (*Mor.* 605D-C; 782A-B; 179E; 179F-180A, 180E, 181B, 188C-D; 331E, 333B); Quintilian (*Inst. Or.* 2.20.3).

41 This problem of friendship and monarchs is identified later by Plutarch (*Mor.* 96B-C). Concerning flattery as an adjunct to power, cf. Plutarch (*Mor.* 53C-D; 57A; 58F and 471E; 60B-C; 65C-F, 472D, and 124C-D). The chastisement of a monarch will always be problematical (*Mor.* 71B-C; [181F]), as will rivalry (*Mor.* 58F; 179D; 181CE; 471E), or serving too well (cf. the suspicions cast on Antipater [*Mor.* 180E; 183F]); cf. Curtius 6.1.17–19; 8.14.46.

42 Compare with Plutarch *Mor.* 826C-D, where the Megarians vote πολιτεία to Alexander.

43 On Curtius' date, there is a vast range of opinion. Baynham (1998) is the most recent full-scale discussion of the text.

3   Readings—Living Fast, Dying Young . . .

1   Cf. Horace *Odes* 1.3.34–40, with all its problematic, heroic Augustan implications. See also Edwards 1993: 176–83, 190–95.

2   *On the Sublime* 33.2. Although 'Longinus' says he is talking about literary criticism, in fact, as Alison Sharrock pointed out to me, his comments apply equally (if not more so) to the political, cultural and military repositioning that characterizes Rome during these centuries (*On the Sublime* was probably written during the first century CE).

3   On the Stoic doctrine that food be eaten for nourishment rather than pleasure, see Cicero, *de Off.* 1.106.

4   Velleius' OTT encomium of Tiberius (2.126.1–130.5) concludes the main narrative.

5   In support of this, we can contrast the positive portrayal of Sejanus, the ultimate military acolyte/rival in Velleius, with the coruscating anger displayed against him by Tacitus.

6   Velleius' decapitated text commences with the Trojan War, and demonstrates an on going concern with a process of history whereby past and present are inextricably connected, e.g. 1.6.3–6, 1.7.2–4, 1.14.1, 1.16.1–18.3, 2.1.1–2, 2.13.1–2.

7   See Woodman 1988:51. Caesar is named in a literary excursus at 2.36.2.

8   Cf. Plutarch *Alex.* 75.

9   Cf. *Concerning Anger* (*de Ira*) 3.17.1–2 (passage 3.6); Plutarch (*Mor.* 71C; 449E; 458B; 781A-B). Also Valerius Maximus (9.3 ext.1). For this incident see also Cicero, *Tusc. Disp.* 4.79: Alexander regrets his behaviour so greatly that he almost kills himself. This passage is part of a letter that deals with the effects of drunkenness on individuals and on the State; for a more detailed discussion see Spencer forthcoming (2).

10 There were parallel but opposed tropes of dining during this period; firstly, the traditional notion of the communal meal as a key performative model for the normative hierarchical status quo, but secondly, a paradoxical belief that meals ought to offer a space that could exist outside these conventions where social distinctions would be set aside (see e.g. Martial 3.60; Pliny *Ep.* 2.6; Juvenal *Sat.* 5). Gowers 1993: 211–19 examines how Juvenal *Sat.* 5 presents the discriminatory dinner as representative of a wider social dysfunction, a corruption of the whole nature of the relationship between patron and client (see also D'Arms 1984; 1990). On poisoning in the imperial family see e.g. Cassius Dio 54.30 (on Augustus); but of course Germanicus and Claudius offer other prime examples.

11 Cf. Tacitus *Germania* 23; Justin 1.8.7.

12 Cf. Suetonius, *Gaius* 52. For potential resonances of Alexander during Claudius' Principate we can consider his reported over-dependence on freedman advisers, which does seem to echo a negative rhetoric associated with Alexander's flatterers. A discourse of the danger of court-flatterers and poetasters was already available via the East and the Hellenistic

kingdoms, with a cyclical and allusive input from Alexander along the way.

13 On the dating of the *de Ira* and Seneca's works in general, see Griffin 1991²:396. That Seneca would have been particularly alert to issues of political chicanery and dirty deeds as they played out at Rome may be deduced from his prowess as an orator (to which Caligula took exception, Suetonius, *Gaius* 53), and thus his participation in civic life. He himself gives almost no clue as to any first-hand knowledge of the events surrounding Caligula's assassination, save for a brief reference at *de Ira* 1.20.8–9. After being found guilty of adultery with Julia Livilla in 41 CE, the senate voted for him to receive the death penalty, but Claudius reduced the punishment to exile. On his exile and recall, see Griffin 1991²: 59–63. The *de Clementia*, dedicated to the young Nero, dates to 55/56 CE; the *de Beneficiis* was composed after CE 56, but completed by 64 CE.

14 'Graecia capta ferum uictorem cepit et artes / intulit agresti Latio.' (Horace, *Ep.* 2.1.156–57).

15 Curtius 4.7.31. Cf. Livy 27.19.4; Cicero *de Rep.* 2.30.52.

16 On this episode, see Spencer 1996:166–81. Cf. Arrian's brusque treatment (3.26.1–3), and citation of Ptolemy as his authority: 'Πτολεμαῖος δὲ ὁ Λάγου λέγει . . .' (3.26.2). Arrian makes no attempt to undercut the 'Ptolemaic' spin.

17 Curtius 8.5.5–8.8.23.

18 Feral imagery characterizes Seneca's descriptions of Alexander's passions. We can compare the emphasis on outdoing Liber and Hercules with *Ep.* 114.62–63.

19 The theme of surrender to passions is used in general by Livy (Book 9) to reinforce Alexander's lack of credibility as enemy for Rome. Italy would have proved no such soft and easily overcome country (9.17.17). This argument is made problematic by the corollary that if Alexander was such a soft touch, why should any country measure its greatness in terms of his defeat? Remember our consideration of Livy in Chapter 2 on kingship?

20 As Griffin 1991²:62–63 comments, we know that Seneca was already committed to becoming Nero's tutor—in accordance with Agrippina's wishes—when he returned home.

21 Habinek 1998:141–42 suggests that the construction of a critique on elite anger is designed to reinforce elite dominance, but reading in Alexander, it becomes a more sophisticated meditation on the possibilities and limitations of authority and autonomy.

22 The Augustan *Lex Iulia de adulteriis* prescribed relegation as punishment for adultery, but Augustus (and afterwards Tiberius) had upped this to exile. Relegation did not deprive a citizen of his property, but exile did. One might agree, of course, that exile was itself a little death, particularly given its effective divorce of the citizen from everything that defined him as such. It is ironic that in the political climate of the

Principate, exile could be constructed as an imperial benefit in contrast to the gung ho blood-lust of the Senate.

23 E.g. Cicero, Ovid, Tiberius, Augustus' daughter and granddaughter (both Julias), Julia Livilla and (Julia) Agrippina.

24 Cf. Pliny, *NH* 8.21.54. This story is accepted in essence by Justin (15.3), and Seneca (here and at *de Clem.* 1.25), but doubted by Curtius (8.1.13–17).

25 E.g. Suetonius *Nero* 19 on that emperor's cultivation of Alexander.

26 That Telesphorus is from Rhodes certainly invokes Tiberius' 'exile', although the connexion is never more than implicit. Perhaps more direct correspondence may be found in stories of Tiberius' treatment of Germanicus' elder sons Nero and Drusus, recounted by Suetonius (*Tiberius* 54).

27 Timagenes was a Greek orator and historian who arrived in Rome as a captive in 55 BCE but subsequently stayed on when freed by Sulla's son Faustus. Although he initially found favour with Augustus, it appears that his 'frankness' was eventually considered too outspoken, and he ended up under the protection of C. Asinius Pollio. We know that he wrote *On Kings*, and an anti-Roman world history up to the time of Caesar, and he is thought to have been the subject of Livy's slur on Greek historians at 9.18.6.

28 It is difficult to know how intentionally ironic Seneca's use of *iratus*— with its overtones of violence, and in the context of Alexander's murderous anger—to describe the shifting relationships between Timagenes, Augustus and Pollio may have been.

29 Compare Seneca's use of the simile 'as if struck by lightening' (*quasi fulguritum*) 3.23.6, with Lucan's similar (if more highly developed) usage in which Pompey—the tottering oak—is juxtaposed with a fulminating Caesar, dazzling and sizzling like a bolt of lightening (*BC* 1.136–57).

30 It might even be possible to argue that Alexander's significance as a prototype for one-man rule, first within the Hellenistic Kingdoms, and later in Rome, marks him out as a symbolic founder of a greater pan-Mediterranean dynasty.

31 Further to a connexion of violence with a climate of flattery: superstitious people hate the gods for fickle cruelty, even as they worship them; thus are despots honoured and courted while loathed. Hermolaus, tried for plotting Alexander's assassination, was Alexander's attendant; Pausanias, executed for Philip II of Macedon's murder, was his attendant; and Chaerea was Caligula's (Plutarch *Mor.* 170E).

32 Note the potential irony in Alexander's relationship with his mother *vis-à-vis* the reputation for power-grabbing that was growing up around the imperial women, particularly under Caligula and after, but culminating in Nero's mother Agrippina.

33 See e.g. Barton 1993 for a modern, and often intriguing study of how the games intersected and informed the Roman psyche. On the increasing

concentration of the right to control who sponsored how many games, see Wiedemann 1992:8. Seneca composed this essay in the wake of Caligula's participation as a gladiator (Suetonius *Gaius* 54.1). On Caligula's provision of spectacles and public benefactions, see Josephus, *Antiquities* 19.130. For the close personal connexion that was drawn between Caligula and gladiatorial combat, see e.g. Suetonius' record of one Roman's promise to take part in the games if the emperor recovered from illness (*Gaius* 27.2).

34 Cf. Seneca *Epistles* 7.3 on the cruelty and inhumanity that infects all who make up an audience at the games. On the degeneration from a Golden Age, see Seneca *Epistles* 90.45, 95.33, 7.2ff.

35 Lucan was born at Corduba in 39 CE, and committed suicide at Rome in 65 CE in the wake of the unsuccessful Pisonian conspiracy against Nero. Another 'hero' dying young, another Alexander parallel? Lucan had been a close companion (though not *necessarily* friend) of Nero, and recited specially written praises (*laudes*) of the *princeps* at the *Neronia* of 60 CE. The split with Nero may have developed from the publication of the first three books of the *BC* (62/3 CE), though this is unclear. What is known is that Nero banned Lucan from reciting his poems in public or speaking in the courts, effectively disenfranchising him politically, and Lucan then joined the conspiracy led by C. Calpurnius Piso.

36 Cf. Lucan 2.632–49 on Pompey's 'easterners'; even Pompey's 'westerners' are not Italians but Hesperii 7.728, 741–42. After Pharsalus Lucan has Caesar's forces conceptualize Rome as *Tarpeiae arces* (7.758) combining the intricate relationship between internal treachery and external attack. But still the emphasis returns to civil war with 7.772–73. Cf. Caesar *BC* 3.3–5 on Pompey's forces, and 3.96 on the luxury of his camp.

37 There are thirty-four references to 'Emathia' in the poem, mainly concentrated in Books 6–9; there are thirteen references to 'Pella', concentrated in Books 8–10.

38 Cf. Statius (*Siluae* 3.2.117–118) for a valediction to Maecius Celer on his way to command in Syria: '*duc et ad Emathios manes, ubi belliger urbis conditor Hyblaeo perfusus nectare durat.*'

39 On Stoic hostility to Alexander in antiquity see Fears 1974:113, 130. Croisille 1990:272, 274–76 suggests that Lucan's anti-Alexander diatribe has closer links to the general evolution of Neronian power, than to specific allusions (cf. Cicero *de Off.* 1.90).

4 Readings—Imaging Alexander

1 Cf. Eder 1990:84–85 on Syme 1939, in contrast to the influential model constructed by Zanker 1988.

2 Eder 1990:87 argues that the Republic continued because Augustus had reinvigorated and reinvented Roman consciousness of their traditional

right and responsibility to rule over the earth. Alexander addresses the Macedonian troops as an independent racial unit – representatives of the leading nation in Europe, victors not so much through his but rather their own determination, and liberators of the world (Curtius, 3.10.4–5; also 4.14.4; 6.3.1–18; 7.7.10–14). Beyond the Hyphasis, Curtius shifts emphasis from group nationalism to an appeal to personal greed and individual loyalty to their leader (9.1.1–4, 2.12–34, 4.19–21).

3 Under Augustus, the scale of cult acts in the eastern provinces far out-stripped that attained by Hellenistic ruler-cults. Cf. Millar 1984:53. Confined to the East (and at a distance), the imperial cult was acceptable in Rome.

4 Cf. Wallace-Hadrill's discussion of Hellenistic monarchs' interaction with and self-representation to subjects. He notes Alexander's positive potential in this context (1982:34–35); this can be compared with the *recusatio* expected from the Roman *princeps* (1982:36–37). In the two full-length narratives of Curtius and Arrian we find that the move from a semblance of monarchical accountability to autocracy is not followed through consistently.

5 Written in 62 BCE, in the wake of Pompey's success against Mithridates, and Cicero's consulship. A. Licinius Archias was a Greek poet (from Antioch) who gained citizenship under the *lex Plautia Papiria* (89 BCE). His citizenship was later contested, leading to Cicero's—successful—speech in his defence.

6 For other versions of Alexander's visit to Sigeum cf. Arrian 1.12 and Plutarch *Alexander* 15.

7 Cf. Cicero, *ad Att.* 1.16.15.

8 As Cicero affirms in passage 4.2, Alexander chose artists well, but on his poetic taste, cf. Horace for a wholly negative view (passage 4.3; *Ars Poetica* 357–60). Rudd 1989:114–15 notes that scholiasts on the *Ars Poetica* (357) suggest that Horace is twisting the 'main' tradition, in which Alexander variously repudiates Choerilus or has him beaten to death (with a ratio of one blow per bad line of verse). Curtius (8.5.7–8) links Choerilus' flattery to the king's desire both to be believed, and worshipped as divine. Statius notes a statue of Bucephalus said to have been Lysippus' work, and later associated with a statue of Caesar (*Siluae* 1.1.84–87 (see pp. 183–4)). Cf. *Siluae* 4.6.59–74 (passage 4.7); Martial 9.43.

9 (Gn. Pompeius) Theophanes of Mytilene accompanied Pompey during the third Mithridatic war, and wrote up his campaigns for him. He later went on to serve with him in the civil war (49/8 BCE). He was posthumously deified in his hometown as 'Zeus Eleutherius Theophanes'. That on receiving the citizenship he would have taken the name of his benefactor serves to heighten the co-dependency of author and subject. In his account of Pompey's campaign he drew a comparison with Alexander's expedition (*RE* V^A 1934.2125), and Pompey's complicity in the

textualization of his own historical afterlife, coupled with his apparent success in propagating the image during his lifetime, were important functions of his links with Alexander.

10 Cf. Plutarch (*Mor.* 531A); contrast with Curtius 4.14.13; 4.4.2, 14.4; 8.8.15. Livy comments on Alexander's great fame (9.17.5, 6, 12, 18.6), only to introduce Roman equals. He ridicules the Greek suggestion that Alexander's name would have been enough to cause a mass surrender of the Roman people (9.18.6). See Plutarch (*Mor.* 85C) for Alexander on Homer. Arrian (4.10.1–2) is unsympathetic to Callisthenes' claim that Alexander's fame is all in the telling.

11 Lucceius prosecuted Catiline for murder in 64 BCE, and published speeches against him, and it is thought that he had some kind of advisory role in 63 BCE. For the dating of this letter see Shackleton Bailey 1977:318–19. He argues that the traditional date (April 56 BCE) is a year out.

12 See Plutarch (*Mor.* 360D) on Lysippus' disapproval of Apelles for his portrayal of Alexander with a thunderbolt, rather than the spear chosen by the sculptor—its glory would remain undimmed, was truthful, and was Alexander's by right.

13 Note the use of 'great' (*magnus*) to describe Lucceius in the final line of the extract. Lucceius is not only out-Homering Homer, he is also taking on Alexander's attributes.

14 Maslakov 1984:440 n. 6 on *exempla* comments: 'When Cicero gives his catalogue of examples he does so when the tradition invoked serves immediate political ends. . . . He also assumes in his audience a ready familiarity with the monumental counterparts of these rhetorical stereotypes.'

15 Where Habinek 1998:100–2 argues that this poem signals Horace's intervention on the side of literature as a privileged practice of cultural hegemony, I suggest that he is in fact acknowledging the power of the visual, or performative over that of the literary text. On this poem see Barchiesi 1993 and Spencer: forthcoming.

16 In a wider context, the poem is concerned with the debate of old versus new; Rome is lacking in ability to judge artistic and literary merit because inertia and worship of the old is all that is understood (cf. Rudd 1989:2). Conversely, Rome is right in adapting to worship and honour of Caesar.

17 There is some debate as to the identification of this colossus as Alexander—see Menichetti 1986 for the argument in favour—but even if the colossus was not originally Alexander, we still have the trans-formed Apelles images, and another, literary, version of the transfor-mation: Alexander to Caesar (see my discussion of Statius *Siluae* 1.1.84–87 at pp. 183–7 and Geyssen 1996:86 n. 45). On the dedication on the forum, see Anderson 1984:68–69. We may also note that according to Pliny (*NH* 34.48), whilst two of Alexander's 'statuesque'

tent-poles were erected in front of the Temple of Mars Ultor, the other two were placed in front of the *regia* ('palace').

18 Augustus' familiarity with Alexander-imagery, and use of it for propagandist purposes, is no doubt behind Horace's comparison. Cf. Zanker 1988:36, 57–65, 145. An interesting addendum to this exaltation of Alexander's success as an art-critic can be found in Pliny's comment that Alexander was given to talking a great deal about painting, despite not knowing much about it, leading to mockery of Alexander by Apelles' studio-hands (*NH* 35.84–85).

19 *Ep.* 2.1.214–31.

20 For Horatian bombast on Augustus the military man, see 2.1.250–59. Cicero's letters, discussed in chapter 5, are *ad Fam.* 2.10.3 and *ad Att.* 5.20. The lack of anything comparable in scale and imagery to the *Panegyric of Messalla* during the rest of Augustus' Principate is telling. There was no room for other emperors-in-waiting who had the political freedom to indulge in Alexander-style personal campaigns.

21 Curtius 8.6–8. This episode is also narrated by Arrian (4.13–14) and Plutarch (55).

22 'Proskynesis' was a gesture of respect performed in Persia by inferiors to their social superiors. This meant that all Persians owed proskynesis to their king. Different interpretations of what was involved include blowing a kiss in a stylized way with the right hand, going down on one's knees, and full-body prostration. Full prostration seems to have been at issue in the story of Alexander, and this is where trouble started. For the Persians, it's likely that proskynesis was less a cult act (i.e. did not denote cult worship of the Great King) than a social convention of respect. For the Greeks and Macedonians, prostration was only accorded to gods, leading to a belief that the Persians worshipped their king as a god and that by attempting to introduce this practice, Alexander was seeking further acknowledgement of his deity. What he actually intended is difficult to recover. At its most basic level, Alexander may have wanted to standardize court practice—prostration for everyone—but this interpretation still allows some leeway. He may have wished to ensure that all his subjects used the same forms of deference, or he may have hoped to institute Alexander-worship across the board. For different versions of the story see Arrian 4.10.5–12; Curtius 8.5.5–21; Justin 12.7.1–3; Valerius Maximus 7.2 ext. 11.

23 On this disquiet, see Zanker 1988:5–11, 33–77. See Gruen 1993:223–71 on what he terms 'the appeal of Hellas', during the earlier period, although I suggest that his configuration of a wholly normative approach to the appropriation of Greek culture would benefit from some unpicking. Nero's promotion of Greece and Greek culture was closely bound up in senatorial unrest during his Principate, and later, under Hadrian, we see a similar pattern whereby his promotion of Greek culture led to unpopularity at Rome.

24 *'dixisse Callisthenen meminisse debere eos iam uiros esse.'* Curtius
   8.6.25.
25 *'idque ad consolandam patientiam uerberum an ad incitandum iuuenum
   dolorem dictum dictum esset in ambiguo fuisse.'* Curtius 8.6.25.
26 Arrian comments that some of Callisthenes' detractors said that he had
   incited the Pages against Alexander 'τοὺς δέ, ὅτι καὶ ἐπῆρεν αὐτὸς ἐς τὸ
   ἐπιβουλεῦσαι' (4.12.7); although he seems to think that Callisthenes was
   probably not involved in the plot, he does argue that his aggressive
   independence made Alexander's hostility towards him understandable.
   Plutarch is far less ambiguous, coming out openly with inflammatory
   comments made by Callisthenes (*Alexander* 55.4–5) to the effect that
   killing Alexander was just like killing any other man. Ptolemy and
   Aristobulus both claimed that the Pages implicated Callisthenes under
   torture (Arrian 4.14.1), but this may have been a face-saving device on
   the part of two of Alexander's key generals.
27 Lucius Cestius Pius was an outspoken Augustan orator. Papirius
   Fabianus was an orator, philosopher and an enormous influence on the
   younger Seneca. Seneca *Ep.* 100.12 comments on his popularity with
   young people.
28 Marcus Porcius Latro was an orator and close friend of the elder Seneca.
   He committed suicide *c.*4 CE. Seneca tells us that Ovid was one of his
   admirers (*Controuersiae* 2.2.8).
29 That Alexander may have been implicated in the assassination of his
   father, and the emphasis on his mother (who was herself a problematic
   and 'other' figure even in Greek sources) suggests how even the formal
   familial structure is warped in Alexander's case.
30 Rome is introduced explicitly when a poem on Germanicus' voyages (the
   poem was written by Pedo, an officer of the younger Germanicus, and
   therefore presumably about him, cf. Tacitus, *Ann.* 1.60, 2.23–24)
   is quoted (1.15). Perhaps this offers a link between Alexander and
   Germanicus as participants in their own myths?
31 On narratorial destabilization cf. Herodotus 2.146.1, 4.195.2; Livy
   6.12.2–6; Curtius 9.1.34; Tacitus *Annals* 1.76.4; 4.11.
32 *Inst. Or.* 3.8.16. Quintilian states that the argument often first asserts
   that the deed should not be done, even if possible, and second that it
   cannot be done anyway. See also *Inst. Or.* 7.4.2 for Caesar deliberating
   on the Ocean. Cf. Alcock 1994:101–3 on Nero and the Isthmus.
33 Livy 9.18.1–15 (passage 2.1). Cf. Velleius on Caesar (2.41.1: passage
   3.1). The Roman aspiring leader needs to distance himself from this side
   of Alexander, and Velleius seems to imply that Caesar is consciously
   frugal in physical indulgence to counter the problem. Cicero (*de Fin.*
   2.116–17) highlights the contrast between Eastern self-seeking pleasure
   lovers and the nobility of 'true Romans' who act for common good.
34 Livy 9.19.5, 9.19.12. Curtius has Alexander wish Darius had proved a
   worthier enemy (3.12.26).

35 Statius' life is a function of his verse, and apart from Juvenal 7.82–87 we have little external information on his career. Coleman 1988:xv-xx provides a good introduction to the details as we have them. *Siluae* 4 is believed to have been published in 95 CE. Statius' father, a poet and teacher, had tutored Domitian, and the introductory poem in this collection (4.1) celebrates the opening of Domitian's seventeenth consulship (95 CE). This reinforces the connexion between emperor and poet right at the start of this group of poems, but like books 1–3 of the *Siluae*, this book also has a prose dedication, which complicates the direct relationship. Coleman 1988:54 suggests that Statius may have chosen prose so that Domitian retained pride of place as the first poetic subject in books 1 and 4, but we could equally argue that the use of prose is an act of covert subversion. Statius the poet places the Emperor first, whilst Statius the anthologist recognises that even with the Emperor at its head, the collection—and the world it reflects and refracts—is meaningless without his editorial control and justification.

36 Coleman 1988:178 suggests that Statius is engaging in a parody of the stereotypical debate between gourmets found at e.g. Horace, *Satire* 2.2.31ff., but the Saepta as source of luxurious commodities and popular haunt of fashionable Rome undermines his satirical approach.

37 '*multo mea cepit amore / pectora*' 4.6.33–34. In each case, *pectora* falls as the first word of the line.

38 Coleman 1988:181 commenting on line 21 notes that the idea of the statue as unintentionally deceptive is a common topos, but does not explore the implications of wax as the material for 'permanent' art (as against *imagines*). On the public, rhetorical permanence of ancestors and (cultural) ancestry for imperial Rome, see most recently Beard and Henderson 2001:164–75.

39 Compare Juvenal with Statius, *Siluae* 2.7.89–95 (an ode to Lucan on his posthumous birthday): '*o saeue nimium grauesque Parcae! / o numquam data longa fata summis! / cur plus, ardua, casibus patetis? / cur saeua uice magna non senescunt? / sic natum Nasamonii Tonantis / post ortus obitusque fulminates / angusto Babylon premit sepulcro.*' ('O too stern and cruel Fates! / O that a long life is never allowed to the exalted! / why are the elevated most wont to fall? / Why, by cruel vicissitude does greatness not grow old? / It was just this way for the son of the Nasamonian Thunderer / blazing his lightening from sunrise to sunset / when finally restrained to a narrow tomb at Babylon.' On this poem, see Malamud (1995).

40 E.g. The Elder Seneca, *Suas.* 1.2; the Younger Seneca *Ep.* 19.7–8; *de Ben.* 7.2.5–3.1 (passage 3.5).

41 This returns us to the notion of a binary opposition between two parts of the world, them and us, east and west, realms of the mind rather than fixed to any geographical or cardinal points. In this polarized worldview, everything that is not 'us' is automatically a function of this mythic, fascinating and threatening, dangerous sphere.

42 See Suetonius *Iulius* 2, 49.

43 Croisille 1990:272, 274–76; Fears 1974:125.

44 Silius Italicus (*c.*26 –102 CE) connects the two in his vast 17-book epic poem on the second Punic war (*Punica* 13.767–768). Praise of the Flavians in Book 3 of the poem suggests either publication before Domitian's death in 96 CE, or incomplete revision before Silius' death. Silius, a *nouus homo*, prospered under Nero and then Vespasian, and must have been a canny political operator.

45 Lucan 9.585–86. Cf. Pliny on campaign parameters (*NH* 2.67.167–68; 6.45, 51, 58–62, 96, 198; 8.17.44), Alexander did cross the Hyphasis, and dedicated altars on far bank.

46 See Spencer 2001:259–64 on the teetering instability of myth in Augustan Rome.

47 Contrast with Seneca, *Ep.* 91.17.

48 Cf. Seneca, *Ep.* 94.92–93; Plutarch, *Mor.* 326A-C.

49 For some examples of the compass of Alexander in moralistic anecdotes, cf. Plutarch *Mor.* 97C-D; 207D, E; 317F-318A; 326A-C. Cf. Dio Chrysostom *On Kingship* 2.29–32 for Alexander as a literary critic. Rulers and generals, Rome itself, all seem bound up with Alexander when eastern expansion is mooted. As Greek 'Romans', Plutarch and Dio Chrysostom pose other interpretative questions; cf. Pelling 1989:199–232. Other general references to Alexander as conqueror: e.g. Cicero, *de Rep.* 3.14; *de Inuent.* 1.93; Augustine *de Civ. Dei* 4.4.25; Plutarch, *Mor.* 179E,F; 180C-181D; 221A; 240A; 259E-260D; 847C; Seneca, *de Const. Sap.* 6.8. For Alexander's quip that when wounded he feels pain like any mortal see e.g. Curtius 8.10.27–29; Plutarch, *Alex.* 28.

5   Autocracy—The Roman Alexander Complex

1 Tranio, the ghost-story-telling slave, spoke these lines to the butt of his jokes, his elderly master Theopropides.

2 Pompey may have defeated the Iberians, never conquered by Alexander (see Plutarch, *Pompey* 18–20, 45) but in terms of the endgame, Caesar was the ultimate victor.

3 Cf. Henderson 1987:129 for shifting perspective on names and their heritages in Lucan, who perversely robs Pompey 'the Great' to pay Caesar.

4 Cf. André 1990.11–24. Contra, see Green 1989b:199.

5 Cf. Plácido 1990:60, 66–68.

6 Complementary studies by García Moreno 1990:134–42 and Bowersock 1984:169–75 explore the question of how attempts to reconcile eastern and western areas of empire inform Alexander emulation in Rome. García Moreno groups the eastern pretenders as a unit; Bowersock relates the theme specifically to the struggle in Augustus' favours between Gaius Caesar and Tiberius (2 BCE).

7   As Hardie 1983:43 suggests, the development of a formalized structure
    to the Principate led the court to take over, progressively, as the major
    source of patronage and arbiter of taste. Once this began to happen,
    eulogies such as Tibullus' of Messalla, or potentially of other Roman
    aristocrats, could not expect continued toleration. Nero the Emperor
    and Corbulo the potentially 'great' general could not co-exist. Green
    1989b:202 argues that pre-Principate, comparison or identification with
    Alexander could only be made in terms of military endeavour, because
    this was his only image with the Roman public. This would help explain
    the shift that Alexander goes through post-Caesar, but my account
    suggests that he overstates Roman ignorance of other facets.

8   Levi 1977:171 over-emphatically proposes the indivisibility of Roman
    judgements on Alexander from contemporary politics; many of the great
    wealth of references to Alexander have no overt relevance to anything
    other than their own internal logics, though of course allusivity remains
    central to this discourse. On Ocean and world's end cf. Anderson 1928:
    45–46; also Galinsky 1972:126–66. The serpentine Oceanus, limiting
    the potential *orbis terrarum* is a prominent motif in the Alexander myth
    (e.g. *Alexander Romance* 1.11; Plutarch, *Alex.* 63; Curtius 8.5.1; 9.2.26,
    4.17, 9.1; 10.6.36; Arrian 5.25–27), and one that passes to Pompey and
    Caesar (Plutarch, *Pomp.* 38, *Caesar* 58); also *Aeneid* 1.286–87. Cf.
    Romm 1992:12–17, 20–26.

9   There are also potential (and maybe latent) Alexander-tendencies in
    Marius and Sulla, which we ought to be aware of in passing.

10 See Weinstock 1971:188 for discussion and references on this connexion
    between Alexander and Hercules. Ahl 1976:272–73 n. 51 investigates
    the evocation and discusses authorial consciousness; Cato retains his
    credibility at Ammon (unlike Alexander) (9.585–86). The 'snaky' desert
    (9.498–510) illustrates the strongest Alexander/Cato link (compare with
    Arrian 3.2–3, 6.25–26; Plutarch *Alex.* 42; and Curtius' alternative
    version (8.4.15–17). Cf. Plutarch (*Cat. Min.* 71), Tarn (2, 1948.338–46)
    and Weinstock 1957:214.

11 Livy, 35.14.6–7. There is great irony in this when contrasted with the
    description of Perseus' army mustered for war against Rome: '*Satis
    constabat, secundum exercitum, quem magnus Alexander in Asiam
    traiecit, numquam ullius Macedonum regis copias tantas fuisse.*'
    (42.51.11). For Alexander and Scipio, cf. Silius Italicus (*Punica*
    13.762–75; passage 4.10); Alexander's primary attributes: his youth
    (13.762), and his power, are confined to the effect of his reputation. To
    what extent would success under Nero, and that emperor's Alexandrian
    aspirations, have tainted the reference? In a different political world, all
    men could aspire to be Alexander. Cf. Wilson 1993:227–30.

12 For Augustus' visit to Alexander's tomb in Alexandria, cf. Suetonius
    (*Aug.* 18). Also Caligula's association with Alexander's breastplate (Suet.,
    Gaius 52). On supremacy, cf. Juvenal (10.167–73): great gifts destroy
    greatly.

13 See Croisille 1990:266–67.

14 See Johnson 1987:72–73.

15 To create Caesar's visit to Alexander's tomb, Lucan alters the story. Green 1989b:193–94 provides a cogent summary of the strands of critical thought linking or driving Caesar and Alexander apart, but discerns no *imitatio*, only early, vague *aemulatio*. Of particular note is this emphatic differentiation between reported *imitatio/aemulatio* on the part of an individual, and the likening of such an individual by an ancient source to Alexander (*comparatio*).

16 Suetonius, *Iulius* 7. Green 1989b:195 explains this mention of conscious comparison as a result of Caesar's lack of established power (69 BCE) and Pompey's ascendancy, counting this as an example of Caesar comparing himself to Alexander. Cf. Plutarch's variant which gives him a similar reaction to a history of Alexander (*Caesar* 11).

17 Strabo 13.1.27; cf. Plutarch, *Caesar* 58.

18 See Plutarch, *Caesar* 60, 61; *Alex.* 54; Curtius 8.5.9–24; Arrian 4.10–13; Suetonius, *Iulius* 79. These, of course, are 100–150 years after the fact.

19 For the doubters, Green 1989b:196–98, argues a sceptical approach to the development of Alexandrianism from Pompey.

20 See Ahl 1976:190.

21 See Dempsie 1991:154–55 on Curtius 10.5.28. *Clementia* as a Roman virtue cf. Fears 1981; Virgil, *Aeneid* 6.851–53; Livy 33.12.7.

22 E.g. Augustus: Velleius 2.100.4; *Res Gestae* 3.1–2, 34.2; Tiberius: Tacitus, *Ann.* 3.50.2; Germanicus: Tacitus, *Ann.* 2.73.3; Caligula: Dio 59.16.16; Claudius: Dio 60.28.1; Nero: Tacitus, *Ann.* 13.11.2; Seneca, *de Clem.* 1.5.2, 1.11.4, 2.1.1. But note Dio (55.14–21) on Livia's assessment of 'security' through *clementia*.

23 Cf. Fears 1977:140 on *de Clem.* Curtius highlights this with the argument that Philotas *had* to be executed, because if pardoned he would never be able to forget this debt he owed (6.8.5–9).

24 '. . .*impleuit popularis laudibus meritis Scipionis: uenisse dis simillimum iuuenem, uincentem omnia cum armis tum benignitate ac beneficiis.*' ('he filled his fellow countrymen with the well-earned praises of Scipio, saying that there had come amongst them a most godlike young man, conquering all before him not just with arms, but with generosity and favours.' Livy 26.50.13; the setting is 210 BCE). Cf. Xenophon's 'original' casting of this plotline in the *Cyropaedia* when Cyrus resists the temptation of the beautiful Pantheia (5.1.3–18, 6.1.31–49)

25 E.g. Curtius 3.11.24–12.26; Plutarch *Alexander* 21; Arrian 2.12.3–8.

26 Arrian calls the story a λόγος (2.12.6), and says that he has recorded it without ascertaining its truth or falsity ('καὶ ταῦτα ἐγὼ οὔθ' ὡς ἀληθῆ οὔτε ὡς πάντη ἄπιστα ἀνέγραψα' 2.12.8). From what we know of the so-called Vulgate tradition, the group of stories that tend to focus on the more sensational and fantastic, character and adventure-driven episodes in Alexander's life, it was used by most of the Alexander historians to

some extent, but particularly by Curtius Rufus, Pompeius Trogus (and therefore also Justin, who wrote a Latin version of Trogus' narrative), Diodorus Siculus and Plutarch. This could suggest that Arrian was both distancing himself from the more popular tradition *and* distancing Alexander from Roman republican appropriation.

27 Julian's *Caesares* (mid fourth century CE) has a similar focus on the name Caesar, and the text goes on to have Alexander claim Caesar as an imitator of himself, who had done him no credit (322B-C).

28 In Suetonius' *Augustus*, again the opening (1–8) places him first within the Octavii, and then as heir and adopted Caesar. On Antony and dynasticism, see e.g. Plutarch, *Antony* 36.4.

29 On liberty versus tyranny, see e.g. Justin 11.11; Curtius 8.5.5, 7.13–14; also Dio on Antony, 50.25.3. Ceauşescu 1974:162 proposes an interesting link when he ties Alexander's circle of friends who suffered for their attempts to regulate his excesses, to an idealized circle of faithful senators who, in senatorial ideology, might steer the *princeps* in a 'correct' direction (e.g. Pliny, *Pan.* 85–86; Eutropius, *Breu.* 8.4–5).

30 Cicero, *de Diu.* 1.47; Plutarch, *Alex.* 3.3. Anderson 1928:26–28 links this with representations of Alexander with winged serpent and star, and the Romance tradition of his ascent to heaven borne by a serpent followed by an eagle carrying a star.

31 Cf. Wissowa 1912; and Anderson 1928:31–37.

32 Dio (16.39); Polybius (10.2.9); and Valerius Maximus (1.2.1) are all cynical about Scipio's piety; Anderson 1928:32–33 suggests that Alexander's alleged relationship to Ammon, and visit to Siwah, would have connected in Roman popular belief with the Scipio–Jupiter tie. He may be overemphasizing the case, but resonances of some sort were clearly at work. The other big Scipio/Alexander story is the comparison between the receding of the waters in the lagoon on his capture of New Carthage (Polybius 10.8.6–9.3, 11.6–8, 14.7–12; Livy 26.45.8–9), and the supposed *proskynesis* of the waves to Alexander at Mt Climax (Plutarch, *Alex.* 17.3–5; Arrian 1.26.1–2). Cf. Wirth 1976:185–86; Weippert 1972:37–55; Walbank 1967b.

33 Livy 26.19.7,9; see also Gellius 6.1.1.

34 See Wiseman 1974:153, 158–9; but without any discussion of Alexander's relevance to Roman genealogical concerns.

35 Suetonius, *Augustus* 18. We may speculate as to what spin Suetonius, from his second century CE perspective, has put on this moment.

36 29–23 BCE; see Kienast 1969:435 nn. 13, 14; Suetonius, *Aug.* 50; Pliny *NH* 37.10.

37 Cf. Bruhl 1930:208–9.

38 Cicero *Phil.* 5.17.48. Heuß 1954. Cf. Kienast 1969:432–43; Eder 1990: 89–101.

39 A brief but rounded examination is undertaken by García Moreno 1990, who draws on Kienast (1969) for detail, but allows greater leeway for

the relationship between Alexander, Roman discussions of limits to empire, and popular ideology.

40 Once the threat of autocracy becomes concrete, Alexander is more to be feared for his despotic overtones than admired for his militaristic values. Antony's Egyptism, coupled with his propagandist comparisons to Alexander, bears this out. Crassus has potential as an Alexander (cf. Propertius 3.4); he led the Romans east against Parthia/'Persia', but he led Rome to a crushing defeat. Crassus did not return to Rome, and Crassus was not 'great'.

41 Cf. Statius *Siluae* 4.6.59–74 (passage 4.7) and Martial (9.43.7) on Alexander's statue of Hercules.

42 '*Centum hos uersus, quos in equum maximum feci, indulgentissimo imperatori postero die, quam dedicauerat opus, tradere iussus sum.*' ('These hundred lines I've written on the Great Horse, I was ordered to hand over to our most indulgent Emperor, on the day after he had dedicated it.'). Statius, *Siluae* 1 (Dedicatory preface to Stella).

43 Henderson 1998:104–5 discusses Statius' insistence on textual time-tripping in his Preface to the *Siluae*.

44 See *Siluae* 1.1.1–2 (passage 4.7).

45 See Geyssen 1996 on these lines. Pliny tells us that Augustus' horse was granted a funeral mound, and Germanicus composed a poem about it (Pliny *NH* 8.154–55). Caligula's adoration of the horse Incitatus is notorious; according to Suetonius, he wanted to make him consul (*Gaius* 55.3).

46 Excavated on October 24 1831. Two recent and contrasting discussions can be found in Cohen's lengthy study (1997) and Beard and Henderson's pithy modelling of this image as paradigmatic for Alexander's centrality to all Roman responses to the Hellenistic (and classical Greek) world (2001:13–23).

47 See e.g. Ceauşescu 1974:153–57 who has conservative senatorial and traditionalist circles see Alexander as embodiment of despotism.

48 See e.g. Livy 9.18.1–3, 22.14.6, 38.17.12; Justin 12.14.1; Curtius 8.5.14, 9.3.10; Seneca, *de Ira* 3.17.1; Lucan 10.28–29; Valerius Maximus 9.5 ext.1. The principal senatorial anti-Alexander motif is expressed by Curtius in Hermolaus' speech (8.7.13; see 6.6.10 and 8.4.30), the terms of which are echoed, as Ceauşescu 1974 suggests, by Seneca on Caligula (*de Ben.* 2.12.2). Cf. Edwards 1993:92–97 on Roman conflation of effeminacy and Hellenization. On more recent readings of Alexander, see Spencer 1996.186–89. For a perspective from a later 'empire', also at a time of crisis, see Barker 1969:12–16, 113–14 on Alexander and Roman development, and on Alexander, India and the British Empire. British uses of Roman imperialism, paralleling Roman constructs of Alexander, can be seen in action in Lucas 1912; Bryce 1914; Haverfield 1916; Symonds 1986; Brunt 1990b.

49 Pompey's fall (or degeneration) is brought about as a result of his return to Rome. Cf. Anderson 1928.37–38.

50 See Kienast 1969:437–39 for a full exploration of parallels between

Pompey's victories in the east, and Alexander's route, including his defeat of a Median king Darius, and Alexander's similar feat. Plutarch, *Pomp.* 2.1–2, 34.1–36.2, 38.1–3, 45.1–46.2; Appian, *Bell. Mithr.* 103, 106, 117; Velleius 2.40.1; Diodorus 40.4; Pliny, *NH* 7.95–99. Also Zanker 1988:8, 10.

51   See Ahl 1976:226–27; Caesar plays on the licentious ways of foreigners (Greeks) (*BC* 3.110). Cf. Caesar (*BC* 3.95–97) on the grandeur and luxury of Pompey's camp; contrast with Curtius on Darius' camp (3.11.20–23). Weinstock 1971.324–326 suggests that Caesar could legitimately dress as an Alban king (Dio 43.43.2; cf. Suetonius, *Caesar* 45.3), (i.e. tactical role-playing). This allowed him to dress the part of kingship, if only in the east. Compare Suetonius (*Gaius,* 52) with Curtius on Alexander (6.6.4–7,10; also 6.2.1–3).

52   Through the Naumachia organized in conjunction with the dedication of the temple of Mars Ultor, Rome as a cohesive unit could take on the role adopted by Alexander (saviour of the Greeks). See Ovid, *Ars Amat.* 1.171–72; 178–89, 181, 203. *Res Gestae* 23; Dio 55.10. Cf. Bowersock 1984:171–72, 175. The standards recovered from Parthia in 20 BCE were placed in the newly dedicated temple, and linked with Gaius' departure eastwards, evoking imagery of a new '*ultor*' for the Parthian struggle.

53   See Syme 1958; and Walker 1952 as typical of the 'positive' analysis; Shotter 1968, Ross 1973, and Pelling 1993 offer a corrective analysis.

54   Taken with the evidence of P.Oxy. 2435 (if we accept that it does refer to Germanicus). See Tacitus, *Ann.* 2.73. The edict can be found in Ehrenberg and Jones 1955[2] 320 (b), 147–48; see also Lobel and Turner 1959:2435 for the text of the papyrus. The former shows the extent of Germanicus' popularity, and his charm; the latter displays again the rhetoric that might well cause Tiberius to fear Germanicus.

55   See *Ann.* 2.60.1; P.Oxy. 2435 v.10.

56   Cf. Aalders 1961:383; Malissard 1990:334. Germanicus' speech in Alexandria may also have overtones of Octavian's rhetoric on entering the city after Antony's suicide (cf. Gurval 1995:70–71).

57   See Aalders 1961.382, n.3; Curtius' version makes most play on the confused misery that erupts on Alexander's death, suggesting a parallel with Tacitus' version (Curtius 10.5.7–16). Justin's, the only comparable account, concentrates on Persian sorrow (13.1.1–6); cf. Livy (1.29.3); Dempsie 1991:132–34 also notes these correlations. Tacitus/the narrator is careful to state that these are the comparisons and praises of those contemporaries who honoured the deceased Germanicus; the authorial stance is distanced from the compliments.

58   Cf. Treves 1953:161, 168.

59   '*Après la mort de Germanicus, quand commence vraiment le règne des successeurs d'Auguste, les lauriers sont déjà fanés*' (Malissard 1990:338; my emphasis). Malissard offers an extensive discussion of this Tacitean eulogy.

60 See Malissard 1990:330–31.

61 See Pelling 1993:85.

62 Compare Alexander's marriage to Roxanne (and the disfavour shown towards the match in Curtius [6.2.1–9, 8.4.30]) and Antony's union with Cleopatra.

63 Cf. Velleius 2.60.4, 2.61.1; Seneca, *Suas.* 6.10; Florus 4.11.3. And with the rise of Domitian, the problematisation of *dominus et deus* (master and god) becomes acute.

64 Ceauşescu 1974:159, n. 29. In this light, note Curtius' designation of the Macedonian resistance as 'free men' (8.7.1, 14). The same words recur in Seneca's description of the death of Clitus (*de Ira* 3.17.1; also Seneca the Elder, *Suas.* 1.2).

65 Cf. Appian, *BC* 3.16, 19; Plutarch, *Ant.* 4; *Comp. Ant. et Dem.* 3. The best introductions to Hercules and the East are Anderson 1928, and Galinsky 1972:126–52. Compare Arrian 4.10–11, 28–30; *Ind.* 5.8–9; Curtius 8.5.11, 10.1, 11.2; 9.4.1, 21, 8.5. Spencer 2001 suggests how Hercules became an increasingly problematic and unstable figure in the Augustan pantheon.

66 On Antony and Alexandria, see Dio 49.41. On Octavianic propaganda, see Plutarch, *Ant.* 58. Cf. Ceauşescu 1974:163; Gurval 1995:189–208. Suetonius (*Iulius* 79) recounts the disorder caused by rumours that Caesar would move the capital east, and that to defeat the Parthians needed a 'king'. For versions of 'barbarian' enchantresses: Curtius 6.2.1–5, 8.4.29–30; Virgil, *Aeneid* 6.688; Horace, *Epode* 9.11–16; Ovid, *Met.* 15.822–28; Propertius 3.11.29–35; Lucan 10.59–60; Dio 50.5.24–25, 26.1–3. On barbarian allure Dio 50.25.1; 51.6.6–13; Plutarch, *Ant.* 73; Horace, *Odes* 1.37.10; 3.5.5–12; Caesar, *BG* 3.110. Roman 'fear' of Cleopatra is bound up, as Gurval (1995: 196, 207–8) suggests, in the shame of fearing a woman. This theme closes the Hercules/Alexander/Antony loop when we compare Hercules' enslavement by Omphale with the spin put on Antony's liaison with Cleopatra; see Spencer (2001).

67 See Plutarch, *Ant.* 33.2–3. Rose 1924:25–30 and Scott 1929:135, 137–39, provide opposing views of the propaganda campaign with Rose arguing for a continued threat from Antony's memory even after his death.

68 Plutarch, *Ant.* 75.3–4. See Rose 1924:29–30.

69 Dio 50.5.3, 25.2–4. See also Cicero (*Philippic* 2); Plutarch (*Ant.* 9.3); Seneca (*Ep.* 83.25). Scott 1929:137 ties these references to a general hostility to the Dionysiac cult, manifest in the *S.C. de Bacchanalibus* (187 BCE). Horace's version of Antony and Cleopatra (*Odes* 1.37) emphasizes the force that this must have conveyed in Octavianic propaganda. Zanker 1988:57–61 provides a fluent narrative of the shifting propaganda battle, noting Propertius (2.15.39–47) on how an alternative, pro-Antony constituency could equally have been engendered. Gurval 1995.87–111 argues that the Augustus/Apollo identification dates from the post-Actium restoration.

70 See Kienast 1969:437–55.

71 Gurval 1995:67, 69–70 connects this foundation with Alexander's victory-foundations (Suetonius, *Aug.* 18.2; Dio 51.1.2–5; Pausanias 5.23.3; 10.38.4; Strabo 7.7.6; also Plutarch, *Ant.* 80.2). Antony, with Cleopatra at his side, attempted to create a dynasty with Alexander Helios and Cleopatra Selene as its second generation (Plutarch, *Ant.* 36.1–4). Gurval 1995:54–55 discusses 'Actium-Typus' portraiture, commenting on the 'Alexandrian' style apparent in Octavianic coinage; cf. Pollini 1990: 350–351.

72 *Aeneid* 6.791–807; See Norden 1957 for how this passage is closely related to Alexander-encomium, and how this reflects on Augustus and his imagery. On Tibullus 1.7, cf. Cairns 1979:43–44; on Propertius 3.4.1–10, cf. Cairns 1972:186–87.

73 Virgil, *Aeneid* 6.795–6; Dio 56.36.2f. Cf. Curtius on the Macedonian troops' refusal to continue past the Hyphasis: '*extra sidera et solem ... quae mortalium oculis natura subduxerit*' (9.4.18). Also Seneca *Ep.* 94.63.

74 Cf. Ceauşescu 1974:164; Gurval 1995:70–71, 135–36.

75 Fears 1977:48, 64–65, 90–99 characterizes Alexander's monarchy, and those of the Diadochoi, by a 'theology of victory'. Having broken free from the ties of tradition and conservative senatorial opinion, Caesar was in many ways in a similar position, and the role was remade for Octavian.

76 Green 1989b:207 discusses Caesar's Parthian ambitions.

77 Lucan, *BC* 1.273–351; Virgil, *Aeneid* 3.85–89. Ahl 1976:200–2 develops this to show how Lucan builds on this simplicity of cause to attract the common soldier, integrating himself into Roman national aetiology. See also Campbell's discussion of the emperor as 'fellow-soldier' 1984: 32–59.

78 Cf. Johnson 1987:92, 95–96.

79 Gilmartin 1973 gives a detailed analysis of Corbulo's career, dealing with Tacitus' account, while making comparisons with Dio's version. Hammond 1934 is also helpful for a broad analysis, including a discussion of information relating to Corbulo's earlier life. Schur 1926 proposes that Nero engaged with the eastern campaigns purely as a result of his desire to take on the mantle of 'new-Alexander'. Tacitus juxtaposes Agrippina's growing influence with his narrative of eastern affairs (*Ann.* 13.5–6). These political tensions and oppositions at home are the backdrop for how foreign policy will come to be determined.

80 *Ann.* 13.6–7. Gilmartin 1973:599 explores the stand-off between emperor and general, contrasting Nero's debaucheries (14.20–22) and Corbulo's march on Tigranocerta (14.23.1). There is no overt irony in Dio's general representation of events (62.19.2–4, 23.5; see also 63.6.4). Hammond 1934:101–2 takes this to mean that this sentiment was common in Rome, where Nero would have been the preferred popular Emperor. Cf. Tacitus (*Hist.* 2.76).

81 Tacitus, *Ann.* 13.35. Gilmartin 1973:592 suggests a comparison between Tacitus' positive description of Corbulo, Sallust (*Iug.* 96.3), and earlier

Tacitean phraseology (*Hist.* 1.23.1, 5.1.1). Corbulo bends the troops to his training through the force of his personality and demeanour. The incident of the frozen limbs, also highlighted by Gilmartin (ibid.) recalls Curtius 8.4.1–17.

82 Corbulo's enemies in the East are given a comparable build-up to that created for Darius by Curtius (*Ann.* 13.37.1): compare with 13.40.1; 14.23.1; and 1.70.1 on Germanicus. Gilmartin 1973:594 notes the emphasis on Tiridates (cf.13.35.4), but does not develop a link with Alexander. The parallel between himself, Pompey and Lucullus (13.34.2) echoes Cicero and Livy.

83 Tacitus, *Annals* 14.23.1–2. On fame and the reality effect, see Curtius 8.8.15. On Alexander's clemency see especially Curtius on the treatment of Porus (8.14.41–46) and Darius' family (3.12.24–25). Gilmartin's emphasis on the development of a conflict of interests between emperor and general (14.26.1) is particularly significant in terms of Curtius' representation of Alexander's uneasy relationship with Antipater (6.1.17–19; Gilmartin 1973:603 and n. 43).

84 Cf. Gilmartin 1973.621 n.25.

85 Arrian 7.8–11; Plutarch *Alexander* 71. Another potential comparison can be drawn between Curtius 10.2 (Opis mutiny), and Tacitus' treatment of Germanicus in a similar situation (*Ann.* 1.34–35, 41–44). Carney 1996: 31–42 discusses Alexander and mutiny, commenting on how Curtius has the officers represent the troops, not their own interests, at the Hyphasis. Not knowing when Curtius wrote makes it difficult to plot parallels between his account of Alexander and Lucan's Caesar, but given the likelihood that both men were contemporaries, it is clear that some kind of dialogue on mutiny as a *locus* for thinking about identity and power is taking place.

86 Curtius 10.2.27–30. See Carney 1996:35–37.

87 See Fantham 1985:120 and Curtius 10.2.27.

88 E.g. Caesar *BC* 3.73; Suetonius, *Iulius* 69–70; Plutarch, *Caesar* 39.51; Appian 2.47.194, 2.93.388–96; Dio 41.27–35, 42.52–55 (cf. Suetonius *Aug.* 25). The mutiny at Placentia is conspicuous, in Caesar, by its absence (*BC* 2.22). For a detailed description of the historical tradition of this mutiny see Chrissanthos (2001).

89 See Caesar *BC* 3.6.1, 74.2; 3.91, 95.1, 97.1; 3.47.5–48. Cf. Carter 1993: 11–12.

90 *BC* 3.68–73; 1.52.3; *BG* 7.47–52.

91 Cf. Ahl 1976:200; Fantham 1985.123, 126–31.

92 Cf. Ross's reading of the Tacitean Germanicus (1973). Dio (55.5.2–3) gives an alternative version, where Germanicus decides not to commit suicide because it would not solve the problem.

6   Alexander *After* Alexander

1   For a more extended treatment of Alexander's development through the ages, see Spencer 1996 and Bosworth and Baynhan 2000.

2   For the most developed modern example of Alexander as a propagator of a dream of the unity of mankind, see Tarn 1948.

3   For example: Foucher 1986; Moynihan 1985; Hartog 1988; Nicolet 1991; Romm 1992. On Romans and barbarians see Thompson 1979, 1989; Walbank 1972; Dauge 1981. For the extension of geographical to literary *termini*, recent work on closure (e.g. Roberts et al. 1997) becomes particularly important.

4   Romm 1992:83. On the narratives of Iamblichus, Antonius Diogenes, and the history of Apollonius of Tyre, see Reardon 1971, 1989.

5   See Cary 1956; Stoneman 1991, 1994a, 1994c; also Ross 1988².

6   Examples of its influence include Gower, *Confessio Amantis* 6.1789–2366, Chaucer, *The House of Fame*, 860–861. See Stoneman 1991.

7   See Spencer 1997 and Baynham 1998 for extended discussions of Curtius.

8   Cary 1956:78–79. Though isolated in themselves, anecdotes and epigrams can create distinct ontologies for Alexander, available for application in diverse contexts, within a larger pattern of knowledge.

9   Stoneman 1994c. For Ctesias, see Jacoby 1957:688. Also, Halbfass 1988, and Karttunen 1989.

10 For example 'The Correspondence of Alexander and Dindimus' plays upon an acceptance of Alexander acting as a signpost for discussion of contrasting lifestyle choices (a Latin text of this narrative is referred to in the eighth century CE). Cary 1967:79, breaks the genre of Alexander stories into four groups of authors: philosophers (morals, metaphysics and government); theologians and mystics (concerned with historical and religious truth); writers of *exempla* (didactic and edificatory); and secular (romance and lyrics). For our purposes a two-way split is sufficient.

11 See Cary 1967:118–142, 183–189 on Alexander in these terms.

12 Seventh or eighth century CE or earlier. See Stoneman 1994c for texts.

13 Cf. Phillips 1988, N.B. chapter 7.

14 As an example, see Cary 1967:95–98, who traces the story of Alexander's encounter with the pirates from an anecdote ascribed to a lost section of Cicero's *De Rep.*, through St Augustine (*De Ciu. Dei*) and John of Salisbury (*Policraticus* 3.14), to Chaucer (*The Manciple's Tale* 226–34), Gower (*Confessio Amantis* 3.2636ff.) and François Villon (*Le Testament*). From a condemnation of the injustice and illegality of Alexander's dominion, the narrative eventually comes to illustrate his mercy towards a malefactor.

15 Cary 1967:260–72 provides a detailed explanation; see also Storost 1935. Examples of secular Alexander-works of this era are Walter of Châtillon's *Alexandreis* (J.P. Migne, *Patrologia Latina* 209 [Paris 1944–64]); and the *Roman d'Alexandre* (Armstrong 1937). The qualities of *magnanimitas*

and liberality are of particular importance to this development; cf. West
1938. Cary 1967:218–10 discusses Alexander and courtly love.

16 This was picked up in the twentieth century in the 'Camelot' imagery
surrounding Kennedy's American 'court'.

17 An example of the way in which engagement with Alexander was shifting
in emphasis can be seen in Petrarch's negative portrait of Alexander in
De Viris Illustribus. Cf. Cary 1950:43. See also Starn 1988:70: 'With the
erosion of communal institutions and the conversions of the party boss,
ambitious noble, or upstart oligarch into princes, cults of personality and
dynasty and the cultivation of the rhetoric and iconography of heroism
were often inseparable . . . the city states had to borrow and transform
models for representing heroes—in particular the body heroic—from
rival sources of authority.' We might also note the influence of Lucian's
Dialogue of the Dead 12 from the second century CE. This has Minos
interrogating Alexander, Hannibal and Scipio as to which is the greatest.
This was first translated into English by Jasper Mayne in 1663.

18 Pietro della Vecchia: Figure 2; Veronese: Figure 3. For more detailed
discussion, see Spencer 1996. Other images (from a vast selection)
include e.g. Giuseppe Bazzani's *Alessandro Magno e la famiglia di Dario*,
Charles Le Brun's *Alexander and Porus*, and Giambattista Tiepolo's
Family of Darius Before Alexander (a companion piece for his
Continence of Scipio).

19 The secular name of Paul III (1534–49) was Alexander. He also issued a
medallion with his image on one side, and that of Alexander worship-
ping the High Priest Jaddus, at the gates of Jerusalem, on the other
(British Museum P513.37).

20 The most accessible discussion is in Schama 1995:401–5. For the story
of Deinocrates, see Vitruvius' *De Architectura* 2. For an alternative, contemporary use of Alexander in the mediation of secular authority see Le
Brun's depiction of the successes of Louis XIV alongside Alexander's
triumphal entry into Babylon (Figure 4). Le Brun's magnificent Alexander-
cycle was turned into a series of tapestries by the Gobelins workshop.

21 See Schama 1995:426–27, and Wood 1993:19–23, 201–02.

22 McFarland 1981:xi. See Spencer 1996.

23 For wider discussion see Shaffer 1975, and Schwab 1950.

24 See McFarland 1981:14 n. 7—discussion and references. See also Aske
1985. McFarland 1981:15 provides a catalogue of early deaths among
the Romantics; another facet of this theme is the tendency towards
'intentionally' fragmentary works, e.g. Coleridge's 'Christabel' (and
'Kubla Khan'), Byron's 'Don Juan', and Shelley's 'Prince Athenase. A
Fragment'.

25 'To the reflective mind, pondering on the general course of history, the
British connexion with India cannot but appear one of the most astonishing things in the record—more astonishing than the conquests of
Alexander, which carried Greek culture, for a time, into India, and even
diffused its influence in Turkestan and China.' (Barker 1969[2]) Barker's

wartime reflection, published originally in 1941, demonstrates tacitly one of the problems posed by Alexander as an imperial comparative: impermanence.

26   The explorer Richard Burton also fulfils many of Alexander's characteristics as 'scientific' explorer, exemplifying the adoption of 'Classics' as the keystone of British imperialism in the late nineteenth and early twentieth centuries.

27   On the 'Nantucketers': 'And thus have these naked Nantucketers, these sea-hermits, issuing from their ant-hill in the sea, overrun and conquered the watery world like so many Alexanders' ch. 14; prefiguring our first meeting with Ahab: 'Nor will it at all detract from him, dramatically regarded, if either by birth or circumstances, he have what seems a half wilful over-ruling morbidness at the bottom of his nature. For all men tragically great are made so through a certain morbidness. Be sure of this, O young ambition, all mortal greatness is but disease.' Ch. 16 Hermann Melville *Moby Dick*. Thanks to Gideon Nisbet for drawing Melville to my attention.

28   Obvious examples include the new Rome of Mussolini, and the development of a monolithic neo-classicism in Nazi Germany, but these more recent developments also reflect a trend evident in the early evolution of the United States.

29   See e.g. Beard and Henderson 1995.

30   Reports in the *Sunday Times* (8/11/1998) link Oliver Stone with one project in which Alexander is apparently to be portrayed as a brutal war criminal killed in a coup, and closely compared with John F. Kennedy. As is so often the case, most of the information on these projects comes from the internet, but the *Observer Review* 28 October 2001:8 does mention both films, in conjunction with a version proposed by Dino de Laurentiis for Ridley Scott. For internet sites currently hosting information, see: http://filmforce.ign.com/articles/36042p1.html (a review of the Scorsese script; this project was initiated by Christopher McQuarrie (Jude Law was a previous choice for Alexander); http://movies.go.com/movies/A/alexander_2003/index.html (general gossip); http://film.guardian.co.uk/News_Story/Exclusive/0,,523525,00.html; http://www.hollywoodreporter.com/hollywoodreporter/film/brief_display.jsp?vnu_content_id=857176 (on the Ridley Scott film); http://film.guardian.co.uk/News_Story/Exclusive/0,,579367,00.html (on the Scorsese/diCaprio film). Much of this is collected (and updated) on Tim Spalding's fascinating 'Alexander the Great' web pages (http://www.isidore-of-seville.com/alexander/11.html). http://www.geocities.com/philalexandros/fun.html suggests casting options . . . For a synopsis of the Indian *Sikander* (1943), see http://www.pothos.co.uk/alexander.asp?keywordID=19 Perhaps more offbeat, we can read Alexander as a model for Xena (http://whoosh.org/issue4/richan.html), or watch an animated 'Alexander' mini-series (http://www.ani-alexander.com/english/index.html).

31 It is an interesting correlative of this position that Renault's writings are
    frequently categorized within the genre of gay literature. Public per-
    ceptions of her work could be seen to conflate Renault's own sexuality
    with her choice of subject matter in such a way as to render her vision
    of history a product of her sexual politics.
32 On praise for Renault, see McEwan 1987. The personal identification on
    Renault's part is highlighted in David Sweetman's recent biography of
    Renault, Sweetman 1993.
33 For example: 'His experience at the Aigai Dionysia is invented, but
    expresses, I think, a psychological truth' Fire From Heaven, 375. On
    Alexander's lack of provision of an heir: 'This psychological block, in a
    man with immense plans meant to outlast his life, will always be an
    enigma' Funeral Games, 272; and 'We know as little as we do about his
    love affairs, partly because they were few, partly because he was a good
    picker; none of his partners involved him in scandal' The Persian Boy,
    410. I cite Penguin editions (see Bibliography), but see p.219 for details
    of first editions.
34 Renault's diatribe is particularly compromised by its comparison between
    the actions of Hitler and Curtius. Whether such comparisons are appro-
    priate is an issue for debate, but for a late twentieth (or early twenty first)
    century reader, the emotive qualities of her language and choice of parallel
    are inescapable. Submerged in this passage, of course, is an implicit par-
    allel between the fate of Alexander at the hands of his biographers, and
    the Jews at the hands of Hitler.
35 Renault says that if Alexander had in *truth* been corrupt, the mutineers
    at Opis would have dragged him down and killed him; that instead they
    sought his forgiveness 'is not *fiction* but *history*' (my italics; The Persian
    Boy 413).
36 See Bann 1990:64–81; also Hutcheon 1992:87–101, 158–77.
37 See Peter Green's review, Green 1989a.
38 Green 1989a:152 suggests, plausibly, that the title of the venture as a
    whole originated with Time Inc. (co-sponsors, with the National Bank of
    Greece).
39 Yalouris 1980:10–20.
40 See e.g. Patrick Comerford, *Irish Times*, 13/08/1994:9; Liam McDowell,
    The Guardian, 'Europe' 30/03/1993:16. Also, extended discussions of
    Cowan 2000, Karakasidou 1997, Shea 1996.
41 Cf. James Dean, Marilyn Munroe, Marc Bolan, Jim Morrison, Princess
    Diana, Kurt Cobain. For Alexander, similarly, see Curtius Rufus
    3.5.11–13; 4.4.1–2; 5.1.36; 6.7.1.
42 See Manchester 1983, for a hagiographic treatment of Kennedy's life and
    the 'Camelot' analogy surrounding his presidency, playing the metaphor
    out in full.
43 Two notable television outings, now, sadly, extremely difficult to gain
    access to, are the 1961 BBC remake of Terence Rattigan's *Adventure Story*
    (first made in 1950), starring Sean Connery as Alexander; and ABC's

1964 pilot for a proposed mini-series on Alexander (*Alexander the Great*), shown only once (in January 1968) and then shelved. This version starred William Shatner as Alexander, with Adam West as Cleander, and John Cassavetes and Joseph Cotton also on board.

44 See the tie-in volume, Grabsky 1993.

45 Ironically, the series did have web pages (no longer live) as part of the BBC Online service: http://www.bbc.co.uk/education/archive/walden/alex.shtml

46 In particular, see Wood 2001:12–15. On East versus West see Wood 2001:237–38. For an earlier, twentieth century eastern slant on Alexander, the 1941 Indian film *Sikander* (directed lavishly by Sohrab Modi, with epic production values) produces an Alexander whose conquests have strong overtones of British imperialism. It was banned in some theatres. We could also compare Michael Wood's retracing and recreation of Alexander's route with Freya Stark's rather more minimalist (but perhaps no less self-dramatizing) account of her own post-Alexander travels in *Alexander's Path* (1958).

47 *Hello!* 343 18/02/1995:16–17.

48 Montagu Don, *Observer* 'Life' magazine 23/10/1994:65.

49 Ezard, John, 'Talk of Alexander and of others too' *The Guardian* 8/06/1995:2. Matthew Engle ('In the pink on the road to gold', *The Guardian* 'Friday Sport' 24/06/1994:4–5 has a less positive slant to offer in his coverage of the Gay Games IV, held in New York: Alexander is described as wiping out the Sacred Legion of Thebes (described as pairs of male lovers), a band of fearsome warriors. Positively glowing details on 'gay' Alexander can be found at http://www.gayheroes.com/alex.htm, where Alexander is joined by Lawrence of Arabia (http://www.gayheroes.com/law.htm).

Bibliography

Abbreviations of journals are those used in L'Année Philologique.

Aalders, G.J.D., 'Germanicus und Alexander der Grosse' *Historia* 10 (1961), 382–84.

Ahl, Frederick M., *Lucan: An Introduction* (Ithaca, 1976).

Albrecht, Michael von, *A History of Roman Literature: From Livius Andronicus to Boethius, With Special Regard to its Influence on World Literature*, 2 volumes, trans. Ruth R. Caston and Francis R. Schwartz, revised by author and Gareth Schmeling (Leiden, 1997).

Alcock, Susan E., 'Nero at Play? The Emperor's Grecian Odyssey' in Elsner and Masters (1994), 98–111.

Alessandrì, Salvatore, 'L'*imitatio Alexandri* augustea e i rapporti fra Orazio e Curzio Rufo' *SCO* 18 (1969), 194–210.

Alfonsi, L., 'Sul passo Liviano relativo ad Alessandro Magno' *Hermes* 90 (1962), 505–6.

Alston, Richard, *Aspects of Roman History AD 14–117* (London, 1998).

Anderson, Andrew Runni, 'Heracles and His Successors: A Study of a Heroic Ideal and the Recurrence of a Heroic Type' *HSPh* 39 (1928), 7–58.

Anderson, J.C., *The Historical Topography of the Imperial Fora*, Collection Latomus 182 (Brussels, 1984).

André, J.M., 'L'otium chez Valère-Maxime et Velleius Paterculus ou la réaction morale au début du principat' *REL* 43 (1965), 294–315.

———— 'La conception de l'État et de l'Empire dans la pensée gréco-romaine des deux premiers siècles de notre ère' *ANRW* II.30.1 (1982), 3–73.

———— 'Alexandre le Grand, modèle et repoussoir du prince (d'Auguste à Neron)' in Croisille (1990), 11–24.

Anson, Edward M., 'The *Ephemerides* of Alexander the Great' *Historia* 45 (1996), 501–4.

Arafat, K.W, *Pausanias' Greece: Ancient Artists and Roman Rulers* (Cambridge, 1996).

Armstrong, Edward C., *The Medieval French Roman d'Alexandre*, six volumes (Princeton, 1937–76).

Aske, Martin, *Keats and Hellenism* (Cambridge, 1985).

Astin, A.E., *Scipio Aemilianus* (Oxford, 1967).

Atkinson, J.E., 'Curtius Rufus' Historiae Alexandri and the Principate' *Actes de la XIIe Conférence d'Études Classiques Eirene* (Amsterdam, 1975), 363–67.

———— *A Commentary on Q. Curtius Rufus' Historiae Alexandri Magni Books 3 and 4* London Studies in Classical Philology 4 (Amsterdam, 1980).

———— *A Commentary on Q. Curtius Rufus' Historiae Alexandri Magni Books 5 to 7.2*, *AClass* Supplementum 1 (Amsterdam, 1994).

Badian, E., 'Some Recent Interpretations of Alexander' in Bosworth (1976), 289–94.

Baehr, Peter, *Caesarism and the Fading of the Roman World: A Study in Republicanism and Caesarism* (New Brunswick, 1998).

Bakhtin, M.M., *The Dialogic Imagination: Four Essays*, Holquist, M. (ed.), trans. C. Emerson, and M. Holquist (Austin, 1981).

Balsdon, J.P.V.D., *Romans and Aliens* (London, 1979).

Bann, Stephen, *The Inventions of History: Essays on the Representation of the Past* (Manchester, 1990).

Barchiesi, Alessandro, 'Insegnare ad Augusto: Orazio, Epistole 2, 1 e Ovidio, Tristia II' *MD* 31 (1993) 149–184.

Barker, Ernest, *The Ideas and Ideals of the British Empire* (New York, 1969[2]).

Barrett, Anthony A., *Caligula: The Corruption of Power* (London, 1993).

Barthes, Roland, *The Rustle of Language*, trans. Richard Howard (Oxford, 1986).

————— *Mythologies*, trans. A. Lavers (London, 1993).

Barton, Carlin A., *The Sorrows of the Ancient Romans: The Gladiator and the Monster* (Princeton, 1993).

————— *Roman Honor:The Fire in the Bones* (Berkeley 2001).

Bartsch, Shadi, *Actors in the Audience: Theatricality and Doublespeak from Nero to Hadrian* (Cambridge, Mass., 1994).

————— *Ideology in Cold Blood: A Reading of Lucan's* Civil War (Cambridge, Mass., 1997).

Baynham, Elizabeth J., *Alexander the Great: The Unique History of Quintus Curtius* (Ann Arbor, 1998).

Beard, Mary, 'Looking (harder) for Roman Myth: Dumézil, Declamation and the Problems of Definition', Colloquium Rauricum Band 3, *Mythos in mythenloser Gesellschaft: Das Paradigma Roms*, Graf, Fritz (ed.) (Stuttgart, 1993), 44–64.

————— and Alan K. Bowman, Mireille Corbier, Tim Cornell, James L. Franklin Jr., Ann Hanson, Keith Hopkins, Nicholas Horsfall, *Literacy in the Roman World, JRA Suppl.* 3 (1991).

————— and Michael Crawford, *Rome in the Late Republic* (London, 1999[2]).

————— and John Henderson, *Classics: A Very Short Introduction* (Oxford, 1995).

————— and John Henderson, *Classical Art From Greece to Rome* (Oxford, 2001).

Bellinger, Alfred R., 'The Immortality of Alexander and Augustus' *YClS* 15 (1957), 93–100.

Bengtson, Hermann (ed.), *The Greeks and the Persians: From the Sixth to the Fourth Centuries* (London, 1969).

Bieber, Margaret, *Alexander the Great in Greek and Roman Art* (Chicago, 1964).

Bloomer, W. Martin, *Valerius Maximus and the Rhetoric of the New Nobility* (London, 1992).

Bosworth, A.B. (ed.) *Alexandre le Grand, image et réalité* Fondation Hardt *Entretiens* 22 (Geneva, 1976).

————— *A Historical Commentary on Arrian's History of Alexander* 2 vol (Oxford, 1980/1995).

————— 'History and Rhetoric in Curtius Rufus' *CPh* 78 (1983), 150–61; review of Atkinson (1980).

————— *Conquest and Empire: the Reign of Alexander the Great* (Cambridge 1988a).

————— *From Arrian to Alexander: Studies in Historical Interpretation* (Oxford, 1988b).

Alexander and the East: The Tragedy of Triumph (Oxford, 1996).

————— and E. Baynham (eds) *Alexander the Great in Fact and Fiction* (Oxford, 2000).

Bowersock, Glen, 'Augustus and the East: the Problem of Succession' in Millar and Segal (1984), 169–88.

————— *Fiction as History: Nero to Julian* (Berkeley, 1994).

Boyle, A.J. (ed.), *Roman Literature and Ideology: Ramus Essays for J.P. Sullivan* (Victoria, 1995).

Braccesi, Lorenzo, 'Livio, Curzio Rufo e Petrarca (per la fortuna dell' *excursus* su Papirio)' *Athenaeum* n.s. 65 (1987), 237–39.

Brenk, Frederick E., 'Antony-Osiris, Cleopatra-Isis: The End of Plutarch's *Antony*' in Stadter (1992), 159–82.

Bruère, R.T., 'Silius Italicus Punica 3.62 and 4.763–822' *CPh* 47 (1952), 219–27.

Bruhl, Adrien, 'Souvenir d'Alexandre le Grand et les Romains' *MEFRA* 47 (1930), 202–21.

Brunt, P.A., *Roman Imperial Themes* (Oxford, 1990a–c).

————— 'Augustan Imperialism' in Brunt (1990a), 96–109.

————— 'Reflections on British and Roman Imperialism' in Brunt (1990b), 110–33.

————— 'Roman Imperial Illusions' in Brunt (1990c), 433–80.

Bryce, James, *The Ancient Roman Empire and the British Empire in India: The Diffusion of Roman and English Law Throughout the World* (London, 1914).

Cairns, Francis, *Generic Composition in Greek and Roman Poetry* (Edinburgh, 1972).

————— *Tibullus: a Hellenistic Poet at Rome* (Cambridge, 1979).

Cameron, Averil, (ed.), *History as Text: The Writing of Ancient History* (London, 1989).

Campbell, Brian, 'War and Diplomacy: Rome and Parthia, 31 B.C.–A.D. 235' in Rich and Shipley (1993), 213–40.

Campbell, J.B., *The Emperor and the Roman Army 31 B.C.–A.D. 235* (Oxford, 1984).

Carlsen, Jesper, et al. (eds), *Alexander the Great: Reality and Myth* (Rome, 1993), *Analecta Romana Instituti Danici*, Suppl. 20.

Carney, Elizabeth, 'Macedonians and Mutiny: Discipline and Indiscipline in the Army of Philip and Alexander' *CPh* 91 (1996), 19–44.

Carr, E.H., *What is History?* (Harmondsworth, 1973).

Carter, C.J., 'Valerius Maximus' in Dorey (1975), 26–56.

Carter, J.M., (ed.), trans., comm., *Julius Caesar: the Civil War Books I and II* (Warminster, 1991).

————— (ed.), trans., comm., *Julius Caesar: The Civil War Book III* (Warminster, 1993).

Cartledge, Paul, '"We are all Greeks"? Ancient (especially Herodotean) and Modern Contestations of Hellenism' *BICS* 40 [n.s. 2] (1995), 75–82.

Cary, George, 'Petrarch and Alexander the Great' *Italian Studies* 5 (1950), 43.

————— *The Medieval Alexander* (Cambridge, 1956).

Cascon Dorado, A., 'La labor desmitificadora de Curcio Rufo en su Historia de Alejandro Magno' in Croisille (1990), 254–65.

Ceauşescu, Petre, 'La double image d'Alexandre le Grand à Rome: essai d'une explication politique' *StudClas* 16 (1974), 153–68.

Charlesworth, M.P., '*Pietas* and *Victoria*: the Emperor and the Citizen' *JRS* 33 (1943), 1–10.

Chrissanthos, Stefan G., 'Caesar and the Mutiny of 47 BC' *JRS* 91 (2001), 63–75.

Cizek, Alexandru, 'The Function of the Heroic Myth in the Encomium', *Actes de la XIIe Conférence d'Études Classiques Eirene* (Amsterdam, 1975), 295–305.

Clarke, M.L., 'The *Thesis* in the Roman Rhetorical Schools of the Republic' *CQ* 45 / n.s. 1 (1951), 159–66.

Cohen, Ada, *The Alexander Mosaic: Stories of Victory and Defeat* (Cambridge, 1996).

Coleman, K.M., (ed.), trans., comm., *Statius: Silvae IV* (Oxford, 1988).

Conte, Gian Biagio, *Latin Literature: A History*, trans. Joseph B. Solodow, revised Don Fowler, Glen W. Most (Baltimore, 1994).

Cowan, Jane, *Macedonia: The Politics of Identity and Difference* (London, 2000).

Croisille, J.M., (ed.), *Neronia IV: Alejandro Magno, modelo de los emperadores romanos*, Actes du IVe colloque international de la SIEN, *Collection Latomus* 209 (Brussels, 1990).

————— 'Alexandre chez Lucain: l'image du tyran. Notes sur Ph. X.1–52' in Croisille (1990), 266–76.

Crook, John, *Consilium Princeps: Imperial Councils and Counsellors From Augustus to Diocletian* (Cambridge, 1955).

Cunningham, David Robertson, *The Influence of the Alexander Legend on Some Roman Political Figures* (Unpublished PhD Diss. Washington, 1971).

D'Arms, J.H., 'Control, Companionship and Clientela: Some Social Functions of the Roman Communal Meal', *Echos du monde classique* 28 (1984), 327–48.

———— 'The Roman *Convivium* and the Idea of Equality' in Murray (1990), 308–20

Dahlmann, H., 'Studien zu Senecas Consolatio ad Polybium' *Hermes* 72 (1937), 301–16.

Dauge, Y.A., *Le Barbare: Recherches sur la conception romaine de la barbarie et de la civilisation* Collection Latomus 176 (Brussels, 1981).

Dempsie, W.A.R., *A Commentary on Q. Curtius Rufus Historiae Alexandri Magni Book X* (Unpublished PhD Diss. St Andrews, 1991).

Dihle, Albrecht, 'The Conception of Asia in Hellenistic and Roman Literature' *PCPhS* 190 (1964) 15–23.

———— *Greek and Latin Literature of the Roman Empire: from Augustus to Justinian,* trans. Manfred Malzahn (London, 1994).

Dorey, T.A. (ed.), *Latin Biography* (London, 1967).

———— *Empire and Aftermath: Silver Latin II* (London, 1975).

Dunkle, J.R., 'The Rhetorical Tyrant in Roman Historiography' *CW* 65 (1971), 12–20.

Eder, W., 'Augustus and the Power of Tradition: The Augustan Principate as Binding Link Between Republic and Empire' in Raaflaub and Toher (1990), 71–122.

Edwards, Catharine, *The Politics of Immorality in Ancient Rome* (Cambridge, 1993).

Edwards, M.J. and Simon Swain (eds), *Portraits: Biographical Representation in the Greek and Latin Literature of the Roman Empire* (Oxford, 1997).

Ehrenberg, V. and A.H.M. Jones (eds.), *Documents Illustrating the Reigns of Augustus and Tiberius* (Oxford 1955²).

Elsner, Jaş and Jamie Masters (eds), *Reflections of Nero: Culture, History and Representation* (London, 1994).

Fairweather, Janet, 'Fiction in the Biographies of Ancient Writers' *AncSoc* 5 (1974), 231–75.

———— *Seneca the Elder* (Cambridge, 1981).

Fantham, Elaine, 'Caesar and the Mutiny: Lucan's reshaping of the Historical tradition in *De Bello Civili* 5.237–375' *CPh* 80 (1985), 119–31.

Farrell, J.G., *The Singapore Grip* (London, 1978).

Fears, J. Rufus, 'The Stoic View of the Career and Character of Alexander the Great' *Philologus* 118 (1974), 113–30.

———— *Princeps a diis electus: the divine election of the emperor as a political concept at Rome* Papers and monographs of the American Academy in Rome 26 (1977).

———— 'The Cult of Virtues and Imperial Roman Ideology' *ANRW* II.17.2 (1981), 827–948.

Feeney, D.C., 'Towards an Account of the Ancient World's Concept of Fictive Belief' in Gill and Wiseman (1993), 230–44.

Feldherr, Andrew, 'Livy's revolution: civic identity and the creation of the *res publica*' in Habinek and Schiesaro (1997), 137–57.

———— *Spectacle and Society in Livy's History* (Berkeley, 1998).

Flower, Harriet, *Ancestor Masks and Aristocratic Power in Roman Culture* (Oxford, 1996).

Foucher, M., *L'invention des frontières* (Paris, 1986).

Fox, Matthew, *Roman Historical Myths: The Regal period in Augustan Literature* (Oxford, 1996).

———— 'Dialogue and Irony in Cicero: Reading *De Republica*, in Sharrock and Morales (2000), 263–86.

Fraenkel, Eduard, *Elementi plautini in Plauto* trans. Franco Munari (Florence, 1960).

Frazier, Françoise, *Histoire et morale dans les Vies parallèles de Plutarque* (Paris, 1996).

Frye, Northrop, 'New Directions From Old' *Fables of Identity: studies in poetic mythology* (New York, 1963).

Gabba, Emilio, 'The Historians and Augustus' in Millar and Segal (1984), 61–88.

Galinsky, G. Karl, *The Herakles Theme: The Adaptations of the Hero in Literature from Homer to the Twentieth Century* (Oxford, 1972).

———— *Augustan Culture: An Interpretative Introduction* (Princeton, 1996).

García Moreno, Luis A., 'Alejandro Magno y la politica exterior de Augusto' in Croisille (ed.) (1990), 132–42.
—— 'Hellenistic Ethnography and the Reign of Augustus in Trogus Pompeius' AncW 24 (1993), 199–212.
Garnsey, Peter, 'The lex Iulia and Appeal under the Empire' JRS 56 (1966), 167–89.
Geiger, Joseph, Cornelius Nepos and Ancient Political Biography (Historia, Einzelschriften 47, 1985).
Gelzer, Matthias, Pompeius (Munich, 1949).
—— Caesar: Politician and Statesman, trans. P. Needham (Oxford, 1969).
Geyssen, John W., Imperial Panegyric in Statius: A Literary Commentary on Silvae 1.1 (New York, 1996).
Gill, Christopher, 'The Question of Character Development: Plutarch and Tacitus' CQ 33 (1983), 469–87.
—— and T. P. Wiseman (eds), Lies and Fiction in the Ancient World (Exeter, 1993).
Gilmartin, Kristine, 'Corbulo's Campaigns in the East: An analysis of Tacitus' account' Historia 22 (1973), 583–626.
Goldhill, Simon (ed.), Being Greek under Rome: Cultural Identity, the Second Sophistic, and the Development of Empire (Cambridge, 2001).
Goldstein, Laurence, Ruins and Empire: The Evolution of a Theme in Augustan and Romantic Literature (Pittsburgh, 1977).
Goukowsky, P., Essai sur les origines du mythe d'Alexandre (336–270 av. J.-C.), 2 volumes in 1 (Nancy, 1978/1981).
Gowers, Emily, The Loaded Table: Representations of Food in Roman Literature (Oxford, 1993).
Grabsky, Phil, The Great Commanders (London, 1993).
Green, Peter, Alexander of Macedon 356–323 B.C.: A Historical Biography (Harmondsworth, 1974).
—— Classical Bearings: Interpreting Ancient History and Culture (London, 1989a/b).
—— 'The Macedonian Connection' in Green (1989a), 151–64.
—— 'Caesar and Alexander: Aemulatio, imitatio, comparatio' in Green (1989b), 193–209.
Greenhalgh, Peter, Pompey: The Roman Alexander (London, 1980).
Griffin, Jasper, 'Propertius and Antony' JRS 67 (1977), 17–26.
—— 'Augustus and the Poets: Caesar Qui Cogere Posset' in Millar and Segal (1984), 189–218.
—— The Mirror of Myth: Classical Themes and Variations (London, 1986).
Griffin, M.T., Seneca: A Philosopher in Politics (Oxford, 1991)².
—— Nero: The End of a Dynasty (London, 1996³).
—— and Jonathan Barnes (eds), Philosophia Togata: Essays on Philosophy and Roman Society (Oxford, 1989).
—— 'Philosophy, Politics, and Politicians at Rome' in Griffin and Barnes (1989), 1–37.
Gruen, Erich S., The Last Generation of the Roman Republic (Berkeley, 1974).
—— Culture and National Identity in Republican Rome (London, 1993).
Gurval, Robert Alan, Actium and Augustus: the Politics and Emotions of Civil War (Ann Arbor, 1995)
Habicht, Christian, Pausanias' Guide to Ancient Greece (Berkeley, 1985).
Habinek, Thomas N., The Politics of Latin Literature: Writing, Identity, and Empire in Ancient Rome (Princeton, 1998).
Hägg, Tomas, The Novel in Antiquity (Oxford, 1983).
Halbfass, William, India and Europe (New York, 1988).
Hamilton, J.R., Plutarch: Alexander, a Commentary (Oxford, 1969).
—— Alexander the Great (London, 1973).
Hamilton, Paul, Historicism (London, 1996).
Hammond, Mason, 'Corbulo and Nero's Eastern Policy' HSPh 45 (1934), 81–104.

Hammond, N.G.L., *Three Historians of Alexander the Great* (Cambridge, 1983).
———— 'The Royal Journal of Alexander' *Historia* 37 (1988) 129–50.
———— *Alexander the Great: King, Commander and Statesman* (Bristol, 1989).
———— *Sources For Alexander the Great: An analysis of Plutarch's Life and Arrian's Anabasis Alexandrou* (Cambridge, 1993).
———— *The Genius of Alexander the Great* (London, 1997).
Hammond, N.G.L., G.T. Griffith, and F.W. Walbank, *A History of Macedonia*, 3 vol. (Oxford, 1972–88).
Hannestad, Niels, 'Imitatio Alexandri in Roman Art' in Carlsen (1993), 61–69.
Hardie, Alex, *Statius and the Silvae: Poets, Patrons and Epideixis in the Graeco-Roman World*, ARCA Classical and Medieval Texts, Papers and Monographs 9 (Liverpool 1983).
Hardie, Philip, *Virgil's Aeneid: Cosmos and Imperium* (Oxford, 1986).
Harris, William V., *Ancient Literacy* (Cambridge, Mass., 1989).
Hartog, Francois, *The Mirror of Herodotus*, trans. Janet Lloyd (Berkeley, 1988).
Haverfield, F., 'Some Roman Conceptions of Empire' *Occasional Publications of the Classical Association* 4 (Cambridge, 1916).
Heckel, Waldemar, *The Marshals of Alexander's Empire* (London, 1992).
Henderson, John, 'Lucan/The Word at War' *Ramus* 16 (1987) 122–64.
———— 'Livy and the Invention of History' in Cameron (1989), 64–85.
———— *A Roman Life: Rutilius Gallicus on Paper and in Stone* (Exeter, 1998).
———— 'From Megalopolis to Cosmopolis: Polybius, or there and back again' in Goldhill (2001), 29–49.
Herrero Montero, S., 'La religiosidad de Alejandro en la historiografía latina: el testimonio de Q. Curcio' in Croisille (1990) 339–50.
Heuß, Alfred, 'Alexander der Große und die politische Ideologie des Altertums' *A&A* 4 (1954) 65–104.
Hoffman, Werner, *Das Literarische Porträt Alexanders des Grossen im Griechischen und Römischen Altertum* Leipziger Historische Abhandlungen 8 (Leipzig, 1907).
Horst, John Russell, *A Critical Index to References to Alexander the Great in Roman Literature* (Unpublished PhD Diss. Boulder, Colorado, 1987).
Hutcheon, Linda, *A Poetics of Postmodernism: History, Theory, Fiction* (London, 1992).
Hutchinson, G.O., *Latin Literature from Seneca to Juvenal: A Critical Study* (Oxford, 1993).
Isaac, Benjamin, *The Limits of Empire: The Roman Army in the East* (Oxford, 1992[2])
Isager, Jacob, 'Alexander the Great in Roman Literature from Pompey to Vespasian' in Carlsen (1993), 75–84.
Jacoby, F., *Fragmente der griechischen Historiker* (Leiden, 1957)
Jaeger, Mary, *Livy's Written Rome* (Ann Arbor, 1997).
Jameson, Frederic, *The Political Unconscious: Narrative as a Socially Symbolic Act* (London, 1981).
———— *Postmodernism, or, The Cultural Logic of Late Capitalism* (London, 1991).
Jenkins, Keith, *On 'What is History?': From Carr and Elton to Rorty and White* (London, 1995).
Johnson, W.R., *Momentary Monsters: Lucan and his heroes* (Ithaca, 1987).
Jones, A.H.M., *Studies in Roman Government and Law* (Oxford, 1960).
Jones, C.P., 'Towards a Chronology of Plutarch's Works' *JRS* 56 (1966), 61–74.
———— *Plutarch and Rome* (Oxford, 1971).
———— *The Roman World of Dio Chrysostom* (Cambridge, Mass., 1978).
Karakasidou, Anastasia, *Fields of Wheat, Hills of Blood: Passages to Nationhood in Greek Macedonia, 1870–1990* (Chicago, 1997).
Karttunen, Klaus, *India in Early Greek Literature* (Helsinki, 1989).
Keitel, E., 'Plutarch's Tragedy Tyrants: Galba and Otho' in R. Brock and A.J. Woodman (eds) *Papers of the Leeds International Latin Seminar* 8 (1995), 275–88.
Kennedy, David, 'The East' in Wacher (1987), 266–308.

Kennedy, Duncan F., '"Augustan" and "Anti-Augustan"': Reflections on Terms of Reference' in Powell (1992), 26–58.

Kennedy, George, *The Art of Rhetoric in the Roman World: 200 B.C.–A.D. 300* (Princeton, 1972).

Kienast, Dietmar, 'Augustus und Alexander' *Gymnasium* 76 (1969), 430–56.

Kierdorf, Wilhelm, *Laudatio funebris: Interpretationen und Untersuchungen zur Entwicklung der römischen Leichenrede* (Meisenheim am Glan, 1980).

Kilpatrick, Ross S., *The Poetry of Criticism: Horace Epistles II and Ars Poetica* (Alberta, 1990).

Kraus, Christina Shuttleworth (ed.), *Livy: Ab Urbe Condita VI* (Cambridge, 1994).

Lane Fox, Robin, *The Search For Alexander* (London, 1980).

———— *Alexander the Great* (Harmondsworth, 1986).

Lassandro, Domenico, 'La figura di Alessandro Magno nell'opera di Seneca' in Sordi (1984), 155–68.

Laurence, Ray, 'Rumour and Communication in Roman Politics' *G&R* 41 (1994), 62–74.

Leeman, A.D., *Orationis Ratio: The Stylistic Theories and Practice of the Roman Orators, Historians and Philosophers*, 2 vol (Amsterdam, 1963).

Levi, M.A., *Introduzione ad Alessandro Magno* (Milan, 1977).

Lintott, A.W., 'Provocatio: From the Struggle of the Orders to the Principate' *ANRW* I.2 (1972), 226–67.

Litchfield, H.W., 'National *exempla virtutis* in Roman Literature' *HSPh* 25 (1914), 1–25.

Lobel, E, and E.G. Turner, *The Oxyrhynchus Papyri* 25 (London, Egypt Exploration Society, 1959).

Lowenthal, David, *The Past is a Foreign Country* (Cambridge, 1995).

Lucas, C.P., *Greater Rome and Greater Britain* (Oxford, 1912).

Lühr, Franz-Frieder, 'Zur Darstellung und Bewertung von Massenreaktionen in der lateinischen Literatur' *Hermes* 107 (1979), 92–114.

Lyotard, Jean-François, *The Postmodern Condition: A Report on Knowledge*, trans. Geoff Bennington and Brian Massumi (Minneapolis, 1984).

McCormick, M., *Eternal Victory: Triumphal Rulership in Late Antiquity, Byzantium, and the Early Medieval West* (Cambridge, 1986).

McEwan, Neil, 'Mary Renault's Fire From Heaven, The Persian Boy, and Funeral Games' *Perspectives in British Historical Fiction Today* (London, 1987), 58–78.

McFarland, Thomas, *Romanticism and the Forms of Ruin: Wordsworth, Coleridge, and the Modalities of Fragmentation* (Princeton, 1981).

McGushin, P., *C. Sallustius Crispus Bellum Catilinae: A Commentary* (Leiden, 1977).

MacMullen, Ramsey, *Enemies of the Roman Order: Treason, Unrest and Alienation in the Empire* (Cambridge, Mass., 1967).

Malamud, Martha A., 'Happy Birthday, Dead Lucan: (P)raising the Dead in Silvae 2.7' in Boyle (1995), 169–98.

Malissard, A., 'Germanicus, Alexandre et le début des *Annales* de Tacite: À propos de Tacite, *Annales*, 2.73' in Croisille (1990), 328–38.

Manchester, William, *One Brief Shining Moment* (London, 1983).

Mannoni, O., *Prospero and Caliban: The Psychology of Colonialisation* (London, 1956).

Marincola, John, *Authority and Tradition in Ancient Historiography* (Cambridge, 1997).

Maslakov, G., 'Valerius Maximus and Roman Historiography: A Study of the *Exempla* Tradition' *ANRW* II.32.1 (1984), 437–96.

Masters, Jamie, *Poetry and Civil War in Lucan's Bellum Civile* (Cambridge, 1992).

Maxwell O'Brien, John, *Alexander the Great: The Invisible Enemy, a Biography* (London, 1992).

Mayne, Jasper, *Part of Lucian made English from the Originall* (Oxford, 1663).

Mayor, John E.B., *Thirteen Satires of Juvenal with a Commentary* (London, 1886[4]).

Melville, Herman, *Moby Dick: or The Whale* (London, 1920).

Menichetti, M., 'La testa colossale della Pigna, il Colossus Divi Augusti e "l'imitatio Alexandri" in età giulio-claudia' *MEFR* 98 (1986), 565–93.

Mette, H.J., ' "Roma" (Augustus) und Alexander' *Hermes* 88 (1960), 458–62.

Michel, D., *Alexander als Vorbild für Pompeius, Caesar und Marcus Antonius: Archäologische Untersuchungen* Collection Latomus 94 (Brussels, 1967).

Millar, F., *A Study of Cassius Dio* (Oxford, 1964).

———— *The Emperor in the Roman World (31 BC–AD 337)* (London, 1977).

———— and E. Segal (eds), *Caesar Augustus: Seven Aspects* (Oxford, 1984).

———— 'State and Subject: The Impact of Monarchy' in Millar and Segal (1984), 37–60.

———— *The Roman Near East 31 B.C.-.-A.D. 337* (Cambridge, Mass., 1993).

Milns, R.D., *Alexander the Great* (London, 1968).

Moles, J.L., 'Truth and Untruth in Herodotus and Thucydides' in Gill and Wiseman (1993), 88–121.

Momigliano, Arnaldo, *The Development of Greek Biography* (Cambridge, Mass., 1971).

———— *Second Thoughts on Greek Biography* (Amsterdam, 1971).

Montgomery, Hugo, 'The Greek Historians of Alexander as Literature' in Carlsen (1993), 93–99.

Moore, Philip, *Quintus Curtius Rufus' Historiae Alexandri Magni: A Study in Rhetorical Historiography* (Unpublished DPhil, Oxford, 1995).

Morgan, J.R., and Richard Stoneman (eds), *Greek Fiction: The Greek Novel in Context* (London, 1994).

Mossman, J.M., 'Plutarch, Pyrrhus and Alexander' in Stadter (1992), 90–108.

———— 'Tragedy and Epic in Plutarch's *Alexander*' in Scardigli (1995), 209–28.

———— (ed.), *Plutarch and His Intellectual World: Essays on Plutarch* (London, 1997).

Moxon, I.S., J.D. Stuart and A.J. Woodman (eds), *Past Perspectives: Studies in Greek and Roman Historical Writing* (Cambridge, 1986).

Moynihan, R., 'Geographical Mythology and Roman Imperial Ideology' in R. Winkes (ed.), *The Age of Augustus* (Louvain, 1985), 149–61

Murray, Oswyn, 'Herodotus and Hellenistic Culture' *CQ* 22 (1972) 200–13.

———— *Sympotica: A Symposium on the Symposion* (Oxford, 1990).

Nicolet, Claude, *Space, Geography and Politics in the Early Roman Empire* (Ann Arbor, 1991).

Norden, Eduard, *P. Vergilius Maro Aeneis Buch VI* (Stuttgart, 1957).

Oakley, S.P., *A Commentary on Livy Books VI-X* (Oxford, 1997, 1998).

———— 'Single Combat in the Roman Republic' *CQ* n.s. 35 (1985), 392–410.

Pédech, Paul, *Historiens compagnons d'Alexandre: Callisthène, Onésicrite, Néarque, Ptolémée, Aristobule* (Paris, 1984).

Pelling, Christopher, 'Plutarch's Method of Work in the Roman Lives' *JHS* 99 (1979), 74–96.

———— 'Plutarch's Adaptation of his Source Material' *JHS* 100 (1980), 127–49.

———— 'Plutarch and Roman Politics' in Moxon, Stuart and Woodman (1986), 159–87.

———— 'Plutarch: Roman Heroes and Greek Culture' in Griffin and Barnes (1989), 199–232.

———— (ed.), *Characterization and Individuality in Greek Literature* (Oxford, 1990).

———— 'Childhood and Personality in Greek Biography' in Pelling (1990), 213–44.

———— 'Tacitus and Germanicus' in T.J. Luce and A.J. Woodman (eds) *Tacitus and the Tacitean Tradition* (Princeton, 1993), 59–85.

———— 'Plutarch and Roman Politics' in Scardigli (1995), 319–56.

———— 'Plutarch on Caesar's Fall' in Mossman (1997), 215–34.

Phillips, J.R.S., *The Medieval Expansion of Europe* (Oxford, 1988).

Picon Garcia, V., 'La figura de Alejandro en la biografía latina' in Croisille (1990), 361–78.

Plácido, Domingo, 'Alejandro y los emperadores romanos en la historiografia griega' in Croisille (1990), 58–75.

———— 'L'image d'Alexandre dans la conception plutarchéenne de l'empire romain' *DHA* 21/2 (1995) 131–38.

Plass, Paul, *Wit and the Writing of History: The Rhetoric of Historiography in Imperial Rome* (Madison, 1988).

Pollini, J, 'Man or God: Divine Assimilation and Imitation in the Late Republic and Early Principate' in Raaflaub and Toher (1990), 334–63.

Pollitt, J.J., *Art in the Hellenistic Age* (Cambridge, 1986).

Poulsen, Birte, 'Alexander the Great in Italy during the Hellenistic Period' in Carlsen (1993), 161–70.

Powell, Anton (ed.), *Roman Poetry and Propaganda in the Age of Augustus* (London, 1992).

Prandi, L., 'L'Alessandro di Plutarco (Riflessioni su 'De Al. Magn. Fort.' e su 'Alex.')', *Rhetorical Theory* (2000) 375–86.

Putnam, M.C.J., 'Horace *Carm.* 2.9: Augustus and the Ambiguities of Encomium' in Raaflaub and Toher (1990), 212–38.

Quint, David, *Epic and Empire* (Princeton, 1993).

Raaflaub, Kurt A. and Mark Toher (eds) *Between Republic and Empire: Interpretations of Augustus and His Principate* (Berkeley, 1990).

Rawson, Elizabeth, *Intellectual Life in the Late Roman Republic* (Baltimore, 1985).

———— 'Roman Rulers and the Philosophic Adviser' in Griffin and Barnes (1989), 233–57.

Reardon, B.P., *Courants littéraires Grecs des IIe et IIIe siècles après J.-C.* (Paris, 1971).

———— *Collected Ancient Greek Novels* (Berkeley, 1989).

———— *The Form of Greek Romance* (Princeton, 1991).

Renault, Mary *Fire From Heaven* (Harmondsworth, 1972).

———— *The Nature of Alexander* (London, 1975).

———— *The Persian Boy* (Harmondsworth, 1980).

———— *Funeral Games* (Harmondsworth, 1983).

Reynolds, L.D., *Texts and Transmission: A Survey of the Latin Classics* (Oxford, 1983).

Rice, Ellen, 'The Glorious Dead: Commemoration of the Fallen and Portrayal of Victory in the Late Classical and Hellenistic World' in Rich and Shipley (1993a), 224–57.

Rich, J.W., 'Dio on Augustus' in Cameron (1989), 86–110.

———— and Graham Shipley (eds), *War and Society in the Greek World* (London, 1993a).

———— and Graham Shipley (eds), *War and Society in the Roman World* (London, 1993b).

Richard, Carl J., *The Founders and the Classics. Greece, Rome and the American Enlightenment* (Harvard, 1994).

Richardson, J. S., '*Imperium Romanum*: Empire and the Language of Power' *JRS* 81 (1991), 1–9.

Roberts, Deborah H, Francis M. Dunn, and Don Fowler (eds) *Classical Closure: Reading the End in Greek and Latin Literature* (Princeton, 1997)

Robinson, Charles Alexander Jr., *The Ephemerides of Alexander's Expedition* (Providence, RI, 1932).

———— *The History of Alexander the Great*, Vol. 1 (Providence, RI, 1953).

———— *Alexander the Great: the Meeting of East and West in World Government and Brotherhood* (Connecticut, 1984).

Romm, James S., *The Edges of the Earth in Ancient Thought* (Princeton, 1992).

Rose, H.J., 'The Departure of Dionysus' *Annals of Archaeology and Anthropology* 11 (1924), 25–30.

Rosenstein, Nathan S., *Imperatores Victi: Military Defeat and Aristocratic Competition in the Middle and Late Republic* (Berkeley, 1990).

Ross, D.J.A., *Alexander Historiatus: A Guide to Medieval Illustrated Alexander Literature* (Frankfurt, 1988²).

Ross, D.O., 'The Tacitean Germanicus' *YClS* 23 (1973), 209–27.

Rudd, Niall (ed.), *Horace: Epistles Book II and Epistle to the Pisones ('Ars Poetica')* (Cambridge, 1989).

Rutland, Linda W., 'The Tacitean Germanicus: Suggestions for a Re-Evaluation' *RhM* 130 (1987), 153–64.

Sacks, Kenneth S., *Diodorus Siculus and the First Century* (Princeton, 1990).

Said, Edward, *Orientalism* (Harmondsworth, 1991).

———— *Culture and Imperialism* (London, 1993).

Saller, Richard, 'Anecdotes as Historical Evidence for the Principate' *G&R* n.s. 27 (1980), 69–83.

Scardigli, Barbara (ed.), *Essays on Plutarch's Lives* (Oxford, 1995).

Schama, Simon, *Landscape and Memory* (London, 1995).

Schur, W., 'Die Orientpolitik des Kaisers Nero' *Klio* 20 (1926), 215–22.

Schwab, Raymond, *La Renaissance orientale* (Paris, 1950).

Scobie, Alec, *Hitler's State Architecture: The Impact of Classical Antiquity* (Pennsylvania, 1990).

Scott, Kenneth, 'Octavian's Propaganda and Antony's de sua ebrietate' *CPh* 24 (1929), 133–41.

Scullard, H.H., *From the Gracchi to Nero* (London 1991⁵).

Serres, Michel, *Rome: The Book of Foundations* (Stanford, 1991).

Shackleton Bailey, D.R. (ed.), *Cicero: Epistulae Ad Familiares, Vol. 1 62–47 BC* (Cambridge, 1977).

Shaffer, E.S., *'The Oriental Idyll', 'Kubla Khan' and the Fall of Jerusalem; The Mythological School in Biblical Criticism and Secular Literature 1770–1880* (Cambridge, 1975)

Sharrock, A and H. Morales (eds) *Intratextuality: Greek and Roman Textual Relations* (Oxford, 2000).

Shea, John, *Macedonia and Greece: The Struggle to Define a New Baltic Nation* (Jefferson, 1996).

Shotter, D.C.A., 'Tacitus, Tiberius and Germanicus' *Historia* 17 (1968), 194–214.

Sordi, M. (ed.), *Alessandro Magno tra storia e mito* (Milan, 1984).

Spencer, Diana, 'Alexander the Great and the popular (anti-)hero' in Lorna Hardwick and Stanley Ireland (eds), *The January Conference 1996: The Reception of Classical Texts and Images* (Open University 1996), 174–95. [http://www.open.ac.uk/OU/Academic/Arts/CC96/ccfrontpage.htm].

———— *The Roman Alexander: Studies in Curtius Rufus* (Unpublished PhD Diss. Cambridge, 1997).

———— 'Propertius, Hercules, and the Dynamic of Roman Mythic Space in *Elegy* 4.9' *Arethusa* 34 (2001) 259–284.

———— 'Horace and the Company of Kings: Art and Artfulness in *Epistle* 2.1' (forthcoming).

———— 'Telling it like it is: Alexander and Advice-giving in Seneca' (forthcoming (2)).

Spranger, Peter P., 'Der Große: Untersuchungen zur Entstehung des historischen Beinamens in der Antike' *Saeculum* 9 (1958), 22–58.

Stadter, Philip A., *Arrian of Nicomedia* (Chapel Hill, 1980).

———— 'Fictional Narrative in the *Cyropaideia*' *AJPh* 112 (1991), 461–91.

———— (ed.), *Plutarch and the Historical Tradition* (London, 1992).

Stahl, H.P., 'The Death of Turnus: Augustan Vergil and the Political Rival' in Raaflaub and Toher (1990), 174–211.

Stark, Freya, *Alexander's Path: From Caria to Cilicia* (London, 1958).

Starn, Rudolph, 'Reinventing Heroes in Renaissance Italy' in Robert I. Rotberg and Theodore K. Rabb (eds), *Art and History: Images and their Meaning* (Cambridge, 1988), 67–84.

Stephens, Susan A. and John J. Winkler (eds), *Ancient Greek Novels: the Fragments* (Princeton, 1995).

Stewart, Andrew, *Faces of Power: Alexander's Image and Hellenistic Politics* (Berkeley, 1993).

Stoneman, Richard, tr. *The Greek Alexander Romance* (Harmondsworth, 1991)

———— 'Oriental Motifs in the Alexander Romance' *Antichthon* 26 (1992), 95–113.

———— 'Romantic Ethnography: Central Asia and India in the Alexander Romance' *AncW* 25 (1994a), 93–107.

————— 'The Alexander Romance: From History to Fiction' in Morgan and Stoneman (1994b), 117–29.

————— tr. *Legends of Alexander the Great* (London, 1994c).

Storost, J., *Studien zur Alexandersage in der älteren italienischen Literatur* (Halle, 1935).

Stuart, D.R., *Epochs of Greek and Roman Biography* (Berkeley, 1928).

Sullivan, J.P., *Literature and Politics in the Age of Nero* (Ithaca, 1985).

Sussman, Lewis A., *The Elder Seneca* (Leiden, 1978).

Swain, Simon, *Hellenism and Empire: Language, Classicism, and Power in the Greek World AD 50–250* (Oxford, 1996).

Swain, Simon (ed.) *Dio Chrysostom: Politics, Letters and Philosophy* (Oxford, 2000).

Sweetman, David, *Mary Renault: A Biography* (London, 1993).

Syme, Ronald, *The Roman Revolution* (Oxford, 1939).

————— *Tacitus* (Oxford, 1958).

————— *Anatolica: Studies in Strabo*, Anthony Birley (ed.) (Oxford, 1995).

Richard, *Oxford and Empire: The Last Lost Cause?* (London, 1986).

Tarn, W.W., *Alexander the Great* 2 vols (Cambridge, 1948).

Tatum, James (ed.), *The Search for the Ancient Novel* (Baltimore, 1994).

Thompson, Lloyd A., 'Strabo on Civilization' *Platon* 31 (1979), 213–30

————— *Romans and Blacks* (London, 1989).

Toher, M., 'Augustus and the Evolution of Roman Historiography' in Raaflaub and Toher (1990), 139–54.

Too, Yun Lee, 'Educating Nero: a reading of Seneca's *Moral Epistles*' in Elsner and Masters (1994), 211–24.

Treves, Piero, *Il Mito di Alessandro e la Roma d'Augusto* (Milan, 1953).

Tsigakou, Fani-Maria, *The Rediscovery of Greece: Travellers and Painters of the Romantic Era* (London, 1981)

Vance, William L., *America's Rome* (New Haven, 1989).

Vasaly, Ann, *Representations: Images of the World in Ciceronian Oratory* (Berkeley, 1993).

Vermeule, C., *Alexander the Great Conquers Rome* (Cambridge, Mass., 1986).

Veyne, Paul, *Writing History: Essay on Epistemology*, trans. Mina Moore-Rinvolucri (Manchester, 1984).

Wacher, John (ed.), *The Roman World* Vol. 1 of 2 (London, 1987).

Walbank, F.W., *A Historical Commentary on Polybius* 3 vols (Oxford 1957, 1967a, 1979).

————— 'The Scipionic Legend' *PCPhS* 193 (1967b), 54–69.

————— 'Nationality as a Factor in Roman History' *HSCPh* 76 (1972), 145–68.

Walker, B., *The Annals of Tacitus* (Manchester, 1952).

Wallace-Hadrill, Andrew, 'Civilis Princeps: Between Citizen and King' *JRS* 72 (1982), 32–48.

————— 'Time for Augustus' in M. Whitby, P. Hardie and M. Whitby (eds), *Homo Viator* (Bristol, 1987), 221–31.

————— 'Pliny the Elder and Man's Unnatural History' *G&R* 37 (1990), 80–96.

Warmington, B.H., *Nero: Reality and Legend* (London, 1969).

Weber, F., *Alexander der Große im Urteil der Griechen und Römer bis in die konstantinische Zeit* (Unpublished Diss. Giessen, 1909).

Webster, Graham, *The Roman Imperial Army of the First and Second Centuries AD* (London, 1969).

Wehrli, C., 'La place de Trogue-Pompée et de Quinte-Curce dans l'historiographie romaine' [res.] *REL* 39 (1961), 65.

Weinstock, Stefan, 'Victor and Invictus' *HThR* 50 (1957).

————— *Divus Julius* (Oxford, 1971).

Weippert, Otto, *Alexander-Imitatio und römische Politik in republikanischer Zeit* (Published PhD Diss. Würzburg, 1972).

West, C.B., *Courtoisie in Anglo-Norman Literature* (Oxford, 1938).

Wheeldon, M.J., '"True Stories": The Reception of Historiography in Antiquity' in Cameron (1989), 33–63.

White, Hayden, *Metahistory: The Historical Imagination in Nineteenth Century Europe* (Baltimore, 1973).

—————— *Tropics of Discourse: Essays in Cultural Criticism* (Baltimore, 1978).

—————— '"Figuring the Nature of Times Deceased": Literary Theory and Historical Writing', in Ralph Cohen (ed.), *The Future of Literary Theory* (London, 1989), 19–43.

—————— 'The Question of Narrative in Contemporary Historical Theory' in Mark Currie (ed.), *Metafiction* (London, 1995), 104–41.

White, Peter, *Promised Verse: Poets in the Society of Augustan Rome* (Cambridge, Mass., 1993).

Wiedemann, Thomas, *Emperors and Gladiators* (London, 1992).

Wilcken, Ulrich, *Alexander the Great*, trans. G.C. Richards, intro., notes, biblio., Eugene N. Borza (New York, 1967).

Williams, Gordon, *Tradition and Originality in Roman Poetry* (Oxford, 1968).

—————— *Change and Decline: Roman Literature in the Early Empire* (Berkeley, 1978).

Wilson, Marcus, 'Flavian Variant: History. Silius' *Punica*' in Boyle (1993), 218–36.

Wirszubski, Chaim, *Libertas as a Political Ideal at Rome During the Late Republic and Early Principate* (Cambridge, 1960).

Wirth, Gerhard, 'Alexander und Rom' in *Alexander le Grand: image et réalité; sept exposes suivis de discussions* (*Entretiens Hardt* 22, Geneva, 1976), 181–210; discussion 211–21.

Wiseman, T.P., 'Legendary Genealogies in Late-Republican Rome' *G&R* n.s. 21 (1974), 153–64.

—————— *Clio's Cosmetics: Three Studies in Greco-Roman Literature* (Leicester, 1979).

—————— *Catullus and his World: A Reappraisal* (Cambridge, 1985).

—————— 'Julius Caesar and the *Mappa Mundi*' in *Talking to Virgil* (Exeter, 1992), 22–42.

—————— 'Lying Historians: Seven Types of Mendacity' in Gill and Wiseman (1993), 122–146.

—————— *Historiography and Imagination: Eight Essays on Roman Culture* (Exeter, 1994).

Wissowa, G., *Religion u. Kultus der Römer* (Munich, 1912).

Wood, Christopher S., *Albrecht Altdorfer and the Origins of Landscape* (London, 1993).

Wood, Michael, *In the Fooststeps of Alexander the Great* (London, 2001).

Woodman, A.J., 'Velleius Paterculus' in Dorey (1975), 1–25.

—————— *Rhetoric in Classical Historiography: Four Studies* (Croom Helm, 1988).

—————— and Jonathan Powell (eds), *Author and Audience in Latin Literature* (Cambridge, 1992).

—————— 'Nero's Alien Capital: Tacitus as Paradoxographer (*Annals* 15.36-7)' in Woodman and Powell (1992), 173–88.

Woolf, Greg, 'Becoming Roman, Staying Greek: Culture, Identity and the Civilizing Process in the Roman East' *PCPhS* 40 (1994), 116–43.

Yalouris, Nicholas, 'Alexander and his Heritage', *The Search For Alexander: An Exhibition* (catalogue produced by NY Graphic Society, Boston; exhibition: Washington, Chicago, Boston, San Francisco, 1980–1982).

Yavetz, Zwi, *Julius Caesar and his Public Image* (London, 1983).

—————— 'The *Res Gestae* and Augustus' Public Image' in Millar and Segal (1984), 1–36.

Zanker, Paul, *The Power of Images in the Age of Augustus*, trans. Alan Shapiro (Ann Arbor, 1988).

Zecchini, G. 'Alessandro Magno nella cultura dell' età antonina' in Sordi (1984), 195–212.

Zwierlein, Otto, 'Statius, Lucan, Curtius Rufus und das hellenistische Epos' *RhM* 131 (1988), 67–84.

General Index

Achilles (see also Homer; Troy) 6, 11, 123–4, 127, 169
advice 57–8, 61–2, 63–9, 73, 79, 102–4, 108, 110–2, 170, 190, 232 (n. 12)
Aeneas (see also Troy; Virgil) 2, 11, 27, 34, 169, 196, 199
Alexander Helios 24
Alexander Mosaic ii (illustration), 188–189, 204, 209
Alexander I of Epirus 49, 143–4, 227 (n. 9)
Alexander—III of Macedon—the Great (see also Alexander Helios; *Alexander Mosaic*; Alexander I of Epirus; Apelles; Aristotle; Caesar, C. Iulius; Clitus; flattery; historiography: Roman and Imperial Greek; Lysippus; Orientalist constructions of 'the East')
admired by Napoleon: 210
alcoholism: 85–6, 87, 91–3, 95, 108, 118, 152–3, 227 (n. 4), 232 (n. 7)
and Aristotle: 61–2, 64, 72–3, 102
and Callisthenes: 68, 97, 127, 128, 136–8, 206, 230 (n. 32), 237 (n. 10), 239 (n. 26)
and Cato: 168, 170, 200, 116, 117, 242 (n. 10)
and Clitus: 85, 91–2, 102–3
and Darius' family: 84, 172–4
and Lysimachus: 85, 97, 102–5, 110–11, 128
and modern Macedonia: 2, 213–5
and mutiny: 201–3, 249 (n. 85)
and proskynesis: 178, 199, 238 (n. 22)
as addressee of Stoic admonitions: 110–1

as benchmark for Roman expansion: 2–4, 34, 83, 119, 121, 138–9, 141, 146, 163, 167, 180, 189, 199, 241 (n. 6), 244–5 (n. 39)
as Christian emblem: 206–7, 250 (n. 14)
as compulsive conquistador: 39–40, 48–9, 75, 95–7, 119–21, 138, 140, 142–4, 157, 166, 241 (n. 49)
as counterfactual antagonist of Rome in Livian declamation: 43, 51–3, 233 (n. 19)
as descendant and emulator of Achilles: 6, 123–4, 127, 146, 169
as exemplar for British imperialism: 210, 245 (n. 48), 251 (n. 25), 254 (n. 46)
as exemplar for Roman imperialists: 14, 40, 63, 75, 118, 119, 122, 138–9, 141–2, 147, 162, 165, 168, 180, 190
as explorer: 160–1, 169, 205
as focus of personality cult: 3, 84, 107,
as glory-crazed individualist: 146–8, 157
as humanist Renaissance Man: 208–9, 251–2 (nn. 17–20)
as military paragon: 87, 121, 166, 169, 180–1, 195, 241 (n. 49), 242 (n. 7)
as monarch and statesman: 2, 39–40, 41, 44, 47, 50, 83, 88, 92
as namesake of Paris of Troy: 4
as negative template for Antony in Octavianic propaganda: 24
as novelistic adventurer in the fabulous East: 205–8, 250 (n. 10)
as paradigmatic autocrat and tyrant: 2, 52, 75, 76–7, 78–9, 85, 100, 102–5,

Index of chief passages discussed